HUMANITARIAN AFTERSHOCKS IN HAITI

HUMANITARIAN AFTERSHOCKS IN HAITI

MARK SCHULLER

RUTGERS UNIVERSITY PRESS
New Brunswick, New Jersey and London

Library of Congress Cataloging-in-Publication Data
Schuller, Mark, 1973–
    Humanitarian aftershocks in Haiti / Mark Schuller.
        pages cm
    Includes bibliographical references and index.
    ISBN 978–0–8135–7424–0 (hardcover : alk. paper)—ISBN 978–0–8135–7423–3
(pbk. : alk. paper)—ISBN 978–0–8135–7425–7 (e-book (epub))—ISBN
978–0–8135–7426–4 (e-book (web pdf))
        1. Haiti Earthquake, Haiti, 2010. 2. Earthquake relief—Haiti. 3. Non-governmental
organizations—Haiti. 4. Neoliberalism—Haiti. I. Title.
    HV6002010.H2 S38 2016
    363.34'95097294—dc23
                                                            2015011172

A British Cataloging-in-Publication record for this book is available from the British
Library.

Visit our website: http://rutgerspress.rutgers.edu

Manufactured in the United States of America

CONTENTS

ILLUSTRATIONS AND TABLES

ILLUSTRATIONS

TABLES

ACKNOWLEDGMENTS

First I thank the many camp residents for their time, generosity, and inspiration, and also the grassroots organizations and their members whose activism not only makes this research possible but offers hope for other visions for Haiti.

I offer a hearty thank you to the "dream team" of research assistants Marie Laviode Alexis, Sabine Bernard, Théagène Dauphin, Jean Dider Deslorges, Mackenzy Dor, Jean Rony Emile, Junior Jean François, Robenson Jn-Julien, Sandy Nelzy, Adlin Noël, Rose-Mercie Saintilmot, Stephanie Semé, Roody Jean Therlius, Tracey Ulcena, Castelot Val, and Jude Wesh for going to the field in often difficult conditions. The intrepid Jimmy Toussaint typed up thousands of pages of Creole interview transcripts, which the Faculté de Linguistique Appliquée translated into English, and Scott Freeman and Shawn Smith read and coded into N-Vivo.

Michael Barnett, Beverly Bell, Karl Bryant, Marc Cohen, Trude Jacobsen, Liza McAlister, and Dawn Pinder as well as Rutgers University Press's external reviewers offered valuable insights on the manuscript. The Northern Illinois University writing group—Andy Bruno, Laura Heideman, and Emily McKee—offered comments on chapter drafts as well as moral support. This project benefited immensely from comments on chapters by Beth Currans, Elaine Enarson, Hillary Haldane, Jane Henrici, Jennifer Wies, and Tiffany Willoughby-Herard. Participants of the Royal Holloway University of London Seminar Series and University of Iowa Anthropology Department's Colloquium Series offered useful critiques on chapter 4, first presented at a plenary of the 2012 Haitian Studies Association and published in *Feminist Studies* as "Pa Manyen Fanm Nan Konsa: Intersectionality, Structural Violence, and Vulnerability Before and After Haiti's Earthquake" (2015).

A draft of the introduction was presented at the London School of Economics, and research was presented at several conferences, including a December 2012 international conference on International Aid and IDP Camps at the Faculté d'Ethnolologie and a 2013 panel on Humanitarianism at FOKAL. I offer a heartfelt thank you to Ilionor Louis for co-organizing the latter discussions.

Activist comrades working in Haiti—*blan* and Haitian alike—offered invaluable support, advice, and critique: organizations like AVS, BAI, FRAKKA, GARR, and KOFAVIV, as well as individuals Beverly Bell, Olga Benoit, Nixon Boumba, Jean Claudy Caristil, Camille Chalmers, Eramithe Delva, Jackson

Doliscar, Alexis Erkert, Sony Esteus, Patrice Florvilus, Ellie Happel, Jessica Hsu, Margo Joseph, Mario Joseph, Amber Munger, "Ti Paul" Christian Namphy, Nicole Phillips, Jane Regan, Reyneld Sanon, "Ti Mak" Snyder, and Malya Villard. Practitioner and scholarly colleagues in Haiti like Rachel Beauvoir-Dominique, Jean-Yves Blot, Lise-Marie Dejean, Fritz Deshommes, Jean-Reynold Elie, Yolette Etienne, Nirvah Jean-Jacques, Ilionor Louis, Josette Perard, Michèle Pierre-Louis, Chevalier Smail, Charles Vorbe, and Georges Werleigh, helped shape these ideas and sharpen my analysis. Blurring these boundaries, the evening sessions at "Kay Joris" were sustaining, inspiring, challenging, and motivating. The late Janil Lwijis, who was murdered minutes before the earthquake, was an inspiration for this research and a would-be collaborator. Rachel Beauvoir-Dominique led the path for this work both intellectually and institutionally. Jean-Yves Blot played a particularly helpful role in helping to set up the "dream team." Chevalier Smail helped design the gargantuan data management systems. Collaborator and department chair Ilionor Louis has been a consistent colleague, comrade, mentor, and friend.

Offering consistent ongoing support and advice were friends and colleagues outside Haiti as well, like Manolia Charlotin, Tony Oliver-Smith, David Lewis, Lilianne Fan, Antonio Donini, Valerie Kaussen, Gina Ulysse, Kendall Thu, Barbara Rose Johnston, François Pierre-Louis, Claudine Michel, Alessandra Benedicty, Faye Harrison, Gregory Button, Benjamin Junge, Alex Main, Brian Concannon, Melinda Miles, Peter Redfield, Jennifer Kirker-Priest, Laura McDowell Hopper, Rachel Drochter, Tania Levey, Selena Rodgers, Michele Gregory, Mychel Namphy, George White, Kelly Josephs, and other comrades and colleagues at the African American Resource Center at York College. The Haitian Studies Association also plays an invaluable role in providing space for in-depth discussion and support for me and countless others. Chapo ba to director Marc Prou.

Research was made possible from the National Science Foundation (#1122704), CUNY Haiti Initiative, the Professional Staff-Congress, CUNY, and the UCSB Center for Black Studies Research for their support of Poto Mitan. Support for the writing of this book was generously provided by the Rockefeller Foundation's Bellagio Center Resident Scholar Program. The staff at Bellagio offered an absolutely perfect experience, and participants offered feedback, support, and friendship: Mahnaz Afkhami, Sadik Alfraji, Rae Armantrout, David Brody, Eduardo Diniz, Thomas Farley, Naresh Fernandes, Gauri Gill, Edmund Malesky, Luiz Martinelli, Robert Orr, Bernadette Searle, Romulo Paes de Sousa, and Roy Steiner. I also to gratefully acknowledge Northern Illinois University for their support for the publication.

ACRONYMS

CAJIT: Committee to Support the Youth of Impasse Thomas, one of the eight camps in the study

DINEPA: National Directorate for Drinking Water and Sanitation

FOKAL: Foundation of Knowledge and Liberty

FRAKKA: Reflection and Action Force on the Housing Cause in Haiti

IDP: internally displaced person

IHRC: International Haitian Reconstruction Commission

IOM: International Organization for Migration

ITECA: Institute for Technology and Community Organizing

KOFAVIV: Commission of Women Victims for Victims

MINUSTAH: United Nations Mission to Stabilize Haiti, multinational "peace-keeping" military force

NGO: nongovernmental organization

UN: United Nations

USAID: United States Agency for International Development

WASH: Water, Sanitation, and Hygiene

HUMANITARIAN AFTERSHOCKS IN HAITI

INTRODUCTION

January 12th, I was leaving work. Around 5:00, when I almost got home, I felt the earth shake. Then I raised my head. I looked up and saw a cinderblock falling on me. I went unconscious. When I came to, I saw that I was leaning against a wall. There was a slab of the house behind me. Just then it fell and landed on my stomach. In other words, all my lower body was trapped under the rubble. At that time, I thought I was going to die. I was trapped under this slab. I couldn't see any life for me anymore. I didn't know what to do. People were walking up and down the street, all crying for help. I raised my hands and asked Jesus to help me. Jesus help me. I didn't see any life for me.

After a few minutes someone saw where I was buried. So someone looked for a way to get me out of there. But they couldn't. After they left, another group of people came, and they couldn't either. After that another group came by with many tools and they pulled me out. And they dug me out and removed the rubble. After this they pulled me up but I couldn't stand on my feet. They carried me on their back and put me in a room to await transport to the hospital. Someone with a car said, "Everything is destroyed. All the hospitals are destroyed." Where were they going to go with me? After that they returned and dropped me off where they found me. But after they put me on the ground, they had me lie down. After a few minutes, I couldn't feel my body. Everything was totally blocked, everywhere. I couldn't do anything. After that I went to the hospital to check out my legs. My legs weren't broken but I had a minor fracture in my ankle.

I spent a month and a half in the provinces, at my family's. But then I returned, and finally went back to work. After we went to the hospital one and a half months later, I made a lot of effort to walk but that wasn't good.

I need to mention that my house was destroyed, so we pitched a tarp. A tarp, not a tent. We slept under a tarp, like this blue tarp that we bought. We saw that the tarp couldn't do anything at all. So we bought a few sheets of tin. We did it on our own. The situation isn't good for us.

No one is secure! In a tent, when you would like to leave, if you left any valuables inside, well! Someone could take a little razor, cut the tent, and take it. No one at all is secure! No one is safe!

All Haitians have the right to a house, but only the people who owned their houses will have them in the future. You who didn't have one will never have one.

What's worse in the camp is all this mud. That is, last week they came by to lay down a little gravel. But after that, nothing anymore.

We hear that a lot of money has been given but in this camp—we don't know if others got some of the aid—but except for the water, we haven't gotten anything at all.

What changes would I ask of NGOs? They know they are here to bring about change. But when the money comes in their hands they just keep it for themselves. It's like the old saying, *lave men, siye atè*— "washing your hands to wipe them on the ground." But they aren't doing anything serious.

I hope that foreigners would come to visit this camp, to see what is not happening, to see what's going on, to see what's missing in the camps.

My last message to share with foreigners is that, even though they send aid, it's true. But only a portion of people see it; the rest of us don't. I would like foreigners to take this seriously, to fulfill their responsibility.

—"Marie-Jeanne"[1]

Marie-Jeanne became officially classified as an "internally displaced person," an IDP, when she returned to Port-au-Prince. At the peak in the summer of 2010, there were 1.5 million IDPs living in more than a thousand camps across the country, about one in every six people. Marie-Jeanne's interview was in July 2010, six months after Haiti's earthquake. Marie-Jeanne has since been kicked out of her camp: "A pastor was responsible for the camp. So when the pastor came, they forced everyone out. We didn't yet have time to take our sheets of tin. But the pastor sent someone with a bucket of gas to set fire to the rest of the houses that hadn't been destroyed." This was in November 2012. Marie-Jeanne was reduced to another statistic: the number of people no longer living in camps, in this case through violent forced eviction.

Marie-Jeanne's final hail calls the question: Who bears responsibility in the wake of disaster? This has been the subject of a heated debate. The earthquake that struck Haiti on January 12, 2010, will forever be remembered as one of the world's deadliest disasters. For thirty-five seconds the earth shook and reduced a nation—already struggling with the historical weight of slavery, underdevelopment, imperialism, and intense internal divisions—to rubble. Although precise figures of the death toll remain elusive (estimates range from 65,000 to 316,000),[2] Haiti's earthquake remains one of the deadliest disasters in recorded history. One in seven people was rendered homeless. Haiti dominated the airwaves and cyberspace for weeks, bombarding world citizens with words and images at once contradictory, controversial, consuming, and ultimately confusing: the earthquake seemed to have as many meanings as people with access to a blog.

The earthquake was a tragedy that gripped the nation and the world. The outpouring of solidarity within and outside Haiti was extraordinary. United Nations Office of Special Envoy Bill Clinton pledged that the world would help Haiti "build back better." These promises notwithstanding, many people in Haiti, like Marie-Jeanne, experienced the disaster as a two-step process. The first was the earthquake. The second was the multibillion-dollar aid response, which triggered a range of negative unintended consequences, including rupturing Haitian sociocultural institutions and even increasing violence. This second, ongoing disaster is best described as many people like Marie-Jeanne experienced it: as humanitarian aftershocks.

As this book details, the events of January 12, 2010, also demonstrated Haiti's long-standing tradition of *youn ede lòt*, Haitian Creole for one helping the other. Throughout the earthquake-affected region, not only Port-au-Prince but the area to the south, including Léogâne, Jacmel, Petit-Goâve, and Grand-Goâve, the first emergency response came from people themselves: complete strangers pulling out children or elderly persons half-buried under slabs of concrete. Neighbors pooling together what scraps of food, utensils, charcoal, and water they could find, sleeping next to one another on the ground, in the street. Community brigades pulling out material goods and living and dead bodies from the remains of houses. Makeshift clinics set up under borrowed tarps or bedsheets. Store owners giving out stocks of candles, water, batteries, and medicines to passersby. Huddled meetings assessing the damage, the loss of life, needs, and community assets. Homeowners opening their *lakou*—the family compound—to family members, fellow churchgoers, neighbors, coworkers, and friends. Teams of able-bodied young men and women clearing debris from roads and corridors. Stories like these were not the exception: this was the story of how the Haitian people put away their economic and political differences and worked together, in dignity and solidarity, to collectively survive.

Unfortunately this wasn't the story that was broadcast into people's living rooms across the world. News from within Haiti first trickled out through Twitter, because the earthquake damaged other satellite-based Internet and cell phone towers. Soon thereafter, CNN reported the earthquake nonstop for more than a week, capturing the most horrific scenes and broadcasting them throughout the world. The images—edited for maximum impact—could not have been more graphic. It was presented as hell on earth. Lending their international star power, Hollywood celebrities embraced the cause and helped raise its profile. George Clooney won an Emmy award for his *Hope for Haiti Now* telethon, which raised more than $57 million. Wyclef Jean re-recorded Michael Jackson's "We Are the World" using stars of this generation. And the day before Sean Penn was set to present the Best Actor award at the Oscars, he unveiled his plan to help Haiti: the Jenkins/Penn Haitian Relief Organization (J/PHRO), which adopted one of the largest IDP camps at an exclusive country club, the Pétion-Ville Club, home to some fifty thousand people.

Overall, the response to Haiti's earthquake was one of the largest humanitarian efforts ever mounted to date. Citizens and governments the world over responded with unprecedented levels of aid; more than half of U.S. households contributed $1.4 billion in 2010, despite an acute recession and unemployment (Preston and Wallace 2011). Eighty percent of African American households gave to Haiti relief efforts. The UN Office of the Special Envoy (2012) reported that worldwide, private individuals gave $3.06 billion. At a March 2010 UN conference, donors pledged $10 billion for reconstruction. The Special Envoy's office reported that official donors allocated $13.34 billion to Haiti, having disbursed just under a half, $6.43 billion, as of December 2012. How have international aid agencies evaluated this effort?

FOCUSING ON IDPS

It should be noted from the outset that Haiti was an aid regime—often called a "Republic of NGOs" (nongovernmental organizations)—even before the earthquake. One obvious change to Haiti's social landscape specifically brought by the earthquake serves as its most powerful symbol. The city of Port-au-Prince bore on full public display scars (called "tent cities" or "camps") of the extended misery. For a range of reasons, camps for IDPs like Marie-Jeanne became visible symbols of the humanitarian crisis. The camps remain visual reminders of the failures within the international aid response, eyesores that got in the way of selling Haiti as being "now open for business," as President Michel Martelly boasted in May 2011. IDPs' mere existence brought visibility to profound social problems, such as the extreme depravity and deep class hostility that has always beset Haiti but had been swept under the rug. The official count of people living in camps was conducted by the International Organization of Migration (IOM), the agency that defined who is an "internally displaced person," an internationally recognized term carrying some loosely defined "rights" codified in the UN "Guiding Principles" (United Nations Office for Coordination of Humanitarian Aid [OCHA] 2001). IOM's regularly conducted censuses showing a gradual decline in the numbers of internally displaced became *the* barometer of the success of the international humanitarian response. The official statistics often lead communiques from the Haitian government, Bill Clinton, international agencies such as USAID, and NGOs as signs of progress.

As I write this introduction in January 2015, five years after the earthquake, the IOM reports that there are 85,432 IDPs, 6.3 percent of the peak population. This singular focus on the statistic of who counts as an IDP provides a powerful incentive on the part of international actors to push people out of camps, to show that their efforts worked. However, official relocation efforts accounted for only a sixth of this decrease in camp population (CEPR 2015). The Shelter Cluster also reported in October 2014 that 9,032 houses were built with international support, a small percentage of the 105,000 houses completely destroyed and 188,383 houses collapsed or badly damaged (UN Special Envoy 2012). This number also deliberately excludes Kanaran/Canaan, an informal settlement area built around Corail Cesselesse, where residents of Sean Penn's camp were relocated in April 2010. The Haitian government declared in June 2013 that three hundred thousand people lived in Kanaran, making it one of the country's largest cities. The decrease in people living in camps includes people like Marie-Jeanne, who were forced out through violence. Her eviction can hardly be considered a success.

ASSESSING PROGRESS, FIVE YEARS LATER

January 12, 2015, the fifth anniversary of the earthquake, provided a marker in time, an opportunity to assess progress of the multibillion-dollar international effort. Dozens of international journalists flew to Haiti to mark the occasion and establish yardsticks. Coincidentally, it was also the end of an official period of soliciting written feedback on the Assessing Progress in Haiti Act, which President Barack Obama signed into law on August 8, 2014. Notwithstanding the valiant effort during the immediate emergency phase, progress was limited. True, hundreds of miles of roads were either rebuilt or newly asphalted, and more than nine thousand homes were rebuilt. But the living conditions of the majority of Haitian people failed to improve much, and some were worse off. To put it simply, Haiti was not "built back better" as promised, despite the billions in aid. The $16 billion question was often where did the money go?

Figure 1.1 is of a large camp called Karade (Carradeux), at the site of a press conference on the morning of January 12. Officially, according to IOM, it is not one but seven camps. A large sign saying (in French) "Welcome to Carradeux Village" was painted on the wall next to the front entrance. "Village" is a political term, an assertion and erasure. It makes a claim to permanence, erasing the identity of being a *kan*, a camp. As this book details, living in a camp—being defined an IDP—carried stigma. The word *village* is also a declaration of not being a *cité*, a "city" in French but denoting the status of shantytown or "slum" (see Pierre-Louis, forthcoming). Like a handful of others, notably the informal Kanaran and the planned Morne a Cabrit, visible in the background of the photo, this village was a creation of the international aid effort. A major concern voiced by residents themselves and aid workers (Haitian and foreigners alike) was that these creations were to become the slums of tomorrow, like the infamous Cité Soleil. They seem on their way to the same path, with no public investment in institutions, infrastructure, needs called "basic" such as water, sanitation, or electricity, and those deemed "social" like schools, health care, or jobs.

Figure 1.2 shows that the "village" built of plywood temporary shelters was artificially fenced off from neighboring camps, with even less NGO aid, where residents had to fend for themselves. Both the "have-littles" (not quite "haves") and "have-nots" overlook the city of Tabarre below. Also visible in the photo, two buildings rise above the sight line: on the left is the campus of the Aristide Foundation and on the right, the U.S. Embassy. It is almost as if they are each staring one another down: Karade is on land adjacent to the Aristide Foundation, declared public by former president Jean-Bertrand Aristide in 2002, to expand the campus. Aristide was forced out of office in 2004 by a mobilization that WikiLeaked documents verified had received funding, coordination, planning, and support from the United States. Explaining this situation, several residents cited a Haitian proverb, *rat konnen, chat konnen: barik mayi a rete la*, literally translated as "The rat knows, the cat knows: the corn barrel is just sitting there." In other words, a stalemate.

High above both, visibly demanding to be seen although often left out, are the residents of Karade. Being called a "village" like Kanaran could be an attempt to literally define them out of existence. But they do exist. Residents aren't going anywhere. They fought back an attempt to forcibly remove them in the middle of the night April 10, 2014. Since then, residents organized a *brigad vijilans*, a "vigilance brigade," that conducts nightly patrols. At a press conference the morning of January 12, 2015, living on land declared public by Aristide, residents assert their rights to remain and become homeowners. Resident leaders also denounced that millions in aid came to only one sector of the camp, while abandoning the rest. They also demanded that any remaining funds be given to support the individual families and that the community become self-sufficient.

FIGURE 1.1. Karade (Carradeux) camp, July 2011. Photo: author

FIGURE 1.2. Karade camp, January 2012. Photo: author

POLITICS AND THE BLAME GAME

Figure 1.1 and the five-year commemoration in one of the few remaining camps thus demonstrates many questions and unresolved issues about the earthquake, sharpening the focus on the question of responsibility that Marie-Jeanne brought to the fore. This standoff is a metaphor, a microcosm, of larger structural issues. Discussions about the obvious shortcomings quickly led to assigning blame. Where *did* the money go? To many individuals profiled in this book, one thing was clear: it didn't go to them. Assuming that all pledges materialized, were sent to Haiti, and were distributed to every person there regardless of impact from the earthquake, it would have totaled $1,600 per individual, $8,000 for a household of five.

Journalists who flew to Haiti for the fifth anniversary found another story to cover. Also on January 12, terms for the legislature expired, leaving President Michel Martelly to rule by decree. The prime minister post became vacant only weeks before, and there was some question about the validity of a constitutional amendment that UN Special Envoy Clinton had championed in 2009 that granted the Haitian president the power to name prime ministers without full parliamentary ratification. The last time a Haitian president, René Préval, ruled by decree in 1999, foreign agencies cited this as the reason to suspend aid pending a democratic election. But that was then. Although it is too soon to predict as I write this, many of my colleagues argue that this state of affairs serves foreign interests in two ways. First, it clears the way for mining companies that Parliament blocked following a grassroots social movement mobilization and high-end tourist companies blocked by peasants defending their rights to land. Second, it allows the story about the international aid response to be blamed on Haiti, turning attention away from foreign responsibility. A week before the quake anniversary, a judge ruled that the United Nations was immune from responsibility for introducing cholera to Haiti in October 2010. The best epidemiological (Piarroux et al. 2011) and genetic (Hendriksen, Price, and Shupp 2011) evidence pinpoint the source as infected UN troops who spread it through defective sanitation systems on their base. According to the Ministry of Public Health, the epidemic killed 8,774 people as of December 2014.

In addition to the government, Haitian people and culture were also often blamed by people like conservative U.S. televangelist Pat Robertson and more mainstream journalists like *New York Times* columnist David Brooks. Many aid agencies also highlighted the role of people like Marie-Jeanne in their own degradation. Several stories emerged questioning their status as "legitimate" IDPs, arguing that many were "faking it" or gaming the system. Stories like these received widespread attention, in part because of international agencies' greater access to resources, including media. Even if international agencies weren't actively promulgating these stories, they *were* expending quite a bit of effort on detailing their good intentions. When the lack of progress was evident, many foreign media consumers and potential donors resolved their cognitive dissonance by resorting to negative stereotypes of a mass, singular, undifferentiated "Haiti." These stereotypes also easily slot into long-standing racist narratives about the world's first free Black republic (Trouillot 2003; Ulysse 2010). Haiti is often put in a category of its own: exceptionalized (Clitandre 2011; Trouillot 1990). I have heard many people, shaking their head at the evident lack of progress, say that "Haiti is just a basket case."

Haiti also reappeared in U.S. partisan politics; it will be likely only to garner more attention in the lead-up to the 2016 presidential election. Mary O'Grady, a columnist for the Rupert Murdoch–owned *Wall Street Journal*, has long been critical of the Clintons. A May 19, 2014, article titled "Bill, Hillary, and the Haiti Debacle" openly called into question the failure of the Clinton experiment on Haiti, pointing out the obvious conflicts of interests in having Bill Clinton as UN Special Envoy and Hillary Clinton as U.S. secretary of state. In effect, the Clintons' legacy hinges in part on how they spin the work in Haiti. Therefore any criticism risks being fodder for the Republican nominee (as of this writing, Hillary Clinton is all but assumed to be the Democratic candidate). Testifying to the contests over how to understand "the Haiti debacle," I was interviewed for a local radio station in New York City. Near the end of the interview the host (whom I later found out was also a Fox News producer) noted that she had just seen the film *Haiti: Where Did the Money Go?* (Mitchell 2012), and she steered the conversation toward the moral shortcomings of foreign aid workers. The outrage she felt was real, but most definitely misplaced.

Setting aside the partisan politics—the United Nations has also been a perennial target for the Republican Party—the line of questioning about where the money went often leads to a morality tale, like my interviewer's. Vilifying international aid workers for their bad intentions, just as blaming Haitian individuals who "game the system," is a dead end. The issue is not whether or not people who work for aid agencies are good people or bad people but the impact they had on the ground. Good people, even with good intentions, can do bad things. Or better for some. Or have bad side effects.

This same outrage was later fanned following a scandal involving the American Red Cross. The title of a June 3, 2015, NPR exposé was "How the Red Cross Raised Half a Billion for Haiti and Built Six Homes." Media coverage exploded, focused on the misrepresentations of the world's largest humanitarian agency about the overhead and administrative expenses used and of the touted statistic of "providing homes" for formerly displaced persons. Also at issue was a near total opacity of "Where did the money go?"—some of which apparently went to address its $100 million deficit. A press conference in Haiti served only to deepen suspicions, inspiring U.S. Representative Nick Dolan (D-MN) to call for a formal congressional inquiry. The tenor of the conversation—still ongoing as final edits to this book were made—was one of shock and outrage, focusing on issues of financial management and outputs. The majority of the discussion did not bring to light the underlying structural issues, the reward structures, the inequalities and exclusions built into the system. The Red Cross was singled out for criticism, apparently for its success at collecting money and its continued need to tout its successes in spending it, reproducing a "good NGO"/"bad NGO" dichotomy. The Red Cross, in its defense, critiqued this black-and-white absolutism, attempting to point out shades of gray. The Red Cross did provide relocation assistance to many camp residents, including some discussed in this book. Should this count as providing housing? Report authors Justin Elliot and Laura Sullivan clearly think not. The Red Cross also pointed out that their assistance included trainings and materials to help people rebuild or construct their own homes. Would this not count as building homes, or were only those built by Red Cross employees?

The sensationalism of the discussion, fueled by humanitarian agencies' presumed moral inviolability (Fassin 2011), risks preventing a deeper understanding and interrogation into the structure and culture of humanitarian action itself. What about this scandal is unique to the Red Cross, and what is endemic to an increasingly mediatized, well-resourced humanitarian enterprise? What are the long-term impacts? What do beneficiary populations think about this aid? What would they have done? What ideas do they have? Asking these questions requires a sober analysis of the system and a patient, inclusive methodology. At issue is the structure of the response and cultural imperialism that combine to shut out beneficiaries and their families, communities, organizations, and government from any real decision making, prioritizing, or agenda setting. To get answers, a structural analysis of the system, and not assessing individuals' (or individual agencies') morals, is needed.

BEYOND HAITI

As dramatized by the earthquake response, humanitarianism is big business. Although funding for international development has declined, certainly since the global recession that began in 2008, funding for humanitarian aid has held steady and even grown. In 2013, the industry was worth $22 billion, up from $17.3 the previous year (Development Initiatives 2014). As Didier Fassin (2012) has argued, it has become a leitmotif for our age, defining a new "moral economy." Following the end of the Cold War and increasingly in a post-9/11 world, wars have increasingly been justified on humanitarian grounds (for example, Duffield 2014; Fassin and Pandolfi 2010; Terry 2014; Woodward 2001). A critique admitted and/or leveled by practitioners is that humanitarian assistance is often used as a "fig leaf" to cover the naked inequalities, poverty, and violence of the prevailing economic world order that augments and stokes ethnic divisions that can spiral into armed conflict (Feldman 2008; de Waal 1997). Michel Agier (2003) has called humanitarianism the "left hand of empire" (see also Hardt and Negri 2001). Humanitarian agencies—often invoking standards of neutrality, impartiality, and independence—have nonetheless fallen prey to forces of instrumentalization, being used as tools for other purposes (Atmar 2001; Donini 2012). In response, to maintain their independence, many agencies have at least tacitly adopted a "state-avoidance" approach, retreating from activities that cloud their humanitarian mandate of "saving lives," often to the detriment of long-term development (Macrae et al. 1997; Macrae and Leader 2001).

Michael Barnett (2011) has noted that humanitarian aid has an extraordinary ability to maintain unscathed faced with criticism. Fassin (2011) noted that this might be because of humanitarianism's moral untouchability. What might be called "do-gooding" does not open itself up for interrogation and critique, which might also explain some of the indignant reactions blaming Haitian people. Nonetheless, there have been calls to reform humanitarian aid, specifically to address its shortcomings and myopia. "Development" agencies have been making declarations (2005 Paris, 2011 Busan) about the need for local "ownership" and a role for host governments. Humanitarian agencies have more recently made similar moves to link development and humanitarian aid (Mosel and Levine 2014). The 2004 Indian Ocean tsunami relief effort, notably in the Aceh province of Indonesia, inspired a rethinking of humanitarian approaches, "Humanitarianism 2.0." The same Bill Clinton played a similar cheerleader role in Aceh, where he launched the expression "Build Back Better." Although there were mistakes, especially in the early phase regarding coordination, "Aceh" was generally deemed a success. With an even greater media profile (at least in the so-called West, given colonial and imperial ties), the earthquake in Haiti provided the next major opportunity to field test these new models and optimism.

Things did not go according to plan. An impulse, at least initially, was to blame "Haiti" for the missteps, failures, and shortcomings just noted. Eventually, aid agencies like the United Nations did take stock of their experience in Haiti: the Special Envoy's webpage is called www.lessonsfromhaiti.org. Three such "lessons learned" are that successful aid delivery requires effective coordination, by a functioning local government, and that the "humanitarian toolkit" needs to adequately develop tools to respond to urban disaster settings. The UN's humanitarian experience in Haiti was also cited as the inspiration for its "Transformative Agenda." Thus, the experience in Haiti is of central importance to future humanitarians. It was widely known that *the* place to launch a humanitarian career was in a "mission" in Haiti.

As such, the stakes are much higher than Haiti: experience in Haiti reveals larger structures, patterns, and logics of humanitarian aid in general. Not all these good policies were followed, or lessons applied. Why, despite these stated policies for local ownership and coordination, were beneficiaries like Marie-Jeanne excluded from decision making? Why did foreign agencies implement expensive, inefficient, unsustainable "solutions" that deepened dependency, dehumanized or infantilized the population? Haitian people's own experiences, analyses, and understandings demand that we interrogate the humanitarian enterprise even further. A closer look from a diverse set of Haitian people's perspectives exposes other humanitarian "principles" not openly professed: the tendency to "just do something," always with an eye to the photo op in no small part because of the competition over funding, within an underlying capitalist market logic. On top of these underlying structures are cultural concerns. Haitian aid workers and their local knowledge were also similarly marginalized by what one employee called an "internal colonization" or another, an "invasion" of often young, inexperienced foreign employees in supervisory positions. Humanitarianism, which professes a universal subject of "humanity" (Agier 2010), is nonetheless a product of a "Western" worldview (Barnett 2011; Bornstein and Redfield 2011). Given that foreign humanitarian workers imposed their own culturally specific ideas, solutions, definitions, and frameworks, the billions in aid triggered a range of sociocultural changes: humanitarian aftershocks. This book discusses several.

AFTERSHOCKS

Thus, the question is not only where did the money go but also what did it do? Noted earlier, cholera was introduced by UN troops. *Humanitarian Aftershocks* attempts to explain why and how good intentions not only failed to achieve desired outcomes but also triggered some important long-term consequences, what Haitian sociologist Ilionor Louis (2012a) termed "social fractures." Aid policies, like the blind support for shutting down camps at all costs, created large informal settlements, like Kanaran, well on their way to becoming shantytowns, and often the site of violence. Evicted camp residents with no other alternatives also increasingly have swelled the existing shantytowns building up steep mountainsides.

Arising from a multiyear study of aid within the IDP camps like Karade, *Humanitarian Aftershocks* focuses on the sociocultural changes observable in this context. This book demonstrates how the groundswell of everyday solidarity noted earlier was replaced by a top-down, NGOized, depoliticized, international system of international humanitarian aid. One key element of this disruption in solidarity was the fissioning of Haitian households, resulting from a reward structure regarding food aid. Many households in Port-au-Prince followed the flexible, multigenerational *lakou* model, whereas aid agencies envisioned "nuclear" families as the norm. Given that the same amount of food aid went to a household of two or eight people, many families decided to split up, and the average household size decreased by two people. Policies about food aid prioritizing women were also factors in an increase of violence against women. Although the food aid went to women, they had to obtain a ration card in order to receive it, often waiting in long lines. They could be targets for acts of violence at the end of the line, but many women were also asked to grant sexual favors to the men who distributed the cards. Aid agencies created a system of camp committees that were dominated by men. Although knowing very little about these committees, foreign agencies granted them absolute power to select recipients. If an unflattering picture of the realities of aid delivery, analyses by Haitian beneficiaries and aid workers offer necessary questions for self-evaluation and critique. Given the singularity of the media attention and therefore generosity, it is tempting to once again exceptionalize Haiti. However, Haitian people's analyses also offer insights into other humanitarian situations. Haiti's case is more visible and therefore the contradictions within the humanitarian system are easier to notice. But these questions are applicable far beyond Haiti: these humanitarian aftershocks offer an opportunity and duty for reflection, analysis, and self-critique. Haitian people also offer solutions to these problems.

CONDUCTING THIS RESEARCH

How to document these experiences, perspectives, understandings, analyses, critiques, and suggestions? The first research was a six-week, mixed-method study of 108 camps, one in eight in the metropolitan area in July and August 2010, resulting in a self-published report (Schuller 2010). This research was conducted by a team of eight students at the Faculté d'Ethnologie, l'Université d'État d'Haïti, the School of Ethnology of the State University of Haiti, where I have been affiliated since 2003 and teaching since 2004, for three reasons. In addition to the scale—while I visited thirty-one camps that summer, I couldn't conduct a systematic review of more than a hundred—I attracted a large crowd wherever I showed up. My foreign, white body was read as aid worker or journalist; I heard several people say *sa blan an vle?* (What does the *blan*, the foreigner, want?) and at one large camp, when walking across the street, I heard, *men li menm!* (Here he is!) as people pointed and scurried across the street. Also important was the necessity to rebuild the capacity of a public institution to conduct research. In January 2011, after the October 2010 outbreak of cholera, the research team went back to the same camps and noted only a minimal improvement. The results—discussed in this book—were published in a follow-up report (Schuller 2011). One such result was that camps with an NGO management agency (a fifth of the total) were more likely to have services such as water, toilets, or a clinic. However, they also had lower resident participation and awareness. What explains this? What does this mean?

This was the starting point of the four-year ethnographic study, begun the summer of 2011. The research was conducted in eight camps, selected from a purposive sample of eight camps, four with NGO camp management agencies (Hancho I, Karade, Kolonbi, and Plas Lapè) and four without (CAJIT, Meri Dikini, Nan Bannann, and St. Louis). A team of five Haitian American students at York College were paired up with a team of eight students at the Faculté d'Ethnologie to conduct the five-week fieldwork. In total, 791 families responded to a fifty-six-question household survey (see humanitarianaftershocks.org for link to the research tools). Following this was a semi-structured interview with at least ten individuals from each camp, for a total of eighty-eight. The teams conducted observation, noting the economic activity, social organization, leisure activity, any aid distribution, conflicts if they arose, and anything particularly noteworthy. I visited the camps nine separate occasions over the next four years. As of 2015, the only remaining camp was Karade. In addition, I conducted fifty-seven interviews with agency staff from the front lines to "LogBase"—the UN logistics base where the twelve humanitarian clusters met and were headquartered.

STRUCTURE OF BOOK

This book centers on these people's analyses and lived experiences. Each chapter, like this introduction, begins with an extended transcript of an interview. Answering the questions about the significance of the earthquake, understanding the humanitarian aftershocks, this book is organized into eight chapters. The first, "Haiti's Unnatural Disaster: Neoliberalism," outlines the production of Haiti's vulnerability to disasters. Following a large historical sweep, this chapter argues that neoliberalism triggered centralization, a massive urbanization, and what Mike Davis (2006) called "slumification." However, Haitian people also have a collective tradition of solidarity, known in disaster literature as "resilience," a discussion of which ends the chapter.

Chapter 2, "Racing from the Rubble: Constructing 'IDPs,'" discusses the event itself and people's moving into camps. It begins with stories of survival to highlight how all too real the difficulties are, sharing the pain that people carried with them to the camps even as they had to leave much behind, including loved ones and material possessions. Disasters are often mistakenly seen as "leveling" events; however, people's experiences of the disaster are refracted by the many layers of inequality that remained standing. As Rebecca Solnit (2009) reminds us, disasters can also be stages for extraordinary human growth and solidarity. Haiti's earthquake was not by any means an exception, despite the fact that stories of solidarity and Haitian people's everyday acts of survival went largely unnoticed by international press and humanitarian agencies.

Chapter 3, "Hitting Home: Humanitarian Impact on Haiti's Households" disentangles the ways in which the humanitarian apparatus splintered Haiti's *lakou,* discussed earlier, drawing on detailed analyses from many people, especially IDPs. This chapter discusses these interconnected phenomena, how camp life, including the policies behind humanitarian aid, fissioned many households. Now that the majority of IDPs have left the camps, are families reuniting? Are they living better than they had while in the camps? Combining quantitative data from the 791-household survey with participant observation, recorded interviews with IDPs and aid workers, and follow-up research conducted in the summer of 2012, chapter 3 aims at answering these questions.

The title of chapter 4, "*Pa Manyen Fanm Nan Konsa*: The Gender of Aid," refers to a popular song from now-president Michel Martelly, "Don't touch the woman like that." This chapter teases apart the ways in which the aid was gendered, reproducing stereotypes noted earlier. Building on insights from chapter 3, this chapter interrogates the role that the gender of humanitarian aid—rooted in foreign agencies' own culturally, socially, historically, and economically specific conceptions of gender—contributed to the very increase in gender-based violence (GBV) that Haitian and foreign agencies combatted.

Chapter 5's title, "*Pòch Prela*: Camp Committees," refers to a slur many IDPs in a particular camp used to denote the committee: literally "pockets of tarps," the expression critiques these opaque, unaccountable structures for pocketing billions in aid. Haitian forms of solidarity discussed in chapters 1 and 2 are "hybrid," adapting to the new urban realities. How they mutated in the camps, becoming "genetically modified" organizations, is the focus of this chapter. Like the camps themselves, camp committees were a new social phenomenon in Haiti. Chapter 5 attempts to understand how they came to be, how they functioned, and why. The chapter includes quantitative survey data, but the bulk of the chapter attempts to tease out, analyze, and understand the many perspectives of the IDPs.

Chapter 6, "*Aba ONG Volè*: The 'Republic of NGOs'" interrogates the failures of aid delivery. From the point of view of many within the beneficiary population, NGOs were depicted as "thieves" profiting from their misery. This chapter organizes residents' thoughts about NGOs, beginning with the distinctions some people make between NGOs. This leads into the discussion of people's "appreciation" for NGOs, even though the population identified other priorities. Similarly to the committees, residents fault NGOs for poor communication. Many individuals shared a critique that NGOs take their names and make money off them. Some went further in this critique, identifying inequalities and hierarchies inherent to NGOs. However, some individuals identify the Haitian government as ultimately responsible.

Chapter 7, "Colonization within NGOs: Haitian Staff Understandings," discusses the perspectives of thirty Haitian NGO employees, from front-line worker in the camps to director. Hearing the analyses of people who worked to implement NGO aid after the earthquake gives some clues to what might be behind some of the shortcomings identified in the previous chapter. This chapter is organized into two sections, clustering analyses from front-line workers and middle management, because these two institutional locations tended to play the largest role in shaping responses. Front-line workers tended to focus their analysis "downward," with the beneficiary population, whereas middle management tended to focus "upward," on their relationships with their foreign coworkers and supervisors. Interviews with the latter population tended to be longer and more involved; a couple of front-line workers literally looked over their own shoulders during their interviews. Program supervisors, who all had experience working in NGOs before the earthquake, shared their analyses of how the post-quake aid response differed. Several commented on an "internal colonialism" within their agency as they saw decision making and other positions of authority taken by expatriates, often younger and all less experienced than they, at least in Haiti. Workers share their frustrations at being "led into error," as one employee put it, often arising from a situation of cultural imperialism. Some of these organic intellectuals began theorizing about a common experience or knowledge systems, in effect a "culture" within aid agencies.

Residents in one camp called UN troops stationed there "photocopies" because it is as if they hung on the wall, doing nothing. This is an appropriate metaphor for the continuing military occupation and the proliferation of—and competition between—imperialist interests. This is the focus of chapter 8, "*Fotokopi*: Imperialism's Carbon Copy." The plan for Haiti was to repeat the successes of the response to the 2004 tsunami, especially in Aceh, while continuing the same failed policies that brought Haiti to the brink of disaster. Many individuals working in the postquake response had in fact come fresh from Aceh with their supposedly universal, generalizable experience, dubbed "Humanitarianism 2.0." By implication of the supposed universal applicability, failures in delivery were not due to the model but to Haitian culture. Chapter 8 analyzes the many differences in context, notably the heavy imprint of the United States and its imposition of what many in Haiti call "the American Plan," which led to a diminishing of state functions and the creation of the "Republic of NGOs." Provincializing "Western" humanitarianism, this chapter specifically analyzes the cultural specificity of the humanitarian toolkit.

The conclusion pulls together the theoretical "lessons learned" from a critical understanding of the humanitarian aftershocks in Haiti. Following a discussion of how various strands within humanitarian scholarship contribute to understanding the Haiti earthquake and how Haitian people's analyses contribute to these strands, the conclusion assesses Haitian scholarship on humanitarian aid. Answering these questions requires that we question humanitarianism itself: the logic of the photo op, the disaster narrative, the structures, "culture," and the power dynamics inherent to the gift. Also drawing from the perspectives of Haitian people in this book, the conclusion outlines strategies for imagining a new way of doing humanitarian aid that respects its highest ideals. Haitian experience and Haitian people's analyses demand fundamentally challenging the assumptions, worldview, logic, and structures of the current system. The humanitarian aftershocks in Haiti suggest a reboot, a new operating system: humanitarianism 3.0.

I am writing *Humanitarian Aftershocks* to inspire dialogue, self-critique, and I hope changes to the ways in which the international humanitarian enterprise is conducted. The lessons that we should have learned in Haiti are applicable well beyond. The warning signs documented in this book—if heeded—can empower Haitian women and men, organizations, movements, and government to make a rupture with the current system and be able to participate actively and fully in the reconstruction. Doing so demands attention to people's rights, like Marie-Jeanne's, a focus on justice and solidarity. A final element to humanitarianism 3.0 is that it should be about our shared connections to our common humanity, dignity, and self-worth. Struggling for justice and rights of people like Marie-Jeanne demands we envision and create a world where our shared humanity is valued, respected, and defended.

1 · HAITI'S UNNATURAL DISASTER

Neoliberalism

My parents didn't have the means to raise all of us kids. They sent us away. They sent some of us to Port-au-Prince and others to Jacmel. I came to Port-au-Prince. I used to live somewhere else, but then I couldn't afford it. So I came here. People pile on top of one another. Garbage piling up. Even if you clean up today, there will be more garbage to pick up tomorrow. That's how life is here. Life is bad. Bad for our health, for our economic problems, and bad for our material needs. This is how it is; our living conditions are not good at all.

I created a little store in the house that helped me pay for rent. After January 12, the store was destroyed. I didn't have anything anymore. After January 12, we slept several days in the street. Our brother came to look for us. We went to live in the provinces for a couple of months.

People say that we're just abusing the system but it's not true at all. If I had the means I would leave. I could leave if I had a job that amounted to something. So now, for me to rent a one-room house in Port-au-Prince, I will need at least 50,000 gourdes (about $1,150) in my hand to rent for a year. Before January 12 you could rent a house for 20,000–25,000 gourdes.

In Nazon where I used to live, it was 30,000 a year. I paid for it every six months. I could never scrape up enough to pay for one year.

What explains the increase in rent? A lot of houses were destroyed. The people are in the street. That's why when President Martelly and all the NGOs moved people out, many people took the 20,000 gourdes ($460) from them to rent a house. Really they couldn't find a house. It's the same thing, people who are displaced from this camp just go to another camp. Because they can't find a house. That's why even now many camps are still full because there aren't really any houses. And some landlords don't really give the house to rent.

So I have a choice to return to Bainet, Mark, you hear? My mother is dead. I don't have any children in the country. I have a brother and a sister you just visited. You saw how things are. You saw the state of my brother's house three and a half years after January 12, that he's living in a house that's destroyed. You saw it's not possible.

What needs to happen? We are almost ready to leave but we would need to have a place to live. And after a house, people need the ability to earn money to meet their needs. The earth is tired: it is starting to die, to no longer give. Today you plant and tomorrow the crops burn. There's nothing. No economic activity at all. You can believe me.

For the youth over there to stay, they should open a high school. Kids from the provinces come here for high school. If there was that, Port-au-Prince would never have gotten overcrowded like this. They should also open a health clinic. If someone has a problem they have to go to Jacmel (two- to-three-hours walk). If there was a clinic or a hospital, a university hospital, do you think people would die en route? People would be saved.

—Frisline, *Poto Mitan*

Frisline powerfully explains the social construction of risk that produced one of the deadliest disasters in modern history. She was one of the many people who swelled Port-au-Prince in the past several decades because of limited educational and economic opportunities. Frisline also was among the 630,000 who fled the rubble in the capital after the earthquake (Bengtsson et al. 2011). With these "push" factors remaining unaddressed despite billions in aid, she returned to the capital and lived in a camp. Directly engaging a "blame the victim" discourse that became increasingly shrill as hundreds of thousands languished in camps as the years wore on, Frisline identifies the central problem of housing, and skyrocketing of rents, before and after the earthquake. Through her story, we begin to understand that the "disaster" was the result of human action, producing Haiti's extreme vulnerability, which this chapter details.

Many commentators in Haiti don't use the word *katastwòf* (catastrophe) or *dezas* (disaster) to discuss the earthquake. For a long while people did not use the Haitian word *tranblemanntè* (earthquake) to discuss the seismic event, out of respect for the dead and also to not relive the memories: it was known as various names, including *Douz* (12), *bagay la* (the thing), *evenman nan* (the event), or *goudou-goudou* (an onomatopoeia mimicking the rumbling sound of the earth moving).

Haitian scholar Myrtha Gilbert is succinct: the title of her 2010 book is *La Catastrophe n'était pas naturelle* (*The Catastrophe Wasn't Natural*). Many commentators, be they activists, scholars, or people living in the camps, pointedly drew the distinction between "the catastrophe" and "the event." This language mirrors social science scholarship, which discusses triggering "events" as only one part of the disaster. Haitian intellectuals, including those whom Antonio Gramsci (1971) termed "organic intellectuals," individuals like Frisline and the dozens of others in this book whose experience and reflection represent marginalized people's interests, distinguish the *kriz estriktirèl* (structural crisis) from the *kriz konjonktirèl* ("conjunctural" crisis, of the intersection of contemporary issues with the structural).

This chapter discusses the *kriz estriktirèl*, what disaster scholars term "vulnerability," the socially produced conditions that augment destructive impacts of hazards, either natural phenomena like hurricanes or earthquakes or human creations like oil spills. A key text in disaster studies, *At Risk* (Wisner et al. 2004), discusses disasters as the combination of hazards and vulnerability. The book also outlines three levels of vulnerability, what the authors call "root causes," "dynamic pressures," and "hazardous conditions." Using this frame, this chapter outlines the production of Haiti's vulnerability to disasters. However, Haitian people also reinforce local resilience, the ability of individuals and communities to respond and rebuild (Alexander 2013; Gaillard 2007), through collective action. This discussion of resilience concludes the chapter.

KRIZ ESTRIKTIRÈL: VULNERABILITY

The extreme loss of life and physical damage following the earthquake in Haiti cannot be explained by the sheer power of the earthquake alone. The Haitian government estimated that 316,000 people perished on January 12, 2010, and most donors cite a lower figure of 240,000. Declaring the number to be around 64,000, an unpublished report commissioned by USAID (Schwartz, with Pierre and Calpas 2011) triggered a debate about the precise death toll, bringing up larger issues such as official state recordkeeping. However, there is no question that the event on January 12 was far deadlier than an earthquake 500 times more powerful that occurred in Chile six and a half weeks later and killed 525 people according to official sources. One of the reasons for the dramatic difference in death was the proximity of the quakes to urban centers (Oliver-Smith 2012). For an even clearer example of this difference, in September 2010 an earthquake of similar magnitude to the one in Haiti and similar proximity to an urban center occurred near Canterbury, New Zealand. No one died (Crowley and Elliott 2012). The temblor of January 12 reveals the clearest example of sociopolitically produced vulnerability to disasters.

This chapter traces the factors that led to Haiti's extreme vulnerability to natural hazards. To begin this discussion, a few words on the concept would be in order. As David Alexander (1997) noted in a twentieth-anniversary issue of *Disasters,* "vulnerability" successfully entered the conversation in policy and aid circles regarding disasters. However, as Frerks and Bender (2004) point out in the conclusion to *Mapping Vulnerability,* reducing vulnerability had not been included in development institutions' stated goals and agendas. Doing so was an explicit advocacy item at the UN's World Conference on Disaster Reduction in Kobe, Hyogo Prefecture, Japan. The resulting Hyogo Framework for Action noted that official development programs can lead to greater vulnerability (Wisner and Walker 2005). Other scholars such as Anthony Oliver-Smith (2010) have made this same observation. Greg Bankoff (2004) offers a critical reading of the concept's popularity among international agencies. He points out the continuity within discourses of "contagion" with which the global North (he uses the term "West"[2]) painted the Global South as dangerous or deficient. "Hazard" is the current term to replace the "disease" metanarrative of the seventeenth century, or "poverty" of the "development" era. The "Western" cure is Western science. In the same volume, Oliver-Smith (2004) theorizes vulnerability within a global context, attempting to de-link natural events from sociocultural disasters. Oliver-Smith challenges scholars and practitioners to address the issue of uneven experiences of risk and vulnerability, and particularly the geographical distance between producers of risk—those who reap benefits from exploitation of natural resources—and those who are subjected to increased hazards. In an increasingly global economy, this distance increases, as the headquarters of multinational corporations that emit toxic waste are thousands of miles away from populations—workers and residents near factories—exposed to that waste, often across national borders. The same can be said for climate change (O'Brien et al. 2006). Countries most at risk tend to be tropical areas with large urban centers near coastlines, but they are by far not the biggest emitters of carbon dioxide, an aspect of what Rob Nixon (2011) calls "slow violence." For example, Haiti is ranked third most vulnerable to climate change (Kreft and Eckstein 2013).

At Risk includes a model for understanding various levels of analysis in vulnerability (Wisner et al. 2004). The authors describe "root causes," "dynamic pressures," and "unsafe conditions." Vulnerability can be thought of like a car: the root causes level is the engine, such as the system of inequality imbedded in colonialism or global capitalism, or the ever-increasing sea temperatures as a result of industrialization. The dynamic pressures are like the transmission, applying forward motion from the pistons to the wheels, for example, how colonialism stoked ethnic conflict, including between the Hutus and Tutsis in a Belgian colony that was to become Rwanda, or a sustained drought there that increased competition over scarce resources. The unsafe conditions occur when the rubber hits the road, the visible decisions by policymakers or an aggregate of households, including the building of settlements along a flood zone because of rapid urbanization and a lack of adequate available land or zoning. Because of the time scale, and because of disasters' visibility, media coverage tends to focus almost entirely on this level of analysis, obscuring the dynamic pressures and certainly the root causes (Button 2010). The model provided in *At Risk* is useful for understanding the various factors that translate into Haiti's high level of vulnerability. The rest of the chapter uses this frame to explain these various levels. I focus more on the "dynamic pressures," in part because of the rapid changes within the previous two decades, but also because as an anthropologist this is the data I have collected, from interlocutors' own life histories, like Frisline's.

HAITI'S "UNTHINKABLE" POSITION

In the wake of the temblor, televangelist Pat Robertson claimed it was God's punishment for Haiti's "pact to [*sic*] the devil." Although this wasn't Robertson's first such statement following a disaster—he made similar comments following Hurricane Katrina—this discourse gained wide currency. The "pact" Robertson referred to was the ceremony at Bois Caiman, on August 14, 1791, that ignited the Haitian Revolution. Robertson was half correct: Haiti *was* punished for this act of defiance that ended slavery and frightened the British into abolishing the slave trade three years after Haiti's independence in 1804. But not by God.

This section of the chapter addresses the "root causes" of Haiti's vulnerability to disasters, a long-term process of exploitation by foreign powers. This vulnerability began with the violence that went into producing the "pearl of the Antilles," the world's most profitable colony. The brutality of the Caribbean plantation system has been well documented,[3] if often forgotten in Euro-centric historical constructions.[4] The white planter class in Saint Domingue and other French colonies was so brutal that metropolitan France—all the while benefiting from the wealth that slavery had created—had to offer legal frameworks such as the Code Noir (Black Code) to limit the violence. Many within the local white—male— planter class forced themselves on slave women, and from these "monstrous intimacies" (Sharpe 2010) an intermediary class was born, alternatively known as *affranchis* (enfranchised), *sang-mélé* (mixed-race), or *mulâtre* ("mulatto"). Within French colonial society, unlike the "one-drop rule" of the British or the *mestizaje* of the Spanish,[5] such mixed-race individuals could be on either side of the color line, an inherently unstable category (Price-Mars 1956; Trouillot 1994). Many members of the affranchis class inherited the plantations—and slaves— from their white fathers and continued the brutality of the slave system.

Within the slave population there was also a division between *kreyòl* ("Creole," island born) and *bosal* (Bossale, born in Africa). Creoles were products of the plantation system and more Europeanized, with at least some basic capacity in colonial language, and thus greater ability to navigate colonial society and culture. Also important, Creoles did not know any other life besides slavery (Price-Mars 1956, 1983). By contrast, Bossales were born free and remembered the horrors of the Middle Passage, spoke one of several African languages, and kept alive traditional religious practices. It was not by an accident that the revolt began at a traditional drumming ceremony (now solidified at least in the anthropological imaginary as Vodou and in popular discourse, "Voodoo") on August 14, 1791, led by a non-Christian Bossale.

These colonial divisions were to remain powerfully intact after independence. Michel-Rolph Trouillot (1990b) discussed how the proto-state in the revolutionary leadership of Toussaint Louverture, a Creole, began to display tendencies to exclude, suppress, or exploit the formerly enslaved population, the proto-nation.[6] Trouillot underscored the continuities between Toussaint's plan of ostensibly "free" plantation labor and post-independence strategies and disparate development, what he called "State against nation."[7] Other writers emphasized different aspects of this division; David Nicholls (1996) focused on the differences based on color, Robert Fatton (2007) centered his analysis on despotic rulers and the authoritarian *habitus* (Fatton 2004), and Alex Dupuy (1989) highlighted the role of international capitalist forces in stoking this division and favoring elite populations.

Although Toussaint was able to rise to the level of governor general, effectively ruling over the island nation, he never questioned his colonial status and attachment to a "French" identity that was never fully accepted. In one of the most well-known analyses of the Haitian Revolution, Trinidadian revolutionary C.L.R. James (1989, 288) critiqued Toussaint for his "failure of enlightenment." The revolutionary vanguard was slow to see the need for independence from France, but it was not coincidental that Bossale slaves first called for independence. Later, the vanguard joined in: Jean-Jacques Dessalines was the general who finally ripped the French from Haiti's social fabric and declared independence, on January 1, 1804. Vilified by his contemporaries and mulatto historians for his brutality, Dessalines's response to colonialism was similar to Frantz Fanon's (1965) at the beginning of his scholarly career, allegedly *koupe tèt, boule kay* ("Cut the heads, burn the houses"). However, Dessalines also promoted an alternative vision for the State, *Leta Byennèt* (Lwijis 1993), the "well-being" State, a century before the social welfare state promoted by European social democratic movements and John Maynard Keynes. Haiti's first coup d'état was triggered by Dessalines's attempt at land reform, to offer former slaves rights to land. Mulatto leaders recoiled, claiming the titles they inherited, to which his response was, "And those of us whose fathers were slaves? We are to have nothing then?"[8] The question of land rights was thus "settled" by reactionary force.

To recap this, what historian Laurent DuBois (2012) called "the aftershocks of history" in terms of vulnerability: Haiti's state apparatus was in the hands of two competing elite populations, a black military elite based in the North and a mixed-race mercantile elite based in the Port-au-Prince metropolitan area. After Henri Christophe—whose Sans Souci palace was destroyed by an 1842 earthquake—committed suicide in 1820, his efforts at continuing Dessalines's Leta Byennèt in providing education and health care died with him.[9] Subsequent State leaders were called a "kleptocracy" (Lundahl 1989; Rotberg 1997) or a "predatory" republic (Fatton 2002; Lundahl 1984). The State was used to support elite groups' exclusion of Haiti's poor majority, denigrated as *moun andeyò*, literally "people outside." In this traditional social hierarchy, following colonial patterns, cities were de facto restricted to elite and middle-class populations, and rural life was dominated by *grandon* (large landowners, from the French *grand homme*, literally "big man") who controlled access to the most arable land. Peasants, heritors of the Bossale tradition, engaged in small acts of resistance, rejecting Creole society, both capitalist and European-ized (Barthélémy 1990; Blot 2012; Price-Mars 1919; Sheller 2004, 2012).

Present-day commentators, particularly foreigners, are quick to point to this "state failure" in explaining Haiti's vulnerability and justifying the "invasion" of NGOs (Étienne 1997). Missing from this binary state-versus-society analysis of *only* focusing on the state is a consistent foreign domination. Also missing is the role of elites: the two elite groups had different orientations to foreign capitalist powers, often animated by a barely hidden white supremacy: the black military elite built and maintained a military apparatus whereas the mulatto merchant class—whose interests were directly tied to monopolizing foreign trade—accommodated foreign interests. Mulatto leader Alexandre Pétion offered France an indemnity while Christophe prepared militarily, building the Citadelle, which is still standing today. Jean-Pierre Boyer, a counter-revolutionary mulatto leader, took over the south of Haiti following Pétion's death in 1818, the whole of Haiti in 1820, and the entire island following his 1824 invasion of the Spanish colony now known as Dominican Republic.[10] One of Boyer's first acts was to negotiate Petion's offer of an indemnity with France in exchange for the former colonial power's recognition of Haiti's independence. This 1825 indemnity, originally 150 million gold francs but reduced to 90 million, plunged Haiti into a debt that would, after U.S. refinancing, take until 1947 to pay off. Dupuy (2014) argued that the mulatto elites used this indemnity to solidify their property claims. When "the West" was industrializing, building railroads and later roads, telegraph, and telephone lines, and modern irrigation and sewage systems with the surplus generated in part by colonialism and slavery, Haiti was forced to pay up to 80 percent of its public revenue to service this debt. In political economic terms, this transfer of wealth was unprecedented. Both mulatto and black leaders dutifully paid off the debt, using a regressive coffee tax that primarily affected small-scale peasant farmers to finance it.

With the threat of French reconquest abated,[11] Haiti was still an "unthinkable" (Trouillot 1995) beacon of freedom in a sea of plantation colonies, in the shadow of a rising world power of the United States, also built on slavery. In 1823, the United States declared its dominance in the region with the famous Monroe Doctrine and undermined regional solidarity by boycotting the first Pan-American Congress scheduled for 1825 even after host Simón Bolívar caved to US pressure to deny Haitian participation. Ironically, the Latin American liberator had accepted help from Pétion's Haiti, a debt that Venezuelan President Hugo Chávez often acknowledged. South Carolina Senator Hayne explained the U.S. foreign policy toward Haiti in 1824 when presenting a gag rule in Congress, preventing the word *Haiti* from being uttered: "The peace and safety of a large portion of the country demands it" (Schmidt 1995, cited in Farmer 2004, 312). Before the U.S. Civil War, eight U.S. presidents owned slaves while holding office;[12] they felt that the example of the Haitian Revolution had to be silenced if the so-called peculiar institution was to survive. During the Civil War, following the Emancipation Proclamation, the United States formally recognized Haiti in 1863.

Recognition had no impact on the United States from militarily intervening to protect U.S. trade interests. The United States invaded Haiti twenty-six times from 1849 to 1915, when U.S. Marines landed and occupied the country for nineteen years. Several commentators have written extensively on the impact of the U.S. Occupation (for example, Plummer 1988; Polyné 2010; Renda 2001; Smith 2009). In addition to setting the stage for the 1957–1971 François Duvalier dictatorship and opening land for foreign ownership, the U.S. Occupation centralized economic and political power in Port-au-Prince, to the detriment of regional economies and provincial cities (Etienne 2012; Jean-Baptiste 2012). Haitian historian Eddy Lucien (2013) points out that although the processes of political and economic centralization began before, the U.S. Occupation accelerated urbanization, albeit without the promised "modernization." One can read the nostalgia in the late Haitian historian Georges Corvington's eight-volume history of his hometown, *Port-au-Prince au cours des ans* (*Port-au-Prince throughout the Years*), particularly his last, published in 2009, chronicling the elegance of the capital city in the 1950s (Corvington 2009).

In addition to its brutality and inhumanity, plantation slavery was also destructive to the local environment. Haiti's mountainous terrain is almost entirely deforested, retaining only 2 percent of its original forest cover. Looking from afar, commentators such as Jared Diamond (2005) place the onus of deforestation on policies of the second half of the twentieth century, specifically those of dictators. However, the process of cutting down trees began in the colonial era to make way for environmentally unsustainable sugar production. One difference between Haiti and the Dominican Republic, for example, was the intensity of plantation slavery before independence. The Spanish were more interested in prospecting for gold and turned its imperial attention and resources to continental Latin America. Long after the Haitian Revolution ended slavery, indeed following British emancipation in 1838,[13] the "plantation complex" (Curtin 1990) intensified in the Spanish Caribbean (Cox 1948; Knight 1970, 1997).

This abridged account of Haiti's history fleshes out the "root causes" of Haiti's vulnerability (Wisner et al. 2004): slavery, colonialism, U.S. (and other countries') imperialism, and white supremacy, with collaboration from local elite populations and the State. The legacy of this foreign powers–state–elite "ménage-à-trois" (Schuller 2007a) is environmental destruction, land conflicts, social exclusion, extreme inequality, centralization in Port-au-Prince, and a state that did not invest in social development, all of which amplified the destructive force of natural hazards such as earthquakes and hurricanes, both of which are endemic to the region.

Addressing these root causes requires a long-term framework based on justice, equity, and reparations. Reparations as a framework and remedy include a range of specific foci: slavery and the slave trade, colonialism, and agencies such as the World Bank. These measures aimed at redressing uneven development or capital accumulation (Harvey 2006; Smith 1984) are decidedly unpopular in the Global North, raising uncomfortable issues and histories. In the lead-up to the 2004 ouster of Jean-Bertrand Aristide, it is significant that France, not the United States, first called for Aristide to step down. Although it is possible that France was trying to mend relations with the regional hegemon over the rift triggered by the unilateral U.S. invasion of Iraq, French commentators note that Aristide's call for $22 billion in restitution for the 1825 indemnity threatened to destabilize France's overseas *départements* (the equivalent of states) and territories, particularly in the Caribbean.[14] Indeed, one such department, Guadeloupe, erupted in 2008, with striking workers denouncing French colonialism (for example, Bonilla 2012). The 1825 indemnity was the best documented, but certainly not the only such case for reparations. Scholars have been documenting such a case at least since Eric Williams's *Capitalism and Slavery* (1961) and Walter Rodney's *How Europe Underdeveloped Africa* (1972). There is such a movement for reparations against slavery, particularly against banks and insurance companies that profited off of slavery, in the United States (see, for example, Robinson 2001). Undeterred by *Realpolitik* considerations, in October 2013, fourteen Caribbean governments formally called for reparations from the U.K. and French governments for slavery. Hilary Beckles, whose 2013 book documents the case, led the commission.

"MONSTROUS" URBANIZATION

Images of the earthquake circulating on the Internet focus on the piles of concrete slabs, former buildings, in the nation's crowded capital, and particularly its *bidonvil*, from the French *bidon-ville*—literally, phony city, or shantytown. This was not the Port-au-Prince of the time before the U.S. Occupation's centralization of political and economic resources, and not even of Corvington's youth. In interviews several commentators, more of them foreign, used some variant of the word *monstrous* to describe the contemporary state of Haiti's "macrocephalic" (word used by many Haitian scholars, meaning a medical condition of an oversized head) capital city where an estimated three million people now live. Haitian American sociologist Alex Dupuy pointed out that the metropolitan area grew fourfold since the mid-1980s, from 732,000 to 3 million as of 2008 (2010, 17). Like other scholars (for example, DeWind and Kinley III 1988; Deshommes 1995, 2006), Dupuy attributes this rapid urbanization to the impact of neoliberalism. In a report about Hurricane Jeanne (2004), Haitian anthropologist Rachel Beauvoir-Dominique (2005, 16) noted a similar hyper-urbanization in the city of Gonaïves, the regional center of the Artibonite Valley, Haiti's "bread basket." In 1982, Gonaïves had 35,000 residents, up to 130,000 in 1997 and 170,000 in 2000. Mike Davis (2006) argued that across what he calls the "developing world," neoliberalism has triggered hyper-urbanization and slumification. The following section of the chapter details these "dynamic pressures," the second level of the *At Risk* model of vulnerability (Wisner et al. 2004), as lived through the many participants in the study.

"Devil's Bargain": Neoliberal "Push" and "Pull" Factors

Neoliberalism—the ideology and practice based on the assumption that the free market, unfettered by regulation or government interference, is the best engine for growth and fairest distributor of wealth—is so embedded in the social fabric of the United States and increasingly Europe that it is often difficult to remember or imagine alternatives. As David Harvey (2005), followed by Naomi Klein (2007), argued, neoliberalism advances following crises. University of Chicago economist Milton Friedman seized upon the opportunity created by the September 11, 1973, coup against socialist Chilean president Salvador Allende that brought General Augusto Pinochet to power. Friedman trained a generation of economists—often called "Chicago Boys"—employed at international financial institutions (IFIs) as well as economy or finance ministries across the Global South. These IFIs, most notably the World Bank, the Inter-American Development Bank, and the International Monetary Fund (IMF), impose neoliberal policy measures through what used to be called structural adjustment programs—austerity measures and macroeconomic "reforms"—in exchange for temporary debt restructuring.

The imposition of neoliberalism in Haiti fits the general pattern. As Haitian economist Fritz Deshommes (1995) notes, the rupture caused by the popular uprising against the dictatorship of Jean-Claude "Baby Doc" (1971–1986), who fled the country on a U.S. plane on February 7, 1986, provided an opening for a rapid acceleration of neoliberal policy changes. The U.S.-backed military junta that ruled Haiti following Duvalier's ouster placed "Chicago Boy" Leslie Dela-tour as the minister of finance and former World Bank employee Marc Bazin— who just before his death apologized for his role in neoliberalism, calling it bad for the country—at the Ministry of Economy (Bazin 2008). One of Delatour's first moves was to float Haiti's currency. People still refer to the concept of a "Haitian dollar," because up until this time the national currency, the gourde, was fixed at a rate of five gourdes to the dollar. The junta's neoliberal team also began lowering Haiti's tariffs and loosening restrictions for mass-produced, often subsidized, foreign goods to be sold. Haitian economist Myrtha Gilbert (2010) notes the steady decline in rice production, directly tied to neoliberal pol-icies (see also DeWind and Kinley III 1988) often imposed by the United States as conditions on food aid (Richardson and Grassroots International 1997). In a March 2010 testimony before the Senate Foreign Relations Committee, former U.S. President Bill Clinton, acting as UN Special Envoy, apologized for what he called a "Devil's bargain": "It may have been good for some of my farmers in Arkansas, but it has not worked. It was a mistake. . . . I had to live everyday with the consequences of the loss of capacity to produce a rice crop in Haiti to feed those people because of what I did; nobody else."

This "Devil's bargain" of neoliberalism all but destroyed local rice production. In documentary video *Poto Mitan: Haitian Women, Pillars of the Global Economy* (Bergan and Schuller 2009), Haitian economist and director of PAPDA (the Haitian Platform to Advocate for Development Alternatives) Camille Chalmers explains, "We are a small country that's always called the 'poorest country in the continent.' We're also the fourth largest importer of U.S. rice in the world! It's a veritable scandal. Today we import 340,000 metric tons of rice each year, 82 per-cent of the national consumption. Yet, we can produce this rice. We have the capacity and ability to produce rice of very high quality." In recent years Haiti has ranked higher—third largest and sometimes second highest. In total, Deshom-mes (2006) estimates that 800,000 jobs were destroyed since the application of neoliberal policies (also quoted in Bergan and Schuller 2009).

No discussion of rapid urbanization would be complete without noting the role USAID played in destroying the local pig population. Following an out-break of swine flu—known today as H1N1—in neighboring Dominican Repub-lic, the U.S. government pressured Duvalier to kill the Haitian pig population

(Diederich 1985; Farmer 1992). Hélène, one of Frisline's peers in the women's organization profiled in *Poto Mitan*, reports, "The story of Creole pigs is a cancer for Haiti because Creole pigs were the bank accounts for almost every Haitian. People sold healthy, fattened pigs. With this single pig you could afford to feed, clothe, and send your child to school." So the destruction of the swine population, adapted to foraging table scraps, represented Haiti's "great stock market crash" (Smith 2001, 29) Documents resurfaced that outlined a deliberate U.S. strategy to use this as an opportunity to render Haiti more economically dependent on U.S. agribusiness: "to eradicate once and for all the Haitian model of swine raising, whose 'primitive' conditions may at all times be a source of nuisance for the modern swine industry of North America" (Allan Ebert, cited in Bell 2013, 68). This "stock market crash" played a role in people's rising up against the father-and-son Duvalier dictatorship, which at this point had lasted more than twenty-five years.

In the 2011 household survey, one of the first questions we had asked camp residents was to tell us where they were born and, if outside the Port-au-Prince metropolitan area, when they came and why. Of the 791 people who participated in the household survey in the eight camps, 71.5 percent were born outside of Port-au-Prince,[15] the majority displaced by neoliberalism. Half of these people came to Port-au-Prince by 1996, the median year. Haitian development professional Yolette Etienne (2012, 28) estimated that 12,000 to 15,000 people move to Port-au-Prince each month. Of 458 people in the 2011 study who moved to the country's capital, 222 (48.5 percent) left the provinces for economic reasons. Franck, who spoke with the research team from his tent in the Kolonbi camp ("Colombia," across a ravine from a camp called "Jamaica"), near Port-au-Prince's industrial park, describes his journey to the capital:

> Humm, man! I've been working since my early teens because my family members were farmers and vendors. My mother was a street vendor. My father was both a carpenter and farmer at the same time. After his death in 1984, I began working in a company in Damien called UPV from 1986 to 1987. Agriculture was not too profitable because our crop was sold at a low cost.
>
> I came to Port-au-Prince in order to join the army. And in 1990 there was a war between the National Palace and the army. After that, I was transferred and I toured the country.
>
> Then, in 1994, when President Jean Bertrand Aristide returned, the army was "demobilized." I remained jobless for a long period of time. After that I went to International School [the name, in English] to study to be a mechanic. When HASCO [the Haitian American Sugar Company] was closed I found a job at the international port, in customs, delivering cars. In 2002, because of insecurity that was rampant in the zone, I gave up the job. I spent about two years without having a job. In 2004, I found a job at a bank, and I've been working there ever since.

Through Franck's story we discover several important historical events. Franck was one of the 800,000 people whose rural livelihood was destroyed by neoliberalism. Damien is the location of the School of Agronomy, and also the nickname of the ministry housed in the same building. When the campus was built during the 1915–1934 U.S. Occupation it was outside of the Port-au-Prince metropolitan area; the city has since grown up around it. Again, Franck lost his job because of privatization of the sugar company, one of the State's last remaining productive resources. The new private capitalist owners saw greater profit in shutting the factory down (see Gilbert 2012 for more information and analysis). HASCO's empty structures cast a large shadow over Cité Soleil, initially built to house HASCO workers and now the country's largest shantytown, sometimes sensationally (and incorrectly) called "the most dangerous place on Earth" (for example, Leth and Loncarevic 2006). Points also worth noting are Franck's tenure with the army, which was linked with human rights violations, including massacring people on election day, November 29, 1987, and the September 30, 1991, coup d'état against Haiti's first democratically elected president. Former army officers like Guy Philippe and Louis Jodel Chamblain—let go or "demobilized" by Aristide—shouldered a heavy role in the 2004 coup against Aristide. Also of note is that Franck worked at a bank for seven years at the time of his summer 2011 interview. Even though Franck held a steady job, he lived in a camp, highlighting the diversity of people categorized together as IDPs.

Faced with this loss of livelihood, many people decided to leave the countryside to try their luck with neoliberalism's "pull" factor. DeWind and Kinley (1988) argue that this is part of a coordinated strategy; the title of their book is *AID-ing Migration*. Jean-Claude Duvalier vowed to turn Haiti into the "Taiwan of the Caribbean" by promoting export processing zones, exploiting Haiti's "comparative advantage" of extremely low wages and its proximity to the United States. According to the Worker Rights Consortium (2013) Haiti's prevailing wages are third lowest in the world, behind Cambodia and Bangladesh.[16] A World Bank study documented that during its heyday, Haiti's export processing zones sewing clothes for U.S. companies employed 70,000–80,000 people (Hachette 1981). With neoliberal policies' destruction of 800,000 jobs, this spells out a net job loss for 720,000 families. As PAPDA director Chalmers puts it, "Most of the people pulled from the countryside aren't given jobs. This creates a massive unemployment. We can therefore say that Cité Soleil is a child of the Industrial Park." Generally speaking, the insecurity Franck brought up also has a relationship with neoliberalism and loss of livelihood, as Yolette Etienne notes: "We won't say that misery and poverty create violence, but misery and poverty facilitate violence. Furthermore, inequality increases violence. Excluding and marginalizing the youth creates a time bomb. If we don't get involved, create alternatives for these youth, we will not get at the roots of this violence" (*Poto Mitan*).

Frisline was one of the lucky few who had a job. She recalls, "I spent more than fourteen years in the factory. So the experience wasn't good at all. Because the factories, the bosses, when you hear that they have a job, they don't really give the money they promised you. Nothing is left in my pocket after fourteen years." Floating Haiti's currency benefited foreign companies who employed people in Haiti based on the local currency. In 1972, Thérèse, Frisline's colleague in the women's organization also profiled in *Poto Mitan*, earned six and a half gourdes a day, $1.30 at the time. The wages stayed relatively stagnant, being raised only following large mobilizations. In 2003, wages were raised to 70 gourdes, about $1.75 at the time. In 2009, wages were increased for the export-processing zone to 125 gourdes a day, around $3, following a unanimous vote of both houses of Haiti's parliament to raise it to 200 a day.[17] Since 2013, workers have been demanding an increase to 500 per day; on May 1, 2014, International Labor Day, wages went up to 225 gourdes per day, less than $5.

Even if they have incrementally gone up compared to the U.S. dollar, wages have not kept pace with inflation. Thérèse notes that, in 1972, "With 5 gourdes you could feed yourself: make juice, cook chicken, because everything was cheap." This was definitely not the case in the twenty-first century, as Frisline explains: "You work for 70 gourdes per day, but a gallon of gas is more than 200 gourdes. Here you can work two full days and still can't afford a gallon of gas." Her statement was prescient: in 2008, Haiti made world news because of "riots" protesting *lavi chè a*, the high cost of living, or inflation. As the most open economy in the hemisphere, with the lowest tariffs, a low tax base, and productive resources being drained to pay off debt[18]—all linked to neoliberalism—Haiti was extremely vulnerable to fluctuations in the global food market, particularly the spike in grain prices because of biofuels (Mazzeo 2009). Although then-president René Préval arranged for a temporary decrease, food prices continued to go up after. Jean-Jacques, one of the camp committee leaders in Kolonbi, explained that a small bag of rice used to cost 400 gourdes in 2004 (about $10). In June 2013, at the time of our conversation, it cost 1,250 ($28.57), more than double the price (600) in 2008 when people took to the streets.

Neoliberalism imprints heavily on people's other expenses. One of the explicit directives in structural adjustment is forced reduction in social spending. These "austerity measures" require governments to cut spending, such as primary schools and health care. In 2001, the IMF demanded that Haiti reduce its social spending from 3 percent of the gross domestic product to 2 percent (Duhaime 2002).[19] Raw wages are lower in China, but the government provides for necessities such as schools, education, and even housing, which is why "purchasing power parity," measuring spending on consumer goods, is a more appropriate measure. In Haiti, individual workers bear all of these costs. Factory worker Marie-Jeanne, whose story began the book, recalled, "School is my biggest expense. I pay 550 gourdes [$15] per month for school." At (2007), Marie-Jeanne was earning Haiti's minimum wage of 70 gourdes p or 1,400 per month. In other words, to send her one child to school cost alm 40 percent of her salary at the time. She continued, "If you look around, a lot o children in Haiti can't go to school because schools have become too expensive. Kids who can't go to school are in the street; that's why the country is in crisis. It's not their fault their mother can't pay for school. They're just trying to survive, to eat." Child care was even more expensive; it is why Marie-Jeanne quit her job in 2012: "I left the factory because the way things were there. I would have quit a long time ago but I needed to work. But after, when I became pregnant with this baby, when I left to give birth I just quit. I didn't go back again. If I was to work I would need to pay someone to look after him, and the money I need to pay a babysitter I don't even earn in the factory."

Processes parallel to neoliberalism's push-and-pull economic factors, certainly not helped by the forced reduction in state spending, also centralized schools in Port-au-Prince. This in turn was another primary motivation for people's migration to the capital. In the 2011 survey, an additional 128 people (27.9 percent) left because of schools, like Hélène, also profiled in *Poto Mitan*: "My family came to Port-au-Prince for school. While there are schools in the provinces, once you pass grade school there are no high schools." Pierre, who like Franck lived in the Kolonbi camp, left the countryside for similar reasons: "I wasn't born in Port-au-Prince, but these kids were born here. Myself, I was born in the countryside, Bonbadopolis. I was attending school. After graduating from elementary school there, I moved here to pursue my studies."

Jobs and schools combined make up more than three-quarters (76.4 percent) of the reasons why people came to Port-au-Prince. But are other reasons linked with neoliberalism? There are other major responses, such as "family" (148 responses, or 32.3 percent), and 45 said that they were "forced." One weakness of quantitative research is that these categories are too broad. This is one of several reasons why we followed up with semi-structured interviews. Manoucheka lived in a camp called Hancho I—in a shantytown called Cité Jacques Roumain, named for one of Haiti's most celebrated novelists and a Marxist political leader and founder of the Faculté d'Ethnologie. Cité Jacques Roumain sits on the border between Delmas and Cité Soleil, on the other side of the Industrial Park from Kolonbi; the camp was on two parcels of factory-zoned land, empty, surrounded by high factory walls. Manoucheka recalled what brought her to the city:

I am from Jeremie. I came here in '92. I came for my older sister's wedding, then I stayed. So I started school. I didn't finish, I stopped my first year of high school. I was staying at someone's house, then I moved out and so I didn't finish school. Well then, I started having children. Instead of accomplishing

ing backward. I can't get ahead. I have these kids, and I
. I see that my life is miserable. My mother is with me,
h me, I can't do anything for her either. Well, I am not

multiple motivations and migrations. Like Manou-
sehold survey were children when their families
...en looked at from the perspective of the household and not the
individual, responses of either being "family" or "forced" could be recategorized
as either economic or educational reasons. But even if no one who migrated for
family reasons could be tied to neoliberal policies, more than three-quarters of
people in the study coming to the capital for jobs or education are results of neoliberal economic policies. Noted previously, Mike Davis (2006) details these
same patterns across the Global South.[20] Discussing Port-au-Prince, Lilianne Fan
(2012) argues that humanitarian agencies need to take into account insights of
critical urban theory when planning shelter intervention. Saskia Sassen (2001)
wrote of "global cities," including New York, London, and Tokyo. At the other
end of processes of global accumulation are cities like Port-au-Prince, whose
deteriorated living conditions can also be called a type of "global city." Understanding these processes is crucial to addressing vulnerability.

Unsafe Conditions

Geographer Craig Colten (2006) argued that there is a geographical component to vulnerability: some physical areas are more at risk of hazards than others. This uneven geographical distribution usually maps onto axes of inequality
in society. For example, the Lower Ninth Ward and the Seventh Ward in New
Orleans, where low-income African Americans and recent immigrants disproportionately lived because of formal and informal housing segregation, was
not coincidentally the area with greatest flood risk and therefore deaths following
Hurricane Katrina. A fundamental contribution of political ecology—particularly
environmental justice—is the understanding that environmental benefits and environmental risks are not distributed equally (for example, Checker 2005, 2008;
Watts and Peet 1996). This is particularly useful to understanding disasters like
Haiti's earthquake.

Viewed through a political ecology lens, Port-au-Prince's rapid population
growth alone can't explain the city's extreme vulnerability. Also relevant is the
socioeconomic status of the city's new residents as well as the physical spaces
they inhabited. Traditional status categories equated the city with Haiti's small
elite and middle classes, and the rural areas with Haiti's poor peasant classes.
This marginalization and social exclusion were not limited to spatial segregation:

language is also a powerful means of reinforcing the ruling classes' hegemony (Gramsci 1971). French became Haiti's only official language in the constitution imposed during the U.S. Occupation that a young Franklin Delano Roosevelt bragged to have personally written. Only Haiti's educated elite and middle classes are fluent in French. The popular movement that brought down the Duvalier dictatorship also succeeded in a "National Project" of "re-founding" the nation, the 1987 constitution (Deshommes 2006, 2011). This constitution specified the right to housing (article 22) and education (article 32), also elevating Kreyòl, Haitian Creole, to equal status as an official language to French.[21] Also in the late 1980s, community radio stations began to spring up, with Kreyòl on the airwaves, for the first time including the population in the national conversation (Esteus 2013).

When the two million displaced peasant farmers came to Port-au-Prince, they were greeted with social exclusion. Mike Davis (2006) notes that in other postcolonial settings, certainly former French colonies in Africa, colonizers kept the urban centers for white settlers, deliberately suppressing growth by limiting infrastructural development. Eddy Lucien (2013) argues that the city's postcolonial urban elites followed in this pattern of limiting infrastructural development.

Faced with this "invasion," a typical response was to "give the city to the people" as one NGO director who married into an elite family put it. Haiti's elite and middle classes moved up the mountain, to the suburb of Pétion-Ville, and even higher, all the way up to Kenscoff, 1,800 meters above sea level. In this case, physical geography mirrors higher or lower socioeconomic status. Centre-ville, downtown, had been inhabited by new residents, many of whom were first- or second-generation displaced peasants who had unsuccessfully sought work in the export processing zones. In a process not too unlike U.S. "white flight," as a result of their moving up the mountain, elite families disinvested in the city's urban core, taking their capital with them. Before the earthquake, the brightly painted buildings on Grand Rue (the "great street," National Route #1, named after Dessalines), remnants of an earlier era, were covered in dust and exhaust, many of them empty except for merchandise stored by *timachann* (street merchants). In an autobiographical book, Haitian American novelist Edwidge Danticat (2007) noted how an established neighborhood, Bel-Air, which overlooked the National Palace and the Champs-de-Mars, the national plaza, had become a *katye popilè*, a "popular" (poor) neighborhood during her father's lifetime. Haitian American anthropologist Michel Laguerre (1982) discussed the "popularization" of these neighborhoods, the process by which lower-income residents settled. By 2003, when my two years of fieldwork began, spanning a political crisis that included Aristide's forced departure, these patterns were fully in place, with "down" and "low" signifying not only the proximity to the port but also one's presumed socioeconomic status. These "lower" neighborhoods were also the sites of conflict—labeled "red zones" by the United Nations—between UN troops and armed groups. If a neighborhood was declared a red zone it endured severe travel restrictions, including forbidding foreign aid workers to travel and not insuring car rentals, effectively targeting the NGO and international agencies who were (and still are, as of the time of this writing) the primary customers of rent-a-car agencies.

These decapitalized urban neighborhoods weren't the only red zones. Even with this process of popularization, Port-au-Prince couldn't have quadrupled in the two decades since neoliberalism without the building up of shantytowns. The largest is Cité Soleil, originally named Cité Simone in honor of the wealthy wife of President-for-Life François "Papa Doc" Duvalier (1957–1971). Cité Soleil grew alongside the industrial park, both the state-owned SONAPI [official park] and the private factories that built up around it (see Bernard 1996; Maternowska 2006, for more detail about the history of Cité Soleil). SONAPI itself was anchored by the new international airport, which Duvalier named for Ethiopian leader Halle Selassie I, a transnational Black Power symbol immortalized by the Rastafarian religion. Cité Soleil is certainly not the only shantytown in the metropolitan area, only the most visible. Aristide made Cité Soleil into a commune, an official municipality with its own mayor and *deputé* (representative in the lower house of Parliament), in 2003. Throughout the city, shantytowns are tucked away, particularly on marginal land because it is too close to the port and where waste settles (like Cité Soleil, La Saline, Cité Eternelle, and lower Martissant); on a steep mountain slope like Mòn Lopital (which includes shantytowns such as Jalousie, Canapé Vert, Decayette, and upper Martissant); or tucked away in hilly areas not serviced by roads (like Fort-National, Nazon, Delmas 30, and Bobin). Yolette Etienne (2012, 28) pointed out that some shantytowns such as Jalousie, at 43,475 people per square kilometer, are more densely populated than Mumbai (Bombay, India).

Overcrowding is not the only contributing factor to vulnerability. Geographically based factors such as capital flight, urban disinvestment, elite control of land, and a lack of infrastructure combine with economic forces of neoliberalism, including the high cost of social services, job loss, poverty, and inequality, to make up the "unsafe conditions and livelihoods," the third and final level of vulnerability in the *At Risk* model (Wisner et al. 2004). Sanitary conditions in the shantytowns leave much to be desired. Because shantytowns typically lack running water, people have to haul buckets up and down them, sometimes up steep hills, to the nearest tap. Corridors—often no wider than a foot and a half, just enough for a person to pass—divide individual houses, and these corridors also serve as sewers. When it rains, the lack of sewage systems mean that ravines often fill up with trash that washes down the mountainous terrain. All of these conditions complicate getting in and out in case of emergencies, either that of an individual who needs medical attention or of a neighborhood-wide evacuation in the case of a disaster.

In addition to neighborhood environmental conditions, poverty increases individual households' vulnerability to disasters. Nearly four-fifths (78 percent) of people in Haiti earned less than US$2 per day, and 55 percent of people survived on an average of a dollar a day. The majority of people displaced from the provinces because of neoliberal policies were not employed in the formal sector. Among these 70 percent of people working in the informal economy, the labor is often gendered, with street merchants being predominantly women, and chauffeurs, day laborers, and *bòs* ("boss," skilled labor for hire) being predominantly men. With this low income, either fixed as a stagnant minimum wage or fluctuating in the informal economy, individual households make choices based on the realities and constraints in front of them. Already discussed was *lavi chè*, literally "expensive life" or inflation, also denoting the mobilizations in 2008 protesting the high cost of food staples for which prices are steadily rising, as Jean-Jacques details. Marie-Jeanne brought up the expense (almost 40 percent of her income) of sending one child to school. Ghislaine, who at the time of her interview lived in the camp on the grounds of St. Louis de Gonzague, a well-heeled private school for boys in the middle-class neighborhoods of Delmas 31/33, described the choices she was forced to make:

> This is how I have been living as a woman: I never found a man who stuck around and did anything for me. I had my first child, and her father left me when she was seven months old. Now she is twenty-one years old. I've been the one to pay her school fees. I worked in the factories to pay her school fees and rent. I have never been able to build a house, because I could not afford both school fees and construction.
>
> So, like this, I am still toiling away in the factory. Sometimes, when I don't feel strong enough to operate the machines, I run a small business to survive with my kids. I work hard in the factories. I rented before the earthquake struck. The house where I lived fell to the ground. I lost everything I had and I was obliged to . . . well! Now I am under a tent.

Like many parents, Ghislaine prioritized schooling for her daughter. Because of this, like many other parents, Ghislaine had little money left over for housing. Ghislaine also discussed how, given traditional gender roles, she was held responsible for raising her daughter (see chapter 4 for a more detailed discussion). She had another child, a son, with another man who died while she was still pregnant. Also of note are the ways in which factory work was temporary, replaceable by running a small business. In the household survey, most people, like Ghislaine, were street vendors before the earthquake.

Unfortunately there is a "blame the victim" (Ryan 1971) element in much theorizing about the intersection of poverty and vulnerability. Paul Collier, whose report (2009) after having spent a few days in Haiti, served as the blueprint for development and now the earthquake recovery, talks about the "poverty trap" (Collier 2007). It should be evident from the previous discussion that larger political economic forces, the collusion between foreign agencies imposing structural adjustment and a local elite who often identify with and benefit from monopolizing trade with foreigners, limits choices for the vast majority of people like Ghislaine. Commentators from afar like Hernando de Soto (2000) argued that the informal housing market represents a wealth in unsecured capital. It may be true that densely populated shantytowns have higher real estate value than often acknowledged, and even higher than other apparently wealthier areas. However, de Soto's analysis does not take into account that though individual households build the dwellings, they often have to pay someone else to rent the land. The earthquake exposed the problems with land titles; in addition to the state of the archives and the almost nonexistent cadaster, title registry, multiple claims to the same plot of land were not uncommon. Although in a long-standing settlement such as Jalousie, with residents going back as many as eighty years, occupants (sometimes called "squatters" in other contexts) might have defendable claims to the land and certainly do not pay a landlord, in most inner-city shantytowns wealthy or middle-class families who laid claim to the land assert the right to collect rent.

Given all of these pressures, individual households often construct housing as cheaply as possible, because this was the one expense that households had some measure of control over, unlike food, health care, and rent. The fact that many people prioritize education despite its high costs—at least until they cannot afford it—speaks volumes to a hope that education is an investment in a family's future. Given these high costs, one way to stretch limited funds was to have higher percentages of sand to concrete in the cement that was used for houses, sand being of abundant supply in Haiti because of unregulated mountainside mining. When these individual household-level decisions based on structural forces are put side by side with the fact that many shantytowns were on marginal land in the first place, it is therefore not surprising that the earthquake almost completely leveled some shantytowns like Fort National and Nazon. Yolette Etienne (2012, 29) reported that 86 percent of the houses destroyed in the earthquake had been built since 1990.

So far this chapter has detailed how the more visible actions by individual households, notably housing construction, that amplified the quake's destructive effects, are only understandable in the context of long-term geographical, political, economic, and social factors. These factors like urban disinvestment, hyper-urbanization because of neoliberalism, and long-standing social exclusion are harvests of seeds sown both nationally and globally. So to focus on earthquake-resistant housing design and construction only or even primarily as a technical solution to prevent further catastrophes misses important realities. Indeed, the problem was not the lack of a building code; Haiti had such a building code on the books (see also Katz 2013). The problem was the lack of enforcement, caused in no small part by the elected governments—succeeding the twenty-nine-year Duvalier dictatorship that according to the IMF's own accounting took funds for personal gain and the paramilitary apparatus (Ferguson 1987, 70)—being systematically undermined through privatization.

Port-au-Prince, for all its overcrowding and inequality and occasional violence, is also where people live, make their homes, earn a living, raise families, organize leisure time, and build communities. Although it is crucial to fully comprehend the factors that led to the extreme vulnerability, it is also important to understand people's resilience, their capacity to survive and rebuild after catastrophic events.

SURVIVING ON THE MARGINS

The stories shared here were samples of dozens more like them we heard during our research. Reading through the transcripts, it is not hard to find other poignant examples of survival strategies and solidarity, often spoken in the same breath as the narratives of suffering and misery. Common to many camp residents' life histories is the matter-of-fact spirit of *kenbe la*, hanging on (see also Bell 2001). It is important also to keep in mind the context of the telling of these stories. They were told to student research assistants in a setting constructed and surveilled by humanitarian agencies to varying degrees. People who were being asked questions had become frequent objects of research, usually conducted by people working for aid agencies. At this point many camp residents were tired of research; many specifically asked what benefits would accrue to them. Some asked the student interviewers which NGO they worked for, disbelieving that they were students conducting scholarly research. All this is to say that these should be understood, like all research, as coproductions of thinking, reflexive people for particular purposes, an aspect of what Haitian American anthropologist Gina Ulysse (2002, 2008) called a "reflexive political economy."

Sandy, who found herself in the Nan Bannann (in the banana trees) camp nestled in a crowded mixed neighborhood in Delmas 32, discusses the importance, and flexibility, of the household as both an economic and residential unit:

> I was living in Tigwav with the guy I was in love with. And then I became pregnant. The father said the child was not his and he would not take care of him. I decided to sell lemons, oranges, and avocados to take care of my child.

When I was in my mother's house, she kicked me out. My father has many houses in the *lakou* [yard] where we lived. He took me to his house, and I took care of myself and my child. And then I said to myself: I have one child, I will not have a second one because of the difficulties encountered. Now I have only one kid. Afterward, I came here [Port-au-Prince] and left her with my mom to work as a maid. After January 12, I stopped working.

Like Ghislaine, Sandy points to the ways in which traditional gender roles meant that she was saddled with child care responsibilities. Sandy cites the importance of the *lakou*, the traditional family compound, in her survival. Although initially being punished by her mother, Sandy was able to set up another house in the *lakou*. In this way, the *lakou* functions as a safety valve to ease tensions within families like the flexible residences in Samoa Margaret Mead (2001) discussed. It offers a degree of autonomy within extended households, while providing for a common pool of resources to share for survival (Bastien 1961; Laguerre 1973— see also chapter 3 for a more detailed discussion on the household and family).

Many people described the solidarity provided by the flexible, "extended" *lakou* household system. A young woman, Edwidge, sought shelter in a "site"— residents distinguish the term from a "camp" because of its negative connotations and assumptions made of residents—in the hills above the national highway in the Paloma neighborhood of Carrefour. The site was called CAJIT, the name of the committee: the Committee to Support the Youth of Impasse Thomas. Edwidge shared the importance of her family: "Because of my aunt I still stayed connected. Our family bond has not yet broken and I think will never break. I am living in a family, and I have not yet had a child. I am not married yet, I don't have a partner and I don't have a fiancé." Edwidge's confidence that her family bond will never break is interesting, because she also hints at the possibility of severing the residential ties: if she were to establish a family of her own. The *fwaye*, the "foyer," is a term many people use to describe their household, physical house, or both, as distinct from the *fanmi*, "family," which also represents an important base for solidarity. Charlène, a neighbor of Edwidge in CAJIT, discusses how "the family made it possible for them to get help. Now when you have kids, you cannot do anything for your family. You have to provide for children." This suggests that the term *fanmi* ("family") is thought of differently than one's own children, who are often understood as the priority.

Although obviously constrained by the lack of available urban space, the lakou system, at least the cultural logic of a flexible household unit (*fwaye*) and extended sharing ties within the family (*fanmi*) survived urbanization, as Laguerre (1982) documented. Since neoliberalism and the resulting population explosion, even within the newly created shantytowns, these sharing relationships continued. It was not uncommon to find six, seven, or sometimes eight extended family members living in an eight-foot-square single-room cinder-block house. The average in the 2011 survey was 5.37 people per *fwaye* before the earthquake. Recorded interviews explain why: "We lived all together in that little place because we helped each other out," began Magalie, a twenty-four-year-old mother of two who had lost two members of her household to the earthquake. "You know there were never many jobs in the country. So if one of us made money then we all ate. You see?" As the next two chapters detail, people survived by sharing food with family members, friends, and neighbors.

Although life in Port-au-Prince, like that in any city, can be characterized by a certain anomie and atomization not found in rural settings, there were dense networks of solidarity before the earthquake.[22] In addition to the sharing rela-tionships described earlier, there are other collectivist traditions. Interestingly the word "community" (in Haitian, *kominote*) does not seem to have meaning among many people interviewed, or be associated with the phrase "international community." That said, people maintained social ties among physical neighbors, members of the same church, or the same organization. A close look at the sur-vey reveals diasporas of people who migrated to Port-au-Prince from the same area: in the area behind the industrial park in Delmas there are neighborhoods called Site Okay and Site Jeremi, referring to the two provincial capitals in the "Grand South"—Okay (Les Cayes) and Jeremi (Jeremie). When we asked peo-ple where they lived before the earthquake, these neighborhood names often came up, and often they corresponded to people who grew up in the home-town of the same name (people from the rural South province often said they were from Okay, and later specified the *bitasyon*, or hamlet, or *seksyon kominal*, communal section, the smallest administrative unit). Obviously there is far less "social control," informal regulation of individual or group behavior, in urban neighborhoods than in rural hamlets, where one's extended family and church community could account for half of the area population. However, to assume, like many aid agencies do, that *nothing* in Port-au-Prince is worth doing because of the lack of community,[23] because of the anonymity of the big city, is not only wrong; it is dangerous.

In addition to details about solidarity within what would be called the "extended" family in the United States, stories given by camp residents reveal two thriving collectivist traditions stemming from rural community orga-nizing practices such as the *konbit*—collective work groups (see also Smith 2001)—suggesting that urban poor had more "social capital" than donors and mainstream NGOs acknowledged.[24] Even during the worst urban violence of Haiti's turbulent transition period (2004–2006), *gwoupman katye* (neighbor-hood associations) from various sections of the city organized collective work groups to fix minor infrastructure problems such as drainages or potholes. Fac-tory workers organized *sòl*, solidarity lending groups, in which members pool their biweekly pay, and one member receives all of the funds for that period, to pay a child's school fees, the annual rent, or a funeral. The *sòl* is a widespread practice, often organized once per pay period among coworkers, once a month in a grassroots organization, or even daily between street vendors, called *sabotay* (see also Bell 2013). As Solange testified, "With a sòl, I can afford a better house for my family than I could on my own." This interest-free, completely autonomous institution contrasts with donors' increasing promotion of Grameen Bank–style microcredit programs that some scholars, for example, Karim (2011), noted have increasingly professionalized management and coercive repayment measures.

Neighborhood associations were complex and often contradictory institutions even before the earthquake (see Schuller 2012a for more detail). With data from the registry at the Ministry of Social Affairs, it is possible to pinpoint the impetus for creation of a neighborhood association—an NGO wanting to work in the area—because a dozen would be founded within a month of an NGO project in a given neighborhood. The vast majority of officially recognized neighborhood associations in a particular district had been closed as of 2009, when the research team visited. This is indeed an important part of the analysis. But following Jennie Smith's (2001) analysis of peasant associations (*gwoupman peyizan*), it is best to think of neighborhood associations as "hybrid," blending Haiti's *youn ede lòt*, or one-helping-the-other "genetic material" and support and direction from foreign (at least foreign-funded) NGOs. With an ethnographic eye trained to look for other, more culturally specific forms of civil society, a broader definition of local civil society emerges, and existing collectivist efforts become visible. Researchers overlooked community water taps, for example, failing to see the neighborhood-run associations as "institutions" because they were neither housed in buildings, nor were the managing community groups necessarily officially registered. But when we returned to these taps with digital recorders to ask people about their history, a more complex picture emerged. Whenever the public water was turned on in the area, the neighborhood committee would collect fees from users to fill their bucket, a specific type of a general set of practices called *kotizasyon*. This grassroots practice of *kotizasyon*, voluntary contributions, allowed the group not only to pay the water bill but invest in road repair, maintenance, or trash cleanup. That this group existed under the radar might have been a part of its continued existence, because the Duvalier dictatorship forced a clandestine approach in many arenas.

With a culturally sensitive ethnographic lens rendering visible existing sociality, other collective projects could be seen before the earthquake. In neighborhoods across the city, groups of workers (almost always men) would work to fix potholes on busy streets and intersections and collect voluntary contributions from the users of the streets. Several neighborhood associations provide electricity to residents by purchasing an account, counter, and transformer and letting residents plug into the main line. This is also an example of *koti-zasyon*. Other forms of community organizing were invisible to the research team because they occurred at night. Block parties, *ti sourit*, are social gatherings animated by music. Not explicitly political, they can also be platforms for *brase lide* (literally, stirring ideas, community discussions) or *konsyantizasyon* (consciousness-raising) sessions, sometimes using skits or short films.

Given the modified, urbanized forms of Haitian collective institutions beginning with the *lakou* and extended family structure and continued through the *sòl* and neighborhood associations, people in Port-au-Prince practiced forms of solidarity that allowed them to survive on the margins. These practices constitute "resilience," often understood as a community's capacity to "bounce back" (Guest Editorial 2011; Oxfam 2013). Scholars have sharpened the concept, arguing that reinforcing resilience is one of the most important interventions regarding disasters (for example, Barrios 2014; Gaillard 2007; Tobin and Whiteford 2002). It is also described in a Haitian proverb: *nou se wozo; nou pliye nou pa kase* (we are like a reed; we bend but we don't break). The term *resilience* is recently gaining popularity among agencies and scholars, but there is a flip side to the discourse: it can depoliticize inequality and demobilize efforts to reduce vulnerability (Henrici forthcoming). The term was overused following the earthquake, often serving as an excuse to do less because Haitian people need less, because they can get by, and therefore deserve less (for example, Clitandre 2011; Panchang 2012; Ulysse 2011). For these reasons and others, my Haitian colleagues tended to prefer the word *solidarity*.

CONCLUDING REMARKS

This chapter has argued how centuries of exploitation and isolation from foreign powers benefited kleptocratic leaders, constituting the "root causes." Neoliberalism triggered a massive urban migration and slumification of Port-au-Prince, the "dynamic pressures." And, finally, individual household decisions to make do with what they had reinforced "hazardous conditions" as well as solidarity or "resilience." The stories discussed in this chapter attest to a certain variation in individual experiences migrating to the capital as well as some commonalities. The various people we heard from in this chapter testify to how neoliberalism encouraged a massive rural exodus and urban poverty. The living conditions in the shantytowns and particularly the low-cost housing, both direct outcomes of global and national neoliberal policies, rendered Port-au-Prince and many popular neighborhoods extremely vulnerable to disasters. In addition to the neoliberal underpinnings encouraging the city's hyper-urbanization, a close reading of people's life histories suggests that people's migration—or to use another term, "displacement"—was a relatively common occurrence, such as Ghislaine's testimony highlights. This does not mean that as recent migrants, poorer new residents of Port-au-Prince should have less a sense of place, lesser attachment, to their new homes than the comparatively well-off older urban dwellers have (Low and Lawrence-Zúñiga 2003). Understanding the difference between space and place, and using this analysis, we can interrogate not only the geographical construction of vulnerability but also resilience and solidarity, both before and after the earthquake.

How did the earthquake and the international response affect these relationships and solidarity institutions? How did these individuals, many of whom were already displaced by neoliberalism, come to be defined as internally displaced persons, and what did this mean for their lives? This is the focus of the following chapter.

2 · RACING FROM THE RUBBLE

Constructing IDPs

The house was destroyed on January 12. But I was renting, pregnant with this child here. Then the house crashed down. I was with my sister-in-law, we looked for a place to put the ... The child's father left this tent for me but at that time I was in my hometown to give birth. And when I came back, I found he had left this tent for me. But he didn't look for a spot for me to pitch it.

I broke up with him. We stopped talking ever since I became pregnant with his child. Actually, we were in different places when the earthquake happened. At that time, he was in his hometown; I was the only person in the house.

Someone told me that [the baby's father] had a tent in HENFRASA [an outdoor fitness facility], by St. Louis. He's been working there since the earthquake, you know? They showed me the tent but regardless, I didn't want to live under that tent, because I was alone with the baby. I said to myself that I don't know anyone around. If I want to buy anything, I don't have anyone to watch over my baby!

Then, my sister-in-law told me: "You have a baby." She looked for a spot for me so that I could pitch the tent, but to tell you the truth, since the earthquake, I have gone so many places before getting here. Because the place I pitched the tent, it's like ... there's a house in there, but there's a big yard around that house.

The landowner had five children who died in the earthquake, so the landlord ... then ... in the yard ... you know ... nobody cared about the burial. He dug a hole in the yard and buried the children and definitely went away. He left the house.

So we were walking and looking for a place to pitch the tent and my sister-in-law—that is to say, she had a child with my brother, and her child is living with her—we four were to live in the tent: my baby, my sister-in-law, her kid, and myself. So then we found the spot and we saw two people who made a roof out of a bed sheet and we told them that we're going to put the tent here. Then we pitched the tent. After that, one morning, we saw a police officer coming up to us.

When I realized that the place where we were wasn't appropriate—when it rained, I couldn't sleep—then I was obliged, I moved here [to St. Louis, where the interview took place]. I'm looking after the baby alone... this other child wasn't here, to tell you the truth, he was in the countryside. He came here after the earthquake. So, I have two kids to watch over. I'll send him back to the provinces because I don't have money. I'm obliged to keep the little one [laughing]. That's the way it is.

All my belongings were destroyed. I can no longer pay my rent. I'm waiting. I'm not the only one in this situation. The main reason why I'm unable to pay the rent now is because I have this baby. If it weren't for that, I could've... I could sell things and be part of any sòl so that I can pay my rent, but I have the baby and I have nobody to leave him with.

—Claudine, St. Louis de Gonzague

As a survivor, Claudine lived to tell her story, unlike those who live on only in the memory of loved ones. Claudine outlines the importance of solidarity to her survival: not related by blood but by marriage, and shared motherhood, with her sister-in-law. As in many istwa—stories (see Bell 2001; Schuller 2007a)—from the previous chapter, Claudine underscores the traditional tie to her children. Whether or not her relationship with her sister-in-law was strong before the earthquake, in Claudine's retelling at least, Claudine's newborn cemented a bond and helped secure assistance in finding shelter. Paradoxically, like many narratives within the previous chapter, her pregnancy played a role in her breakup with her partner, who at least provided the tent for their child.

Claudine's testimony also highlights the difficulties in finding a secure place to pitch the tent. We don't know how the father of Claudine's child obtained the tent; it is inferred that he had access because of his job. The biggest challenge Claudine's new fwaye, her household, faced was a place to pitch this tent. Casually noted in Claudine's retelling was the way in which the landlord lost five children, burying them himself, ensuring they wouldn't go into a mass, nameless grave. Gina Ulysse (2010) discussed the ways in which this trauma and the dehumanizing process were mistranslated, misinterpreted, by foreign journalists. In Claudine's story it is possible to read a sense of helplessness faced with the enormity of the calamity, which other testimonies in this chapter also show. But the police officer's presence was a reminder that lines dividing private property were not all crushed in the earthquake. The previous chapter discussed the problems with inequality and the politicization of land ownership, increasing vulnerability before the earthquake. It also made life more difficult after, as Claudine describes. Presciently, one of the largest postquake informal settlements—and certainly the largest settlement still standing as of this writing—is called Kanaran, or in French, Canaan—the promised land. Kanaran stands alone, defiantly refusing easy categorization, the subject of scholarly analysis such as that of sociologist Ilionor Louis (2012b, 2013), chair of the Development Sciences Department at the State University of Haiti, and of a novel by Kettly Mars (2013).

Tracing the themes Claudine brings up, this chapter discusses people's transition to becoming "internally displaced persons," or IDPs. This chapter begins with stories of survival to highlight how all too real the difficulties are, sharing the pain that people carried with them to the camps. Disasters are often seen as "leveling" events—witness Claudine's landlord losing his children; however, people's experiences of disaster—like Claudine's migrating from place to place until she settled in St. Louis—are refracted by the many layers of inequality that remained standing. As Rebecca Solnit (2009) reminds us, disasters can also be stages for extraordinary human growth and solidarity. Haiti's earthquake was not by any means an exception, despite the fact that stories of solidarity and Haitian people's everyday acts of survival went largely unnoticed by international press and humanitarian agencies. Continuing the work of Ulysse (2011) and Haitian writers (for example, Jean-Baptiste 2012; Lahens 2010; Montas-Dominique 2011; Trouillot 2012; Victor 2010), this chapter aims to correct this.

Unfortunately, there is a serious gap in research on local communities acting as first responders to disasters. This chapter documents Haitian people's roles in saving their own and their neighbors' lives in an attempt to inspire disaster researchers to focus more attention on this critical if underacknowledged aspect of disaster response. The political divisions that six years prior ripped the country apart were at least temporarily suspended. Glimpses of another Haiti that fulfilled its revolutionary slogan, emblazoned on its flag, *l'union fait la force* (Unity creates strength) were visible, as the spirit of *youn ede lòt* (one helping the other) was so poignantly expressed.

Nevertheless, being rounded up into camps, IDPs quickly became objects of scorn, both internationally and from local elite and middle classes. Camps—residents' homes and neighborhoods, even if temporary—were subjected to an increasingly invasive foreign humanitarian gaze. Conditions in these camps varied along a series of parameters; the eight in the present study offer a range that is instructive. Even the best among them lacked basic services and were described as inhumane by residents. Residents felt as though they were being treated, and thought of, as animals, subhuman, delinquent. IDPs were reduced to aid: the word *sinistre* was used to describe both disaster aid and victims. As a new identity category, being a *deplase*, an IDP, subjected one to humiliation, harassment, and discrimination. Being labeled an IDP was a form of "social death," ostracism from Haitian society and an annulment of full humanity (Patterson 1982). This chapter interrogates why.

"THE DIFFERENCE IS THAT I AM NOT BURIED YET": STORIES OF SURVIVAL

Mackenson, speaking from his shelter in the Karade (Carradeux) camp, expressed poignantly what many others inched toward: "The way I was living compared to the way I'm living now, I consider myself to be a dead man. The difference is that I am not buried yet." I begin here, choosing to cite the stories hereto remind readers that whatever the debates about the death toll, whatever the dehumanizing policy jargon or disembodied human suffering bombarding the airwaves, Mackenson, Claudine, and all others in this book are real, living, surviving human beings, and deserve no less than their full humanity and dignity. The tons of concrete slabs that killed tens, if not hundreds, of thousands of people, were a form of violence. The previous chapter outlined the human actions and decisions, recategorized, rationalized, and sanitized, behind these deaths, a form of structural violence (Farmer 2004; Galtung 1980; Harrison 1997).

Although their deaths may have been senseless, and may not have even counted, they were human beings: loved ones, neighbors, friends, students, colleagues, family members, and fellow parishioners. Their living relatives and relations have made extraordinary efforts to rebuild their lives. Many continue to struggle, on the belief and hope that their suffering will not be in vain, for a better life. As a fellow human being responsible for this research, I feel an obligation to share these stories, to honor the time and pain in retelling them, and trust in the research team, but also in the hope that IDPs' humanity and dignity can be recognized, to document the almost unimaginable situations that forced them into camps, lest we too become dehumanized in our hopelessness and cynicism. And ultimately their stories of survival, despite monumental challenges are—and should be understood as—achievements. Maud, Mackenson's neighbor in Karade, recalls:

> January 12th was something extraordinary because ten of us in a three-story building nearly died. First the ground floor crumbled down. Then the second floor split into two parts and fell on a neighbor's house. My sister's bedroom and mine were in the back of our building; both were falling apart. God saved us.

Two babies lived inside: Magalie and her cousin who was hardly one month and five days old. The floor over ours fell down, I mean, split into two parts, with the bricks crashing down. Despite all this, nothing happened to us because God got us out of there with our children.

That day, we finished cooking dinner, but we didn't have time to eat. I spent about fifteen days with no food, even though I was breastfeeding my baby. I was so scared that I couldn't eat anything. When I got back to St-Michel, my mother prepared some home remedies for us. I happened to feel a little better, but the ground was still shaking and I was afraid. With everybody around giving a piece of their mind, we were traumatized and scared. Since January 12th, up to this day [July 2011], we have not returned to normal.

Aftershocks continued for several weeks after the event. Lise, my neighbor across the street, lost her house—which survived January 12—to an aftershock. Maud also reports that she, like Frisline and Marie-Jeanne, left the crowded capital to go back to her hometown. As noted in the previous chapter, they were part of a reverse migration of 630,000 people (Bengtsson et al. 2011). Also worth noting is the care Maud received—a home remedy. When other systems, including those set up by international agencies, fail, falter, or take a while to set up, Haitian people turn to one another. As Chenet Jean-Baptiste (2012) decried, this solidarity and caregiving went unrecognized and uncompensated, by the Haitian government as well as international agencies.

Some have attempted to document people's survival stories. Not surprisingly, solidarity played a central role. Michèle Montas-Dominique, a journalist who was UN Secretary-General Ban Ki-moon's spokesperson,[1] led a campaign, "Si M Pa Rele" (Montas-Dominique 2011), "If I Don't Speak Out," which the United Nations translated as "voice for the voiceless," later the title of an International Organization for Migration program (see Kaussen 2012). The purpose of the project was to document Haitian people's perspectives in advance of a March 31, 2010, UN donors' conference. Noted previously, several Haitian novelists of varying ideological stripes published accounts, including Gary Victor, Yanick Lahens, Kettly Mars, and Edwidge Danticat. Gina Ulysse (2011) edited a special issue of *Meridians* called "Pawòl Fanm sou Douz" ("Women's Words on the 12th"). The Latin American Studies Association facilitated a collaboration between UCLA and the Université d'État d'Haïti to document people's oral histories. Historian Robin Derby is preparing the narratives for publication. History graduate student Claire Payton interviewed dozens of survivors and uploaded the interviews on a website, http://haitimemoryproject.org. Other projects include http://asoapboxinhaiti.com and Beverly Bell's *Fault Lines* (2013). Several people used their artistic talents to share these stories, including Ulysse, Myriam Chancy, Lenelle Moïse, and Kantara Souffrant.

As many stories document, concrete—cheaply constructed—was the main killer in Port-au-Prince. According to official estimates there were 19 million cubic meters of rubble. Since this figure is hard to grasp, media accounts cited the statistic in terms of volume (for example, five Superdomes, referencing Hurricane Katrina) or distance (for example, paving a road from London to Cairo). Rubble also had an all-too-human impact. Earlier, Marie-Jeanne described how she was knocked unconscious when a concrete slab fell on her. Maud was lucky enough not to have been inside her house when the quake struck. Thousands of others, like Suze, were not as fortunate:

> Yes. My leg was struck here, don't you see? They had to remove us. We—my grandchild and I—spent eight days under a house, eight days without food, without drink. We didn't feel hungry and we didn't feel thirsty: we were only hoping to save our lives. When we were trapped under the house, we heard voices but they were far away. But when they started banging and breaking up concrete, we told them we were here. The little child was on top of me. I said, "The little child is here on top of me. My head is here!" They struggled to bring the thing to pull us out and remove the ground [by bulldozer]. Now I started to find a hole so they could see me, and I reached my fingers to them, to say "I am here! I didn't die." Yes, we were crushed. We were crushed up against cinderblocks, blocks pushed against us here and there. My whole body was eating me.

Suze's house was near Fort National, which sustained the most damage in the quake. She found emergency shelter in a camp called Plas Lapè—Peace Plaza—in the low-income neighborhood of Delmas 2. Fortunately Suze and her granddaughter made it out alive when a public works team began chipping away at the remains of her house. During her interview, Suze pointed to an injury. Thousands of others, like Rose-Mercie, the housekeeper employed by my Belgian flatmate, sustained serious enough injuries that, when the foreign aid flotilla did arrive, their legs had to be amputated. A newly visible identity category of *andikape*, "handicapped," demanded attention. Although it is definitely true that many in Haiti lived with a physical disability before the earthquake, the issue became highly visible following, with some resources dedicated to it. Rose-Mercie, for example, had two prosthetic legs given to her by different agencies. One fit better, but it was peach colored, ostensibly a color to match the manufacturer's idea of their typical patient. Rose-Mercie preferred not to wear that one at first. She eventually improvised a nylon sock that more closely matched her skin tone.

Tens of thousands of others fared even worse. Rose-Mercie was cleaning an apartment of a women's NGO worker whom I knew from my previous research, Edele. Edele rented her apartment from Myriam Merlet, cofounder of feminist

NGO Enfofanm. According to Rose-Mercie, Myriam was, like Suze, trapped, pushed against concrete slabs, for several days. Unlike Suze, who happened to have been found by people chipping away at the house, Myriam was not found alive, despite her sending dozens of SOS texts. Because of her international stature as a leader within Haiti's feminist movement, Myriam's death was one of the few commemorated.

Myriam and tens of thousands of others didn't die because people didn't care. Robenson, a college student who found shelter at the St. Louis de Gonzague camp, a private school for boys, describes the pain of not being able to help:

> While passing by Université Caraïbes, at Delmas 19, I heard people crying out for help. Even if you try, you can't do anything for them. Huge slabs of concrete were on top of them. With a lot of regret, you see people asking for help, but you realize you can't do anything. And so you have to go.
>
> I volunteered to learn first aid. I went up to Delmas 64 [about 3 km up the hill], by the Villa Imperial, to a vocational school. I went inside a room. It was like, you see, like a restaurant, a big kitchen, where they . . . they took chickens to cook, hung upside down. You found all kind of corpses under the beams, their eyes already starting to swell. Everybody was dead, even the principal of the school.

Robenson was traumatized as he retold this story to two other college students, one in Haiti and one in the United States. These two students, similarly overwhelmed, shared this story over a breakfast training meeting. As dutifully shown by foreign press agencies, Port-au-Prince was, in the words of several people in this study, "brought to its knees," a triple entendre, meaning the physical gesture with people having been jostled to the ground, people's reflex to pray, and the concrete slabs brought down. Several Haitian commentators like filmmaker Raoul Peck criticize the metaphor of the country being brought to its knees, forced to beg for international aid. In documentary *Fatal Assistance*, Haitian President René Préval said, "I can't negotiate like that. I have a weak state."

In part, I am sharing this story to show my own impotence and discomfort about my own ability to do anything. As a middle-class, white man in the United States, with a PhD, I don't often feel this powerless, in large part because of my privilege and greater access to resources (Schuller 2010b). But it wasn't, it isn't, enough (Schuller 2014). I arrived in Haiti on one of the first flights the U.S. military allowed to land, on January 20, eight days after the earthquake, as part of a thirteen-person medical team organized for a local clinic, Hospice St. Joseph, in Christ-Roi, the mixed-income neighborhood where I had lived. When our aid flight arrived on the ground, and after we picked up our bags, the situation was more orderly than I had ever remembered it, only a week following the earthquake. Because ours was a small grassroots effort, we didn't have big walkie-talkies, military escort, or an SUV, and we had to make our way out into the open on our own. We had a few troubles, with some other foreign aid groups taking some of our supplies, including water, and some attempts to woo our doctors. Eventually we made it out of the airport, thanks to the Haitian staff who picked us up.

The ride from the airport, around three kilometers, took more than an hour, not because of the *blokis*, the traffic jams that often occur, but because the main thoroughfares all were either torn up by the earthquake or concrete buildings had fallen down and blocked the road. Access from the roads explained the difference between Suze's and Myriam's situations, literally the difference between life and death, in these crucial days that followed.

In the van, I was struck by the medical masks that the Haitian staff wore. "Why is this?," I inquired of them, hoping that my query wouldn't upset the team of foreign doctors, trauma specialists who didn't speak a word of Haitian Creole. At any rate, they had put on their own masks because that's what the driver was doing. There were two reasons for the masks: first was a range of airborne infectious diseases, and second was the smell. In the low-lying areas and especially the shantytowns, some two hundred thousand bodies were still decomposing, trapped under the rubble. Thankfully it had been "cold" (only 75 degrees), and our neighborhood of Christ-Roi, though it was one of the most damaged by the earthquake, was high enough to have some breeze.

Of eighty-five people who lived on my block, twelve people died, including all inhabitants of the house on the top of the hill where a local band sometimes played. Trauma specialists walked the area to identify houses that still had dead bodies trapped underneath.

Some of the dead were never unearthed. Such was the case in the informal CAJIT settlement in a remote neighborhood in the suburb of Carrefour closer to the epicenter. In our first meeting in August 2010, CAJIT president Linda explained that "Carrefour is blessed with many natural springs. However, here, the water is putrid because it flows over cadavers." Over the past several years, Linda has been in and out of the United States for medical treatment. Fortunately for her, she had already had a U.S. visa because of her profession of being a *madanm Sara*, an informal commercial importer (Ulysse 2008).

As noted in the previous chapter (see also Katz 2013), the destruction of people's houses was in many cases predictable, as Sabine, who lived in CAJIT at the time of the August 2011 interview, recalls:

Goudougoudou[2] (Earthquake) had passed. The house was destroyed. Oh! It had a big impact because when the earthquake passed, we had a little child under the house debris. We thought she had died. We had two children in our house.

Our other child did not die; we found him in the middle of the night. We acted quickly and pulled him out. He was two years old.

My sister has a child who died. It seemed like she had breast milk constantly spilling all over her chest that drove her crazy. Even I was, like, I was going crazy. I recovered after that, they made some remedy for us. Another sister who was here, she was away for two to three days. She thought we were dead. When they told her that the house was destroyed, she knew the house was already in bad condition. She thought that we died. We were like crazy people. Goudougoudou (Earthquake) acted strongly upon us.

Sabine herself was able to recover; she refers to a "remedy"—not a *medikaman* (medicine) or *konprime* (pill). One could only imagine her sister's pain.

Some people didn't need to imagine this pain, like Marjorie, who was staying at St. Louis camp: "Also I can say that due to January 12, I was pregnant before January 12th . . . that baby would have been one year old this coming August. I had a miscarriage. I lost her." Marjorie was most definitely not alone in this pain. On the other side of the city, in CAJIT, Yves recounts:

This is where it happened. This is where I've been living ever since I left my hometown [literally, "my country"]. Now, I have a small tent. I was very shocked, because we didn't see it coming. I went down to see how my wife was doing.

When I got there, as it [the earthquake] was happening, houses hadn't yet collapsed. Nobody was killed yet. Now, when I went to that side, I took a look. Houses were falling down here and there, people were shouting for help.

When I got there, my wife was injured by a part of the wall where she was sitting. It struck her in her leg . . . it hit her in her leg and it dislocated it. When that happened, she was pregnant. The shock from what happened caused . . . she was eight months pregnant, and as a result she lost the baby. When the baby died, God himself took it out. He saw the way people were losing their life. That's what caused the death of the baby. He helped her to push the baby out.

Now the baby . . . fortunately there was a hospital, but hospitals were not letting people in. Now when I took my wife to a traditional healer, now when she pushed the baby out, then . . . God saved her for me. She's alive, but the baby died, just . . . but my wife was very sick. She was very sick. She was treated with appropriate traditional medicine in the countryside. I took her to her mother in the provinces, she gave her traditional medicine, and she recovered.

Although Sabine's treatment was unclear, there is no ambiguity in Yves' wife's. She was saved by a *doktè fèy*, a traditional healer with specialized knowledge about leaves, an herbalist. Yves points out that—at least in the immediate aftermath, at least near him in Carrefour—the formal, "Western" health care system was not functioning.

There are many other stories that could also be shared. But these chosen highlight the extreme difficulty, the emotional toll, the fear, and the loss, and most also highlight the solidarity that saved their lives from Goudougoudou. The deaths, and near deaths, were all because of concrete. Noting its role in death, some commentators renamed the Republic of Port-au-Prince—itself a critique of the country's centralization—the "Republic of Concrete." The huge slabs of rubble left uncleared, houses left demolished, even at the time of this writing four years later, are like gravestones, visible reminders of the trauma of January 12. Over my visits during the past four years the mounds of concrete have gradually—*very* gradually—diminished. There was a rumor, repeated by former Venezuelan president Hugo Chávez, that the United States had a secret "earthquake weapon," HAARP, that triggered Haiti's earthquake. Although the science behind this rumor was roundly critiqued by U.S. media, notably Fox News, the fact that it could be repeated and people would be willing to believe it suggests a persistent and powerful critique of U.S. policy toward Haiti and countries like Haiti. One needn't imagine the world's "sole remaining superpower" with this kind of weapon to acknowledge people's anger and pain at these senseless deaths (Rosaldo 1984). The anger isn't that far displaced: staring down the rubble and contemplating, like many in Haiti have, how the "Republic of Concrete" came to be, staring back are neoliberal policies of the United States (and others, notably the World Bank), coming back to the crumbled surface, as the previous chapter demonstrated.

Unfortunately for Myriam Merlet, Sabine's niece, and Marjorie's or Yves's unborn children, and hundreds of thousands of others, this structural violence is all too real: this is what neoliberalism looks like.

INEQUALITY

Claudine recounts how her middle-class landlord lost five children. The exclusive Hotel Montana was flattened by the earthquake, as was the Caribbean Market. Before the earthquake, the Montana, on a hill overlooking Pétion-Ville, was one of the most exclusive, most expensive luxury hotels in the country. On one of the main roads down from Pétion-Ville, the Caribbean Market was the largest, best-stocked, and certainly one of the most expensive supermarkets before the quake. The United Nations lost 102 individuals in the seismic event, including the military mission chief Hédi Annabi. These facts lend credence to the oft-repeated meme that disasters are equalizing events, a point Solnit (2009) doesn't dismiss. Unfortunately, this isn't the case. One of the most human, cathartic uses of technology after the earthquake was a wiki, listing people who were known to be either alive or dead. However, unlike Yves or Sabine, likely only those with access to technology and international contacts could use this service.

Not all deaths—just as not all lives—are given the same value. The fact that there could have even been a debate about the death toll highlights that some lives literally don't count: they weren't registered by the state, and therefore their deaths weren't enumerated. My block was not the worst hit: worse were shantyowns such as Nazon and Fort National. Entire rows of houses stacked on top of one another were destroyed, like Frisline's in Nazon, or Suze's in Saint Martin. For some of these worst-hit areas, with one rubble pile indistinguishable from the next, even estimating the number of houses lost—where possibly entire families lie dead within them—is a difficult task.

The severity of the damage, and one's ability to recover, or even find a place to pitch a tent, as Claudine shows, is shaped greatly by one's place within the social order. We have heard how gender works to place greater burdens on women. Allande, who was living in Kolonbi at the time of his 2011 interview, pointedly recalls another axis of social inequality: "I pulled my family out from under the rubble. Some had their feet fractured . . . some had arms fractured, even one of my sisters who had a baby . . . a light-skinned baby [literally, *blan*, white]. The baby died. I would rather one of the youth die than this baby, for we don't know what this baby would have become in the future . . . that saddened me a lot."

Allande didn't enumerate the circumstances of his lighter-skinned nephew. But numerous commentators such as Jean-Robert Cadet (1998) recall that lighter-skinned children of darker-skinned parents are often whispered about, assumed to be progeny of absentee fathers, inviting suspicion about who he is. Cadet became a *restavèk*, a child servant. Some use the term *slave*. Michel-Rolph Trouillot (1994) terms the father's "clear" features his "somatic capital." Trouillot argued that in relationships that transcend the color line, at least those that are formally recognized, the man would be "upwardly mobile," bringing other forms of capital to the relationship. The father of Allande's nephew fits another pattern that Caribbean feminists point out has existed since the plantation system, where a white (or lighter-skinned) man takes a white woman as wife, a mixed-race woman as a mistress, and a darker-skinned woman as lover (for example, Kempadoo 2004; Ulysse 2008). In Allande's calculation, his nephew might have been able to leverage his somatic capital to benefit his family greater than the youth whom he had time to know. Allande is far from alone in this belief (or hope): many times I have turned my head when I heard someone call out the word *blan*, white person (also foreigner—see Schuller 2010b, for a larger discussion) only to find out that a Haitian of slightly lighter features than her or his peers was being hailed. Curious, I often asked "Blan" to tell me more. Many people with this nickname did report preferential treatments from parents, teachers, and friends.

As Trouillot (1994) and others have argued, color has an ambiguous and debated legacy of inequality in Haiti. Other factors can mitigate somatic referents, as the proverb *nèg rich se milat, milat pòv se nèg* (A rich black person[3] is mixed-race [literally mulatto], a poor mulatto is a black person) highlights. Trouillot argued forcefully against the one-to-one mapping of racial and class inequality, as argued François Duvalier (Denis and Duvalier 1965), who ascended to the post of "President-for-Life" in part because of popular anger against the light-skinned elite propped up by the U.S. Marines.

Economically, Haiti is the most unequal nation in the Western Hemisphere. Although the data are old (2001), well before the earthquake and the infusion of billions of dollars in aid, the CIA World Factbook lists Haiti as the seventh most unequal in the world (all six ahead of Haiti are in sub-Saharan Africa, including number two, South Africa).[4] Although just under four in five people lived on less than $2 per day, Haiti is also home to the most millionaires per capita in the hemisphere. What some—perhaps unfairly, certainly unself-critically—call the "morally repugnant elite" pay as little as they can in taxes, not investing in public infrastructure; some within this group attempt to depose the state when they see their financial interests threatened. As for those at the other end of the inequality spectrum, as Faye Harrison (1997, 2008) has argued, neoliberal economic policies have structured a choice between low-paid work in free-trade zones or often lower-paying work in the unstable informal economy. Faced with this choice, many feel obliged to try their luck at getting one of the few jobs in the factories. Allande's neighbor Jorel said, "Living in Port-au-Prince is hard if you don't have a business or a job. That's the worst situation ever."

But working in the factories was not easy. This was exacerbated after the earthquake, as Ghislaine, who lived in St. Louis, explained: "After the earthquake, the house didn't fall on me, but it shook me real hard because I was ... Before I could manage to get out, a door hit me. Since then, I feel that my bones are no longer strong enough to operate the machines. I intended to keep working in the factories, but I can't. I can't work, because sometimes I can feel my bones cracking when my body really hurts." As Marie-Jeanne detailed in the introduction, working in factories didn't spare people from the earthquake. Paul, who like Allande and Jorel lived in Kolonbi, spells this out:

> I was working in a factory. The building collapsed in January. I was told there were injured people. I could have been victim if I was there. A lot of people died in the factory. They scheme and throw the bodies away at night. When the parents of these people came and asked for them, they show the parents the employee list and tell them those people weren't done working. Your life is good for nothing when you are working there.

Although his story is hearsay, accusing factory owners of covering up the dead is too serious to ignore. It suggests a logic of trying to avoid responsibility for the deaths. The earthquake struck at 4:53, after many factories in the free trade zone had closed. Most people are paid by piece work, as Solange detailed: "When the pants are completely done, they sent them off as your quota. When everyone makes quota you earn 125 gourdes. If it's not met, you earn 70 gourdes. All that work you did was for nothing." Paul's analysis suggests a "blame-the-victim" response from factory owners: if workers were still around after the factory closed, it was their own fault, because they didn't work fast enough. However, the Worker Rights Consortium (2013) found that overtime was a very common practice.

Discussing the evident lack of progress, camp resident Jhon theorizes from his experience in CAJIT: "Except those who had put some of what they had aside, but for . . . how can I say this? Eighty-five percent of the population will have to start all over again." Marie-Jeanne specified, "All Haitians have the right to a house, but only people who owned their houses will have them in the future. You who didn't have one will never have one." Marie-Jeanne is referring to Haiti's constitution, article 22, that outlines the right of Haitian citizens to housing. For obvious reasons, with 105,000 houses completely destroyed and 188,383 houses badly damaged, the issue of housing became central to political and social movement discourse. Critical analyses from Marie-Jeanne and others are reminders about Haiti's socioeconomic divisions that also spelled out differential impacts of the disaster and differential access to the billions of dollars in aid. People like the landlord in Claudine's story, or my middle-class neighbors who vacated the block, had houses belonging to other family members to visit, either in another area within Port-au-Prince, or overseas. On top of an already difficult situation combining poverty and inequality, the people whose stories are discussed in this chapter had many fewer options.

"IT MADE ME THINK ABOUT A LOT OF THINGS": IMPETUS FOR CHANGE

Rebecca Solnit, prolific U.S. writer of place and environment, published a compelling and unorthodox study of disaster in 2009, months before Haiti's earthquake. Drawing primarily on five major North American cases, and pulling insights within sociology, Solnit details how disasters can be the platforms for extraordinary communities, outpouring of solidarity, and glimpses into utopia. She writes, "The desires and possibilities awakened are so powerful they shine even from wreckage, carnage, and ashes" (Solnit 2009, 6). This is so, she argues, not because of our choices or political affiliations, but because disasters "drag us into emergencies that require we act, and act altruistically, bravely, and with initiative in order to survive or save the neighbors, no matter how we vote or what we do for a living" (7). Her optimistic and unapologetic reading of human nature, a term she reclaims from postmodernism (she does not mention anthropology nor Marxism, both of which have challenged an essentialist human nature for over a century), holds that disasters are opportunities for these utopian communities because the systems and structures that normally repress this imagination and collective yearning are temporarily suspended. In their place is privatization, a term she does not limit to economics but includes people's imagination toward private satisfaction (8–9). Media accounts portray individuals as either hysterical or selfish.

Although noting that mainstream media and scientific accounts fail to confirm it, Solnit argues that people's experience shows that human nature postdisaster is "resilient, resourceful, generous, empathetic, and brave" (8). As the Haitian authors noted earlier documented, Haiti's earthquake highlights these qualities in individuals, even as the mainstream story was colored by isolated incidences of looting and violence, in at least one case triggered by the team of journalists themselves by throwing aid on the ground and rolling the camera, according to a Haitian cameraman. This racialized coverage is not unique to Haiti: following Hurricane Katrina, journalists described white families "finding" and black families "looting" food. This next section of the chapter is divided into two sets of people's stories that highlight individual and collective responses to the earthquake, respectively. Seen from the ground, from the eyes of survivors, Solnit's thesis makes more sense than Leviathan or the apocalypse.

Chapter 3 discusses some of the economic and familial impacts of the quake and the humanitarian aid that followed. But first, actually reading people's stories demands that disaster scholars take at least some of Solnit's insights seriously. Michèle, who was living at the Hancho camp outside of Cité Jacques Roumain at the time of the July 2011 interview, explained how the earthquake was the impetus for life changes:

> I use to love hanging around; I never liked to stay at my house. And I used to smoke. Since January 12 happened, I don't do this kind of stuff anymore. I think about my life as if it was an ant where any foot can step on it and kill it. And this started to make me think about a lot of things. The earthquake made a big change in my life. Since January 12, what happened, I changed, point blank.

For Michèle, the earthquake was a wake-up call, a reminder about the fragility of her life. Another positively valenced story about the impact of January 12 comes from Yolette, who shared this insight from St. Louis de Gonzague:

> Well . . . the January 12 earthquake affects me in only one way: it teaches me another life. Some people lost their head after the quake; some lost all their

families in the earthquake, some people lost all they possessed and that affects them severely. I saw the house I rented collapse with all my belongings, and I said this is an opportunity to restart my life. This is the only objective I have after the earthquake. I did not want January 12 to be the end of my life, but an opportunity to restart my life.

Yolette discusses people losing their heads before family or possessions. Unlike Michèle, whose story highlights her actions, attitude, and behavior, assessing the impact of Yolette's goal of "restarting" her life is somewhat more complicated, as this would obviously also depend on external forces and opportunities beyond her control. Reading farther down the transcript of Yolette's interview does not reveal an unambiguous success in her life chances. As she pointed out in the interview, the fact that she was still living in a camp was a sore spot for her, because she wanted a better life.

Yolette's neighbor Robenson discussed how the seismic event encouraged solidarity:

I survive. I am surrounded by people who understand me, who share food with me. While camp life teaches me a new lifestyle, it has taught me how to get along with people. And I learned the meaning of sharing.

If you walk in someone's shoes you'll have the opportunity to lead her or him. This is an unfortunate fact but a good one also. . . . Through a misfortune you get a good thing, a new lifestyle. This is what I can testify or confess while I am currently in the camp.

Robenson, whose earlier testimony highlighted his regret at not being able to help, both underscores and challenges Solnit's ideas. Robenson, too young to remember life outside of Port-au-Prince, didn't say that the quake reinforced already-existing values and practices of solidarity. His new collective life, with even less privacy than in the shantytowns, provided a template for a new, hybrid, urban collectivist habitus/praxis.

"THAT'S WHAT WE DID": STORIES OF SOLIDARITY

Robenson's story suggests not only changes to individuals but also expressions of solidarity between individuals. Lolo, who lived in Karade, the only remaining camp five years after the earthquake as I edit this, stated this new collectivism in pragmatic terms: "There are people from different backgrounds living here but we become familiar with one another . . . but for the time being, it's quite a different situation because 'when one doesn't find what one likes, one likes what one has.'"[5] This is an example of people *reziyen*, resigning themselves. Code-switching to

French demonstrates to at least the interviewer, a Haitian college student, that Lolo, like Robenson, is one of 10 percent of people who had at least a high school education. The fact that Lolo lived in a camp not only demonstrates the diversity of people living in camps—that camps include people with high levels of education—but also that people who make it to college are also more diverse than a simple stereotype. Many of my students at the State University of Haiti lived in shantytowns, several also in camps. Carine Exantus, for example, at the Human Sciences School, blogged about her experience in the large camp by the National Palace, in Champs-de-Mars (Exantus 2010). Perhaps this newfound solidarity had to be learned by people (both young men, at that) who were on a "bootstraps" trajectory, trying to succeed despite monumental obstacles.

To others, like Manolia, solidarity seemed to be a reflex, at least in her narration:

> For myself, the earthquake shook me a lot. I was taking a walk in the Brooklyn[6] market in Cité Soleil. I was with two other women. We separated and went off in different directions to take a walk. Myself, I went my way. Right after we separated, the thing [*bagay la*] happened, shaking the ground. I reached out my hand so my friend could hold it, and she was reaching out her hand to me so I could hold it, but we couldn't hold each other's hand.

As noted in the previous chapter, Cité Soleil is the city's largest shantytown, now its own city. Manolia's residence as of the interview was Hancho, also in a "bad" neighborhood,[7] both distinct from at least the public perception of Delmas 31/33, where St. Louis de Gonzague (which is certainly a space for upper classes) was situated, and Karade. It is possible that as a woman, and as a person who inhabits spaces identified as lower *kouch sosyal* (socioeconomic status; see Jean 2002), Manolia didn't need to "learn" a new collectivist behavior.

Manolia is definitely not alone in her desire for human connection. Beyond reaching for another to hold one up from the quaking ground, people shared what they had with one another to make sure everyone ate. Remène, Manolia's Hancho neighbor, recalled, "I'm still going through difficult times. That means we managed to get by: myself, the other people with me, and my children. When we cook some food we share it with them, and when they have some food they give us some. That's the way it was. That's what we did to get by. That's how we lived after January 12." Remène's statement was matter-of-fact about sharing food, saying simply "That's what we did" and "That's how we lived." In this retelling we don't know whether Remène lived like this before January 12. Some changes in people's living situation seemed to engender a greater social bond, and people used different language, like Anne, who also lived in Hancho: "Ever since that happened we have been living here, we're like a family. That means, for example when a family cooks some rice, they share it with us, but we don't complain if they have nothing." Several people used similar expressions to describe relationships within the camp, that it was like a family. Some, like Alix, who lived in Plas Lapè, found themselves surprised at the level of newfound familiarity with others who happened to share space in the public square. He explains: "I sit here. If no one makes food to give me a spoonful, then I don't eat. Because when I came here, I couldn't imagine that if a person was cooking food for me, it wouldn't be my family. Well, this is how my life has played out."

From "This is what we did" to "This is how my life played out" suggests slight differences in approach. Remène's statement is more active, while Alix's is passive, as he explains a newfound dependence on people whom he would have considered strangers before the earthquake. Gender, with different roles being expected of men and women, might explain this difference. Nadege, who like Robenson took residence on the school grounds of St. Louis de Gonzague, detailed solidarity at many levels:

I have many friends, you know? I sold dishes in the street [before the earthquake]. Some of my friends gave me a stockpot, others buckets. And people even gave me beds. They gave me covers. Even clothes, even though they don't fit me. They gave me dishes. The day after, I borrowed a stockpot to cook my meal. I borrowed plates. I borrowed spoons.

We put up the tents in a place where they used to throw garbage. Mr. Louis said that he will lend me the land. He lived there too. So, we're all living there. A police commissioner gave me two or three pieces of wood along with a little tarp. . . . I pitched a tent.

They were removing rubble from the house. Every single item I found, I took it and put it there, where Mr. Louis lives. Then, there was a woman whose name is Nadege, my namesake, who generally gives me something to eat. She just . . . didn't give me anything last June. She didn't have anything. There's also a brother at the church. He used to provide a lot for me. When he gives me stuff, he gives me some rice, beans. He also used to give me clothes. He told me if I don't want to wear them, I can donate them. I'm a generous person. If a person doesn't have anything, I share. This woman, she's a friend of mine. I used to give them to her children. For example, I used to share with other people around as well.

Nadege explains how her many friends enabled her to slowly regain her livelihood. Nadege described both people sharing resources with her as well as sharing resources with others. In this, she is a lot like Paul, who lived in the Kolonbi camp: "I can tell you that sometimes I get a gift of 50 [Haitian] dollars[8] [250 gourdes, around $6] thanks to good friends, according to the way I used to live with them. Because I wasn't a stingy person. And more, God says, 'When you give you will receive.'" Both Paul and Nadege describe a situation of reciprocity (Polanyi 2001), but Paul's is more "balanced" (giving with at least a minimal expectation for getting in return—the original Haitian phrase attributed to the almighty was *fòk ou rekòlte*, "You need to harvest"). Nadege is both the giver and recipient of generalized reciprocity (Sahlins 1972), in part because of a difference in status. Interestingly, Nadege's social relationships span boundaries of *kouch sosyal*. She refers to a Mr. Louis, who was also a government minister who had a house near the St. Louis camp. The church brother is also someone of professional status. Her namesake's class situation is not clearly situated in Nadege's story, but one can surmise a more egalitarian sharing relationship, with sharing plates of cooked food as opposed to uncooked food rations from Nadege's religious community (see also McAlister 2013). Sending plates of food for neighbors was common practice before the earthquake.

These stories of solidarity certainly reveal elements of a human nature that is "resilient, resourceful, generous, empathetic, and brave" (Solnit 2009, 8). Unfortunately these stories failed to pierce the consciousness of foreign agencies, both media and aid groups. The story often told in safely expat spaces such as nightclubs, gyms, beaches, or pool sides is one of Haitians acting selfishly, short sightedly, often with *blan* trying to outdo each other. Of course, some of these stories aid workers told one another are also true, as not every Haitian always acted with solidarity. Several spoke of a "dog-eat-dog" reality, and several others expressed present fears of theft or rape. However, one must not overlook the lessons Robenson and Alix said they learned. Solnit's book is a challenge to rethink how communities act after a disaster. The earthquake in Haiti was the first major catastrophe following the publication of her book. As a case study, it generally supports her idea, which also guards against Haitian exceptionalism in the positive sense (Clitandre 2011), romanticizing being the "liberal" variant of what Trouillot (2003) termed the "savage slot." However, a deeper reading of the stories reveals variations in emphasis, ideology, practice, and what precisely was new after the earthquake across social boundaries of gender, location, and socioeconomic status.

Moving into camps is one expression of this solidarity, as Anne-Marie explained, describing moving into Hancho: "We settled in one place because the situation was difficult. We slept on the same sheet. We used the same sheet as cover. We ate the same food, because the situation improved for the small group that we formed." These stories of solidarity offer examples of communities as first responders; as Solnit argues, these are more common than acknowledged. How did people take this solidarity into the camps? What impact did this new setting have on this solidarity?

PITCHING TENTS

The story of how camps came to be is complex. In his hard-hitting critique of the international humanitarian response, AP correspondent Jonathan Katz (2013) hinted that the system of camps was an artificial creation of aid agencies. Georges, whom I knew for years from his work at an NGO I studied for my dissertation, worked for a UN agency after the earthquake. Georges offered another example corroborating Katz's suspicion in his Léogâne neighborhood that had a large number of camps, home to people fleeing Port-au-Prince.

Each of the eight camps in this study has a distinct story; see Table 2.1. Each was situated on a particular parcel (or parcels) of land, and vary among a range of factors. Alluded to earlier, some like Hancho and Plas Lapè are in low-income neighborhoods or shantytowns. Others like St. Louis de Gonzague and Karade are in mixed or middle-income areas. Some camps are on public park land, like Meri Kafou or Plas Lapè. Some are sandwiched in between, and stretched across, private properties, like Nan Bannann or CAJIT. Only two of the eight—Kolonbi and Karade—remained in 2014, in no small part because they are out of the way: of foreign dignitaries, business owners, journalists, and NGOs. Finally closed in November 2014, Kolonbi was situated in the sprawling Delmas industrial park, at the end of a corridor, pushed against a ravine. Karade was on land declared public by former president Aristide in 2002, and at the top of a hill away from any main road. Some was used for a planned "relocation" site in April 2010, for residents of St. Louis. Sometime in 2014, Karade was rebaptized a "village," in part to signify the end of NGO aid, in part to lower the number of people living in "camps."

Given this diversity, there is not one story of how the camps came to exist. Based on the eighty-seven interviews with the IDPs themselves, however, some patterns do emerge. First, because of the aftershocks, some of magnitude 5 or

Name of Camp	City	Neighborhood	Number of Families	NGO Management?
CAJIT	Carrefour	Paloma	178	No
Hancho	Delmas	Cite Jacques Roumain	140	Yes
Karade	Delmas	Carradeux, Terrain Toto	4360	Yes
Kolonbi	Delmas	Industrial Park/Delmas 19	285	Yes
Meri Dikini	Carrefour	Diquini	240	No
Nan Bannann	Delmas	Delmas 32	160	No
Plas Lapè	Port-au-Prince/ Delmas	Delmas 2	4900	Yes
St. Louis	Delmas	Delmas 31/33	512	No

TABLE 2.1   Eight Camps in the Study with Some Characteristics

greater, that continued for a couple of weeks, many people, even whose homes were luckily standing, sought a place on the ground. My neighbor Lise's house survived the January 12 earthquake but not an aftershock. Another common story is that many people slept the first night where goudougoudou happened to take them. Many, like Manolia, had to first find their families. Finally, a common thread is that people like Claudine sought refuge together in spaces that could accommodate them.

Reconnecting with people and rebuilding these solidarity ties took some time. In the 791-person household survey, 461 people, or 61.6 percent of responses, reported coming to the camp on January 12. An additional 84, or 11.2 percent, came the first week. This statistic includes the planned relocation camp of Karade. Once respondents from Karade are taken out of the sample, the figure is 69.3 percent arriving the first day and 81.9 percent the first week. This figure still includes 54 people (8.1 percent) who noted that they lived in another camp before the one where they were interviewed. In other words, 90.0 percent of people were in the camps by the first week. In the overall sample, 9.1 percent of people said they arrived in April 2010, which is when six thousand residents were moved from St. Louis to Karade. Taking Karade out of the sample the number shrinks to 1.8 percent.

Living in camps was outside of many people's experience, as Emile recalled: "I would never imagine that we Haitians would live in Plas Lapè [Peace Plaza], because this is where they used to play soccer." Figure 2.1 shows this field. Despite the unimaginable living situation it posed, people still found their way to places they felt they could safely find shelter. IOM counted 1.5 million people at its peak in an official census of May 2010, which represented a sixth of Haiti's entire population. Some had to buy their own tarps or tents, like Sabine:

> After that goudougoudou [the earthquake] had passed, the house was destroyed. It killed my sister's kids here inside. As for us, God saved us. Well, we are here because a cousin invited us here. We found a little shelter that we bought. We heard they were giving out shelters but we up the hill never had that possibility. We brought those little shelters. The life we lived here was very miserable. After that, we found an organization over there, and so we found ourselves in a camp.

Sabine's story shows that many people went to the camps to reunite with family. Sabine also highlights the difficulties of finding shelter, like Claudine. Not every camp was created by NGOs because, simply, not every camp received NGO aid. Explaining this discrepancy, Linda noted above that CAJIT was hidden away from the main road: "They have forgotten about us! I don't know if it's because NGOs are afraid of climbing the hill or they can't get credit because we're not visible, but no one ever comes by." During my first visit, in July 2010,

FIGURE 2.1. Plas Lapè camp, July 2011. Photo: author

Linda thanked my colleague and me for making the trek, a little surprised. Because of its invisibility, CAJIT didn't officially exist until months after the earthquake. According to Linda, the first distribution of tarps didn't occur until after our visit. This is why people like Sabine had to purchase their own tarps.

Hancho straddled two properties, neither of which had been in use. Residents couldn't easily identify the landowners: a few names of rumored landowners surfaced, including former army officers and Tonton Makout—dictator Duvalier's secret police—who had left the country. Given the surprise return of "Baby Doc" in January 2011, many wondered whether his paramilitary would also return from exile and claim their land, a reason proposed by some for Duvalier's sudden return. In the collective memory of people living in Cité Jacques Roumain, the land had been empty since people migrated from the provinces. Sharing residents' detailed stories about how Hancho came to be offers a greater understanding of general processes. Not surprisingly, human relationships and solidarity action played an important role in the gradual settlement. Following are excerpts from three interviews, with women we have already heard from: Manoucheka, Manolia, and Michèle. My hope is that through sharing these particular stories, with a sense of familiarity, readers can get a glimpse of their humanity, understanding that they are real people doing their best to survive:

On January 12, we had . . . I was doing laundry. The ground was shaking under my feet. I was holding a child; I couldn't run. Anywhere I tried to run to . . . just then, a huge piece of concrete ceiling fell onto the bed. Then, when the ground stopped shaking, we ran outside. I spent three days wearing the same clothes without bathing! I didn't take a shower. Things were hard for us.

When we finally came here, we spread some sheets on the ground. We slept on garbage, we slept on the weeds on the ground. Things weren't good for us. We used pieces of torn sheets. Our situation was horrible: caterpillars, mosquitoes, and other types of bugs were biting us. Some people didn't escape with anything. We didn't have money, so we were obliged to collaborate with our neighbors. That means when they fix some food they give us some. (Manoucheka)

When we realized that the sun was coming down, we stood up and set out on foot. We walked a lot and we got there, in front of the airport. We got there on foot and slept there. We went there on foot, carrying only the clothes we had on. We were dirty out there on the streets. We slept on the ground in the open air, in front of the airport. When we were done, while we were sitting at the plaza, the thing [aftershocks] started. Every now and then the ground shook a little. We were cold. It was like hell. All night long, every now and then, the ground shook. We were suffering. At dawn we set out, and I decided to go home.

When I went back home, I didn't know if the house was destroyed, so now, that's when I got back there. When I got there, I saw two single room houses standing. All other houses, all of them collapsed! They were destroyed. Now, ever since the houses collapsed, I've been living on the streets.

A friend of mine called for me. She told me, "Anyway, Manolia, you can't continue walking around like this without a place to rest your head." She added, "The house where I used to live was destroyed. I don't have money to rent an apartment. The children are in my hands. I'm left alone, I don't have any family." She had me join her. She managed to make a shelter with some sheets. She was lying down. She told me to join her, and I lay there with her. While I was there I made a small tent and I stayed there. (Manolia)

Well after January 12, we came here. The only things here were weeds and swamp. We raked the land. We set up the sheets. But the first place, during January 12 . . . when it took us inside, the event took us off guard. We just spread some blankets and slept outdoors like this.

Afterward, the Haitian Red Cross and the Spanish Red Cross came over. After that we haven't received anything. The population themselves did their best to get by, to be able to send their kids to school. (Michèle)

Manoucheka's, Manolia's, and Michèle's stories highlight the first, informal phases of setting up camp. Manoucheka and Manolia point to the human relationships that brought them together to this particular place. They all note sleeping on the ground and all share difficulties of negotiating with the land itself. All three "got by" with what they could salvage—sleeping on and under single bedsheets. Unlike Karade—at least St. Louis Displaced—Hancho never received temporary shelters, called "T-shelters," made of plywood. Unlike even nearby Plas Lapè, in a similar neighborhood, Hancho never received a distribution of tarps. So the physical layout of the built environment was much like the rugged natural environment: irregular, jagged, and particular, as Figure 2.2 shows.

As can be inferred from this discussion, people's experiences of the camps' physical layout varied. And certainly the people relocated from St. Louis to Karade had a much different experience moving into the camp. Their experiences mirror more those documented in Peck's *Fatal Assistance*. Two unforgettable images in the film are of UN troops rounding up people to move from the Pétion-Ville Club, managed by Sean Penn's NGO, packing them into buses, and, later, the look on one of the people displaced again, when seeing the new relocation camp built for them, Corail Cesselesse (French for "endless coral"; indeed the space was a desert).

However, in all eight camps people told similar stories of their first coming together. In the household survey we had asked where people were living on January 12. The list of neighborhoods shows that people did migrate together, seeking the closest space where a family like Claudine's could pitch her tarp (or bedsheets). Urban geography played a role in this, particularly the availability of open land. On the block where I live, people slept on the street because there was no large open space. But down the hill was a large camp either called KID (referring to the political party who had used the space for their headquarters) or Christ-Roi. It was the closest location for many in Nazon, areas of which were totally destroyed, like Frisline's neighborhood. In some camps, a second phase was initiated when humanitarian agencies began distributions: of tarps, water, toilets, hygiene kits, "starter" kits including kitchen supplies, and food. But during the first phase there wasn't that great a distinction. Given camp conditions, many people reported "not sleeping well."

Not Sleeping Well

Once living in camps, as Robenson and Lolo noted, people had to adjust to a much different lifestyle. Although there is certainly a greater solidarity in camp life, with people sharing food, utensils, and other necessities, there is also much less privacy. Carolle notes that not everyone who is by necessity living next to one another, literally *kwense*, "coinciding" or "squeezed," is welcome: "Imagine, if

FIGURE 2.2. Hancho I camp, July 2011. Photo: author

it wasn't for January 12, there are certain people you wouldn't come across. There are certain places you shouldn't be. The way you were living when you were in your own home isn't the same as living here." This lack of privacy is connected to the difference most noted by people: the physical structure of the houses. Living under a tent, tarp, or bedsheet meant that people couldn't sleep well. Nadege from St. Louis began:

> My children don't sleep well, the way you do in a concrete house. They no longer have that comfort. You see what I mean? It rains, my bed covers and other items are . . . I don't care about that. Sometimes, my kids complain about lying too close to each other. I don't worry about that. But one day, the situation will change. You see what I mean? Before the earthquake, we didn't use to sleep in the same bed.

Nadege stopped herself from discussing the problem of rain, as her primary concern is about the close proximity and total lack of privacy. The Haitian word most often used is *pwomiskite*, which could be translated as "promiscuity," because they share a cognate. Some, particularly outsiders referring to IDPs, might use the term in this judgmental connotation. Although there was evidence of a class bias, I was told again and again that the meaning of this word is that people inside tents, and the tents themselves, are crammed next to one another. In some cases the sexual connotation might have indeed been intended, because these conditions reinforced unwanted sexual contact, as detailed in chapter 4.

Although Nadege may not "care about that," the reality of tropical rains was a primary concern for people. Evrance showed the research team in Kolonbi her family's makeshift solution to the rain: "This is the little bowl that we use to protect ourselves from the raindrops when it rains. After it stops raining, we go to bed." Tropical storms can last for hours, sometimes through the night. Wedly, Evrance's neighbor in Kolonbi, discussed the fragility of tarps, not only for rain: "We're not living well because at night we can't sleep. Thieves rip open the tarps. And when it rains, water gets through the tarps. Things . . . it's a headache! We're not living well! We're not living well! Our situation is terrible!"

Their neighbor Paul was reluctant to grant the research team an interview: "All our things got wet last night because it rained a lot, even our bed sheet. My wife had to cover the bed with an old dirty sheet. I'm ashamed to have you come inside. . . . Everything is wet. All these are our struggles." Paul's shame cut deep, as traditional values place a premium on hospitality. I was consistently moved by this, people with barely enough to eat often going out of their way—according to them happily—to welcome a stranger. Not having chairs to offer a guest was also a source of shame. I told them I was *alèz*, comfortable, with sitting on a broken brick, which surprised many coming from a *blan*. But it was just as, if not more, important to show that one could receive a guest.

Sometimes this discomfort was so obvious, the shame too great, that they tried to improve their situation by making demands of the research team. France, who was at CAJIT, was direct: "Because I don't have a place to live, the rain is falling on me and I get wet under a tent, I don't have a place to stay, which means that I would like you to help me find a place to stay with the kids." This was a major concern while conducting the research. People were *bouke*, fed up, with research. Too often, the research conducted didn't do anything to change their life circumstances. In daily meetings with researchers we would discuss this at length. I couldn't offer much more solace, and I certainly couldn't promise anything other than that we are trying to find solutions and that I would share their stories with people who might be able to make changes. This was only magnified when I would go to the field. Often a crowd of up to thirty or forty people would form immediately upon my arrival. People saw my white skin, heard my U.S. American-accented Haitian (Creole), and correctly surmised that I had greater access to resources. I was usually at least initially mistaken for an NGO worker, so people would express their frustrations with the way the system isn't working.

"We're Not Used to This Kind of Life"

Yolette, from St. Louis, offers a poignant reminder of the importance of maintaining a clean house: "Yesterday I was talking to a friend. I told her that I don't remember the last time I cleaned a house, the last time I mopped my house. I told her that this is starting to bother me." Like Manoucheka's discussion of not bathing, Yolette talked about the lack of cleanliness as an affront to dignity. Foreign commentators, including a pastor who recently watched documentary *Poto Mitan*, are often surprised about Haitian people's dignity and self-presentation, commenting on both posture (Hefferan 2007) and cleanliness (Gold 1991). Leaving aside interrogating the source of the surprise—Is it racism about U.S. Blacks or media-fed stereotypes of poor people generally, or Haitian people specifically?—this pride in keeping one's self or one's *fwaye* clean is part of what Ulysse (2008) calls "reflexive political economy."

Because taking good care of what one can represented a refraction of basic human agency and dignity, camp life posed challenges to residents, as Eveline, who lived in Nan Bannann detailed:

> The children's clothes are dirty and we aren't used to leading this kind of life. We are accustomed to renting a house to live in, but now we can't afford to do that. The children are running, the adults are in the street, fooling around as street children. I feel sad and I am not at peace. I don't feel at ease. Now, I am short of money, there is no job to rent a house. Things are upside down, and we are still under the tents.

Detailed in chapter 4, there are so many things outside of one's control in the camps. Sanitary conditions leave much to be desired. This leads to people feeling that they are being thought of, and treated, like animals.

"Like Animals"

There are other environmental problems within the camps. Emile, from Plas Lapè, recalled, "There are reptiles and big rats all around. On Good Friday, for example, I had two little chickens. I decided not to eat them because it was Good Friday. But five rats ate the chickens. You can lie down here and the smell of rats prevents us from breathing." Adlin Noël (2013) reported that rats ate through a child's diapers in Plas Lapè. Many people expressed frustration not only with the animals they were forced to contend with, but described their living conditions themselves as subhuman, as living "like animals," like Manoucheka:

> But ever since, we've been living on this land . . . like animals, because there are no lights here. There's no water supply. We don't have any house, so we're living

under tarps. It's not good for us, it's hot. We get sick because of that. It causes headaches, fever. The kids here can't go to school because we're jobless. Ever since that's the way we've been living.

Anyway, people used to drop by. They always said they would do something for us; they would help us leave this place. But up to now nothing has been done! We'd like for this place to change, because this place is not appropriate for us. We can't continue living in such conditions. We can't take it anymore!

Manoucheka and Emile were far from alone in their frustrations: in our study, 722 of 786 (91.8 percent) preferred to leave the camp. IOM commissioned a study (2011) noting that 93 percent of IDPs wanted to leave. The discourse of living like animals was quite common; at the State University, students and faculty invoked Giorgio Agamben's (1998) concept of "bare life" to describe how human beings were reduced to bare, biological, survival. Living conditions were often inhuman: the heat, lack of sanitation, mud, complete lack of privacy, the smell, and limited opportunities. Skin rashes were a common occurrence, as people's bodies attempted to fend off pathogens in the environment. I contracted a rash in the summer of 2010 because of my own exposure, far more limited than people like Manoucheka. Some people like Yves, from CAJIT, argue that people are treated worse than animals:

I'm not supposed to be living in a tent. If I had some money, I would look for an apartment to rent, and I would live in it because you get humiliated when you're living in tents. We're here, in tents, because of what happened on January 12. Some people look at us like we're dogs. Actually, dogs in foreign countries are valued more than us. The amount of money that's spent on them in one week would be our income for four or five months.

Many people describe the stigma attached with being an IDP. Nadege explained, "My children didn't use to live in that condition! There are words that people say I don't like. I don't appreciate that. It's just because of the earthquake. . . . You see what I mean? I have two young girls. They didn't use to go out. They go out now. You really see what I mean?" Allande decried, "Just because we're living in a camp, the way people see us, people liken us to delinquents." Frisline, who also lives in Karade, revealed, "Sometimes you get on a bus and you hear people speaking badly about people living in the camps. You can't speak because you are one of them." Frisline, Yves, and others outline a powerful stigma attached to being a *deplase*, the identity of being an IDP (Brun 2003; Duncan 2005).

Why is this? In no small part, the camps remain visual reminders of the failures within the international aid response, eyesores that get in the way of selling

Haiti as being "now open for business," as President Michel Martelly boasted in May 2011. More fundamentally, the people struggling to survive under the heat of the tarps or temporary shelters were committing the ultimate indignity: they existed. IDPs' mere existence brought visibility to profound social problems, such as the extreme depravity and deep class hostility that has always beset Haiti but had been swept under the rug; they were what Hardt and Negri (2001, 294) called "disposable people," or Michel Agier (2011), "undesirables." The hypocrisy, misery, and inequality could no longer be ignored, now that it was in plain view, especially at the Champs de Mars, the National Plaza surrounding the crumbled remains of the National Palace: a visible demand to be seen.

On top of Haiti's deep-seated social divisions temporarily suspended after the earthquake, foreign aid agencies added to this denigration of IDPs. In most of my interviews and in informal conversations, foreign aid workers were quick to point to a case of an individual trying to take advantage of the situation. Usually this was a single individual, and always this was the prelude to a general assessment of IDPs. This assessment either justified the agency's disciplinary, even punitive, approach to management of IDPs or explained the failures in the aid system overall. These weren't just conversations with me. Humanitarian agencies attempted to shape the conversation, shifting the "blame" for the obvious lack of progress onto the IDPs themselves. Echoing former First Lady Barbara Bush's comments about the Katrina displaced living better in the Astrodome, on May 10, 2010, Assistant Secretary of State Cheryl Mills said that "people seek to remain in the temporary communities because, as surprising as that might seem outside of Haiti, life is better for many of them now."

Mills's comment highlights a persistent discourse that people like Manolia, Michèle, and Frisline were only living under tents in order to get free services: How else would living "worse than dogs" be possibly considered better? Foreign aid workers expended quite a bit of energy to expose this. For example, anthropologist Tim Schwartz declared there to be only 42,608 "legitimate" IDPs in a report commissioned (and later rejected) by USAID, but leaked to the press and finally published on May 27, 2011, by Agence France-Presse, AFP (Troutman 2011). Dozens of news stories, including in large-circulation media like the *Washington Post, New York Times, Newsweek,* and *Time,* repeated this finger-wagging, more editorializing than news reporting. Schwartz's critique of the Haitian government was based primarily on its lack of transparency in its research methods; however, the leaked report was similarly opaque. For its part, USAID distanced itself from the most controversial claims, citing inconsistencies and irregularities within Schwartz's research methods (Daniel 2011). Only two stories that made it to Google's daily news alerts reported this critique, despite the dozens that used the leaked report to lodge a critique against the Haitian government, many drawing on familiar narratives of Haitian incompetence, adding to Haiti's unending bad press (Lawless 1992; Trouillot 1990; Ulysse 2010). The debate was primarily focused on the death toll, leaving the other unsubstantiated claims about the "legitimate" IDPs and incendiary statements such as people living in the camps only for the free access to services unaddressed. The total silence, the attention deflected away from this discussion of the "illegitimate" IDPs, was an insidious outcome. The inflammatory and controversial allegations about living IDPs, whose rights were actively being challenged by a range of actors, became tacitly accepted by the lack of scrutiny.

Recall that 90 percent of people in the survey came to the camp within the first week and even more wanted to leave the camps. True, some tried to use the aid system to their advantage. In the 791-person survey, sixteen people, or 3.5 percent, had come to Port-au-Prince since 2010. These individuals were not IDPs in the strict legal sense, having come to Port-au-Prince after the disaster. However, broadly speaking, they were displaced: the previous chapter discussed the quadrupling of Port-au-Prince since the 1980s, in large part because of neoliberal policies. The two million new residents are in many real senses "internally displaced." But the critical difference is that as victims of "structural violence" they do not have rights loosely defined in the United Nations Guiding Principles on Internal Displacement (United Nations Office for Coordination of Humanitarian Aid 2001), not officially under IOM's mandate. Even these "rights" are tenuous; the UN language is vague, calling them "guiding principles." This is because as *internally* displaced the United Nations doesn't claim jurisdiction, respecting at least *de jure* national sovereignty, compared to refugees who are protected by international law.

DEHUMANIZATION

Although these loosely defined rights were not universally granted, once thus categorized as IDPs, as *deplase*—people like Claudine, Paul, and Michèle can have their humanity taken away, their actions scrutinized, monitored, and controlled; their intentions questioned and vilified, and their survival stories forgotten. They become in short easy targets, scapegoats for failures in aid delivery or eyesores to be removed by force by local governments. Intentional or not, this characterization of people only suffering rats' eating diapers or scheming to have pots catch the rain water so as not to ruin people's bedsheets or baby pictures in order to obtain free services was useful to many actors. Landowners and government officials such as Delmas Mayor Wilson Jeudy, who actively sought to close IDP camps, found justification by painting IDPs as "illegitimate" (Charles 2011). Days after the APF's May 2011 story that uncritically quoted him, Jeudy again destroyed an IDP camp on public land in his municipality, his second violent act within two weeks, citing a similar refrain of the IDPs not being "real" victims but criminals (Let Haiti Live 2011). Jeudy employed armed private police to rip people's tents and destroy their belongings.

As these stories demonstrate, IDPs lived a precarious existence. At any moment they can be woken up in the middle of the night by rain, by rats, to be moved out, their tents burned, robbed, their bodies or children raped, to have their pictures taken to continue receiving aid, or by helicopters trying with an infrared camera to count how many warm bodies are still surviving under the heat of the tarps in the Caribbean sun. I have hoped to humanize these survivors, beginning with their survival stories, and collective solidarity, followed by difficulties of camp life, which even to many IDPs themselves was unimaginable. In addition to (I hope) inspiring empathy, this chapter outlines the challenges faced, begging the question of what was going on. Why did well-intentioned people come to distrust people like Manolia? And what long-term impacts do people like Yolette face? To begin to answer these questions, the next chapter starts with the impacts on people's livelihoods and families.

3 · HITTING HOME

Humanitarian Impacts on Haiti's Households

The house where I used to live, someone else was in charge of it. When he rented it out, he used to give me some money because I was the housekeeper. Now, the house was destroyed.

Now then, I fell on my knees and cried out, saying "I'm lost! All my children died inside!" along with a woman who lived below named Naomi. A policeman came by; I asked him to rescue Naomi. He said he couldn't. He said he couldn't. Naomi's child ... he put a piece of wood under a block, he lifted the block. I can't talk about this stuff! Ever since I have stopped having my period!

He threw Naomi's son behind a wall. I didn't realize he was dead. I said, "Why would you throw him like that?" He said, "Yes, he's dead."

I eventually found most of my children, but then I yelled, "Woy! I am missing a child, a seventeen-year-old boy!" He was hiding under my bed. The roof of the house didn't collapse. It rested on my barrels, where I stored my merchandize. He was crying for help because he said he was looking for me in the house. He said that's the reason why he cried out the most, so that I could get out. But ever since, he's been through hard times and never found a job.

We put up the tents in a place where they used to throw garbage. The man said he would lend me the land. He lived there too. So, we're all living there. A police commissioner gave me two or three pieces of wood along with a little tarp. ... I pitched a tent.

They used to rip tents open and steal things inside. My daughter can't stand that. When she borrows my sandals, like this black one here that I'd given her, someone rips open the tent and steals the sandals. Ever since, she tells me, "Mom, this is not a place for you to live in. Let's go to the country-side." I answered her, "No, I won't go to the countryside. I was born in the provinces but my whole life is here." I had come here with my mom. I have no resources in the country. If I took my five children to the countryside, what would they eat?

My younger boy told me he doesn't want to live by people who smoke. And the odor makes me nauseous. I asked a neighbor to watch over them for me. My neighbor told me that the kids can't live there. Find a place to live.... The kids can't follow you.

I have these young girls. I can't let them sleep alone. My oldest daughter can't sleep here. Guys are fresh in St Louis. Then, my twelve-year-old was crying. She was afraid. I sent her to Cap Haitian. She was crying because she didn't want to stay there. She came back to find me here again.

Then I said, I moved on with five children. When I'm here, I'm hungry. I left the oldest ones. Each of them is somewhere different. I came here with two of them. Both of them, along with a little one who is twelve years old, whose name is Linda, I came here with her.

There was a woman I was on good terms with. I used to leave one of the little ones at her place. I don't leave them there anymore. I realized that people in the area over there are making trouble, so I keep them with me. Now, I'm the only one here.

Now they tell me they are moving people out. I would choose a shelter, but Mr. Louis told me that he can't let me put it on his spot because it's not his land.... They don't recognize his title [literally, "don't see him"].

—Nadege, St. Louis de Gonzague

Nadege was lucky in that her children all lived. Her *fwaye* (foyer, or household) was intact on January 12 while the house she stayed at was no lon-ger standing. Her seventeen-year-old son was literally saved by her business, her merchandise stored at Mr. Louis's house. In the previous chapter Nadege shared how her many friends from different social stations helped to restart her busi-ness, including Mr. Louis himself, a government minister. What the earthquake did not destroy, realities of camp life splintered or fractured Nadege's *fwaye*. Nadege also hints at the relocation phase, which could have been a time for family reunification. This chapter discusses these interconnected phenomena, how camp life, including the policies behind humanitarian aid, fissioned many households. Tied to the disruption of the household is a diminishing of solidar-ity networks, alternatively called social capital or sharing ties. Another meaning of *fwaye* is stove, reinforcing and referencing sharing ties: With whom do you eat or share food? As of 2014, when this chapter was written, the majority of

IDPs (internally displaced persons) have left the camps, are families reuniting? Are they living better than they had while in the camps? Combining quantitative data from the 2011 household survey with participant observation, recorded interviews with IDPs and aid workers, and follow-up research conducted in the summer of 2012, this chapter aims at answering these questions.

LAKOU

Briefly noted in chapter 1, a flexible, intergenerational household system, the *lakou*, developed after the fall of plantation slavery. The word initially served to denote the yard (French: *la cours*, often simply translated as "yard") framed by individual family dwellings (Bastien 1961). Early ethnographies point to the simplicity of construction of rural houses, and observation points to use of outdoor living space shared across what could be called the "extended" family and even others (Price-Mars 1956, 1983). As Jean Price-Mars (founder of the Bureau National d'Ethnologie), Rémy Bastien (dean of the Faculté d'Ethnologie at the time), and other anthropologists noted, the shared use of the *lakou* was simultaneously the source of strong social ties, symbolized by sharing a plate of food, as well as greater conflict, as extended family members could peer into the private affairs of others. According to these Haitian anthropologists, this familiarity inspired and is explained by the proverb *zafè kabrit pa zafè mouton* (literally, The goat's business is not the sheep's business). Anthropologist Gérard Barthélémy (1990) discussed how this system of solidarity was generalized, and the word *lakou* also came to mean the solidarity ties implied and structured by the extended family compounds.[1] Haitian American anthropologist Michel Laguerre (1973) noted that the word *lakou* also took on religious connotations as the house of ancestor worship (he used the word *voodoo* in his article). Laguerre points to the role that these family shrines play in reaffirming bonds with people who can claim common ancestors. Laguerre (1982) also described continuities of this rural social form in urban Haiti, particularly in the Bel-Air neighborhood of Port-au-Prince. More recently anthropologist Karen Richman (2014) specified this point, discussing *demanbre*, the physical spaces where these identities "belong" and overlap. Although obviously constrained by the lack of available physical space, the urban *lakou* or *demanbre* maintains its function as a form of solidarity.

Since Raymond Smith (1956) and Edith Clarke (1957), many scholars of the Caribbean have discussed the concept of matrifocality, an anthropological kinship term referring to households anchored by women as mothers (for example, Mintz 2010; Price 1982; Slocum and Thomas 2003; Trouillot 1992). The latter two articles, both theoretical reviews, critique the stereotyping of the region, overdetermining the response from plantation slavery. Black feminist scholars such as

Hortense Spillers (1987) and Angela Davis (1983a) deconstruct previous racial stereotyping, from Daniel Patrick Moynihan, who as a U.S. senator chaired a commission that ended welfare and called for a "corrective" to the "absent" Black father figure. Women were thrust into a position of centrality in part because of the ways in which slave owners used them to grow their wealth, while tearing fathers away from children to prevent solidarity between slaves. Spillers and Davis point out that plantation slavery systematically destroyed people's identities and family relations; if there was any family at all during and after slavery, this in itself was a monumental cultural achievement. The system that developed in the Caribbean and the U.S. South was more flexible, more multigenerational, more women centered than the so-called nuclear family that was the norm—although increasingly not the practice—in middle-class, white settler societies such as the United States.[2] Christina Sharpe (2010) continues in the line traced by Spillers and Davis, theorizing the brutality in the fashioning of post-plantation social structures, especially the household.

Chapter 1 details the ruptures to Haitian society caused by neoliberal policies and the consequent quadrupling of the population of Port-au-Prince. Laguerre's study of the modified *lakou* system to accommodate an urban neighborhood setting was conducted before the massive rural exodus that displaced more than two million peasants. Chapter 1 also discusses how migration to the capital often created diasporas of people from similar regions, if not hometowns, exemplified by neighborhood names such as Site Jeremi or Site Okay, both proximate to the space that was to become the Kolonbi camp.[3] M. Catherine Maternowska (2006) discusses gender and households within the nation's largest shantytown, Site Solèy. Maternowska's argument focuses on poverty and inequality, notably triggered or increased by USAID (U.S. Agency for International Development) policies. Her discussion of the way survival strategies are gendered teases apart individuals and households: "It is inside households that power, authority, and conflict define the contours of gender relations. Households are terrains of bargaining, and bargaining in turn works through cultural rules" (Maternowska 2006, 44). Underneath this discussion of negotiation is also a recognition that households are the backbone of survival. Kovats-Bernat (2006) discusses "fictive kin" relations that develop among street children, but missed an opportunity to discuss the household logics of poverty and inequality structured by neoliberalism.

In my own published work I did not specifically engage the logic of households; my work was animated to some extent by a poststructuralist, Marxist feminist critique of anthropological analyses of kinship (for example, Collier and Yanagisako 1987; Strathern 1985; Weston 1997), particularly the consequences of a culturalist understanding, for example, the Moynihan Report (Moynihan 1965) or Oscar Lewis's (1966) "culture of poverty" argument (Abu-Lughod

1991; Behar and Gordon 1995; Clifford and Marcus 1986; Said 1979; Spivak 1988; Trouillot 2003). Consequently my only interviews and writings in field notes about households were not systematic before the earthquake. However, post-earthquake aid brought the issue of households to the center of discussion, debate, and praxis.

Definitions of "Family"

Sabine, interviewing from CAJIT, describes her *lakou*: "My sisters are my family. But I have cousins that are married who live in the yard, they are my family. My husband, my children, and then I have a sister here with me. She is like a mother to me." In addition to caregiving, "like a mother" role, many women who also have "bread-winning" responsibilities will define that role as "father." Many women shared that "I am the mother, and I am the father." This is a common discourse across the Caribbean (for example, Clarke 1957). Sabine defines the family in terms of assistance in times of distress, of compassion, literally shared suffering: "I value my family a lot because during all my suffering, they are the ones that help me get through it. Me too: if someone else has a problem, I feel like I have been affected too."

Family is also defined in functional terms. Michaëlle, who found herself in the Nan Bannann camp, said, "A family is like someone who can provide me with something if I'm in need. I can go to their[4] house and they give it to me. If they need something they can also come to my house and I will give it to him." Michaëlle's conception of family is flexible enough to include people with whom she is on good enough terms to share whenever there is a need. Anthropologists used to call this "fictive kin," on the notion that so-called biological relations were primordial (see, for example, Carsten 2000; Schneider 1984 for a critique). This notion of fictive kin can be extended beyond one's personal sphere, as Sophonie, who lived outside the Carrefour City Hall in the neighborhood of Dikini, explained: "Myself, what I consider as my family is . . . God. After God, the government, because the government can decide to do something for us in any circumstance." In addition to housing the city government Dikini is also the location of a large Adventist superplex, which includes a residential university. Many people who sought shelter in the public grounds had ties to the Adventist church, or ADRA, the international Adventist nongovernmental organization (NGO). The student who conducted research at this camp was also Adventist. Their shared religious experience might partially explain Sophonie's answer; when he asked Sophonie about her children, she replied, "Sure, the kids are my family. But they aren't yet able to help me in any way."

People do distinguish between the *fwaye* (household) and the *fanmi* (family), but it is not necessarily the nuclear family that is central, as Sophonie's neighbor Murielle outlines: "My aunt is the one I regard as my family. Well, there are others, my sister and my cousins, friends too, because we're living with some friends." Liline, who like Sophonie and Murielle stayed in the Meri Dikini (Carrefour City Hall) camp, outlined a dual sense to the word *family*: "People I consider as my family are my family and people living in my neighborhood." Other people used the phrase "real family" to denote blood relations, to distinguish between them and the social role of family. In her definition, Nadine, who lived in Hancho, privileged children: "I don't have children, so my family is my mom, my brother, and sister. Well, I could mention my uncle and my cousins." By contrast, Michèle, also from Hancho, defined a family broadly: "These three people get together to form a family. There is the family, which means sister, mother, kids, cousin, father, nephew, niece, and a bunch of other things." Whatever these other things are, Michèle's understanding allows for the action of deciding to come together to create a family. It also leaves open the possibility that families are strung together, what Iris Marion Young (1994) called "seriality." There is no essence to the family—they are like a series only put together by circumstance, like living in the camps. People would often use the word *makomè* (my co-mother) and *monkonpè* (my co-father) when hailing these relations.

Existing Family Structures

Although not systematically investigating households as unit of analysis, I had the opportunity to visit dozens of them while conducting research before the earthquake, and particularly during the making of *Poto Mitan*. Building on Maternowska, I argue that households are not only spaces for negotiation, but also a basic social unit for survival as well as set of solidarity beliefs and practices. Given my focus on women who worked in export-processing factories, these households were mostly supported by a formal wage. In this, they were the minority: in the 2011 household survey, 450, or 56.9 percent, reported a livelihood of *komès*, microcommerce. Individuals were self-employed as street vendors. My research—not to mention my long-term residency as a neighbor—also took me to households with this as a primary occupation. As Frisline noted in *Poto Mitan*, working in the factories didn't amount to much. When she was fired because she had to visit her ailing mother, she didn't attempt to get another factory job. "In the factory, I only saw a penny every two weeks. This little pittance didn't do anything for me. Now, every day, from this store, I earn some money. I get money and invest it here." In 2012, after she gave birth to her second child, Marie-Jeanne quit the factories because her child care expenses would have exceeded her salary. Marie-Jeanne's mother did not move with her to the city, and by 2012 was too old to help with child care.

These stories highlight the fluidity of people's livelihood strategies, and also the diversity of household structures. For example, Hélène lived with her father, sister, her child, and her sister's child in her one-room dwelling. Marie-Jeanne lived with her husband and child. Frisline, who never married or had children, lived with two nieces, one of whom had children. Thérèse, whose husband passed away, lived with her children, and Solange lived with her three children, who had two different fathers. Although the five women were the focus of the film, they were not necessarily the heads of their households. Marie-Jeanne's husband made a living exchanging money on the street; when she had a factory job her family used that predictable income for regular expenses. All the women in the film participated in a *sòl*. The concept of head of household doesn't make much sense in economic terms; as Frisline said, "Today I might be able to contribute, and tomorrow the other person would since I didn't have a penny." We certainly found this diversity of households in our 2011 research of the eight camps. Mackenson, who lived in Karade at the time of our 2011 interview, reported that "on January 12th, we were five in our family: two brothers and three sisters. We rented a house; as you can see there are many houses in this area. Each of us rented a room. On January 12th, during the disaster, we were in the same house." It was not uncommon to find six, seven, or sometimes eight extended family members living in an eight-foot-square single-room cinderblock house.

Sharing Relationships

A core component of many conceptions of family noted above is sharing. Visible to even a casual observer (provided they went inside people's *lakou*[5]) was also a common practice of sharing a plate of food. Cooking traditional Haitian foods such as beans and rice[6] or cornmeal is a labor- and time-intensive process; they are often cooked in large quantity. Almost every time I have been to someone's house in the late afternoon there was still at least one plate of food covered by plastic mesh to protect against flies. In several instances I have seen visitors—neighbors, extended family, or members of the same church—stop by with a plate of food to make sure that my host didn't go to bed hungry. Alix, in Plas Lapè, noted that "whenever neighbors cook, they know my situation isn't good. Anyone who cooks, they bring some for me. The day they don't cook I don't get any, but if they cook they bring some for me. This is how I live." Before the earthquake, nearly half (377 of 791, 47.7 percent) the people counted on family members to share food with them when they needed it. Because families constitute the backbone of solidarity, this is not surprising. People also counted on friends from time to time (144, 18.2 percent), as well as neighbors (6.1 percent). More than one in six people said "no one" gave them food when they were hungry (138, 17.4 percent)—with some saying "*bondye*" (God) or "*Jezi*" (Jesus) gave them food: 54, or 6.8 percent.

On January 1, to commemorate the Haitian Revolution, a singular achievement in world history, Haitian people often make *soup joumou*, pumpkin soup. It is an expensive dish, and on this day people eat meat (see, for example, Smith 2001, 99). Those who can afford it eat beef in their soup; often this is the only time during the year. People who have the means return to their *lakou* to drink soup from their mother's bowl. Following Haiti's massive rural exodus that followed the implantation of neoliberalism, January 1 heralds a temporary return *andeyò*, "outside," the provinces. Indeed, this was true right before January 12, 2010, and one of the methodologies in the studies that showed the reverse migration following the quake (Bengtsson et al. 2011). Another part of this tradition is that this soup is shared; it is a symbol of solidarity. Whom you drink from—on whose *fwaye* or stove the soup was cooked—acknowledges and helps strengthen your social ties. For those who have the means, it is one of the greatest honors to invite guests to visit on January 1 to partake. Neighbors send bowls to one another. A stash of a couple bowls remains in case visitors come. The ambience, even in the crowded capital, is often one of conviviality and reflection. So what—if anything—did the earthquake change? And how did it change this?

"SOMETIMES I LONG TO HEAR THEIR VOICES": IMPACTS OF THE EARTHQUAKE

To begin with the sharing relationships, people counted on their families (40.8 percent), friends (15.8 percent), and neighbors (5.3 percent) less after the earthquake. More people report that no one helps them out (23.1 percent)—or they wait for miracles (literally, "God" or "Jesus," 7.6 percent). One possible explanation for this loosening of sharing ties is the loss of livelihood directly tied to the earthquake, as François related: "Our things are left in storage. After January 12, when the storage got destroyed, those things got lost." François, who was staying at Hancho at the time of the interview, had been a street vendor who sold housewares in the street before the earthquake. People who engaged in micro-commerce for a livelihood were doubly hit when their homes were destroyed. Not only were their personal effects and sense of security destroyed in the earthquake, but they also lost their livelihood. Although it was still possible to sell low-value items such as hard candy in the camps, the physical setup of the tarps represented a risk that many weren't willing or able to take, as Nadege poignantly described with her sandals being stolen. In many interviews, people noted, "All it takes is a razor to rip the tent and come inside." A pen or pencil would also suffice.

This lack of security was a major reason that the number one livelihood strategy, already fragile, was seriously affected after the earthquake. Almost half of the households engaged in micro-commerce lost this livelihood: from 450 before the earthquake to 234 after (29.6 percent). The number of people who worked in factories also diminished, from 57 (7.2 percent) to 24 (3.0 percent), as did the number of people who worked in a school or owned their business. Sixty-one people, 7.7 percent of the sample, engaged in these strategies before the earthquake, while only twenty-five people owned their business (3.2 percent) and thirty-four worked in a school (4.3 percent). Other professions weren't as severely affected, with slight declines in the numbers of people who declared working a trade, from 109 to 95 (13.8 to 12.0 percent). Some professions slightly increased after the earthquake, such as people working as day laborers (3.5 to 4.3 percent), and people doing "service" (1.4 to 2.0 percent).[7]

The most striking difference following the earthquake was the increase in the number of people who reported no livelihood activity whatsoever. This was the subject of a lot of discussion during morning meetings, particularly in the beginning during the pre-test phases, because research assistants, particularly the Haitian university students, had a difficult time imagining that people didn't have any livelihood. The research team was also concerned about people exaggerating their problems as a means to inspire greater generosity from the NGO that they assumed employed the students, because that was IDPs' usual experience with research.[8] We discussed strategies to assure to people that the research assistants were in fact students, that it was academic research unconnected to an NGO, and that people could be honest with us.[9] The survey phase started at least two full days in the field, and began with a pre-survey. Research assistants questioned this, pointing out to the person that she/he somehow managed to eat. In the end the script asked *ki estrateji pou w viv? Ki aktivite ekonomik?* What strategies do you employ to live (that is, your livelihood)? What economic activities do you engage in? All of this is to say that we were far from naïve in the data collection process and could be confident in the statistic. Of the 791 respondents, thirty-two, or 4.0 percent, reported no regular economic activity before the earthquake. This figure shot up ninefold, to 287 people, or 36.3 percent, more than a third, after the earthquake. Given that people's life savings, houses, and personal items were destroyed along with their merchandise and ability to securely store this merchandise in the earthquake, this figure makes sense. One of the answer choices was remittances; there was no appreciable difference before and after the earthquake.

Some individuals, like Nadege, were able to scrape together the means to restart their small businesses. In Nadege's case, she received donations of goods she could sell. Depending on the physical layout of the camps, some *timachann* opened a small *boutik* (boutique, home-based shop) to sell to camp residents. In CAJIT, which was physically spread out, still-standing houses served as a depot (where people could buy in bulk) or a *boutik*. This was also the case across the busy street from Plas Lapè, in concrete structures that remained standing.

But within the camp itself, a handful of street vendors sold low-value items in their tents along the corridors connecting the two main sections of the camps. A small plywood stand was constructed, again along the road, at the entrance of the Meri Dikini camp. The residents in Karade who had been relocated from St. Louis, who had been given a plywood temporary shelter, called "T-shelters," particularly along the main road from the front entrance to the camp by the UN base, set up such businesses. But even in the "have-not" sections of the camp where people slept under tarps, very cheap items were sometimes sold outside a school and church that had been constructed. Residents informed me that these individuals were allowed to stay in the church (constructed of tarps until a South Korean mission visit, when they received concrete, corrugated tin, and plywood) to guard it, and so had a measure of security for their merchandise. It also displayed a relatively better-off economic position, a good omen for a church, certainly a Calvinist one. Gradually, especially after aid agencies pulled out of the camps, the economic activity within the camps, measured both by the number of vendors and the value of the goods being sold, declined. Some camps had no vendors at all; others sold hard candy instead of cooked food, tiny trinkets instead of used clothing, for example. This was true of all camps except for Karade, at least the sector for the St. Louis displaced, the "have littles." A two-story restaurant and multiplex was built at the entrance to the camp in late 2014.

This loss of livelihood obviously affected people's ability to share with others, like Margo, in Hancho: "Well January 12 destroyed every relationship that we had, because we used to eat and sit together. We cannot do that anymore, because misery is beating us very hard. We used to tell jokes to one another. After the earthquake, we now share our misery together." Mackenson, at Karade, details this experience:

When I returned after January 12, I saw only debris in the location where the house was built. No need to tell you about my belongings. A sister of mine had a place to cook and sell food. A big house fell on it; even the cooking pot was broken. When I was hungry, I used to go to my sister's house to have something to eat, even a spoonful of rice. It's destroyed. She's bankrupt [literally, *sou bouda*, "on her ass"]. If I had the possibility, I would give her five gourdes [about 12 and a half cents]. But my business is long gone. If one of us has a problem, none of us can help the other. And everybody is living in the camp together in the same misery.

This financial difficulty places particular strains on families who had already dispersed, some of those, like Lolo's, also from Karade, who were displaced by neoliberal policies like those described in chapter 1:

As for my relatives, we were much closer before the earthquake. We might have spent one or two months without seeing each other because of our respective activities, but we never went three months. Those living in the countryside, those living in town, and those living abroad, we all kept in touch. We managed to see each another anyway. Now, life is getting so tough that nobody cares for relatives any longer.

Lolo's sentiment, if a little hyberbolic, nonetheless described the dip in sharing documented by the quantitative portion of the research. The earthquake itself, destroying dwelling units, also triggered a residential separation in some cases. Some people's families, like Gracia's, split up with some going to the provinces: "The relationships we have, that is, we are divided. Some of them aren't here—some went to another neighborhood, some went to the countryside—and some are still staying with us."

Youyou, who pitched a tent in Karade at the time of his 2011 interview, noted that "many are scattered away. I don't know where they went, but that has a big impact on me because sometimes I long to see my friends. Sometimes I long to hear their voices, but life doesn't give us that opportunity. This is the impact that January 12 has on us because we don't see those friends anymore." This longing—the original word is *anvi*, stronger than *vle*, "want"—seems particularly powerful given the paradoxical isolation amid a forced familiarity with strangers, new neighbors. However, as Alix and others have noted in this and the previous chapter, living in the camps also created new solidarity practices. And many, like Manolia and Manoucheka, reunited with their social network within the camps. Their neighbor in Hancho, Rose-Anne, also notes that her relationships remained unchanged: "Well those people, we used to . . . even if they weren't my family, they were living next to me. Until now, some go out into the street and some don't. We—these people next to me—are still in the same relationship we used to have before." Sandy also maintained a close relationship while living in Nan Bannann:

So! I must tell you that my only remaining relationship is with the old lady I told you about already. When I see her she asks "how are you?" Then I tell her "I am fine." And she may give me a bag with beans, rice, vegetable oil, and cooking ingredients and tells me to prepare some food. Then I come home and cook.

How can we make sense of these seeming contradictions, with some people—especially reported in the previous chapter—maintaining their solidarity ties in the camps, and others reporting that their households were split up? The fact that the physical space of the camps can engender these contradictory realities argues against a simplistic geographical determinism. There must therefore be other factors that explain the breakup of the *fwaye*.

"JANUARY 12 MADE THEM ADULTS": IMPACT OF THE CAMPS

What is it about camp life that engendered a fissioning of the *fwaye*? Although it may seem too obvious to mention, a tarp is not the same as a cinderblock house. Basic chores such as cooking cannot be done inside a tarp, and the majority of tarps were smaller than even the smallest one-room house. This played some role in households splitting up. Evrance, from Kolonbi, explained, "Yes, we are dispersed. My sisters have moved to a place. I myself had to move to another place. And some of us died." Talking with researchers in front of his tarp in Nan Bannann, Manno recalled, "We're divided. My kids are living somewhere, my kid's mom is somewhere else, and myself, I am at another place, but things were not like that before."

Sophonie explained the reason why she split up from her children, who at least stayed in the same camp, Meri Dikini, on the grounds of the Carrefour City Hall: "It's not that I give [my children] their freedom. I am in this little tent, and it's too small to sleep with all of them. So they are here in the camp and when they gave out tarps, they fashioned a tent out of one and they stay together." Sophonie didn't want to leave her seven children unsupervised, but they were too many to stay in her tent. The aid agency's distribution of tarps facilitated this splitting up. In camps that had an NGO acting as camp management agency, tarps were often constructed into identical tents. Only the number the agency spray-painted or tacked onto it to register and organize distributions distinguished between them. A particularly striking visual example is the back portion of Plas Lapè, with tents pitched on a soccer field (see Figure 2.1; see also the book's website, humanitarianaftershocks.org, for a slide show). Although obviously done because of efficiency and deploying humanitarian knowledge about emergency shelter construction methods, and also reinforcing an egalitarian logic wherein each household receives the same, in practice this reinforces inequality. Households of two people had more living space per person than a household of five, for example. So the reward structure put in place by aid agencies encouraged splitting up. In addition, even assuming that the security situation could be somehow resolved and people able to store merchandise to sell, households whose livelihoods depended on micro-commerce had to contend with the same amount of space regardless of merchandise, or lack thereof.

Like Nadege, whose story began this chapter, Franck, who lived at the Kolonbi camp, noted that living in camps forced children to grow up quickly: "There are words that children are not supposed to hear. January 12th turned many people into adults. Just imagine, they came here and took a parcel of land, they found tarps, and they set up tents. Now they are adults as we are." In addition to the lack of privacy, and Nadege fearing for her daughters, people became adults because of the aid policies that facilitated and encouraged setting up new households. Before the Haitian government stopped it in April 2010, emergency food rations were distributed via NGOs through camp committees in the form of ration cards. Because of Women in Development policies that privilege women, the World Food Program set guidelines for women to be recipients of emergency distribution. Again, as with the tents, the size of the ration didn't vary based on household size: as we were told on numerous occasions, from IDPs to foreign humanitarians, the same bag of beans, rice, flour, and cooking oil was distributed to households of three or eight people. Putting these two facts together, many households were "intelligent" (the word *entelijan* in Haitian has connotations of being cunning) and made the decision to maximize their receipt of food aid. So if the multigenerational *fwaye* had a young mother of a child, she became a new head of household.

Early on, in February 2010, a report on the shanties following the earthquake found families splitting up in order to have members in several camps when aid distribution occurred (INURED 2010, 9). A housing study commissioned by USAID (Schwartz et al. 2011) also quoted a camp leader making this same argument, saying that families would splinter in order to have multiple female heads of households. Aid agencies and media outlets widely circulated this phenomenon, often serving to denigrate IDPs as not "legitimate" or not worthy of aid. Noted from the previous chapter, IDPs quickly became stigmatized, and in many discourses blamed for many problems that befell them. This "blame the victim" discourse falls under two major themes: minimizing tropes point to the poverty that Haiti's poor majority had to confront before the earthquake, and exaggerating tropes point to the few instances of people attempting to secure more for themselves given the rules laid out in front of them. Like most discursive constructions, it is possible to find empirical evidence to verify both these stereotypes. My discussions with foreign aid workers were often peppered with an animated retelling of a scenario when they "caught" someone renting the tent so it would be occupied when the official census came around. Either they were attempting to convince me that it actually happens—because as someone with an activist identity and *Huffington Post* blog I needed to be educated on how things really worked—or they were trying to justify their increasingly punitive disciplinary regimes. In any case, the most an individual who was so down on her or his luck and poor as to attempt to bend the rules would have received would be a $500 annual rental subsidy—and it would have gone to their landlord, not to them—the equivalent of two days' per diem for a foreign aid worker.[10] Per diems are technically expenses—lodging, food, transportation, and incidentals—for which the aid worker (or university professor) does not have to present receipts. This is on top of their salaries, often inflated by their (nontaxable) "hazard pay."[11]

Setting aside this double standard, this reward structure that encourages this behavior definitely merits interrogation. Tim Schwartz, the lead author of the USAID report noted, published a book based on his dissertation research that made similar arguments about the impact of aid in rising fertility rates: simply put, if women were given food aid only if they had children, the reward structure is in place for some women to decide to have more children (Schwartz 2009). Building on Greenhalgh (1990), Maternowska's framework of "political economy of fertility" offers a more nuanced and grounded interpretation of similar phenomena, focusing the analysis less on individuals and more on the policies that structure these choices. As a member of a camp committee in Karade put it, "We see some children, teenagers who become pregnant at the age of thirteen, fourteen, and even twelve. Their parents, because they don't have means of support, they just resign and leave the children without supervision. Most children are not safe in the camps, okay?" This discourse of adolescents bearing children because of aid policies was commonplace, although I am unaware of any systematic research conducted to verify it.[12]

It is also helpful to remember the context of loss of livelihoods when considering whether some people attempted to make the most of their situation by skirting around the rules in front of them. The behavior might have also been learned, because Haiti had played host to hundreds of aid projects from a vast array of NGOs even before the earthquake. This aid regime had its own patterns, some of which may have bumped against local kinship and household traditions. One important factor remains people's felt obligations to help others, including family and household; these networks of obligation, including patron–client relationships (Scherz 2013), are powerful motivators of actions. All this is to say that aid programs and projects have social lives (Sampson 1996), especially as they become entangled with local realities, meanings, structures, and systems.

Agencies could have tapped into these local systems. Rather than a roster that could have easily been created with a list of family members, including the number of children, elderly, handicapped, and dead—which in fact neighborhood groups and camp committees often created on their own before receipt of aid—and with this roster coordinating with other aid agencies, agencies appeared with ration cards to give to individual committee members, who were then tasked with distributing to people in the camps, who presented them in exchange for the item. As several people have reported, this system, which was more efficient for NGOs, was rife with abuse, including transactional sex and sexual harassment, as the next chapter details. So individual households made decisions responding to the external rewards system set in place by the aid agencies, in turn responding to the rewards system put in place by their superiors, central offices overseas, and donors. Before the earthquake, the average household size of the 2011 survey was 5.37. This compared to 5.2 in the USAID Housing

Evaluation study, "something so consistent as to arguably be considered a law" (31). Following the earthquake, the household size in the study was 3.36. An average of 0.8 people perished on January 12 per "family," which includes members outside the household. Respondents detailed exactly who in terms of relations (uncle, sister, and so on), so this could have been used to calculate the death toll from the earthquake. However, the death toll from the earthquake cannot by itself explain the decrease of two people per household on average.

Emergency food aid policies also had the impact of creating new households based on convenience, as a member of the CAJIT committee explained: "We get very little aid, especially tents. Those who couldn't receive a tent organized themselves another way, either with their own bed sheets, their things. They arrange themselves to get stuff. We now become a family in the first place." Whatever the original intent behind the policy in reinforcing families, it thus often had the opposite effect: either it split them up or it created new "families" based on convenience, seriality (Young 1994), or "assemblages" (Deleuze and Guattari 1987; Ong and Collier 2005). This discussion highlights often dramatic changes to the *fwaye* in the camps. But why did this happen?

Isolating the Role of Aid

Although it might be argued that the earthquake, and the ensuing trauma, explains the smaller household size, variation between the camps was instructive. Significantly, households in the camp with the least amount of external aid, CAJIT, also diminished the least: from an average of 5.6 people before the earthquake to 4.8 afterward, a decrease of 0.8 per household, less than 15 percent and approximating the loss per family due to death from the earthquake. Recall from the previous chapter that CAJIT was only "discovered" three months after the seismic event and thus never had an NGO management agency and received very little aid. On the other end of the spectrum, Karade, which included a planned relocation site for families who had left St. Louis, had the most consistent NGO and other international agency presence, like MINUSTAH, the UN troops. At Karade, households diminished the most: from an average of 6.1 before the earthquake to 3.6 after, a decrease of 2.5 per household, or more than 40 percent. For an even better confirmation of this trend it would be good to have data from households that never went into camps. The USAID housing report didn't disaggregate or offer raw data. The best information I have is from the block where I live: though people all slept on the street after the earthquake, whether they were middle class or low-income, no one moved to a camp. All the losses in households were therefore because of the earthquake. In July 2010, the one son in the household of my next door neighbor got married, and he built a structure on the *lakou*. After an NGO provided T-shelters on the property claimed by one family, this family charged rent for setting up a T-shelter in remaining spaces. The number of spaces remained the same after the earthquake—because they were less individualized before the earthquake, multigenerational households that had lived side by side now had separate shelters. Although this is obviously a very small sample, and a convenience sample at that, it offers some clues to isolate the variables of humanitarian aid and NGO presence.

So the decades-old multigenerational family structure that allowed the poor majority to survive on the margins was immediately disrupted by foreign assistance from countries that have at least the official promotion of nuclear family units. UN employee Georges was critical of the ways in which aid disrupted Haitian families. At least in his neighborhood, people were told they had to be in tents in order to receive food aid, and they were explicitly told that aid could only be given to matrifocal, nuclear family units. Georges detailed the conflicts that arose when younger women were given the title—or at least the responsibility—of head of household. In the United States, women as recipients of public assistance—sometimes called welfare—are often demonized by media and politicians, especially during periods of economic uncertainty. This discourse is often (even explicitly) racist, typified by the vilification of the so-called welfare queen. In both, recipients are often scapegoated, explaining some of the vitriol coming from some foreign aid workers. One major difference is that in the United States, intervening into what was declared to be a defective family structure was an explicit goal since at least the Moynihan Report. Another major difference is that in Haiti, these changes were triggered by foreign agencies and as such the critiques coming from Haitian people were directed our way. As an NGO representative said, "This is the single biggest disaster that came, and it came after the earthquake: the way aid was distributed destroyed the family. And I suppose you know that the family is the central pillar of our society, our solidarity. This is more important than the buildings that fell down. When the family is crushed, so is society." This representative was obviously a Haitian. When I asked why he didn't speak up, he laughed sarcastically and replied, "The question isn't whether or not we spoke up but whether or not the *blan* [foreigners] listen to us." During an interview with a foreign aid representative who had a degree in anthropology and for whom Haiti was her first tour, I pointed this out. She responded, sheepishly, that she couldn't explain why they had done this—and apparently hadn't thought about it—because she had started with the NGO long after the end of the food distribution. Another early career worker, among the most suspicious and cynical of all I had interviewed, openly challenged my academic naiveté. Sure, he replied,[13] humanitarian aid biases the nuclear family unit typical of the norm—if not the practice—of "Western" societies. To do otherwise would inspire an endless string of cousins and others to claim aid. Where do you stop?, he retorted. I shared the quantitative methodology of this study, wherein we asked people who shared the same household before the earthquake. Well, you could do that, he said. But how would you know people were telling you the truth? His experiences—while never having interviewed Haitian people because of his lack of fluency in Haitian—with the same people who were tired of research as many of those we interviewed explain, showed him that Haitians will tell you anything to get what they want. At least that's what he chose to share with me. Obviously his experience was particular, arising from a specific context that appeared invisible to him. But these sentiments—usually barely hidden—come out when the workers were on the defensive or provoked.

This said, the realities of camp life and certainly the rules structured by the aid agencies encouraged a fissioning of the extended *lakou* model of households for many Haitian families, to which we now turn.

Impacts on Families

The disruption of the multigenerational household had wide-ranging effects on people. In the St. Louis camp, Jozi shared that "my house was destroyed. Now my children are obliged to live far away from me. Before, we used to be in the same place. But now, we live in different places. One is living far away. It's not how things used to be." Jean-Claude, who stayed in Kolonbi, reported that "the relationship became . . . some of us lived close to each other. We separated: everybody moved to different camps, different neighborhoods." Maud, who had lived with her siblings in a single extended-family household, qualified the changes to her family as negative:

> There have been negative consequences on my family, because since January 12th, we have been separated. Even though each of us was married and had children, we lived in the same house together. But after January 12th, we were separated because we lived in different places, in shelters. We might have had a house to live in, but everybody was still afraid of [concrete] houses. Moreover, we lost different family members [to the earthquake]. We have been communicating on the phone without meeting one another for about two or three months.

Karade, where Maud was staying (she had originally sought shelter at St. Louis; she was one of the six thousand people relocated), is tucked away on a hill. To get to where she used to live is at least two *taptap*, two public transportation routes. Travel to Karade was made easier when it became a new *kous* (course, route) for a public transit circuit. But to visit her siblings would take at least two hours out of her day, and at least 30 gourdes. Maud pointed to a common problem, fear of sleeping under concrete, which was compounded by the fact that most people—630 of 783, or 80.5 percent—did not own their homes. Owners of houses tagged yellow (in need of structural repair) or red (slated for demolition) were not allowed to collect rent from tenants. According to the official housing evaluation, 105,000 houses were completely destroyed and 188,383 houses collapsed or badly damaged. This discourse of "faking it," of people taking a free ride living under a tarp, makes less sense considering that people had the opportunity to stay for free. Indeed, the unpublished USAID evaluation estimated that 73,846 of greater Port-au-Prince's 115,384 houses, or 64 percent, slated for demolition were occupied as of a year following the earthquake. The stereotype also fails to account for the fact that rents increased substantially after the earthquake, while at the same time livelihoods diminished.

Testifying to the flexibility of the concept of family being pushed to extremes, Katiana, who lived in a poor neighborhood to begin with, created bonds with her new neighbors in the Hancho camp: "These people are my family, my neighbors are my family. If you have a problem they are the ones that will help me. With Jesus none of my family members died, but the others, they are apart, only I still live here. The others are in living in camps, but I still live here because this is where I used to live." However, not everyone was as easily adept at creating new relationships, as Ti Wobè recalled in his mid-2011 interview:

Where I was living, I was living with a lot of people, people who were like brothers and sisters, because we're all God's children, no? And [I lived with] some relatives but now, I'm no longer living with them. Now, I'm living in a different place, you see what I mean? I still can't tell you how different they are, because I don't know yet whether they are a group of gossipers or not, and they don't know yet whether or not I'm a gossiper either. They came here. They're taking the time to get to know me, as am I. So, I can't compare it yet.

The camp where Ti Wobè stayed, Nan Bannann, was situated on the property of three large private homes. The neighborhood, Delmas 32, was mixed income, like Christ-Roi on the other side of the hill. The inequality in the neighborhood (Ti Wobè did not indicate where he lived before January 12 during the interview) might have been the source of tension but also possibly the opportunity for short-term jobs for the *ti pèp*, "small" people, the expression for very poor, excluded people. Also like Christ-Roi, certainly on the block where I live, the neighborhood around Nan Bannann showed signs of middle-income families leaving the neighborhood after the earthquake, so there might have been fewer of these intermittent jobs. Ti Wobè's concern about gossip becomes more important in the context of a conflict with one of the land owners, who had consistently attempted to force people off his space. A couple of months after this interview, he succeeded in kicking out more than thirty-five families; tents were slashed by machetes in the middle of the night.

Ti Wobè's concern about living among "gossipers" implies an inability to trust his new neighbors. Given people's definition of family, that it entails support, this splintering of the household potentially represents greater vulnerability. Speaking from the Meri Dikini camp outside of Carrefour City Hall, Sophonie elaborated on Ti Wobè's preoccupation:

> The impact of goudougoudou on my family is that I can't help them. I am somewhere, and they're somewhere else. I mean, that's not normal. The kids, when we were in our home, we could keep a good eye on them but because of the earthquake, I stay in a tent, they stay in another tent doing their own thing. So at night, or during the day, I may not be able to watch over them. This is the impact.

Explaining "growing up fast" or "becoming like adults" in the camp, the physical limitations of the tents and Sophonie's children's newfound independence or liberty also potentially put them at risk of acts of violence or theft, detailed in the next chapter. Building on her analysis of physical separation from her children, Jozi from St. Louis reported, "Well, there can never be the same relationship, because they are not living close to me anymore."

Jozi's qualification that things can never be the same calls into question whether some of these ruptures will indeed outlast the emergency phase. What about the relationship was ruptured? To answer this question it is first necessary to take a look at the process of people getting out of camps.

OUT OF THE CAMPS

How long-term are these humanitarian ruptures to Haitian cultural institutions, such as the basic social unit of the household? A bag of beans, rice, wheat, and cooking oil for two weeks is small compared to the prospect of receiving several hundred dollar cash subsidies (albeit for a landlord). As of 2014, when this chapter was written, the IDP population was a tenth of what it had been at the height in the summer of 2010. This steadily declining figure was the single barometer for "success" for donors, the Haitian government, and NGOs alike. But what does this actually mean? With donor support, the newly elected Haitian government unveiled an ambitious relocation plan in May 2011, "16/6," referring to the government closing six highly visible camps on public land and rehabilitating sixteen neighborhoods. A centerpiece to this program was a $500 rental subsidy given to landlords who agreed to rent to IDPs in these strategic camps. This model was first field-tested after the earthquake by the mayor of Pétion-Ville, but it wasn't the first such subsidy in Haiti. Lesly, who was student in my first class on NGOs in 2004, claimed authorship of the policy when he worked in Gonaïves following the 2008 hurricane season, suggesting a subsidy of at least

10,000 gourdes going to landlords (about $250 at the time). One of the 16/6 camps, the Sylvio Cator stadium in downtown Port-au-Prince, was closed in July 2011—before the official start of the 16/6 program—using violent force. Some people were given the opportunity to pitch a tent somewhere else downtown, but residents did not have a choice. UN Independent Human Rights Expert Michel Forst issued a statement saying he was troubled by the wave of forced evictions (United Nations News Centre 2011).

This book began with Marie-Jeanne's story about being violently evicted from her camp in part to draw attention to this issue. Forced eviction was a consistent and growing threat. In 2010, UN Secretary General Ban Ki-moon (2010) reported that 29 percent of IDP camps were forcibly closed, and through the summer of 2011, one in four camps was under the constant threat of forced eviction. IOM (2011) reported that more than a quarter million had been victims of forced eviction. Oxfam GB published a report on December 10, 2012, International Human Rights Day, sounding the alarm for forced eviction (Toussaint 2012). The report noted that 78,000 people living in 121 camps, 96 percent of them on private land, were at risk of forced eviction. Eviction was a more serious threat on private land, because on public land IDPs had at least some legal protection or recourse. Working with local groups like FRAKKA (the Reflection and Action Force on the Housing Issue in Haiti) and BAI (the International Lawyers Office) and solidarity group International Action Ties, Amnesty International published several action alerts about forced eviction from the camps.[14]

The 147,000 people living in the camps as of mid-2014 had to contend with the stated policy of the Martelly administration that all camps are to be closed by the end of the year. In Karade, in the middle of the night on April 10, 2014, hundreds of heavily armed special police forces came to the camp to accompany agents of IOM, ostensibly working with the mayor, conducting a "census" of the population. Residents, on the belief that they had been promised on-site housing from the NGO management agency, stood their ground by singing popular protest chants and church hymns from 1:00 A.M. to 4:00 A.M. A camp committee member also invoked article 2030 of Haiti's civil code, which states that if a person has continual occupancy over a piece of land for a period of ten years, the state recognizes basic property rights. In 2002, President Aristide declared Karade, up the hill from his Aristide Foundation university, a "public utility," nullifying the previous landowner's claim to the land. Nonetheless people still called it "Terrain Toto," Toto's land. "Toto" was a wealthy lottery owner.

The following day, the NGO came to clarify that they had only envisioned enough houses for 125 families, fewer than 5 percent of the people still living in the area. Since that day residents organize a "brigade," a group of people staying up all night in case the police come back again. Frisline said, "You never really sleep. You have to always have one eye open." Karade is a particularly dramatic example of the omnipresent threat of forced eviction, but only one. In Plas Lapè, also in the middle of the night on May 8, 2012, during a planned relocation effort, a fire swept through the camp, destroying more than sixty tents. Because funds for relocation have all but dried up, many IDPs who remain are in a continual state of fear. Near midnight on February 16, 2013, hundreds of people's makeshift homes were burned to the ground in camp ACRA 2 in Pétion-Ville's Juvenat neighborhood near the Karibe Convention Center, one day before the CARI-COM (Caribbean Common Market) assembly, also held at the Karibe Convention Center. Human rights attorney Patrice Florvilus fled the country in late 2013 because of escalating death threats from President Duvalier's lawyer, who claimed the land of one of Haiti's last remaining camps.

This 16/6 approach was deemed a success, and the model was generalized for other NGO relocation efforts. Said Emily, a U.S. citizen who first came to Haiti in August 2011 following a couple of years at a UN agency headquarters and one of the co-facilitators of the relocation subgroup:

> I believe in this program wholeheartedly, and I think we are doing good work. Thinking back on Haitian relief, I just read a statistic that only 23 percent of T-shelters went to people in camps. All of the NGOs, we all say that they target the most vulnerable people. Well, to me, the most vulnerable people are people who do not have access to land. Of course, there are different gradations within that. So it wasn't until two years after the earthquake that we got to the most vulnerable.

Earlier in the interview Emily pointed out that funds were going to landlords, but her larger point that finally aid was getting into the hands of the neediest bears some analysis. Although she wasn't in Haiti during the emergency phase, she argued that the aid hadn't reached the neediest of the population. Her NGO added to the basic 16/6 formula, offering incentives to stay with the program and training and psychosocial accompaniment before asking the head of household to choose which relocation assistance she or he wanted. The NGO conducted evaluations after one month and two months. In her experience, that included Nan Bannann: more than 95 percent of IDPs selected the rental subsidy option. This percentage of people asking for a rental subsidy is consistent with a January 2012 follow-up study in the same eight camps: 95 percent of residents had been renters before the earthquake instead of 80 percent the previous summer. This suggests that most of the people who had the means to leave—who had a home to return to—had left the camps at this point.

However, beneficiaries' points of view call into question the unqualified success of 16/6. First of all, only 3 percent of people we interviewed knew about the 16/6 program. When asked to define it, only 1 percent of residents from these camps—ostensibly potential beneficiaries—could correctly identify it. Most important, the program was far more effective at closing down particular camps than meeting residents like Jozi and Frisline's housing needs. Some used the proverb *lave men, siye ate* (Wash the hands only to wipe them on the ground) to explain the myopia of the program. For example, an April 2014 report from IOM reported an increase in some camps' population. According to an Associated Press story dated April 10, "The IOM reported that many people said they were forced to return because they couldn't afford rents elsewhere after year-long subsidies ran out." Unfortunately Emily's NGO didn't know what would become of the former IDPs after their subsidies ran out, because they didn't have the budget for an evaluation after the one-year point. This raises questions about the long-term impacts of the relocation program.

Answering these questions was the focus of a follow-up study I led in August 2012 (Schuller 2012b). A team of four research assistants, including two veterans of the 2011 camp study, went to four different low-income neighborhoods—two very low-income (Carrefour-Feuilles and Fort National)—and two mixed neighborhoods (Canapé Vert and Maïs Gate), interviewing a hundred households in each, every tenth house from a predetermined central point. More than 70 percent (262 of 371) of residents of these neighborhoods had lived in a camp at one point. Most people reported leaving the camp because of bad conditions, 147 of 262, or 56 percent. Some of these conditions identified by the residents included improper sanitation, a lack of security, and conditions of the shelters, among others. The next most common answer is that people were forcibly evicted by the landlord, often but not always accompanied by the police or local government. A total of 45 of 260, or 17 percent, just over a sixth, left because they were forced. Combined, these two general reasons affected three-quarters of the population. In other words, the relocation, at least to these lower-income neighborhoods, is not an unqualified success, as in Marie-Jeanne's case. Returning to the questions of the impact on the household and solidarity relationships, did the move out of the camps herald a return to previous households?

LONG-TERM IMPACTS ON HOUSEHOLDS

Even if successful in bringing the IDP population down, this relocation assistance has the potential to increase negative long-term consequences of splitting up families. The survey detailed which members of the family a relocated individual had lived with before and after the earthquake. The results showed that almost half, 133 of 281 people (47.3 percent), did not move back in with the same family members before the earthquake. This could suggest that ruptures to the urban Haitian household triggered by emergency aid have the potential to become long-term for almost half of the population. It could also be a temporary phenomenon, as long as rental subsidies are in existence. I too didn't have the funds for a follow-up survey, and as a confidential survey, research assistants did not collect contact information from individual households from this survey to learn whether residents had been relocated. They did, however, during the January 2012 follow up with the eight camps. That summer a research assistant followed up with these individuals, a few of whom are quoted following.

Of the 321 people for whom verified information was obtained, 102, or 32 percent, lived in a different neighborhood than before the earthquake. So there is a small but significant population of newcomers to these areas since the earthquake. There is some variation based on neighborhood, with lower-income neighborhoods being more likely recipients of new people, including IDPs. For example, 43 percent of people in Carrefour-Feuilles had lived somewhere else, suggesting this is a location where IDPs are relocated. By contrast, only 26 percent of people living in Maïs Gaté or Canapé-Vert had lived somewhere else. This might be explained by Carrefour-Feuilles being more damaged from the earthquake. However, that wouldn't explain the difference in return. The data seem to suggest that low-income neighborhoods were where people were steered, either because of discrimination against IDPs or higher rents elsewhere. Several aid agency staff had said anecdotally that other areas, including those that we could not sample because of high levels of violence, like Martissant and Fort National, were recipients of IDPs because of their low rents.

Similar to patterns found in the 2011 camp survey, people reported a reduction in sharing or solidarity ties. Based on discussion with field researchers it was decided to ask *kiyès ki konn ede w* (Who typically helps you?) for the three time periods. In addition to "other," people were given the option to select family,[15] neighbor, friend, church, or organization. They were told to select as many as possible, or no one. Not surprisingly, family was the most common response. However, people report a decline in this support from family since before the earthquake, from 221 (60 percent) to 187 (50 percent). Following this, people reported that friends typically help them out. There was a slight decline, from forty-six (12 percent) to forty-three (11 percent). Before the earthquake, as many people, twenty-three (6 percent), were helped out by members of a church or members of an organization. However, after the earthquake fewer people, 16 (4 percent), count on other members of an organization. Churches play a greater role following the earthquake aid, helping up to thirty-one individuals (8 percent). Churches are the only type of institution that more people said help them out after the earthquake; this possibly is a result of transnational evangelical missionary circuits of aid (McAlister 2013). The smallest support group, neighbors, also diminished the most: from eleven people to six.

These trends become clearer when only the former IDPs and especially those who live in new neighborhoods are considered in the sample, suggesting that relocation reduces people's social ties. Although nearly impossible to quantify and measure, social ties are an important part of people's survival, livelihood, and quality of life. As such these should be a consideration in any relocation effort. Failure to take this important element of people's lives into account results in relocation projects that maybe technically better but still undesirable, such as Corail-Cesselesse or Morne à Cabrit, areas where camp residents were relocated or housing constructed.[16] Jimmy, one of the people moved out from the CAJIT camp, reported:

> It's not like you had a three or four-room house. . . . I have four children, my wife, my younger brother and myself. So in the shelter that I was given there's not even enough room for my four children. Inside the shelter, when we lie down to sleep we are like sardines packed together or bags piled up in a truck. If I'd known that they were just giving me a shelter and nothing else, I really would not have taken it because I would work anyway.

Naromie, one of Jimmy's former neighbors from CAJIT, discussed severed sharing ties: "I used to share food with people. I don't like to receive food from people, because they can remind me of that. Well, they don't come by anymore. They moved to another neighborhood, and I don't see them anymore."

Naromie and Jimmy voluntarily left CAJIT, because there was no formal relocation assistance program. An NGO offered shelters to some residents. These social bonds forged in the neighborhoods before the earthquake, and maintained or built in the camps, were more severely altered in officially relocated camps, like Germanie reported:

> Yes, I feel that there was a break-up, because we used to tell jokes every afternoon. We used to talk to one another, we used to share our food. You see what I mean? It's not the same relationship we had with the previous "neighborhood family" [fanmi vwazinaj]. Now this new relationship is totally different, because now we can't tell any kind of joke. It will take us time to build a close relationship with them like the one we had with the previous neighborhood family, and it also requires caution.

Germanie had been living in the Dikini neighborhood and the Meri Dikini camp. She moved to Martissant, a crowded shantytown in Port-au-Prince. She reported that it was difficult to find a landlord willing to rent to her. Tracey had an even more difficult time. Having lived in the Plas Lapè camp, she felt she was particularly stigmatized by prospective landlords because of the reputation of the neighborhood and the camp. She had to move all the way to Carrefour, on the other side of town. This relocation caused her ties with her family to be even further severed:

All the time, my [grown] children scold me, demanding that I leave this neighborhood. I told them it is what I can afford. Why don't they tell me 'here is some money so you can get out of that area'? They do not want us to live in Carrefour. They prefer Bourdon of Cite Militaire, where they live. They do not live close by.

Particularly Tracey's testimony identifies how ruptures to the *fwaye* were not only not undone after the end of an IDP camp, they were magnified, despite the best intentions of people like Emily.

HOUSEHOLD AFTERSHOCKS

This chapter has detailed the impacts of the earthquake, life in the camps, particularly the humanitarian aid, and relocation on households. The Haitian kinship system was flexible before the earthquake; extended households were the basis of solidarity and collective survival. The post-quake aid ruptured this institution; the greater the aid, the greater the disruption, as evidenced by the differences within the camps and the increasing isolation with the relocation assistance out of the camps, as Tracey told. Tied to the disruption of the household is a diminishing of solidarity networks, alternatively called social capital or sharing ties.

This chapter has demonstrated that humanitarian policies that on paper are meant to be egalitarian, just, and fair have the consequence of splitting up Haitian households. Some foreign agency representatives, ever concerned about being duped by a Haitian recipient, justified the policies. Most were simply unaware of the cultural biases implicit in them—and their differences from Haitian sociocultural systems. Gender—intimately related to kinship—offers an even clearer disconnect between humanitarian agencies' good intentions and their ethnocentrism that leads to insidious consequences, including an increase in violence against women. This is the focus of the next chapter.

4 · *PA MANYEN FANM NAN KONSA*

The Gender of Aid

I was involved with a women's organization since '91. When I was a street vendor, I was in the organization. At that time, there were a bunch of women who were victims during the coup d'état. I became involved to work with women who were victims of rape because paramilitaries came to my house. They took me before I went to Jacmel. When I went, they raped me as well, and they beat my husband badly. For a month, he vomited blood, he urinated a lot of blood, and after a month, he died. So then we left Jacmel. I came here with six children, and I went out and still participated in the organization's activities because I saw that I could become a victim even though I was hidden.

When I was a victim I was in the street. That's all I had in my head: to kill myself under a car. People feel isolated when they are victims of violence. But when people sit together they see that they're not the only one, that they have a support network and they can do something about it.

We created KOFAVIV in 2004. And we gave this service to women who were victims of sexual violence during the 2004 crisis. We meet with women who are victims. The first struggle is to get justice and reparations that weren't done. We offer them psychological, medical, and legal support.

We see that when there is political instability, when one government falls and another rises to power, rapes against women increase.

The earthquake made things worse. We brought rapists to justice and now after the earthquake we're starting at zero. It's *lavi men, siye atè*, washing your hands only to wipe them on the ground.

The earthquake, January 12, 2010, equals misery, rape, kidnapping, violence against women, juvenile delinquency, and unemployment. After January 12, 2010, Haiti has traversed a difficult impasse where fathers lost their children, children lost their fathers, mothers lost their children, brothers lost their sisters, and so on. Since the earthquake, many families were forced to live in a very degrading situation in camps that are unacceptable for human beings to live in.

Why is it these hard-up guys get the cards to distribute? The NGOs are using them to distribute the cards. And they don't give the cards to the women. So now even a young girl in need is forced to sleep with the person for a little card. What does she get with this card? A little rice. Women stand in line for hours, sometimes since 11 P.M. the night before. The women are standing in line and these thieves come and put up a fight, and they take the goods.

That's why we can't sleep. You're always thinking at night, even when you feel like dozing off. The smallest noise keeps you up because you're looking around, because you don't want other people to come inside and rape the children. You are prevented from sleeping.

I need to continue to fight until, even if the violence doesn't stop, all the same there's a solution. But if you stop struggling there will never be a solution.

—Malya Villard-Appolon, KOFAVIV

Malya's analysis highlights links among violence, politics, and economic inequality. Her full, real name is used because she is a very public figure, especially after receiving the 2012 CNN "Hero of the Year" award. A particularly disturbing element is the role the humanitarian aid system played in increasing acts of violence against women. As the previous chapter argued, practices of emergency humanitarian aid ruptured Haitian households, with a worldview often called Western being reproduced in agencies' structure and policies. As feminist anthropologists remind us, kinship operates through and reinforces constructions of gender (for example, Collier and Yanagisako 1987; Strathern 1985; Weston 1997). This chapter uncovers how humanitarian aid is gendered and how this in turn affects Haitian women designated as beneficiaries. Similarly to the hyper-visibility of Haiti's poverty engendered by the IDP camps, the earthquake brought the issue of gender-based violence to the fore. In processes similar to those discussed in chapter 2, the ways in which gender-based violence (often known in professional circles by its acronym, GBV) was defined by international agencies serve to legitimize foreign control while they render Haitian people intelligible within a foreign moral compass: they are either worthy victims in need of foreign help or outlaws in need of foreign punishment. Othered by the process of foreign intervention, which determines which category to place people in, both groups are subject to surveillance and discipline.

The foreign gaze—from both humanitarian and media agencies—thus firmly fixed on the Haitian population exaggerates Haitian people's role in an increase in GBV while rendering invisible larger structural forces showed by Malya's analysis that facilitated, reinforced, and encouraged this violence. These discourses map onto larger stereotypes and negative images, either of Black people generally or reinforcing long-standing Haitian exceptionalism. Countering these othering tendencies, this chapter details these larger structural forces. Building on insights from the previous chapter, this chapter interrogates the role that the gender of humanitarian aid—rooted in foreign agencies' own culturally, socially, historically, and economically specific conceptions of gender—contributed to the very increase in GBV that Haitian and foreign agencies, like KOVAVIV and their solidarity partners, combatted.

DOCUMENTING THE RISE OF VIOLENCE

Feminist performance artist and author of the *Vagina Monologues* Eve Ensler championed the issue of gender-based violence in Haiti in the 2012 V-Day actions and again in the One Billion Rising campaign in 2014. International news, legal, development, human rights, and solidarity agencies highlighted the issue of gender-based violence, which has by all accounts increased since the earthquake (d'Adesky 2012 and Poto Fanm+Fi; MADRE CUNY School of Law, and IJDH 2011; Nolan 2011; NYU 2011). One arena of progress was this transnational effort to confront gender-based violence. As is standard humanitarian practice, aid agencies felt this issue was important enough to merit its own "subcluster." The humanitarian response was coordinated by twelve UN clusters organized by theme (see chapter 8 for more detail). Unlike all but one other cluster (Miles 2012), the gender-based violence subcluster was co-organized by the Haitian government, met outside of a UN military base called LogBase, and held meetings in one of Haiti's national languages, French. In addition, after years of successful efforts by feminists to address women's issues in development, institutionalizing a Women in Development paradigm (Porter and Judd 1999; Zaoudé and Sandler 2001), the World Food Program adopted policies that targeted women for food assistance.

These indicators would suggest a degree of hopefulness in confronting gender-based violence. Yet, how are we to understand and evaluate both the increase in violence against women and the impacts of the activist efforts? As Régine Jean-Charles (2014) documents, the discourse of gender-based violence reproduced troubling, albeit familiar, discourses that tend to trigger either denial or demonization. Scores of reactionary articles blamed the victims, denied the seriousness of the problem, or cast Haitian men as predators. As Jean-Charles argued, this issue also provided a platform for white liberal feminists like Ensler and journalist Mac MacLellan to play the hero by defending victims in part by deploying rhetorical strategies of exaggeration, victimhood, erasure of activism, and demonization of Haitian men. All of which, Black feminists point, out are familiar discourses regarding Black men generally (see, for example, Davis 1983b; Spillers 1987). MacLellan went so far as to claim the need to engage in sadomasochistic sex to deal with the secondary trauma she experienced while conducting research on the camps, for which renowned Haitian American novelist Edwidge Danticat and others called her to task.

Complementing Jean-Charles's discourse analysis to answer these questions, this chapter offers long-term ethnographic engagement—and analyses from Haitian women, mediated through me, a white man—to analyze how these discourses are embodied, materially, and how they contribute to greater vulnerability (see, for example, Bankoff, Frerks, and Hilhorst 2004; Oliver-Smith 1999). I argue that understanding violence—and efforts to reduce it—and women's vulnerability requires attention to analyses of structural violence and intersectionality. Offering this context and bridging these literatures are the nuanced analyses coming from the lived experiences of a diverse group of women, before and after the earthquake.

The title of the chapter, "Pa Manyen Fanm Nan Konsa" (Don't touch the woman like that), is the name of a song from one of Haiti's most popular performers, then known as "Sweet Micky," now Michel Martelly, president of the Republic of Haiti, who took office in May 2011. However, in a landscape that is rife with contradictions, also in May 2011, President Martelly's first choice for prime minister, Daniel Rouzier, publicly declared he would close the Ministry of Women's Condition and Rights. This very public gaffe, quickly reversed in response to a vocal outcry,[1] shows the multiple ways in which Haitian women are being treated. Women's bodies are targets of an intersection of social realities: poverty, inequality, neoliberal globalization, and patriarchy—challenged by an ongoing economic crisis, exacerbated by the earthquake. This chapter poses questions about how the issue of gender-based violence has been handled by international agencies and asks if the response has increased levels of violence experienced by these very women because of agencies' single-issue understandings and because of consequences based on their foreign concepts of gender.

GENDER AND VULNERABILITY

Feminist researchers have made inroads in the literature on disasters, arguing that gender as a social construct renders women more vulnerable in disaster situations (Enarson 1998), particularly to gender-based violence (Anastario, Larrance, and Lawry 2008; Henrici, Helmuth, and Braun 2010). As shown in chapter 1, vulnerability builds on a political ecology perspective that theorizes the interconnection between the political economy and human societies' exploitation of the natural environment. Vulnerability outlines the societal conditions that augment the destructiveness of natural events. However, disaster scholarship specifically theorizing women's experiences and gender has until recently been relatively scarce. Elaine Enarson published a 1998 article in *Disasters* proposing a research agenda that addresses gender when discussing social phenomena like vulnerability. Other scholars like Alice Fothergill (1999, 2004) discussed women's roles in disasters, typically either ignored or stereotyped as either too emotional or stoic. Kathleen Tierney (Tierney 2012; Tierney, Bevc, and Kuligowski 2006) decries what she called "critical disjunctures," lessons not learned about gender and disasters. Although focused on the United States, Elaine Enarson's recent book (2012) presents a gender analysis of issues such as vulnerability, health, housing, employment, and resilience. Lamenting the still-specialist nature of the literature on gender and disasters, Enarson critiques the way many disaster scholars and practitioners treat gender as an add-on, or an "either/or" category of analysis. She argued the lens of women and gender is more like a kaleidoscope, requiring "multiple visions" to become visible (ibid., 196).

Hurricane Katrina inspired a new and sustained interest in disaster scholarship. This is not surprising, given the mega-disaster's imprint that is still being felt in U.S. society. Katrina exposed for people outside the United States, including many Haitian friends, neighbors, and colleagues, the all-too-real inequalities, racism, and poverty within the United States. This "neoliberal deluge" (Johnson 2011) is the subject of many critical analyses that point to the ways in which conscious social policy and racial segregation augmented the vulnerability for residents of the U.S. Gulf Coast, particularly New Orleans (for example, Dyson 2005; Lubiano 2008; Luft 2009; Woods 2010). In addition to the barely hidden racism in media coverage—with white families "finding food" and Black families "looting"—and the response, inspiring Kanye West to utter "George Bush Does Not Care about Black People"—the storm also was a boon for private contractors, a highly visible example of what Naomi Klein (2007) termed "disaster capitalism" (see also Adams 2013).

Hurricane Katrina also sharpened focus on disasters' impact on women's bodies and gender as a social construct. Enarson coedited a book assembling analyses about women and Hurricane Katrina (David and Enarson 2012). The floods—which were not caused by the storm alone but by the levees that broke—had a disproportionate impact on women, particularly on lower-income and/or women of color, because multiple forms of inequality tied women to their families and meant they had less access to means of escape

(Willinger and Knight 2012). Katrina also had an impact on women's survival networks (Litt, Skinner, and Robinson 2012), particularly difficult for those "doubly displaced" by public housing policy (Henrici, Helmuth, and Carlberg 2012). Several authors theorize a rise in gender-based violence, including activists INCITE! Women of Color against Violence (2012) and SisterSong cofounder Loretta Ross (2012), who take their ongoing intersectional work to their chapters. Diverting the highly racialized gaze away from individual perpetrators, both authors identify larger systems such as state violence (imperialist wars as well as police violence against communities of color) and white supremacy as contributing to the rise in violence against women following Katrina.

This rise in violence against women is certainly not unique to Katrina; Enarson (2012, 73–77) notes similar increases following the *Exxon Valdez* spill, the Loma Prieta earthquake, Hurricane Andrew, the Missouri River floods, and the terrorist attacks of September 11, 2001, to name a few. Researchers have also documented how women's bodies have become targets during violent conflicts, including war, detailed by UN Special Rapporteur Rashida Manjoo (Manjoo, Rashida, and United Nations 2011). In Kosovo, rape was a systematic weapon against Muslim minority populations, and in the Democratic Republic of Congo a weapon of war (Maclin et al. 2014). Miriam Ticktin (2011) notes a pattern across several cases in humanitarian crises and calls into question the official response. Malya's analysis outlines parallels in Haiti. All this is to say that the post-earthquake rise in gender-based violence is far from unique to Haiti.

Structuring This Vulnerability before the Earthquake

To understand the narratives and realities Haitian women face, it is critical to first understand what Black feminist scholars and other women of color and their allies have called intersectionality, the multiple forms of oppression and inequality based on distinct but overlapping identities, such as race, class, gender, sexuality, age, and parental status (for example, Collins 1990; Crenshaw 1991). As a result of both intersectionality and structural violence, Haitian women's condition, particularly among Port-au-Prince's poor majority, was markedly worsened. In Haiti, gender inequality is grafted onto economic inequality and desperation, exemplifying the feminization of poverty (Brenner 2000; McLanahan, Sorensen, and Watson 1989). Marie-Josslyn Lassègue, founder of feminist NGO Fanm Yo La and former minister of Women's Condition and Rights, added, "There is also a feminization of unemployment: most unemployed are women." Edele, a self-described "humanist-feminist activist" theorizes women's condition: "There is no justice in the country. . . . I mean, everyone is a victim. Therefore, women are double victims of the situation." Michèle from Hancho continues in this vein:

> Well, when I was young, I used to go to school. After this, I stopped going to school because I gave birth. My life was not fully actualized because after that my life became like a blanket. Every person that comes by takes a little piece and then leaves me in the cold. I would like my life to improve, not remain how it has been. I would like to completely change so I can live a sacred life, because my life is not good.

Chapter 1 shared how Michèle's neighbor Manoucheka also left school to have a child. Leaving school to give birth limited these women's choices, like many others in a society where 70 percent of people work in the informal economy. In such a competitive environment, inequality in schooling can lead to even greater inequality in employment. Education can be one of very few opportunities—or at least hope—for upward mobility, which is why women like Marie-Jeanne will pay 40 percent of their incomes to send one child to school. Several students at the State University of Haiti were raised by street vendors. Myriam Chancy (2010) details her own family's conscientious upward mobility by investing in education.

Given women's traditional role in the household, women formally employed as wage laborers work a "second shift" at home (Hochschild 1989), as Thérèse, a laid-off factory worker and a participant in *Poto Mitan*, argues, "Who does the paid work? Who does the housework, huh? We women, we are everything. It's true, men have their role, but women play the bigger role. Long ago men used to pay for the children's school, but now it's on women's shoulders. Women pay the consequence." This second shift is also exacerbated by the fact that many women are heads of household, the "mother and the father," a common expression across the Caribbean, characterized with having matrifocal households (for example, Clarke 1957). According to the Ministry of Women's Condition and Rights at a 2004 conference, 59 percent of Port-au-Prince households were headed by single women (Cayemittes et al. 2001). This occurs for many reasons, not the least of which is the violence to the family during slavery. Men are also more likely to migrate for seasonal labor, especially to the Dominican Republic and the *batèy*, sugar cane plantations (Simmons 2010). Chancy (2012) discusses these migrations and their impact on women and gendered relationships. There is also a cultural importance of maternity and practice of *san papa*, unknown or nonrecognized paternity.[2]

M. Catherine Maternowska (2006) details these pressures on women, who often are confronted with the choice of having to have a sexual relationship with a male to provide for their children. Nadine, who like Michèle had a conversation with our team in Hancho I, spelled this out:

Well! My life story . . . I've been living in the countryside, like . . . my mom is not with my father. Well, when my father died—I must have been nine—my mother couldn't afford to send me to school, and I was living with my uncle in Port-au-Prince. But he didn't take care of me. They didn't care for me. I was old enough to have a husband, but at that point I didn't have one. Shortly afterward, I got a husband because nobody was helping me. I ended up being with him, but it was a bad experience. I went to the hospital to have an operation, because I couldn't give birth. They didn't solve the problem, so we split up. Men will not stay with a woman if she can't give birth. So I had another husband. I actually have nothing! I have nothing after that. Even though he's fulfilled, myself, I'm not fulfilled because, for example he has children but I have none. So he wasn't supposed to have problems, but every day we clash with each other, just because I have nothing. Now, myself, when I think about my situation, I don't, I'm not living well. I can't continue living like this, because as a young woman, when you don't have children with a man, you're only with him so he can feed you, there won't really be a strong relationship. Deep down I wanted to die, because I can't live like this.

Nadine's story highlights the importance of women's autonomy within intimate relationships and how poverty and patriarchy intersect to limit her access to resources, thus rendering her more dependent on a male partner.

These intersecting inequalities render women like Sandy, Manoucheka, Ghislène, and Edwidge more vulnerable to disasters: they are more likely to have been inside the house working, or under a concrete building working for a factory, when the quake struck on January 12. Like during Hurricane Katrina, gender and particularly women's roles as family caretakers limited their mobility. Being dependent on male providers also renders some women more vulnerable to violence.

Since the Earthquake

Haitian women's organizations have been struggling against violence, including structural violence, long before the earthquake (Benoit 1995; Charles 1995; Gilbert 2001; Racine 1995). Myriam Chancy (2010) penned a poignant piece honoring the many struggles, achievements, and activism of Haitian women, before and after the earthquake, and also defending Haitian women's right for self-representation. Therefore it is dangerous to paint postquake gender-based violence as either exaggerated or exceptional. Listening carefully to women's stories, however, clearly underscores both the continuities since the earthquake and how the situation deteriorated for most women. As inadequate as it is, the official police report shows 794 cases of sexual violence in 2010, up from 218 the previous year (d'Adesky et al. 2012).

As these stories show, gender is always operating and shaping women's lived experience of disasters. Attempting to respond to the many inequities women faced, a large ad hoc coalition of Haitian, Diaspora, and foreign women's groups wrote "The Haiti Gender Shadow Report" aimed at informing and shaping the Post Disaster Needs Assessment (PDNA), the official reconstruction plan for the country.[3] This preliminary report was written in consultation with a coalition of women from diverse backgrounds working in grassroots communities in Haiti as well as in the international arena. Released on March 31, 2010, the same day as the Haiti Donors' Conference held at UN headquarters, it highlights gender concerns absent from Haiti's PDNA, the operative blueprint for Haiti's reconstruction. The report offers donors, international agencies, and other stakeholders human rights–based policy guidelines to promote and protect the rights of Haitian women. Although the PDNA comprises eight themes—governance, environment, disaster risk and management, social sectors, infrastructure, territorial development, production sector, and cross-cutting sectors (including gender, youth, culture, and social protection)—only the last theme addresses gender, and only peripherally so. The Gender Shadow Report addresses a range of issues such as the economy, political participation, grassroots organizations, popular consultation, health care, and education. After the report's publication, and the PDNA's formal adoption and creation of the Interim Haiti Reconstruction Commission (IHRC) to implement it, the coalition disbanded, and the only organized advocacy effort regarding women centered around violence.

Mirroring the pre-quake discussion, and contributing a timely and specific set of gender analyses of disasters, Gina Athena Ulysse (2011) assembled a pathbreaking interdisciplinary set of essays, poems, and autobiographies about the earthquake in a special issue of *Meridians*, titled "Pawòl Fanm sou Douz Janvye" (Women's Voices on January 12). These critical perspectives centering the voices and lived experiences of Haitian and Diaspora women challenge mainstream constructions of the disaster, infusing an intersectional analysis of how the earthquake affected Haitian women and girls in a multitude of arenas: survival, security, their families, and their livelihoods in addition to violence, as well as how these are linked. The remainder of this chapter employs the intersectional analysis of structural violence provided to materially ground understandings of gender-based violence.

GENDER AND CAMP CONDITIONS

Chapter 2 showed that IDP camps became extremely visible symbols of the humanitarian crisis, and indeed they were sites where acts of violence increased. The Small Arms Survey (Muggah 2011) found that 22 percent of women living in the camps experienced violence the first year following the earthquake, compared to 2 percent outside the camps. Many Haitian women activists cited the proverb, *abse sou klou,* "an abscess on an open wound," to describe the increase. Said Malya, "We worked hard to bring rapists to justice before the earthquake. After, it's like we had to start from zero." Activists since Anne-Christine d'Adesky (d'Adesky et al. 2012) began using the term "gender aftershocks" to describe the secondary impacts of the earthquake and how they in turn increased violence against women. As the humanitarian crisis wore on, camps became symbols of the failure of the disaster response, begging the question of where to assign blame. Ulysse (2010), Jean-Charles (2014), and other Haitian feminist scholars have noted that narratives of postquake problems easily slot into longstanding discourses denigrating the world's "unthinkable" first free black nation state (Trouillot 1995).

Following is a discussion of several aspects of camps and the humanitarian apparatus offering aid to the camps, each of which constitute factors in the rise of gender-based violence. These intersecting factors include physical design, lack of basic services, daily interaction, the gendered ways in which aid was delivered, and housing. Based on the widely proliferated discourse that people were only in the camps for the free services, people claiming to be landowners often responded by cutting life-saving services such as water and sanitation. Hélène reported that at her former camp, "The priest kicked out the doctors. He told the Americans not to saturate the grounds" with people like her. As a result of these (in)actions, many residents felt abandoned by NGOs and other aid agencies. Aline Despaines, president of the women's organization Organisation des Femmes Devouées en Action (OFEDA, Organization of Dedicated Women in Action), who lived in a camp, explained, "It's like they forgot this camp. No one has ever passed through here to investigate. We sent a letter to all the NGOs we know: UNICEF, OIM, WPF, World Vision, but we have received nothing. Only Mercy Corps came by to offer people a little water. However, you see the reservoir? It's empty. Water never comes out anymore." Interestingly, Aline refers to UN agencies as NGOs, a common "mistake" I discuss in greater depth in chapter 6. Unfortunately these cases were far from unique; 42.3 percent of the camps didn't have access to water as of August 2010, seven months following the earthquake (Schuller and Levey 2014). Because of these blame-the-victim discourses, camps on private land had less access to human rights to water than camps on public land.

Wherever people may have come from before the camps, camps are often degrading physical environments. A key element of this degradation, feeling treated as subhuman, was the lack of adequate toilet facilities; 29.2 percent of the camps didn't have a toilet as of August 2010. Researchers counted the number of toilets in the camps. Dividing the official population by this number, it was found that on average there was one toilet for every 273 people (Schuller 2010c), despite

Sphere Minimum Humanitarian Standards that say that a toilet be shared by no more than twenty people (Sphere Project 2004). This doesn't even match the goal the United Nations set for Haiti of one hundred people per toilet (Panchang 2012). There were only thirty toilets for 30,400 residents in Plas Lapè as of the summer of 2010. According to the July 2010 Displacement Tracking Matrix, 6,820 people lived in the soccer field outside of the rectory in Solino. Despite this density, residents had to wait for nearly five months for the first toilets to arrive. When asked in April 2010 how people defecate, Anne-Marie held up a small plastic bag usually used to sell half cups of sugar, or penny candy: "We throw it in the ravine across the street." CAJIT fared worse: despite my advocacy and numerous conversations with water and sanitation (WASH) officials, toilets were never installed in CAJIT.

Residents were concerned not only with the number of toilets but how often they were maintained. In the July–August 2010 sample, toilets had not been cleaned at all since January 12 in 26 percent of camps. Several residents reported that NGOs came to install the toilets, dug up pit latrines made of plywood, and then left. Residents were left wondering why, but more important, the agency handed residents a new public health problem in the making. In Kolonbi, toilets were left for ten months without being cleaned before they were finally deinstalled in December 2012. Covered up, they became the site for new residents who were forcibly evicted from other camps. Camp committee president Jean-Jacques explained that the NGO contract had expired, which is why the latrines were left.

This lack of sanitation hastened the spread of cholera following an outbreak in October 2010, the genesis of which epidemiological (Piarroux et al. 2011) and genetic (Hendriksen, Price, and Shupp 2011) evidence show, was infected UN troops at a base with a leaky sewage. Cholera killed over 4,000 people in the first three months (Agence France-Presse 2011); by January 2012 it had claimed 7,025 lives (Ministère de la Santé Publique et de la Population 2012) and by October 2013 there had been 8,361 deaths, with fifty new deaths occurring monthly. Despite the additional media attention and a UN Flash Appeal to raise an additional $170 million, little progress was made obtaining these life-saving services: as of January 2011, 25.5 percent (down from 29.2 percent) of camps still lacked toilets, and 38.6 percent (instead of 42.3 percent) of camps still did not have water. Where the progress was concentrated was instructive; in Cité Soleil, the Haitian government made 100 percent coverage of water and sanitation (WASH) services in the camps a priority. Although it was still NGOs that did the work, they did so under a frame established by the Haitian government. Like the GBV subcluster, the WASH cluster was cochaired by a Haitian government and met off LogBase. Left to their own devices, NGOs added services to an additional 1 percent of camps (Schuller and Levey 2014). And a close look at the data shows that the increase in percentage might have something to do with the number of camps that had closed. In one camp in Carrefour, at an Adventist Church, there were still no toilets when the cholera outbreak began in late October 2010, ten months after the earthquake. Church leaders had been giving verbal warnings for people to leave. People stayed until one day in November, when eight cases of cholera were recorded in the camp. The next day, all 546 people fled the camp. Levi, a camp in Tabarre, was a shell of its former self by January 2011: only 30 of 486 people remained following the cholera outbreak. The camp never had a toilet, so people went to a neighbor's house. Neighbors' generosity has limits, however, especially after the outbreak of the fecal-borne disease. In all, 12 camps in the original sample of 108 closed in the interim five months.

The shortage of public facilities in the camps had a disproportionate impact on women, especially the tactic adopted in many privately run camps to charge camp residents to use the facilities. Malya said, "Imagine! Having to pay for a bathroom! Men can get away with one time per day, but we women! And who is in charge of the children?" Making matters worse is that despite the emergency rations provided by NGOs the first three months following the earthquake, residents of at least thirty-one camps (all I had visited by the summer of 2010) were not offered sanitary napkins or tampons. Said NGO consultant Murielle Dorismond, "Half of the population needs this! It's good that people are finally concerned about the public health concerns of human waste. But what about menstrual blood? Do we not count as people?"

The physical space, design and planning, of the camps contributed to threats against women. In addition to the precariousness of plastic "walls," lighting was a major concern in all of the camps at first. Karade—at least for the space managed by an NGO—had solar-powered streetlights installed with the T-shelters. Plas Lapè also had a few such lamps installed, but the entire back section of the camp, the soccer field, had access to the outside world only through a narrow corridor that around what used to be the concession stand. Residents reported that this area was often "patrolled" by armed individuals. Some referred to them as "gangs." Facilities for people to shower were inadequate, offering no privacy: at Nan Bannann people crouched behind half-crumbled brick walls to bathe as of the summer of 2011. Similarly, no such space was constructed at Kolonbi. Some agencies reported attempting gender-conscious programming, such as providing lighting or locks for stall doors.

Furthermore, the lack of sanitary provisions in the camps presented particular dangers for women, as State University of Haiti student and blogger Carine Exantus outlined for the Champs-de-Mars camp:

> In my camp, there are twelve toilets in the front and twelve toilets in the back for 4,200 people. You can't use the shower: you wash to get dirty. People hardly use

these facilities anymore. Everyone at their tent has a little plastic tub, where they throw water over themselves, or they just shower in public. In my journal I wrote about this: young women suffer sexual aggression because they have to shower in public.

Carine's interview testimony explicitly connects the poor state of public facilities in the camps with the issue of gender-based violence. Theorizing from her own lived experience (Collins 1990, 31–32), Carine articulates the necessity of understanding an intersectional approach, while also highlighting the limited progress within the international aid response. This intersectional analysis of structural violence requires attention to the ways in which the humanitarian aid was gendered, and how this contributed to violence against women.

GENDERED IDEOLOGIES AND PRACTICES OF HUMANITARIAN AID

As a result of women's culturally valorized status of *poto mitan* (central pillars of the family and society) and because of the conscious shifts in donor policies, and years of tireless advocacy from feminists working within aid agencies (Porter and Judd 1999), donors have made policy decisions to favor women, for example, in microcredit and food aid. Said Alex, a (male) USAID employee, "You give money to a man and he's as likely to spend it on beer or a lover as on his family. But if you give to a woman, you're guaranteed that she will prioritize feeding herself and her children." It is unclear whether Alex particularly cared about women or about gender equality beyond the benefits to aid effectiveness a strategic WID (Women in Development) approach offered. The UN Inter-Agency Standing Committee, responsible for organizing all clusters, also had a training on gender-aware disaster response programming and prevention. However, many foreign aid workers shared that the problem was not so much a lack of good intentions, even good policies, but the will (and funding) to implement them. Many noted that like other stated policy concerns, attention to gender became simply a "check-the-box" phenomenon, paying lip service in reports and then moving on.

One such official attention to gender was food aid. Since the earthquake, donors and large NGOs have adopted the World Food Program's guidelines to give food aid exclusively to women, using a system of ration cards whereby camp committees give food cards to women the night before the food distribution by the NGO and UN troops. Figure 4.1 shows such a distribution. In theory, these policies are advantageous to women. However, actual practice is more complicated, as women are not isolated individuals disarticulated from men in their family and community (Bhavnani, Foran, and Kurian 2003), some

FIGURE 4.1. Distribution of food aid, Solino neighborhood, March 2010. Photo: Valerie Kaussen

of whom understandably seek to use this distribution system to their advantage. Additionally, in some cases, declaring women to be heads of household actively discouraged men's responsibility, in fact reifying and reinforcing the stereotype of matrifocality (Spillers 1987). In other cases, women as aid recipients became targets for violence.

As noted in the previous chapter, the system of distributing ration cards, designed by large NGOs as an attempt to establish order and ensure fairness, had several negative consequences because of gendered ideologies and practices. Alex did not appear to consider that giving women food aid might have given a message to men that they are or shouldn't be responsible for their children. Said Giliane, a Haitian aid worker, "It wasn't even hindsight. We Haitian people warned our foreign bosses that if you put everything onto women, this will make women responsible for everything." These ideologically laden policies tethered women even further to their children. This in turn contributed to gendered discourses and stereotypes, and even targeting women for acts of sexual harassment, as camp committees— disproportionately men—held the power to dole out ration cards.

NGOs gave committees the power to decide who to receive aid. The Humanitarian Accountability Project (HAP and IOM 2010) reported that NGOs gave too much power in the hands of these committees while knowing very little about them. These committees were also gendered, with women making up fewer than a quarter of members (Schuller 2010c). In the introduction to this chapter, Malya argued that the practice of powerful men giving out cards leads too often to sexual harassment and even forced sex. She continued, "Already [March 2010] we have heard over two dozen members tell us that they were forced to submit to sexual relations with the guy in exchange for the cards." This situation was not unique to KOFAVIV; an NYU investigation found that at least the discourse of transactional sex, exchanging sex for ration cards was commonplace (NYU 2011). Kolonbi camp resident Evrance, in her fifties, never received food aid. When asked why, she theorized, "It's because the guys in the committee choose young women with large buttocks." The researcher conducting this interview asked for clarification, making sure of what she heard. Evrance replied, "You heard me! Beautiful, beautiful, beautiful, beautiful asses."[4] This was not unique to Kolonbi, as Fabiola details from Plas Lapè. She didn't get a cash-for-work job digging canals: "This is a job for men. I didn't work in the project. We must have sex with them. Such an old woman like me, what can I do for them?" In the St. Louis camp, the Red Cross gave the camp committee president Esaie, a male, the responsibility to give the official list of who was a "real" resident and therefore eligible for relocation assistance valued at $500 or more. According to Sandy Nelzy (2013, 22), one of the CUNY students on the research team, Esaie held this over at least two mothers, one of whom was married, to demand sex: "Because she refused the offer, [Esaie] stopped informing her about the Red Cross visits to the camp and refused to include her name in the list he gave the Red Cross as to who would receive official relocation assistance." The most comprehensive study of gender-based violence—that performed by d'Adesky and Poto Fanm+Fi, the post-eathquake coalition to support women and girls—reports that 37 percent of pregnant women ($n = 1{,}251$) reported having sex for survival, mostly attempting to exchange for shelter but also for food (d'Adesky et al. 2012).

Unfortunately, the NYU report also found that many people reported that incidents of gender-based violence and sex-for-food increased when the official food aid ended in April 2010. Although the researchers did not collect corroborating data, they are investigating whether a causal link exists between food insecurity and gender-based violence. The report by d'Adesky has a much larger data set that also includes the experiences of women in rural areas. It explores the links between food insecurity and gender-based violence in greater depth, but the results are limited because of the worldwide problem of underreporting rape due to fears of reprisals, lack of confidence in the authorities, and stigma. However, the information strongly suggests that the ways in which humanitarian aid was gendered played a contributing role in increasing violence against women.

INTERSECTIONAL SOLUTIONS

Although it might not register with those of us who are not Haitian, many women begin their solutions through their roles as mothers, like Sandy at Nan Bannann: "I raised my child and sent him to school since he was three. Now he is sixteen, I explained to him the situation of misery in which we live. I tell him that his father didn't take care of him, which explains the painful situation we live. Tomorrow he shouldn't do the same."

In addition to these often invisible everyday solutions, continuing a history of engagement described earlier, women's groups are among the leaders in improving living conditions within the camps. Elizabeth Senatus, leader within a women's group l'Etoile Brillante (Shining Star), said, "We might have potential that we weren't aware of. We use what resources we have in hand. We don't wait for millions to arrive, we create." L'Étoile Brillante created a primary school and an adult literacy program, income-generating activities for women such as manufacturing artisanal soaps and jewelry, and weekly plays and movie nights, while engaging men in a common effort against violence. As of August 2010, when I visited the camp, there had been no instances of rape. L'Étoile Brillante was supported by the Haitian-Dominican Women's Movement founded by the late Sonia Pierre and their Haitian Diaspora partners such as Haitian Women for Haitian Refugees. In her July 2011 interview, after the aid like the water stopped, Aline of OFEDA discussed the first case of rape.

> We hadn't had rape or violence in this camp. Last week we recorded a case. The police were behind and the thieves ambushed them here, inside the camp. They stole people's motorcycles. We don't know if it's because people are too frustrated. We organize ourselves, small families who are here. We get together to survive. We need to organize our own security. We close the gates at night. We lock the gates at 9:00 P.M. and open them at 5:00 A.M. Because the government doesn't see us, big people don't see us, foreign services don't see us, we created an activity for people to forget about their stress on Sundays, the women's group called OFEDA [Organization of Dedicated Women in Action].

Solutions, even for gender-based violence, cannot focus only on police patrols and incarceration as stipulated in an injunction by the Inter-American Commission on Human Rights. First of all, as Carine outlines, women in Haiti, as worldwide, are often hesitant to speak out: "There is rape, but people don't want to talk about it publicly because here in Haiti, someone who has been raped is traumatized, and they don't want people to know they've been raped. They are very restrained, so you can't know about it easily." An intersectional approach, one that addresses structural violence, requires attention to multiple issues that may not be readily identifiable as "feminist" to some international agencies. Women's groups in Haiti are also among the forefront of a growing social movement post-earthquake, a coalition of grassroots groups spanning multiple issues and political perspectives. This mobilization poses solutions to Haiti's IDP crisis within a lens of human rights, to demand better from the Haitian government and donors. The first solution is permanent housing, defined by local organizations as a women's issue, because it directly relates to gender-based violence. Haiti's first minister of Women's Condition and Rights, Lise-Marie Dejean, said:

> In 1993, a journalist asked me what the coming government needed to do to meet women's needs. I said housing. One of the emblems we had in the 2000 Global Women's March was a cardboard box because people used to sleep in them. January 12th sharpened the focus on the housing problem and violence. Because now women live in a series of conditions one on top of one another, lack of privacy. They are at the mercy of any vagabond who would want to rape them.

Activists within KOFAVIV, involved in many of the camps, and part of a larger mobilization of activist organizations defending housing rights, described a direct link between violence and housing. Said Malya's cofounder Eramithe:

> I think that if the government provided permanent housing, the incidents of rape and violence would diminish. True, even when people had houses there was still violence. But it was never this bad. I think if someone has a house to stay in she has more security. Now, the person's under plastic. All it takes is someone to come by with a razor and rip the tent, and he can come inside and do what he wants. It's like you're sleeping in the street if you're in a tent.

As of the writing of this chapter in 2014, housing remains an urgent priority. Four years after the earthquake Haitian Prime Minister Laurent Lamothe cited the official statistic of IDPs, praising that it had gone down by 90 percent since peak, also citing the construction of 5,000 homes. The *New York Times* (2014) reported a total of 7,515 built, and the Shelter Cluster outlined 27,000 homes being repaired. This pales in comparison to the 105,000 homes completely destroyed and 188,383 houses collapsed or badly damaged.[5]

ANALYSIS: CHALLENGES TO
AN INTERSECTIONAL APPROACH

This chapter has demonstrated Haitian women's complex, intersectional analyses before and after the earthquake, which although they go far beyond gender-based violence, nonetheless ground understanding of this problem within women's lived realities and pose culturally appropriate solutions that address women's multiple identities. Noted earlier, a coalition of groups advocated for a holistic, multisectoral infusion of gender concerns into the official reconstruction plan. Why has gender-based violence come to dominate all discussions of women and gender, and why have official solutions to gender-based violence been limited to tools of greater police enforcement focusing on individual perpetrators and victims? Posed another way, what processes mitigate against complexity and intersectionality, and against an understanding of gender-based violence as both embodied and structural/intersectional?

Unfortunately political processes work against such an intersectional approach, as Black feminists have long pointed out. For example, the court system—including the international human rights apparatus—tends to flatten complexity and reproduce essentialist concepts within mainstream, "Western" liberal feminism (for example, Williams 1991). Although many women working within humanitarian agencies and certainly activists working alongside KOFA-VIV and other groups advocating for women and girls have a more nuanced understanding, processes linked to NGO-ization (Alvarez 1999; Bernal and Grewal 2014; Lang 2000; Nagar 2006) limit their responses to those that match donors' priorities and classificatory schema even as gender mainstreaming is attempted (Bessis 2001). This is in no small part because of NGOs' dependence on donors. Added to the culturally, racially, and class-specific definitions of gender issues is an inherently hierarchical and bureaucratic structure that shifts decision-making powers upward through a system of intermediaries (Schuller 2012c).

This tendency is being put to the test: Haitian women's groups like KOFAVIV and their solidarity partners brought litigation to the Inter-American Commission on Human Rights. In addition to more patrols of camps that were required by the injunction, the plaintiffs called for more lighting, sanitation services, and grassroots women's participation. Partly owing to this advocacy, international development agencies have begun to invest significant resources in combating gender-based violence. Although this support to groups like KOFAVIV offered necessary tools to curtail gender-based violence, the bilateral support limits the understanding of the issue and its potential solutions to mainstream, single-issue feminism within restraints of the political processes inherent to bilateral aid. The injunction called for greater policing and management efforts such as lighting. According to MINUSTAH, the UN military mission, they had conducted regular patrols of six camps, representing half of 1 percent, because there were twelve hundred camps at the peak before the cholera outbreak. Karade was one of the six camps: though MINUSTAH had a permanent base, their presence was so ineffective at this camp that residents called them "photocopies"—as if they hung on the wall, never doing anything (Ulcena 2013—see chapter 8 for a more in-depth discussion). Permanent housing, affirming the rights of internally displaced persons, and women's participation remained unaddressed in the international court order. A report from the Government Accountability Office (2013) published in June 2013 critiqued USAID for failing to meet its housing objectives while investing $224 million in a new industrial park outside of the earthquake-affected zone. Although Lamothe pointed to a figure that was a tenth of the population of IDPs at peak, this number excludes women like Marie-Jeanne, whose forced eviction—wherein her belongings were destroyed—can hardly be called a success.[6] Forced eviction is also more felt by women. Malya explains:

> This affects women more because you know, normally, women are always more affected by difficult situations. Because women have to take care of children. Women have to go out in the streets and look for a livelihood to give their children food. It affects women when the government or anyone else forces a woman to leave the camp to go somewhere else, with a lot of children in her hands without out knowing where she will go.

Although resources to confront gender-based violence increased, it is important to remain vigilant so that these tools do not cut off solutions such as permanent housing and economic justice, nor do further violence through amplifying negative stereotypes, thus justifying continued foreign occupation and control.[7] Reflecting shifts in political fortune, in 2011 KOFAVIV received a large USAID grant through a contracting NGO. KOFAVIV has not continued to receive large support, as the value attached to what Erica James (2010) called the "economy of compassion" within "the political economy of trauma" has once again diminished. Certainly other NGOs are also downscaling their efforts in Haiti as international funds wither. However, it is also an open question about how KOFAVIV changed as a result of these funds. They have already been set apart from other women's organizations, including grassroots associations with whom they worked before they had their own office. As noted previously, Malya was named a CNN Hero for KOFAVIV's work. This high visibility comes at a price: assailants attempted to kidnap Eramithe's daughter. As she recalled in April 2010:

> A young man came inside the camp to rape my daughter. When we went to the police station right here, they didn't even come, and they never even conducted an investigation when I explained the problem: This guy took my daughter to run away with her, to rape her. The guy returned under the tent and had a weapon in his hand. A police officer said, "I can't say anything. That's [Haitian president René] Préval's problem. Préval has to get involved." The police came to the camp twice, but they only patrolled the perimeter.

Undeterred, KOFAVIV continued their advocacy, but the retaliation against them escalated. In the summer of 2011, Malya and Eramithe were forced to move out of the camp, as Malya explained:

> I decided to leave the camp because I was a victim of violence. A prison escapee pulled a gun on me, pressuring me. He tried to kidnap me. He said that the police is behind him, he uses the police's firearms, that he killed a lot of people, raped a lot of women, and kidnapped many people. That's what he does for a living. This camp has a lot of people who escaped from prison living inside. He said that he wasn't alone; he had a team of some fifty people. After we left the camp we made several attempts at solutions: we contacted the Haitian government, the Port-au-Prince police station and tribunal. We have a lot of formal complaints and a warrant. And the UN [MINUSTAH] and the Bureau des Avocats Internationaux [BAI]. We have the papers for them to follow up on our case, to arrest the prison escapees. Until now—two months later—nothing has happened. So we're still in *marronage*, in hiding. We have a driver pick us up and drop us off in secret.

UNINTENDED RESULTS

In August 2013, KOFAVIV and particularly Malya were again targeted for acts of violence; Malya sought asylum in the United States and was ultimately denied. As she discussed it, the circumstances of her CNN Hero award were the reason. A team of nine foreign journalists accompanied her in camps to film her work. The CNN team spent a full day in a camp called Tapis Rouge, in a rough part of town, Gran Ravin. When she won the prize, these individuals and very many others were made aware of just how much money she won. One woman from Tapis Rouge was waiting for her at the airport, asking for a cut. The death threats began immediately thereafter. A few months later, she narrowly escaped an assassination attempt. Both Malya and Eramithe had to move their children out of the country, and they moved the KOFAVIV office in the middle of the night. Even so they visited the office less and less, and never without a bodyguard. This obviously took a toll on their work, but worse was a diminishing of funds. This admittedly an extreme case, but it is emblematic of how good intentions can lead to disastrous outcomes by not taking account of the cultural context. At the basis of Malya's story is that she was exceptionalized, set apart, from her community, celebrated for her individual achievement. This individualism is structured into a U.S. media response in part because it reflects this value within U.S. society. Similarly, the ways that foreign agencies responded to violence and the ways in which aid was gendered reflect a Western, and often U.S., worldview, including focus on the individual woman disconnected from her family and community

(Ticktin 2011). White liberal feminism tends to also disarticulate gender as the only focus of intervention.

GENDER AFTERSHOCKS

This chapter has discussed the ways in which gender intersects with other forms of inequality, such as poverty and social exclusion within Haiti, but also inequalities within the world system. Although international agencies mounted a sincere and relatively successful effort to combat gender-based violence alongside Haitian women's organizations, including KOFAVIV, their culturally, socially, and historically specific understandings of gender, including gender-based violence, had a range of consequences that were in the end detrimental to women. Foreign agencies' hierarchical relationships and single-issue feminist agenda, complicated by the "check-the-box" phenomenon, failed to account for the multiple issues, identities, relationships, and inequalities Haitian women of the poor majority face. The ways in which aid was gendered failed to take account the on-the-ground realities and constructs of gender. The physical design of the camps and the persistent gaps in services were more seriously felt by women, and were factors in the increasing violence against women.

Intended to benefit women—though if USAID's Alex is any indication, possibly primarily for other concerns—humanitarian agencies' policies of granting food aid exclusively to women increased the opportunity for a range of other problems, including transactional sex and even violence. This is in no small part because the aid was distributed by also gendered camp committees. Particularly when considering the (extra)ordinary outpouring of solidarity from within Haiti following the earthquake discussed in chapter 2, how did the camp committees become the hierarchical, male-dominated, entities wherein some abused their power over women? Answering this question is the focus of the next chapter.

5 · *PÒCH PRELA*

Camp Committees

The camp committee here is a central committee. But it's made up of people who were at St. Louis. When they were in St. Louis there were three groups called OPPS, KAS, and I forgot the last one. When they came up to Karade, they took two from each group from St. Louis, and they created a committee called the Central Committee. But when the organizations that were already working here noticed that it was made of only men, they asked to create an organization to include women. So they created a women's committee, but the men were wily[1] and did everything to make the women's committee fail. So now the women's committee is no longer around, because CRS [Catholic Relief Services],[2] that sponsored them here, almost left. It is no longer in this site/camp because there was a fight. There were these issues. That is, people who are in charge of organizing something, they took money and didn't really do anything with it.

They did not do anything with it; they just put the money in their pocket. And the population didn't even know if there was money being given. The committee took the money and put it in their pocket. When the population became aware of this, they protested.

I was in the central women's committee. But it never . . . that is, every time CRS needed to meet with us, it proposed a bunch of stuff to do with us here. But every meeting they had for the women, the men were always there. CRS said that it won't work with the men because it found that the men were cunning, so it wanted to work with women. So, one Saturday we threw a party for the children; there was some money given[3] and it fell into the men's hands. They did not share it with the women. As a result, CRS has stopped working with us, and since that time we stopped meeting.

Well . . . the men's committee became stubborn. That is, when the women wanted to stand up, it pulled rank on us. The men stated that they had overall responsibility for us. That is to say, if we didn't go through them to have a meeting or sit with another person, we weren't allowed to do it.

Well . . . we said that we would still meet. We decided to leave the central women's committee and organize ourselves under another name. We will create another group. The men said that even though we form another group, if it was about the camp, they will not recognize our group if we don't meet under their auspices. In other words they won't recognize us as an organization in the camp.[4]

Well . . . to tell the truth, this committee works for themselves. If something comes in, like a house, you do not know anything about what it is happening. They keep it for themselves. They do not defend the population!

Well . . . when they have their meetings, they stand up and say they are defending women's interests, but it is not true at all. If there is something to share, we women won't see it. They keep it for themselves, their wives, and their children.

—Maud, Karade

One of the conclusions from the previous chapter is that well-intended policies such as targeting women for food aid can have the perverse outcomes of increasing violence against women because the intermediaries, male committee members, can use this power over women. Why is there this tendency within at least some camp committees? How are we to understand camp committees, especially when considering the stories of solidarity detailed in chapter 2?

As many researchers have documented (for example, Barthélémy 1990; Gabaud 2000; Smith 2001), there are vibrant collective civic organizations in the countryside, which can be considered the "DNA" of Haitian public life. Smith discusses several forms of autochthonous (home-grown) civil society and a hybrid *gwoupman peyizan* (peasants' organization), explicitly organized with a political intent and engaging with official development aid. However, these arrangements have undergone several mutations as worldwide economic patterns have shifted. Chapter 1 details the explosion of Port-au-Prince, particularly the shantytowns, but also notes thriving collectivist traditions stemming from rural collective practices such as the *konbit*, a collective work group.

These forms of solidarity are "hybrid," adapting to the new urban realities. How they mutated in the camps is the focus of this chapter. Like the camps themselves, camp committees were a new social phenomenon in Haiti. This chapter attempts to understand how they came to be, how they functioned, and why. This chapter includes quantitative survey data, but the bulk of this chapter attempts to tease out, analyze, and understand the perspectives of camp residents, analyzing qualitative interviews from people like Maud. Maud was one of very many people—in fact all of them—who lived in Karade and had a lot to say about their camp's committee. The Central Committee was the cause of *pale anpil*, a lot of talk. One of the eleven people interviewed, Nadeve, defended the Central Committee against a rival, the Civil Protection Committee organized by the government, even though she began by saying, "Well, I can't say much about the committee because I am always on the move. I usually leave at 5 A.M. and come back at 8 P.M. Sometimes I leave at 7 A.M. and come back at 9 P.M." Maud's analysis lays out several reasons why Karade's committee triggered the most animated and negative responses from the residents of the eight camps in the study. Once the Central Committee was created it became dictatorial, wanting total control of the camp. Maud's experience as a women's committee member also explained much of the problems with implementation of well-intentioned policies meant to benefit women discussed in the previous chapter. Maud also critiqued the Central Committee's lack of communication and tendency to take all the aid, literally to put it in their pockets. This chapter's title *pòch prela* refers to a situation well beyond deep pockets. This is a sentiment shared by many people across most of the camps to refer to the committees.

That said, there are some variations across the eight camps worth noting. Teasing these out and then identifying underlying themes is the focus of this chapter. The discussion begins with a history of how these committees became organized. Some were chosen by the population, others self-appointed, and still others appointed by the NGO camp management agency. In all cases there was at least a discourse of needing to have a committee in the camp in order to receive aid. Following this is a discussion of residents' understanding of the camp committee's roles and of their effectiveness. This section groups several common themes across the camps: although there are some notable exceptions, residents accused committees of not being proactive, of poor communication, and of wielding their power to benefit *moun pa*, their people. Much of this leadership is highly personalized, or to use Max Weber's (1946) term, "charismatic."

The chapter ends with an analysis of the variations between camps, but also the variations within camps. According to some committee members, residents accuse committees of not working, or pocketing the funds, because of mistaken understandings of the aid system and receipt of aid. It is also easier for people to critique those within one's social sphere or neighbors than institutions that are either foreign or national in scope. Linguistic cues offer insights into this phenomenon that is certainly not unique to Haiti. The chapter concludes with a series of questions: What explains the difference between Karade and other camps like CAJIT? The answers are to be found in the presence and role of

NGOs, certainly acting as camp management agencies (CMAs). In sum, this chapter is a reminder that community is not always a given but it comes into being through practice.

CREATION OF THE COMMITTEES

Each of the eight camps in the study had a unique story of how it came to being. However, there are some interesting parallels that could suggest some underlying policies. The organic outpouring of solidarity described in chapter 2 did not generate bureaucratic structures like committees. People like Yves, Sabine, and Manolia banded together and shared what they had for their common survival. In the neighborhood where I live, before the first water truck was donated, everyone pitched in to document precisely how many vessels people had, and what capacity. More than twenty people contributed over 150 pots, cups, buckets, or tubs to the effort.

Instructively, the aid apparatus—or at least the specter of receipt of aid—was the impulse for the creation of all eight committees. In some instances, the NGOs created the committees themselves. In other cases, residents decided to constitute a "committee" because they saw they were being left out of the aid distribution and wanted to be able to negotiate with aid agencies in the name of the population. Nelson, a member of the CAJIT committee, outlined a two-step process of community organization. In the first phase, people organically came together to support one another in immediate shelter:

> January 12 struck us and immediately people looked for a shelter to cover themselves. In this context, we looked for land, an empty space, a space without houses that could possibly fall on it. This shelter lasted two nights because, after 12 [the earthquake] we saw that the aftershocks will continue. People had to find somewhere to get cover. So in this point of view, we found shelter in these spaces. People saw that they had to also have cover against the sun and for them to find a place to lay down their body at night. So they organized themselves in groups.

This first phase was similar to what Manoucheka and Manolia described at the other side of the city in Hancho, and all over Port-au-Prince. Nelson continued, "We became a family in the first place living together. For those without food, people who had shared with those who didn't. And we arranged ourselves like this, until everyone had a little shelter." CAJIT was up the hill and hidden from the main road, so agencies failed to notice it until April 2010, three months after the earthquake. Despite—or because—of not receiving formal aid, Linda, the committee president, described a range of activities organized by the committee: a clinic, a child care center, and an overnight security brigade.

For security, they volunteer to help. People at night, they walk around, they look around to make sure that there isn't trouble, anyone coming to do anything here. There are babies here. We don't want any trouble at all. They are all volunteers; they don't get anything for doing that. Sometimes if you don't call them they can't even wake up to do half a night because they have their own needs and have no money. They would need us to cook a little food for them in advance. So this one brings some bread, another some fish paste, this one brings oil and we make soup, we make a little something savory. They eat.

All CAJIT's activities were organized by *kotizasyon*—voluntary donations with individuals passing the hat and each contributing what they could—to pay for a meal for the men who volunteered to stay up all night, to buy medicines, or to pay for materials that could be fashioned into children's toys by a volunteer teacher in a makeshift school. CAJIT became "on the grid" in April 2010 as a result of advocacy from the committee. Linda said, "If there's a child with a fever, if we have 5 gourdes, 10 gourdes I buy, we buy a pill for them." In Nelson's retelling of the history of this committee, also called CAJIT (Support Committee for of the Youth of Impasse Thomas, the neighborhood), "We organized ourselves in a committee so we could make requests in the name of the population living in this space that you see here."

During this second phase, the six people who created the committee saw the necessity to formalize because of the lack of aid. They saw that others were getting aid and they weren't. Eventually CAJIT succeeded in securing tarps for the population, but they felt they had to become a committee in order to do so. This sentiment is shared by their fellow residents of Carrefour, those staying outside of City Hall in Meri Dikini. Said Macdonald, one of the Meri Dikini committee members, "We saw that everywhere people were creating committees so they could survive with a bunch of organizations. We too were obliged to create a committee so we could ask for help." At this "focus group" another participant was even more direct: "Because when we saw there were things being given in other places, we could never receive anything. On top of that, ADRA was distributing rice. They asked us to have a committee. That's how we set up the committee."

The term "focus group" is in quotes because *fokis gwoup*—the Haitian term adopted—was used very often by NGOs, often without following any protocol to assure representativeness. One of the most important steps in organizing a focus group is in selecting participants, to assure a variety of perspectives, and that these perspectives mirror the general population in relevant ways. After the earthquake many researchers, under contract from NGOs, let the camp committees themselves select participants. The term was used so often—even before the earthquake—that people expected to be paid to participate. We used the term "group interview" or "a little talk," partly because we knew we couldn't meet the conditions required of the formal methodology, and also because we wanted to minimize expectations and thus competition over who got chosen to participate, and therefore hurt feelings. Although the committee selected itself for their interview, the researcher who had conducted five weeks of fieldwork and conducted a hundred survey interviews and ten recorded interviews selected the group of individuals for the "little talk" for residents. About a half an hour into the interview, a man who turned out to be a member of the committee showed up. Immediately the conversation changed course; people who had criticized the committee immediately silenced themselves. One young man, who was brought to the back of the room by this committee member, later publicly "corrected" his statement about the committee:

> Honestly, the other reason why we set up that committee was because we wanted security in the camp. We wanted to have a watchful eye on the children, on the pregnant women as well, so that the committee can plan for those people and care for them. Committee members are in charge of sanitation in the camp. We have nothing to reproach them. That's the context in which we set up the committee.

Even if the language wasn't flattering, using the word *we* when discussing the committee's creation would still cause one to pause: this was supposed to have been a meeting of ordinary residents, noncommittee members. I'm not clear just how my presence as a *blan*, visibly a foreigner with more resources and privilege, affected this conversation: Did people take me to be an NGO worker? A journalist? A foreign government representative? This conversation took place after five weeks of research, and the researcher had chosen people whom he knew were comfortable being interviewed. I took this opportunity to introduce myself and begin the process of deciding about the "participant gifts" to be given. In effect, I *was* an NGO at that meeting.

Another individual at this meeting said, "What was the process like? All the big notables, the elders in the camp, had a meeting. We would say that everybody was there, they chose and decided." Putting aside the question of just who the "everyone" meant: the "big notables," the oldest, or literally every single resident (or household), this statement is telling, that this camp committee was selected on the basis of being a big notable. Someone during the committee interview confirmed this: "We chose qualified people, 'quality' people to be part of the committee, people who know what they are doing. Because you can't give someone a post that they can't fulfill. We chose qualified people who could make decisions, who could write something in order to find a solution. That how we proceeded." Although the logic of choosing (or self-selecting, or ratifying) people who were literate[5] to represent a camp makes sense from an effectiveness point of view, certainly choosing a person who could "make decisions" because of his or her qualifications, this nonetheless justifies exclusion of the poor majority from participation. Another committee member, who was not among the original committee, shared a concern about this decision to select the most qualified. "The people most in charge of the committee, such as the president, they left the camp to move back home. And also, because of their activities they couldn't stick around. We came to see this as a disadvantage for the camp because when we need them, we can't find them." Another member of the committee admitted, "When they call, sometimes I am not here. Others who have moved out and left the camp for good, they left the committee and had a friend replace them so that the committee could still continue to function." Even if there was a community vote to ratify the original committee nomination process, once constituted it perpetuated itself, with people naming their friends.

The formation of this committee at Meri Dikini thus reveals various social forces: a foreign impetus, both indirect and direct, and an ambiguous set of local processes that privileged educated middle-class individuals. Other committees detailed the role played by foreign agencies.

Foreign Trigger

The process at Hancho was revealing. Rose-Anne, not a member of the committee, shared what she knew: "Well, the camp committee, how it got here, it was when someone came here, a lady, she told us if we want to benefit something here there must be a committee here." Jesula, the camp president, confirmed this story during their "little talk" with the researcher and myself:

> The camp committee . . . it's when the Spanish Red Cross . . . By ourselves, we weren't a committee. We came here because of January 12. For me, we saw we can't get anything, we saw other people . . . the French Red Cross, Spanish Red Cross, MINUSTAH, Americans . . . All of them stopped by to visit us, but they didn't recognize us. We were under bed sheets, it's almost like we were on an island. I went and looked for someone who speaks Spanish. I made a poster and put it up outside, on the street. Not two days later, the Spanish Red Cross came here and asked for the committee. We told them that there was no committee. The lady said that we should have a committee and it should be headed by a woman, so that's why I became the leader. Yes the Spanish woman. She was with the others. Now she told us to form a committee of seven people, and that she would come back the next day to pick up the paper. So we created a committee with seven people, and we gave her the paper. That's the way it was formed.

Similar to CAJIT and Meri Dikini, residents at Hancho felt that they needed to have a committee in order to have aid. So they did the best they could to speak the language of aid: in this case Spanish. For more than a year and a half following the earthquake, all over Haiti hand-painted signs in English hailed foreigners. In Hancho's case, this worked, and it might have influenced which agency was to come by. One of Jesula's colleagues verified the dates: the Spanish sign was painted on Thursday, January 14, and the Red Cross came by on January 16. Hancho is not as public or as visible as Champs-de-Mars, the national plaza, but it is closer to the city center than either camp in Carrefour. Many people discussed the importance of aid agencies "seeing" them. Camps that were far away from the city center or away from main roads like CAJIT were less likely to have services. Ti Georges, a camp committee leader from Pivoine, in the hardest-hit area of Fort-National, said, "Maybe it's because we're hidden away inside that the NGOs have forgotten us, but we're the most affected area! This area, Fort-National and Pivoine, doesn't have a big road so the NGO trucks just don't see us. Maybe they just don't see us." This theory is confirmed by some evidence: in the 2010 survey, camps from municipalities farthest from the city center (Croix-des-Bouquets and Carrefour) were less likely to have services such as water, toilets, and health clinics. Proximity to the city center was among the most statistically significant independent variables shaping the outcome (Schuller and Levey 2014).

Not surprisingly, the most statistically significant variable was the presence of an NGO camp management agency (CMA). Camp residents like Jesula or Manolia had no way of knowing that this would be the case overall. But they clearly understood what they had to do in order to receive aid. And they did what they were told: they produced precisely seven people as requested. And Jesula became the president because the foreign agency wanted to see a woman in that position. This follows a Women in Development (WID) logic, that to employees like Alex following "gender mainstreaming" predicts better outcomes. However, the previous chapter also demonstrated that good policies by well-intentioned actors can lead to harmful outcomes in the implementation. Because of foreign intervention, Jesula was anointed the position of being a broker for the population (Lewis and Mosse 2006; Merry 2006; Richard 2009). The Spanish NGO workers were her *blan*, her foreigners. In Jesula's matter-of-fact retelling, it was only natural she became the president because she was the one who spoke with the woman from the Spanish Red Cross. She also had the power to name who was in the committee: "I selected them. But some people I selected dropped out." By August 2011, during the group interview, Jesula was unable to answer any question that required more than passing knowledge of the situation. Perhaps like the Meri Dikini committee members, Jesula was too busy to be involved. She admitted this during the group interview. As one of the people selected for the "little talk" from the population said, "The former committee, its members found a job, and they went to work. As a result, they didn't have time to fulfill their responsibilities here." Despite this perception, Jesula kept her post as president well after the aid dried up. Jesula was understood by several other committee members, and the population, as a figurehead, a token—although not to her face. A de facto leader was hailed *dirijan* (leader), *prezidan* (president), or *chèf* (chief) whenever we walked the neighborhood together.

NGO Creations

The Spanish Red Cross could claim ignorance of the process by which the Hancho camp committee was formed, as did the representative who visited the camp in his short interview. This individual, a Haitian who didn't speak Spanish, who continually looked over his shoulder during the interview, did not work for the Red Cross in January 2010. Like all other front-line staff I interviewed, he had a month-to-month contract. However, in other camps NGOs not only forced the formation of the committee as a condition of the receipt of aid, they actively chose who was to be on it. Such was the case in Plas Lapè. The Salvation Army had been headquartered in the neighborhood, right next to the plaza, since 1950, and they had relationships with another faith-based organization, Food for the Poor, one of the only NGOs working in Port-au-Prince that had experience with food distribution. So it seemed fitting that they would manage the food distribution. The Salvation Army played a role of camp manager until October 5, 2010. When the Salvation Army was the CMA, the camp committee met at their headquarters every Tuesday. Roldy, the camp manager, chose the people who would serve on the committee: "The committee members are those who . . . they come from, they represent different organizations in the area.[6] And from those members of each organization we [came] up with the committee." An organization in the neighborhood founded the day before the first democratic elections in December 1990 called Men Nan Men (Hand in Hand) had more than two thousand members, a democratic structure, and monthly meetings, according to its president Liza. Men Nan Men was not included in the Plas Lapè committee. To be more specific, Roldy did not select Liza. Roldy explained that "in many cases, they set up the organizations just to do development." Roldy did not say what else besides development he felt local organizations ought to be doing, but Liza theorized the reason she wasn't chosen for the committee was that she wasn't a member of the congregation. Liza critiqued the official camp committee for not living in the camp, like she and many others did. To this point, Roldy said that "most of the committee members also live in the area, but they are not far from this area. Small organizations around the area [make up] the committee." Not only did they not in the camp, Roldy admitted that some camp committee members did not even live in the neighborhood.

Thus, from its inception, the Plas Lapè camp committee lacked an organic relationship with the population. As Liza describes, the committee thus also lacked legitimacy that it would have had like Men Nan Men, who had been present for almost twenty years at that point. This was only made more apparent as time wore on. As Roldy alluded to, the Salvation Army retreated from responsibility for Plas Lapè, creating a void and competition to fill it. Like many others, the other NGOs who had inherited the responsibility for the camp mistook "local" for "grassroots," conflating a geographic area served with a democratic or participatory structure. The committee is best described as "Astroturf," artificial. This is in direct contrast with Kolonbi, as Magalie shared: "They wanted to choose community leaders, people who've been in the area for a long time. I've been here since . . . I grew up in this neighborhood. When they organized meetings, I used to go and participate in their trainings when they spoke. One day, they had an election, and I was elected committee spokesperson."

Tale of Two Committees

Plas Lapè was not the only camp where the NGO chose the committee and its members. The person who brokered the relocation of six thousand people from the St. Louis camp to Karade was Max, an alumnus of St. Louis de Gonzague school, the chair of its alumni association, and who lived nearby. His son also went to St. Louis. Max recalled:

I told the priest that classes must resume. The priest said [Max laughs], "Look at the situation. You can't do that." He said, "You're out of your mind! We're just trying to survive! You can't talk to me about classes resuming." I told him that life should go on. He replied: "You don't see the huge amount of people who are in the yard?" I said that somebody should talk to them, to have them move.

The priest told me, "Well, as you are Haitian yourself, go talk to them." And a friend and I went to talk to them. When I reached the yard I met my mother's cook. She took refuge in the camp. I asked that cook to introduce me to around thirty women so they understood the issue. So . . . the St. Louis thing started via a woman I met in the yard and whom I knew before, because she worked at my mother's house. She introduced me to some other women.

They talked about their problems and we ourselves were figuring out what kind of services to provide to the population. This is what we did . . . we imagined [ways] to help them go back to work. I opened a daycare where we welcomed the children during the day, and this is what allowed us to have good relations with them. We had 150 kids. Thanks to this service we provided to the children, they listened to us when we told them to do something.

So finally we had some of them move.

And we ourselves organized a committee. We proposed the interior minister be part of that committee. So, we have a third party member: we had the government with us, we had NGOs with us.

Max's primary motivation was to move people off the grounds so his son could continue at school. The way Max tells it, he thought of the people staying there as obstacles until running into "that cook." In chapter 2, Nadege shared her perspective of the kindness of someone like Mr. Louis. This personal, human connection allowed Max to see things differently, to see IDPs as people. Although he explained to them the necessity of moving out, they told him their needs and he was able to develop services they needed. And at least the way he remembered it, providing this necessary service (and likely also the relationship with his mother's cook, which he did not explicitly mention) facilitated their ability to move people out. In order to achieve his end of reopening the school, he offered humanitarian assistance. Max employed humanitarian means for other ends, a case of instrumentalization by a small, local organization that was initially no more than an alumni association.

Whatever his motive, this level of cooperation across sociocultural divisions that extended well after the initial survival phase was noteworthy. And this generosity continued as Max had offered his *lakou⁷* to the camp committee for meetings. Although often ignored in disaster response and not even highlighted in the disaster literature, human relationships are central to desired outcomes: in this case, the relationship between Max and his mother's cook cemented the foundation. Max's relations with the school and their connections as alumni were able to secure resources, an example of social capital at work (Bourdieu 1998; Putnam 1995, 2001). The relationship between Max and his mother's cook provided the way forward.

Social capital is often conceived as a "thing" possessed by people that can be leveraged to obtain other desired outcomes, much in the same way as any other form of capital. One problem with social capital as an explanation is that societies are unequal, and relationships between different types of people in a diverse society have different characteristics (Arneil 2006). In this case, the cement of the settlement, the opportunity for dialogue, resulted from random chance. Although the cook might have counted her relationship with Max as part of her social capital, Max certainly wouldn't, at least before the earthquake. This bond across deep social divisions allowed for other options than pressure. Having an open dialogue between the school administration and people who sought shelter on the grounds influenced the relationships both "below" (between camp residents) and "above" (Max, Catholic Relief Services, and the school administration). This dynamic interrelationship, acknowledging how these relationships can influence others, can be called "civic infrastructure" (Schuller 2006).

Max's balanced reciprocity (Sahlins 1972), his instrumentalized generosity, was not the foregone conclusion in other camps, or even in St. Louis. More than a quarter-million people were forcibly evicted from the camps in the first year. By the week after Easter, the first week of April 2010, 11,867 people were living on the St. Louis grounds, thirteen *kawo* (*carreaux*, colonial French measurement, 41.47 acres). Given this, Hélène, a founding member of KAS (the St. Louis Action Committee), pointed out that "there's space for school and there's space for us to live without us ever coming in contact with them." In March, the priest invited Mayor Wilson Jeudy to force people out. According to Hélène, "He gave a deadline of Wednesday [March 24] to leave. If we didn't leave blood would be spilled. *But the voice of the people is the voice of God.*"[8] As briefly noted in chapter 2, Mayor Jeudy was increasingly repressive in forcing people out of the camps. The people resisted, particularly members of KAS. The mayor backed down. Hélène argued that "the priest failed to speak with the committee." Although the people weren't removed, all aid to the camp stopped, according to Hélène: "While the mayor and police didn't return, the priest didn't authorize even a single [6 ounce] water sack to enter the space." The first time I visited, the last week of March 2010, we saw a medical team sheepishly waiting outside for authorization to enter. They were never allowed in. Hélène also reported that the school administration paid to destroy a latrine that was installed by French NGO Médecins sans Frontières. Hélène recalled, "Luckily, no one was in it when it was destroyed." Tensions were high, to say the least. One committee member invoked a slogan attributed to Dessalines, Haiti's liberator: *koupe tèt, boule kay* (Cut off people's heads and burn the houses). These tensions only increased before April 5, the date selected by the Haitian government by which schools had to reopen or lose the school year entirely. The day before our March 31 visit, a representative of the Haitian government visited the camp, accompanied by police, who met with several committees. There were six committees at the time. According to Hélène, "He said that the government told him that we need to create a central committee to arrange ourselves so when we all are forced out that we do so in an orderly fashion." This was the impetus for what was to become the Central Committee noted earlier.

Unbeknownst to me or most St. Louis residents at the time, Max was busy negotiating an alternative to St. Louis. About half of the population, six thousand people, were part of a settlement to move up to Karade. Karade was on land of another St. Louis alumnus, the wealthy lottery owner Toto. Despite the land being declared a public utility by the Haitian government, CRS still negotiated with Toto. CRS agreed to manage the camp, naming Max as the manager, promising the people displaced from St. Louis that they would have temporary shelters, or T-shelters, a clinic, a school, water, security, child care, and electricity. The meetings the last week of March were tense in part because these services were not yet available. As a member of KAS said, "We in KAS work in social [affairs, meaning working with and for 'the people']. We won't leave here to go somewhere else without the necessary conditions. Before anything, we need to visit. They also didn't make the promises to us, no. We won't accept promises. We need to see the school already there." Eventually, with the help of Max playing intermediary, Hélène and the other five committees, including KAS, did accept their promises. This experience cemented Max's reputation as a leader, and CRS offered him the contract as the camp manager. CRS had taken an interest in the camp in part because it was a Catholic school.[9] This ability to broker relationships across deep sociocultural divisions was key to his abilities, but it also meant that he wielded influence on the committees of both camps. "Relationships are the key to everything," he explained. "You have to work with people you can trust." As it turned out, another of Max's relationships had a great impact. Max sat in the bench next to President Michel Martelly while they were both students at St. Louis. Although CRS let go of him to prevent perceptions of favoritism during an election, Max got a high-level job in the new administration, which he helped leverage for Esaie and the committee.

The effort of Max, Hélène, and others created two realities. Because of the tensions with the activist-oriented groups, certainly KAS, Max hand-picked the next committee president, Esaie, an associate, for the half of the people who remained on the perimeter of the St. Louis grounds. The camp, on four of the thirteen *kawo*, was cut in two: half on one side facing Delmas 31 and half on the other, Delmas 33. The main entrance to the school from both sides was cleared. Up the hill at Karade, the "St. Louis displaced" sector was a formal planned relocation site. Although it took several months for the T-shelters and the committee offices to be built, the UN troops set up a base there. Matching maroon Coleman tents were set up in rows, each marked with a number that was to be their location for the T-shelters. A large white UNICEF tent was pitched in front, which was supposed to serve as a clinic. When I visited in July 2010 it sat empty. Said Hélène, "UNICEF knows that the tent is here but they have never negotiated with us to tell us if this will be a center or a mobile clinic."

Despite the slow start that wore on people's patience, late that fall T-shelters were erected around a road cut through the middle of the land. Solar panel lights were installed on the street corners. At the front entrance on the left side was a small brick structure housing the Central Committee. Behind that was a row of T-shelters for each of the constituent committees. At the end of the row, following the last of the five committee offices, surrounded by a chain-link fence, was the UN base. Behind the military base stood the school, clinic, "psychosocial" center, and a community pavilion used to screen movies or hold trainings (and ostensibly community meetings). Although it was still dusty, relatively isolated, and residents had to struggle to make ends meet, many of them, particularly on the main road, set up *boutik*—home-based stores—from their T-shelters, and their basic needs of shelter and electricity were met. From the vantage point of other camps, the St. Louis Displaced sector was far better off.

One problem with this set-up for the people moved from the St. Louis camp is that people had already been living in that space. The Karade site also included other camps, where many people who were attempting to make their way since the earthquake already lived. The benefits that accrued to the St. Louis Displaced did not reach the surrounding sectors. The first thing, shown in Figure 5.1, that was built by the NGOs was a fence separating the St. Louis Displaced from everyone else. This was a powerful visual symbol, a border between "have littles" (not quite "haves") and "have nots." Coincidentally, this area was also on a hill, reinforcing the distinction and hierarchy. The Central Committee felt so entitled that they reappropriated lamps originally destined for other sectors of the camp. Differences were stark, as the "chosen" (a play on Calvinist ideology) peered down at many other residents from their lit "city on a hill." These differences became only more pronounced as the patterns of uneven aid continued. Some of the resentment of the Central Committee might have to do with this exclusion.

The history of the Karade and St. Louis committees is indeed rich and complex. Their destinies are tied, woven together by tensions, struggle, and negotiation, as well as a few key individuals like Max, who were central to the process, and the relationships they formed. Max succeeded in reopening the school in time for his son to finish the academic year. In this process two powerful committees were created, and they brokered material benefits for T-shelters and some basic needs for people who went to Karade, and a peaceful coexistence and promises of a later relocation to a "village" (designating not only being outside the crowded city center but also a planned city, unlike the *cité*, which denoted shantytowns) with prospects of home-ownership and jobs, for those who remained at St. Louis, provided they were loyal, organized, calm, and patient, and "didn't bother the school."

Although demonstrating the unique genealogy and impetus of the eight committees, this history highlights the importance of aid and aid agencies in all cases. At one end of the spectrum is CAJIT, organizing residents to engage in self-help, formalizing in order to make requests of aid agencies. At the other are Karade, St. Louis, and Plas Lapè, that were in varying degrees hand-selected by the NGO managing the camp. This structure was nearly universal. By the summer of 2010, the Displaced Tracking Matrix, IOM's official database, reported that more than 95 percent of camps listed a committee. Did the specific origins of the committees shape their operation? How did the committees function? What was their role? How did the residents, in whose name the committees existed, view their work? To answer these questions the second section of the chapter offers residents' perspectives.

FIGURE 5.1. Fence erected between camps with T-shelters and camps without, June 2011. Photo: author

RESIDENTS' PERCEPTION OF COMMITTEES

Before the earthquake, neighborhood associations often led collective, volunteer public works efforts such as road repair or trash collection, managed community water taps, or organized *ti sourit*, night-time block parties. Aside from these activities, however, neighborhood associations remained relatively invisible. By direct contrast, committees played a central role in camps, having great impact on the lives of IDPs. With the committees so visible, camp residents have quite a lot to say about them. By far, the subject of committees dominated the qualitative interviews. This section of the chapter discusses the population's perceptions of committees' roles, effectiveness, communication, abuses of power, and how committees became highly personalized.

From Defenders to Liaisons: Committees' Roles

The committees played a wide range of roles. Also, there is a diversity of perspectives within in addition to between the eight camps. Within this diversity, however, the majority of people were critical of the committees operating in their camp, and this had to do with their failure to fulfill the roles expected of them. In the case of St. Louis, the primary role was to defend IDPs' rights to emergency shelter and services, loosely defined in the UN "Guiding Principles on Internal Displacement,"[10] as Marjorie explained:

> They wanted to chase everyone out just like that. This committee was not formed yet. It did not exist yet. There was a committee called KAS. After so many negotiations, they said they could not chase people out just like that anymore. Like they took a small group and moved with them to an area called Karade. Now those people who went to Karade . . . I believe they have already built shelters for them. But if it hadn't been for the committee, besides God's help, the priest would have chased us out of here with nothing, and to say it right, with humiliation.

Marjorie's testimony is an important reminder of the context of their work: at any moment the landowner could decide to reclaim his or her land and kick out all the camp residents. In the case of the St. Louis de Gonzague school grounds, there was a clear "public good" justification for reopening the school, and there was no question about the ownership of the land: it was leased by the Catholic Church and administered by the school. In dozens of other cases across Port-au-Prince this was not the case. As attorney Patrice Florvilus (2012) outlined, to forcibly evict someone from their land requires a legal injunction. The first step in the process is to establish legal title to the land, which many people claiming to be landowners can't produce. Given this reality, one of the most important roles of a camp committee is to defend camp residents against this threat.

In addition to this, the primary day-to-day role of a committee was defined by Robenson, also from St. Louis: "The committee is just a liaison between *the people outside and the population in the camp.*" Robenson continued the code switching into French, displaying his status as a university student. Implied in the position of liaison is being an effective conduit for communication, in sharing information, the lifeblood of democracy or participation, which Robenson detailed: "Currently the committee's role is to be the liaison between the Haitian Red Cross and the camp population, to inform them of Red Cross prospects or objectives for the population, and if they agree they let us know and we . . . and the committee will report what the population thinks." Whether Robenson came to this understanding from observing—or participating—in the committee or whether this was the ideal for representative democracy learned in his university education, it nonetheless represents an ideal type for how a committee *should* function in an ideal world, recalling a central debate within political science about representation: Are officials trustees, empowered to vote their conscience, or delegates, voting what their constituents want? Worth noting within this short description is the hierarchical nature of this mediation: an

NGO proposes a series of actions, and the committee has the ability to agree or not. The population has the ability to express what "it" thinks. The word is in the singular, suggesting a belief that the population has one perspective and should have one voice. This leads to problems of representation, wherein one person can be imagined as speaking for the entire group. Even in this idealized relationship, the population is imagined as being only able to react, while the committee can choose to communicate or not. The NGO is the entity that comes up with the proposals in the first place. I use the phrase "ideal type" because many individuals living in the camps do not believe that the committees are meeting this ideal.

Either following the logic of voluntary *kotizasyon* that predated the camps and the committees or mimicking the IOM's official IDP card, or both, some committees like that of Kolonbi had membership dues, as Jorel described: "That means the committee members can go to an institution and defend us using it, but you have to pay thirty dollars ['Haitian' dollars, 150 gourdes, about $3.50] to get it. Yes, we pay thirty dollars to get it. I haven't gotten mine yet because of the fee." According to Jean-Jacques, the committee president, this was the practice before the earthquake of the neighborhood association, which became the camp committee. The committee printed out ID cards for their members, a commonplace practice in Haiti. However, in the context of the IDP camps, where having a committee was obligatory in order to receive aid, being nominally a member of the committee and carrying a card could bring about significant material benefits. This brings up the issue of aid; because committees were created to facilitate the flow of aid, residents held them responsible for aid materializing.

"It Does Not Have Shoes": Actions/Activities

Speaking of the Hancho committee, Rose-Anne was frustrated at the lack of progress or material resources coming to the camp. She said, "Because it's a committee who sits in place. It does not have shoes, it does not move around." Although during the first few days after the earthquake it might have been possible for camps like theirs to post a sign and successfully net an NGO, as time wore on, receiving aid was more difficult. This was certainly true by the time of the July 2011 interview. The first major relocations were being initiated, and the government was increasingly trying to close the camps because they detracted from the impression that "Haiti is open for business." So those still living in camps, like Rose-Anne, expected the committees to go out and look for aid, literally "walk around." Sophonie had this same reproach for the Meri Dikini committee: "You know that God says ask and you'll find, knock and he will open for you. But they [the committee members] don't take their responsibilities seriously." Not surprisingly in a society that has been the target of missionary activities, and certainly after the earthquake (McAlister 2013), many people invoke the Almighty or cite sayings that they attribute to the Bible. For example, "God helps those who help themselves," which is not in the Bible, is a powerful statement of Protestant (more precisely, Calvinist) ideology (Weber 1985), quoted in Ben Franklin's *Poor Richard's Almanac.*

Rose-Anne and Sophonie were critical of what they saw as a tendency of camp committees toward greater dependency. In the 2010 study of 108 camps, more than 70 percent of committees reported not doing anything because of a lack of external aid. Manno reported that this was the case in Nan Bannann: "I remember that CRS placed some latrines, they were paying for them but they removed them. And the committee didn't do anything after that." Speaking to Manno's first point, Claudine, from St. Louis, concluded that "the committee itself depends on the Red Cross. They can't do anything for us." Most people living in the camps were critical of the committee's lack of effectiveness, passivity, and dependence.

By contrast, Jean-Claude described a much more active role in Kolonbi, using the same metaphor of walking around that Rose-Anne did:

> They walk around high and low for aid. I have to tell you that what little they found, they always distributed it. They don't issue the [ration] cards, they just receive a limited number of cards from organizations for a specific day mentioning the kind of items they are going to receive. They always distributed the cards. When there aren't enough cards for everybody to go around, they decide to give some and tell the other ones they weren't successful and go from tent to tent to distribute them.

Jean-Claude spoke favorably about the committee's role in distributing the cards, which was their primary source of power and too often abused, as the previous chapter demonstrated. Charlène noted a similarly active approach from CAJIT, specifically its president: "Linda always goes and looks for us, to find aid. After that she found tarps for us, she got buckets because everything we had was broken. The house was destroyed and our sheets were torn up. She found linen for us, and we gave them for the children to sleep on. But now she is gone." Instead of CRS giving the latrines that Manno spoke of, Charlène favorably described Linda's proactively going to look for aid. In Manno's telling (and several others in Nan Bannann), CRS was the agent; in Charlène's and others in CAJIT, the camp committee, more specifically Linda, was.

Despite being a minority of cases, there were other camps as proactive as CAJIT. L'Étoile Brillante, discussed in the previous chapter, distinguished itself by its active approach, involving searching, according to its president Elisabeth: "We went to an agency that works to save children, and asked for funds for education, child protection, etc. We went through the whole process but they never supported us. So we created our own space." One significant difference is that Elisabeth was a community leader before the earthquake, a member of REFRAKA, a network of women journalists. Possibly because of her skills and contacts as a journalist, she connected with a smaller, human-rights-oriented NGO to support their efforts. Also significantly, the camp was outside of Port-au-Prince, in a *bitasyon* (rural neighborhood) outside of Léogâne, closer to the quake's epicenter and where an estimated 90 percent of buildings collapsed. Gender might have also played a role. L'Étoile Brillante was a women's organization; the CAJIT committee was led by a woman and consisted mostly of women. Both sprang up organically, unlike Hancho, where Jesula was anointed leader (and surrounded herself with men). I tried to have gender, expressed in committees wherein a majority of members were women, as an independent variable in my purposive sample of the eight camps, but there were too few camps in the 108-camp sample for which this was true.

Continuing his criticism, Manno decried that "in 40 [Delmas 40, the Pétion-Ville Club] people have latrines, in Acra and Champs-de-Mars people have them as well. Why can't we have them in Nan Bannann?" Basing his critique on what he understood other camps to have, Manno mentions two nearby: Acra and the Pétion-Ville Club, one of Haiti's largest camps, managed by Jenkins-Penn Haitian Relief Organization (J-PHRO), the NGO Sean Penn cofounded. Manno might have visited either of these camps, or he might have heard about it through *radyo trannde*, radio of thirty-two (teeth, the rumor mill). Manno defined the procurement of aid as the primary point of the committees: "That's why I said there is a committee but it's like there was none." Manno's critique brings the issue of communication to the fore.

Communication

Central to the committees' role of either providing aid or acting as a liaison is communication. Here too camp residents find much lacking. Fritz, from Plas Lapè, who had detailed a series of critiques, paused, asking the interviewer, "What is a committee, my brother? Answer my question so I can answer yours, what is a committee?" Manno's last statement also calls into question the definition of committees, a symptom of poor communication. Ti Wobè, from Nan Bannann, explained quite simply, "I can't give you any information about the camp committee, because while I'm in the camp, they didn't integrate me" in the committee. Although Ti Wobè's analysis places the onus on the committee, the lack of awareness could also be a symptom of a lack of interest. For his part, Franck stayed out of the Kolonbi committee affairs: "There are a whole series of things I don't try and find out because I live neither from organizations nor from aid. Either they are good or bad. I don't know." Franck held a steady job, which is certainly not the case for the majority of camp residents.

How generalized is this lack of involvement? Among the fifty-six questions in the 2011 household survey conducted were seven assessing residents' levels of awareness about the committee. We asked:

Is there a committee in this camp?
What is this committee called?
Who is the leader of the committee in this camp?
What activities or strategies does this committee do?
When does the committee meet?
How did they choose people to join the group?
Do you have the right to participate in the committee meetings?[11]

Just over three-quarters, 75.1 percent, of people agreed there was a committee. Just over an eighth (12.6 percent) said no, like Manno. Like Fritz, or Ti Wobè, 9.7 percent of people said they don't know. Some said that there used to be one, some said not really. A minority of people said they could participate: 36.7 percent said yes, 34.7 said no, and 28.3 percent said they didn't know. The responses, shown in Table 5.1, varied across the camps.

Much of this information can be read as communication: more residents were more aware of the St. Louis committee, affirming that it exists, knowing its strategy, and certainly knowing the leader (although there were two names,

TABLE 5.1   Population's Awareness of the Camp Committee

Camp	Exist?	Name?	Leader?	Strategy?	Meeting?	Participate?
CAJIT	66 (73%)	34 (52%)	59 (89%)	39 (44%)	36 (55%)	57 (86%)
Hancho	88%	1 (1.1%)	69 (78%)	4 (4.5%)	15 (17%)	41 (47%)
Karade	74%	42 (57%)	34 (46%)	0	12 (16%)	22 (30%)
			6 names			
Kolonbi	85%	7 (8.2%)	59 (69%)	51 (60%)	56 (66%)	59 (69%)
		12 (14%)				
Lameri Dikini	80%	7 (8.8%)	69 (86%)	22 (28%)	12 (15%)	17 (21%)
Nan Bannann	45%	0	23 (52%)	19 (42%)	2 (4.4%)	5 (11%)
	No longer	*1 (2.2%)*				
Plas Lapè	72%	2 (2.8%)	18 (25%)	26 (36%)	1 (1.4%)	9 (13%)
		9 (12.5%)	*11 names*			
Senlwi	96%	43 (44%)	92 (94%)	83 (86%)	30 (31%)	53 (56%)
	(98%)	*49 (50%)*	*2 names*			

not just Esaie, in the responses). Most people at CAJIT felt they had the right to participate, and they were second most likely to know about meeting times, the name of the committee, and the leader. Residents at Kolonbi were more aware than others of meeting times. Interestingly, far more people could identify the leader (74.2 percent overall) than the name of the committee itself (22.2 percent), suggesting a personality-based leadership. The table indicates two sets of numbers in some camps; this is because residents named different committees.

Nearly two-thirds of people (66.1 percent) said they didn't know how the committee was chosen. Of the minority who answered this question, this also varied across the camps, as Table 5.2 demonstrates. More residents of CAJIT reported that the committee was either elected or chosen at a meeting. This is in contrast to Hancho, the camp with the highest number of people identifying the camp as self-selected. Almost as many people at St. Louis identified that the committee was self-named as at a meeting. Everyone at Nan Bannann was ill informed about the committee, like Ti Wobè and Manno: not a one could identify how it was selected.

Despite Robenson's characterization of the St. Louis committee's role as liaison, Claudine saw things differently: "When the [NGO] comes here, when they have meetings, they just meet with the committee. The population doesn't take part in the meeting. That means we never know what's happening. For someone to know what's going on, she has to bootlick that man writing down names on the [NGO] program. If you don't kiss ass, you won't get anything that's good." The difference in perspective might be explained in part by Robenson's and Claudine's different *kouch sosyal*, their socioeconomic status. It could also be gender. Recall from the previous chapter that Esaie attempted to do much more than require genuflection.

The differences could also be circumstantial, or random. Lending support to this explanation during their group interview, a Hancho resident said that the committee was *yon dan yon pye*, which can be translated as "off and on" (literally,

TABLE 5.2   How Camp Committees Were Chosen, According to Residents

Camp	Election	Meeting	Self-Named	NGO	Landowner
CAJIT	17	39	1	0	0
Hancho	20	1	37	2	0
Karade	4	2	8	2	4
Kolonbi	2	4	15	0	0
Lameri Dikini	2	4	2	2	0
Nan Bannann	0	0	0	0	0
Plas Lapè	1	4	2	2	2
St. Louis	5	30	26	3	2

a tooth and a foot). When asked what this meant, she explained, "'Off and on' means if they want to work with you they do but if they don't want to, they won't. If they want to involve you in their conversations, in their activities, they call you if they want to. But if they don't want to, they don't." Sharing information is sharing power; as intermediaries this is one of the only sources of power over the population. This is an example of "trickle-down imperialism" (Schuller 2012c), how power operates in a hierarchical, bureaucratic system. Mediating contact between different groups adds to one's own personal power. It can also explain why well-intentioned policies can lead to problematic implementation.

Moun Pa: Personal Relationships

Table 5.1 shows that people were more than three times more likely to recall the name of the person in charge than the committee. This strongly suggests that camp committees were a cult of personality for many. In the case of CAJIT, residents spoke fondly of Linda, its president. In others, the reaction was far more mixed. Claudine from St. Louis professed ignorance about the committee: "Well, I don't know anything about the committee. I just see them. They are not my friends. And who is the committee? I only see that man as the committee. His name is Esaie. After him, I don't see any other committee. I heard that the committee has many people but he's the only one, he's always in charge of everything." Claudine does not here critique Esaie's use of personal power; she simply identifies the power structure as she and many others see it.

More than simply supporting CAJIT's Linda, Jhon actively defended her against others, whom he saw as corrupting influences on the committee:

> Linda had so many problems with committee members. Many committee members were different; they only looked out for themselves. When an organization gave something, they saw that their position could benefit them: they can do business with the aid, sell it. She herself insisted that everyone receives something when an organization comes with some aid for the camp.
>
> Now she's trying to weed out some of them. She later brought in some people whom she could see have good intentions. That's why now we're working together, and we're doing our best so the population may at least receive a little something. When there's a distribution, nobody tries to stash some items to sell later or for other purposes. Everything is distributed.

Linda played an active role in the beginning, and the good functioning and good will of the committee is attributed to her leadership. Unfortunately for her and this harmony, she fell seriously ill in the spring of 2011, before these interviews. Because of the poor state of health care in the country, and because she had a

U.S. passport, she left to New York to stay with extended family while she sought medical care. She returned periodically to the neighborhood until the summer of 2013, when she felt well enough to return to Haiti. Physically drained and weakened, she felt that she could no longer climb the hill to her house in the neighborhood, so she and her husband moved to her aunt's house in another part of Port-au-Prince. In the interim, other committees filled the void left by her absence and established contact with NGOs looking to construct shelters. The well-respected CAJIT was edged out by these newer committees.

The continuing story of CAJIT highlights the fragility of personalized leadership, a phenomenon noted by many other scholars of NGOs and social movements (for exmple, Davis 2003; Edelman 2005; Hilhorst 2003; Nagar and Raju 2003; Tarrow 2011). There are other dangers of charismatic leadership, particularly when the receipt of aid depends on personal relationships. Using the personal power of committees, some distributed aid to *moun pa*, to "their people" (friends or family). This tendency is stronger when the committee is more powerful or centralized in the hands of a strong leader, tendencies that often went hand in hand, as Magalie noted: "I need to tell you that I was part of the committee. I already told you that. But I stopped working with them because they want to favor their families." Kolonbi's committee had its defenders, like Jean-Claude. Like in St. Louis, gender might be an important factor in perception or the relationships themselves, suggested by Evrance's critique of needing a "beautiful behind."

There are literally dozens of quotes that underscore this tendency of camp committees to *moun pa*. On my way back from Dikini in late July 2010, I saw graffiti spray painted to be visible from the main road (Figure 5.2): "Down with the [ration] card thieves. The thieves give out cards at midnight." Although it could have referred to the ADRA camp—there were also unflattering slogans about ADRA—it could have been any camp. This discourse was quite commonplace in 2010 when ration cards were distributed. Fritz (from Plas Lapè) continued his analysis: "There isn't a committee for real! What constitutes a committee? If they give a committee four cups to distribute among us, they give his sister a cup, one for his wife, and one for his mother. He throws the remaining one to the people. Okay, we don't receive." The WID policies of aid were thus technically followed, but the almost entirely male committee members used their positions to benefit themselves. One might argue that Fritz was unhappy only that, as a male, he was shut out of aid because of the policies. If this was the case, however, Josseyln would have also benefited, when she clearly did not:

Pockets of tarps, that means you get up and come here. You make me talk, you take ten children. You say you are going to the camp with them. When I think you take them to the camp, the child comes back with two cups of rice, but a thousand

FIGURE 5.2. Graffiti denouncing camp committees as thieves. Photo: author

bags of rice fell into your hands. When this happens, you take your share, for your mother, for your sister, for your child. You use me! That is a pocket of tarp. When you are filling it, it never fills up.

In Josselyn's words, the committee was so far beyond deep pockets that the only way to describe it was *pòch prela*, pockets of tarps (Noël 2013). Other people referred to the committee as a gang, a *chèf seksyon* (local police chief of the Duvalier era) or even *makout*, referring to Duvalier's secret police. Plas Lapè had some of the lowest indicators of participation and community involvement in the quantitative survey, which Liza predicted given its top-down, exclusionary founding.

Plas Lapè is not alone in this abuse of power, as Maud's testimony that began the chapter highlights. Roody, Maud's neighbor in Karade, agreed:

Well, the aid that used to come to the camp, if the Red Cross came to the camp, we would participate [would receive aid].[12] But if other Haitians, the committee members, are giving [the aid], when they give to the committee to distribute [aid], they divide it among themselves and give it to moun pa [to their people]. Sometimes, many people in the population don't receive anything.

The same people who defended the camp residents in St. Louis, whom people like Marjorie appreciated, became *gwo nèg* (big men) to such an extent that they attempted to leverage their position for extortion, going beyond the personal power expressed in *moun pa*. Roody continued:

> The committee, at times, aid agencies used to come here for distribution. The committee demanded they pay money to negotiate with the committee members before granting access to the camp for the distribution. For example, the Red Cross used to distribute some little things for the population, provided us with some aid because we don't have anything. Whatever little it may be, we feel we're satisfied with it. The committee asked the Red Cross to pay $30,000 before allowing them here to give the little boxes that used to be—helpful. So, the Red Cross stayed away from the camp.

Roody's testimony was the most precise, but many other people living in Karade blamed the Central Committee for the Red Cross's departure. The people living in St. Louis Displaced sector at least had benefited from the electricity, T-shelters, and programming that the committee had negotiated with CRS. CAJIT was literally ignored by aid agencies the first several months after the earthquake, yet people spoke positively about the committee. What explains this apparent paradox?

MAKING SENSE OF THIS CREATION

On the one hand, the fact that NGOs and other agencies even attempted to have camp committees is a sign of trying to have local control. They could have, for example, run camps themselves, without any local structure. Michel Agier (2010, 29) quoted a camp manger saying that "the camp does not need democracy in order to function." On the other hand, like the gender audits noted in the previous chapter, camp committees too often are simply a "check-the-box" solution. Participation has been a buzzword in the aid industry for years (for a short sample, see Cooke and Kothari 2001; Hickey and Mohan 2004; Paley 2001; Parpart 1999).

In at least a couple of Camp Management and Coordination Cluster (CCCM) meetings I was able to attend, assessing and working with camp committees were agenda items. The Humanitarian Accountability Project (HAP) had done a study with IOM of two camps (2010), noting with alarm that NGOs had given committees power to distribute without knowing much about them. The report identified a tendency toward authoritarian leadership and a lack of participation. At the July 2010 CCCM cluster meeting I attended when findings were discussed, a collective sigh of relief was audible: NGO camp managers felt they were finally given permission to discuss this issue in public. The conversation was peppered with (foreign) NGO employees offering many examples of dictatorial committees. The issue was discussed among the NGOs—in English, hidden away at LogBase—as a problem they inherited, not as one they helped to create.

This chapter has demonstrated that far from being innocent victims of autocratic local committees, aid agencies share responsibility for the problem. Although it may have been an attempt at "local participation," the resulting experiment left many beneficiaries, camp residents, confused, frustrated, and even cynical. Ghislaine, from St. Louis, offers another example of fatalism: "Haitians don't like to share." Although obviously an exaggeration and stereotype, this discourse gained wide currency even among aid recipients. It is not difficult to hear a phrase like it escape a Haitian person's mouth. But coming from foreign aid workers, this discourse maps onto powerfully promulgated stereotypes about the world's first free Black republic. This experience and the discourse of lessons being learned have powerful ideological functions, as Nadine, from Hancho, reports: "But if you're smart,[13] you'll see what's going on, and you'll defend your own interests." Although it may not appear ideological to a U.S. reader, this rugged individualism, of looking out for one's own interests, supports and reinforces neoliberalism (INCITE! Women of Color against Violence 2007; Lwijis 2009; Petras 1997; Sharma 2008; Thomas 2013). Handy from Plas Lapè said, "We are obliged to depend on ourselves." Is this the lesson learned after billions of dollars in aid?

Given the clear failures from the perspectives of people within the camps, and their numerous examples, it might be tempting to end the analysis here. Journalists, aid workers, policymakers, and scholars without historical context, knowledge of Haiti before the earthquake, or experience of Haiti outside their own interventions, often do. Indeed, life in Port-au-Prince was far from perfect before the earthquake. However sad the corruption of KAS and the Karade Central Committee may be, there is more to the story than Lord Acton's famous dictum that power tends to corrupt, and absolute power absolutely. To wit, where did committees derive their power? Gladis recounted that life in Nan Bannann could be tranquil, with people cohabiting peacefully: "One moment we are good together, but when there's something being given out, there's conflict. CRS came once and told us to form a committee if they need to give something. One . . . this one creates a group, that one creates a group, that one creates a group. CRS did not agree, and this was destroyed." Like in Hancho, an NGO appeared to tell people who had been sharing with one another and helping each other survive that they had to form a committee. People like Michaëlle and Sandy reported in chapter 3 that even while living in the camp, they had strong ties with neighbors who helped each other out. The reward structure set up by the NGO favored this *chen-manje-chen* (dog-eat-dog) behavior, with high stakes, no supervision, no guidance, no rules, and no model. The kind of person who would succeed in becoming a committee is described by Emily, who came to one of the eight camps during the relocation phase, a "powerful person who is used to pushing people around" instead of the "timid person standing right next to them."

Some people, like Fritz, don't know the system. Like Fritz, François from Hancho didn't understand the word *committee*. When asked if he felt the committee effectively defended his interests, he asked, "Is the committee a part of the Red Cross?" This is an interesting question; given that it was a direct creation, down to the number of members and having a woman head, is it really not an extension of the Red Cross? When the interviewer pointed out the difference, François said that he "didn't see anything of importance." Quite matter-of-factly François concluded that if jobs or something for him to "participate" in (in this case, the word *participate* means to receive aid) didn't materialize, "this means it's not, it's not in my interest at all."

Residents hold committees responsible for the actual receipt of aid. Although no doubt some committees act like *pòch prela*, pockets of tarps, some people like Jean-Claude understand that the committees don't have the resources to be given out. Even CAJIT residents became frustrated, like Yves: "I think, in the beginning, the committee was doing a good job, but now, I actually think that there's no committee. Because it is the committee responsibility to take steps and bring organizations here. They used to take steps. The committee should insist; they should convince the organizations to distribute aid here." Like others, Yves judges the committee by its results. It could be that when Linda left, things fell apart, because like so many others, leadership was personalized. Later in the interview Yves said, "Everything is fine in other camps, the situation in other camps is improving. They always receive stuff, there's always something going on." This discourse of "Everything is fine" was commonplace. I was able to personally visit only around eighty camps. With eight research assistants we were able to visit 108, in July–August 2010. Far from everything being fine, we found that the results were mixed and persistent gaps in services remained.

I do not expect that Yves spoke from empirical evidence, from his own observation. CAJIT is rather isolated, why, he guessed, that NGOs didn't come around: "Sometimes, I wonder if the organizations find that the hills are too high." My interpretation is that Yves's comment was based on what he heard on the radio: that billions of dollars were promised to Haiti. Paul from Kolonbi expressed this sentiment even more clearly: "I suppose that Red Cross goes everywhere. It's only here that they don't enter." Not having access to information, Paul, Yves, and others could not do other than "suppose."

Given the lack of information about the international aid system, it was not unreasonable for Yves, Paul, and others to assume, first of all, that donors' promises were kept. Not understanding how the system works, it would also not be unreasonable to assume that aid would be distributed equally among the camps, or according to population. This would be, after all, fair. Seen in this light, it is understandable that people like Yves and Paul would assume that theirs were the only camps left out. Many people across the city felt this way as well. This interpretation places responsibility for their lack of aid on the committees. In general it is easier for people to critique those who are closest. When poring over hundreds of pages of these testimonies I was struck by a little linguistic clue: people tended to use the word *yo* (them) when referring to the committees, and *li* (it) when referring to NGOs. When referring to a specific action of a committee member, people could use the word *li* to mean him or her, like Linda, Esaie, or Jean-Jacques. This suggests that in people's imagination, the committees were real human beings with whom they could come into contact on a regular basis, whereas NGOs were distant, singular entities. The few instances of the word *it* to describe the committee were in Plas Lapè or Karade, where the committees were both powerful and distant. Real human beings can be brought down to earth, criticized, and blamed for a bad situation.

It is possible to reinterpret some of the population's anger and frustration. When asked why the Nan Bannann committee disbanded, a former member responded quite passionately:

> I myself went around to take the names, ages, grades, the last class in school, of all the children. I submitted the list to UNICEF, but they never came back here. They don't even pick up my calls! But when the population sees that we sent the children's name to UNICEF, they wrongfully think that we pocketed the money! This is the reason why the committee has decided to close. But other organizations that regularly have us conduct these censuses do nothing for the population. I decided to not accept doing that! If an organization wants to do it, it will do it itself.

Rather than pocket the money, it is possible that the aid never arrived. Certainly as Josselyn noted, performances such as responding to surveys, "making us talk," were normalized as part of the process of receiving aid. So absent information— some committees did a bad job of communicating with the population—why wouldn't Josselyn assume that writing down her name on a list meant that aid was coming to her? A committee member at Hancho explained, "Because all the institutions we've contacted are lying to us. Meeting after meeting, sometimes, they would come and have us talk. After talking to them they would tell us that they would come back, but two three months go by and they never come back. Then they return and ask you questions. Then they leave." In the context of this group interview this person was on stage, so the statement about "all" institutions lying to them might be performance or rhetorical flourish. In any case, the other people in the meeting all knew the situation better than the researcher or myself. Even if exaggerated, it is an important reproach and explanation.

CONCLUSION

A Jain parable discusses six blind men each touching different parts of an elephant and drawing different conclusions about what an elephant is. In much the same way, the IDP population can't be expected to see the whole functioning system of international humanitarian aid. They critique what they can see. The Nan Bannann and Hancho committee members have their hands on another piece of the elephant, and it raises new sets of questions.

In such a complex, multifaceted, and large-scale set of phenomena, completely controlling for and isolating variables is not possible, nor, I argue, desirable. However, this chapter has revealed some interesting correlations that demand attention. Karade's Central Committee, created by an NGO, became autocratic and corrupt when they were able to leverage more material aid for the population (the St. Louis Displaced). NGO-managed camps had worse governance and civil society indicators than those without. In the 108-camp survey in 2010, people in NGO-managed camps were slightly less informed about the name of the camp committee (27 percent, compared to 35 percent), less aware of the committee's plan (25 percent, compared to 35 percent), and less familiar with the committee leadership (50.5 percent, compared to 69.0 percent) than those in camps not managed by NGOs. Most interesting, only 39.8 percent of people in NGO-managed camps felt they could participate in the committee's activities, whereas 57.5 percent of those in camps without an NGO management agency felt they could participate.

Although it may be uncomfortable to acknowledge, the patterns in even the qualitative data are hard to ignore. The worst abusers of their power were directly chosen by NGOs. The heavier the hand played by NGOs in the creation of the camp committee, the more likely the committee was to exclude the population. Understanding this also sheds light on the original question, What happened to the outpouring of bottom-up solidarity immediately following the earthquake? From *kotizasyon* (each making a contribution) to *pòch prela* (pockets of tarps), from *youn ede lòt* (one helping the other) to *chen manje chen* (dog eat dog), the ways in which committees were implanted, imposed by NGOs for the receipt of life-sustaining aid, had the consequence of systematically replacing horizontal, bottom-up forms of solidarity with top-down, hierarchical, bureaucratic intermediaries. Anthropologists used to discuss the concept of "segmentarity," or the ability of a family unit to split off and reproduce the exact structure, a concept revived as "fractals" or rhizomes (Deleuze and Guattari 1987).

Intended or not, like Dr. Frankenstein, NGOs created the very monsters that haunted them in the end. Mary Shelley's parable was a warning against the potential abuses of unbridled technology. Translated to the context of the camp, it is a warning that human relationships don't easily conform to quick, technocratic solutions. Seen from this albeit unflattering portrait painted by recipients, call them camp residents or IDPs, camp committees are best described as "genetically modified" organizations. In some cases, like CAJIT, the intervention is slight; in others, like Karade or Plas Lapè they were outright creations of aid agencies.

Humanitarian agencies are hardly "mad scientists," and I hope that hardworking, busy individuals who work for them do not take offense at the analogy. Sometimes it is only through horror that people are inspired to ask questions. The scale of the human misery—and also the international humanitarian response—in Haiti's IDP camps following the earthquake has few equals. Understanding these horrors is necessary if we are to do better. How did this situation come to be? Why did the humanitarian response create this system of committees? To understand what's going on we need to take a closer look at NGOs themselves; in the next chapter, we examine how recipients view them.

6 · *ABA ONG VOLÈ*

The "Republic of NGOs"

My life! I am living with seven children in Plas Lapè. Since the earthquake we had the Salvation Army that was responsible, that gave us rice with ground meat. But they suddenly cut that off. On Good Friday [2010] they gave us two cups of rice, one cup of beans, one little liter of oil.

Currently, Concern gives us water. It's true, it gave us water, but hear this: we have to pay for it. And when you wake up in the morning you don't have a [Haitian] dollar [five gourdes, 12 and a half cents at the time] to give your children food, now you have to pay a dollar for the water. I heard now they are going to raise it from half a dollar, because the money is not enough to pay the driver to a dollar for one bucket of water.

A bucket of water won't last you through the night. You have to bathe, you have to wash. Concern hasn't cut it yet because I hear it had a job to do, and the job isn't done. I will never believe that Concern asked us to pay for the water.

Only water, sweetheart, only water. Ever since the earthquake passed. Now there is nothing anymore. There are other *blan* [foreigners, in this case NGOs] that come, yes, that could give us some aid. We were dependent on the Salvation Army. And then it stopped and sent people away.

That water over there is from Vivario. Vivario gives water and that's it.

The NGOs work with bandits, guys with guns. They make the most money as well, you understand what I am saying? They don't work with normal people.

Many come to give aid but the way they committee treats them, they stop, they go, and don't come back. Concern, the Red Cross. Well, the Red Cross hasn't really given anything here because we don't have the Red Cross card. But Concern takes care of us more here, only Concern.

They make us sing and then they play films. They take our pictures, they pass our image around in cameras with all the adults clapping hands. I hear people singing: "Burn trash ohhh burn trash!" A bunch of nonsense!

Last week they gave us a card. While still stuck in this camp, we took this card because we have nothing else. We woke up in the morning, resigning ourselves. We said that whatever they give us, we will organize ourselves to sell part of it to feed our children. When we got in line, they gave us four bars of soap.

They said it was IOM but I didn't see. I can't say it was IOM, but it gave us the card for the soap and we got gassed while in line. IOM gave us the card but we never received anything from them.

Well, I can say the Red Cross came several times, IOM came several times. But what aid is possible? They bring soap to wash with, they give Aquatabs to treat water. The people saw that it's too small, so they throw rocks, bottles, and then they leave, that's how it always is.

We were standing in the hot sun, after this the *blan* [in this context MINUSTAH, UN troops] gassed us, shot rubber bullets. They weren't real bullets, but rubber bullets. Someone from MINUSTAH [the UN troops] fired because the guys really were throwing rocks and bottles, you understand? Pregnant women got shot. Someone died from a bullet.

For four bars of soap you lost your life.

—Josselyn, Plas Lapè

Josselyn, who coined the phrase *pòch prela* to denounce the camp committee, outlines a litany of agencies working in Plas Lapè. Her frustration is palpable, not only as she reports not understanding precisely which agency is responsible for what, but also as she retells how some members of the population reacted to what they took as an insult after standing all day in line. Though admittedly critical, Josselyn opens this chapter to demonstrate the range of residents' perspectives on aid agencies. Many within the beneficiary population depicted NGOs as "thieves" profiting off of their misery. Graffiti saying *aba ONG volè*—down with NGO thieves—was quite common for at least the first few years following the earthquake, when the presence of humanitarian agencies was visible. However critical many beneficiaries like Josselyn are, this chapter begins by acknowledging the diversity of perspectives. Some people could distinguish "good" from "bad" agencies based on how they felt treated or the concrete results they could identify.

Like the population's perception of the camp committees, their understanding of NGOs is mixed, but a majority of the population had negative impressions of NGOs. Interestingly, around a third of respondents reported not having sufficient information on which to base an opinion. There are some slight variations between camps. It appears subtle differences between men and women exist, with women more likely to express satisfaction or become resigned than men. One variation is residents' understanding of particular NGOs; some individuals could distinguish between those benefiting the population and those who only go through the motions. Some of the most critical perspectives on NGOs, certainly the most detailed, come from members of the camp committees.

This chapter organizes residents' thoughts about NGOs, beginning with the distinctions some people make between NGOs. This leads into the discussion of people's "appreciation" for NGOs, even though the population identified other priorities. As they did with the committees, residents fault NGOs for poor communication. Many individuals shared a critique that NGOs take their names and make money off of them. Some went further in this critique, identifying inequalities and hierarchies inherent to NGOs. Some individuals identify the Haitian government as ultimately responsible.

GOOD *BLAN* VERSUS BAD *BLAN*:
DIFFERENCES BETWEEN NGOS

Some people distinguished between different agencies, like Katiana from Hancho: "NGOs don't come here, only the Red Cross. Well I only know Red Cross. Red Cross is not an NGO." This was almost the exact same response as Manolia's. Someone at the Red Cross might have told residents that the institution is not an NGO. I was once corrected when using the term to describe the Red Cross, founded in 1863, predating the official terminology of NGO, during the founding of the United Nations, to denote agencies that would have consultative status. Despite the nomenclature, NGOs have been around for more than two hundred years (Charnowitz 1997; Davies 2014). According to the International Committee of the Red Cross (ICRC), it has a status of its own as a "hybrid" intergovernmental organization. It "is recognized as having an 'international legal personality' or status of its own," granting the ICRC special rights and privileges (Rona 2004).[1] I was certainly not alone in this misunderstanding; the Red Cross was listed as the first example of an NGO on sites like Wikipedia, for example.[2] IOM is also a hybrid intergovernmental organization, yet in this study camp dwellers referred to it as an NGO. I have taught a class on NGOs at the Faculté d'Ethnologie (the Ethnology School of the State University of Haiti) since 2004. In addition to the generally negative impressions of NGOs, I was most struck by how many individuals classify institutions such as USAID and the United Nations as NGOs. As their professor I dutifully corrected this misconception. As the years wore on and this understanding was generalized I wondered if this "mistake" was better read as an expression of local knowledge and categorization. NGOs are not the *Haitian* government, and in this imagining are all foreign and several have big wallets.

The status of *not* being an NGO was vehemently defended by many full-time employees of "alternative" NGOs (Regan 2003) on the left of the political spectrum. By contrast, UN Special Envoy Bill Clinton's definition of NGOs is decidedly inclusive. In 2009, he declared there to be ten thousand working in the country.[3] I didn't include a question specifically asking people to define NGOs in these interviews, so the best we can do is to see the definition emerge from context. Defining what is and what is not an NGO is not a straightforward nor academic matter: it is a highly politicized question (Bernal and Grewal 2014; Fisher 1997; Kamat 2002; Sharma 2006). One way to read Katiana's and Mano-lia's statement is that the Red Cross was set apart from the mass of unnamed, unindividuated NGOs because the population had some contact with at least a representative from the Red Cross. Nadine offers this clue: "The Red Cross has never really made a decision. They[4] are on their way out. Because I think they have stopped providing us with water. For example, just the day before yesterday they came here announcing that the toilet-related-service[5] they used to provide will also stop." Notice the use of the word *they*, which could refer to specific individuals at the Red Cross, suggesting familiarity as discussed in the previous chapter, rather than an unindividuated mass, *li* ("it").

Behind much of the debates about defining which institutions are or are not NGOs is a desire to reserve some NGOs as "good" because they are grass-roots, advocacy driven, membership based, or independent from official government aid (for example, Étienne 1997; Houtart 1998; Mathurin, Mathurin, and Zaugg 1989; Pearce 1997; Regan 2003). The impulse is understandable because the term includes institutions that have annual budgets in the hundreds of millions—and even billions—working in dozens of countries and small, volunteer-only local organizations. The abbreviation *NGO* defines institutions based only on what they are *not*: governments (Fisher 1997, 441). Critical NGO scholars question this too given that many NGOs receive a majority of funding from donor governments (INCITE! Women of Color against Violence 2007; Lwijis 2009; Nagar 2006; Nagar and Raju 2003). Feminist scholars Victoria Bernal and Inderpal Grewal (2014) discuss "blurring boundaries." Although some may dismiss this discussion as academic quibbling, it is highly politicized: at stake in definitions are legitimacy, access to resources, and accountability. As Bernal and Grewal argue, by defining NGOs based on what they are not, this allows for a productive instability and ambivalence, shape-shifting to fulfill political ends, including the ideology of "a clear divide between public and private realms of power that is consistent with models of the normative liberal state" (7).

Some people in Haiti have a normative classifactory system. In our first meeting, Jean-Jacques, the committee president at Kolonbi, shared, "Good *blan* are those care about development who like Haiti, they like to work. Bad *blan*, on the other hand, came to collaborate with the mafia who is in power in order to make money. The bad ones, the bad ones! There are more bad ones! Bad *blan* monopolize all the resources. They come here to make money, whereas the ones who came for sustainable development may sometimes not have much." Jean-Jacques was an activist well before the earthquake. His statement can be read as a rejoinder to the graffiti saying *aba tout ONG* (down with *all* the NGOs), especially visible in 2010–2011. Jean-Jacques's unit of analysis wasn't NGOs but *blan*, foreigners, although the two might be interchangeable. Deconstructing an essentialist notion of *blan*, he distinguishes us based on our vision and our access to money and power. In his rendering, principled citizen-to-citizen solidarity is still possible, if the minority.

Some people's experience in the camps demonstrated a difference between the efforts and results of various aid agencies. Jhon, from CAJIT, shared this perspective:

For example, ADRA came here. We were not satisfied because it came with bars of soap that cost five gourdes [twelve cents] and a pack of Aquatabs for everybody in the camp . . . hmm . . . and a second time . . . no, before that! It came with a truck, it gave a small blanket and a tarp, but when we looked inside the truck we saw a lot of buckets. And it left with [the buckets]. You see what I mean?

Now the organization that's supporting us is IOM. I don't find fault with what IOM is doing. Because the other day it came here, it lent us three wheelbarrows, three rakes, three shovels, and one pickax so we could clean the camp but it told us, it warned everybody that they weren't going to get money for what they were doing, because IOM didn't plan to pay for that, the thing is we had to put our heads together to clean the camp.

Why we can't say 100 percent is because our goals are different from theirs. Some donors who give some stuff for distribution . . . well . . . I don't want to judge their work by saying that we didn't receive all that we should have, but the only thing is I'd like to thank God and I'd also like to thank them for what I received.

Jhon's discovery of the buckets was material proof for the belief that other camps are getting aid. Jhon did not comment on the irony of being told by this IOM representative, who received a salary, that they will not be paid for volunteer work. Of all the camps in this study, people at CAJIT were most used to volunteerism and collective work groups. Overall Jhon's tone is appreciative, even though he acknowledges differences in purpose or priorities, and that his camp didn't receive all that it should have.

"They Give Us Things That Help Us": Appreciation

Jhon's final note in the previous passage is a word of thanks. But he also outlines unmet needs. People in other camps offered similar gestures of appreciation. A member of the Hancho population had the following to share during the group interview: "A foreigner, an NGO, comes to our aid here when God touches its/her/his[6] heart. When that happens we feel happy." In addition to implicitly defining NGOs as foreign, and foreigners as NGOs, conflating the two, this individual outlined a core reality of NGOs: they are private entities. Rather than obligation the relationship is of voluntary generosity, part of NGOs' traditional ideology (Bornstein 2012; Bornstein and Redfield 2011; Fisher 1997). Unspoken in this quotation but understood is that NGOs can decide not to give when they lack divine inspiration. So the response is gratitude, happiness. Cassandra, also living in Hancho, completed the thought: "Well it's good, it's good, because not giving at all is not good." Though it is "not good," Cassandra didn't indicate any expectation of a reaction from the population nor consequences for not being good. People in Kolonbi were reminded of this every day for almost a year: an NGO abandoned the latrines it installed, creating a public health hazard in Kolonbi (see Figure 6.1). As private voluntary agencies, NGOs can leave at will, when their contract expires. Cassandra and her neighbor speak as if they're on the sidelines, watching, without a sense of entitlement, power, or responsibility for their situation. The French word for this phenomenon, discussed at least in scholarly circles, is *assistancialisme*, the state of being a spectator, watching instead of acting (Thomas 2013). A neologism used by former French president Sarkozy, who was decidedly against public assistance, the term translates into a "culture of dependency."

Rose-Anne, also from Hancho, offers sincere gratitude for the help she and her neighbors received: "We were under bedsheets. [The Red Cross] took us out from under the sheets, and it gave everyone a place to live. We thanked it for that because it did the first move for us. But this could not resolve our problems." Residents' needs didn't end with the emergency shelter. Fewer than 5 percent (37, 4.9 percent) of people said that the NGO responded to the needs of the people in the camp. Residents were able to see more variation in the work of NGOs

TABLE 6.1   Residents' Perspectives on the Effectiveness
              of Groups Responding to Problems

Does This Group Respond to Problems?					
	Yes	In a Way	A Little Bit	No	Don't Know
Committee	6.7	5.5	9.0	66.6	12.2
NGO	4.9	10.3	16.6	61.9	6.3

FIGURE 6.1. State of latrines six months after the NGO that installed them had left in the Kolonbi camp. The latrines stood like this for more than four months after this photo. Photo: author

compared to that of committees, as Table 6.1 shows. It is worth noting that the questions were worded slightly differently; for the committees it was responding to "problems" and for NGOs, "your needs, people living in the camp." Fewer people said they didn't know, and thirty more people answered the question about NGOs. This suggests that camp residents identify NGOs more than committees as parties responsible for aid.

Other camp residents were similarly grateful for what they received, such as Yannick, from St. Louis: "What would I think about other organizations that would like to participate with us? We would welcome them with open arms because we are in need. The reason why I named the Red Cross multiple times is because even though they don't give what we really need, they give us things that help us, that are good for our health." Rachelle, also from St. Louis, had a slightly different tone: "They used to give a kit that contains umm . . . soap, things like that. Though some of them are so-so,[7] as it is something they give you, you're obliged to get them. Shampoo, for example. These things aren't great, but we're obliged, we resign ourselves." These last two examples, certainly Rachelle, are even clearer examples of *assistancialisme*. At least Yannick identified the aid as useful in and of itself, unlike Josselyn, who was interested in resale value, for the exchange value in meeting her priority needs of feeding her children. Rachelle, in contrast, portrayed herself as powerless, resigned.

Fritz from Plas Lapè had a much different tone in his response, which could be either because as a man he might feel a greater sense of entitlement or that the people remaining at St. Louis self-selected to agree to be passive, accepting. The sense of frustration is evident in Fritz's words: "We hear of millions, but they gave two or three toilets! Yes toilets are good! But if we don't eat, how are we going to use the bathroom?" Although readers, particularly those working for humanitarian agencies, might bristle at this ingratitude, recall from chapter 2 that on average there were around a thousand people per toilet in Plas Lapè. Fritz also outlines a reality that the aid given did not match residents' priorities, also suggested by quantitative information from the household survey. Residents' top priority identified was housing (328 people, 41.5 percent); however, the aid most IDPs reported receiving were hygiene kits, like Rachelle's story shows (496 people, 62.7 percent). This being said, the second and third most identified needs matched the second and third most identified aid received, water and toilets. It is worth remembering the context of the interviews; some individuals may have still taken researchers for NGO workers, which could have limited people's imagination of what is possible. Fueling Fritz's frustration was also his understanding of millions (actually, billions) of dollars of aid coming into the country, which also suggests a lack of information coming to him.

What happens when beneficiaries do not express appreciation? A coalition of committees in Karade outside of the Central Committee, in the sectors outside of the St. Louis displaced, were frustrated with a particular agency. Although the population appreciated the hygiene kits this agency provided, the committee asked for things that were a greater priority. "They came with only two bars of soap, two tubes of toothpaste. Do we really need those things? No, we already had those things. They're supposed to give to you what you don't have. You can't always brush your teeth, you need food too! Every day, it's always bathe, bathe, and bathe!" This focus on hygiene was interpreted by many in the population, certainly all committee members at the meeting, as paternalistic, racist even. This is an example of a pattern that sociologist Ilionor Louis (2012) identified as humanitarian aid being infantilizing. Residents suggested jobs. They qualified them as "useful" jobs, not like the cash-for-work wherein a team of T-shirted individuals do make-work, like hauling rubble in wheelbarrows (Ayiti Kale Je 2010). Residents put two and two together: because people in the camps needed housing, why not give jobs to residents who had that skill? "Because people have different kinds of talents here. There are bricklayers, plumbers, carpenters. Giving jobs to us will enable many people to earn a living, to pay school for their children." People also pointed out that there were also nurses, like Hélène from the previous chapter, or schoolteachers. More than falling on deaf ears, this idea of self-help was anathema to the foreign agency: "As soon as a population says that we don't need what you're giving to us, that we need something else instead, they leave. They're gone forever!"

"We're Waiting": Lack of Information

The Karade committee couldn't understand why, if there were billions of dollars in aid, tens of thousands of skilled laborers unemployed, and still great unmet needs, that these couldn't be connected. In general, beneficiaries did not understand the how the international humanitarian system functions because they were not informed. Immediately following the question about what aid came to the camp, the research team asked people, "Did they tell you why they gave that aid?"[8] Only thirty-four people, 4.3 percent, said yes, and a handful of others hazarded guesses about whether it was what they deserved, because of the committee, or others. Many people—around a third of the qualitative interviews—responded in one form or another that they did not know enough about NGOs, varying slightly by camp. People at Meri Dikini were particularly noncommittal about NGOs, like Tatiana, who said simply, "I don't think anything about them." Tatiana's neighbor Marie Marthe acknowledged that there are limits to her knowledge: "Well, in fact, sometimes I'm not around. Maybe they came by while I'm at church, you understand?" Marie Marthe's generosity of interpretation is contrasted directly with one of the participants in the group interview, before the committee member showed up: "I haven't seen any NGO come here to hold a community meeting, to assemble us in order inform the population of what they're doing, projects they have for us, what they can do and can't do for us. Not even one day! If people say there's an NGO here, I'll stand right in their face to contradict them, no matter who they are!" Although his militancy might again rub people the wrong way, it's important not to overlook the model of communication suggested, a *rasanbleman*, a large community meeting. As the previous chapter demonstrated, NGOs put in place a structure of camp committees as intermediaries—miniature NGOs—as opposed to having direct contact.

Jorel from Kolonbi, like Yannick or Rachelle, explains a passive approach, being a spectator: "Well, we don't know. We're just waiting. We're waiting." Jorel held out hope that NGOs would still come, which was increasingly less likely as time wore on, certainly as of his interview a year and a half following the earthquake. People with more experience with NGOs were more circumspect, like Jean-Robert, the new committee vice president in Plas Lapè in October 2011:

At least they used to invite us to some meetings but that doesn't happen anymore. So we can't tell you if Viva Rio is still here or not, what's happening, or what's not happening. We don't know.

IOM gave a card to the population. It hasn't said anything to population about the card since then. The people are very frustrated at IOM. It never says what's going to happen. Is the card for houses? For money? What is it for? So, when the population sees us, they ask us questions and alas we don't know what to tell them. What does that card in their hands mean? For me this is still a question mark. None of us knows what it means.

The purpose behind the cards never became clear, beyond simple identification as IDPs. The July 2011 interview in Plas Lapè with Fritz was interrupted by a visit from none other than the new president, Michel Martelly. Residents and committee members alike reported that Martelly promised to relocate people from the camp to a new development of Zorangé,[9] the site of a 2011 housing expo presented by Bill Clinton. The story of Plas Lapè, always complex, became more so as time wore on. Incidentally, Liza changed her opinion of this camp committee when I last spoke with her in September 2012. Jean-Robert was a respected community leader who as a soccer player enjoyed a following. His manner, unlike the previous committee president (he was still officially vice president), was calm and understated. In my presence he always spoke slowly, quietly, and with a smile on his face. I am well aware that this too might have been a performance for me.

As Fritz's quote demonstrated, basic facts about the aid system and about NGOs did not trickle down to him. This was true even in camps where residents had greater confidence in the system, like St. Louis, as Yolette discussed: "The Red Cross assists us but I don't know where it gets the aid from, which organization, which *enstans* [agency] helps it, how does it get the aid." As noted, the Red Cross is a particularly complex organization. This lack of transparency downward is certainly not unique to the Red Cross or to Haiti (for example, Edwards and Hulme 1996; Pearce 1997; Strathern 2000; Vanderkooy 2004). Chenet Jean-Baptiste calls this process a "mystification." So it is not surprising that Yolette wouldn't know where the Red Cross—the Haitian Red Cross, backed up by the Spanish Red Cross[10]—received its funding. A word about *enstans*: Haitian is an evolving, adaptive, and creative language, also heavily dependent on context. Literally translated as "instance," the word is deliberately vague, used in the place of *agency, organization,* or *institution.* This suggests further insights, another example, in the ever-powerful, vague, category of NGO in the local imaginary, or what anthropologists call "worldview," the ways in which individuals within particular groups make sense of the world.

This lack of information is related to the perceived lack of results. Like Marie Marthe, Manno from Nan Bannann acknowledges his epistemological limitations: "If the NGOs are giving aid, I can't say that they aren't. But they . . . but it never gets to us in this camp." Suze from Plas Lapè based her critique of the *enstans,* the aid agencies, on her own experience:

They said IOM had some money to give us. We never saw them. Some people said they were IOM, others said they were Salvation Army. Some people came and we didn't ask them. For IOM, they made us make fools of ourselves here. They made us take these cards in the hot sun, without food or drink, they said they would send a little money to us. Since December they said they would give us something. Until now nothing. They said would send food for us, until now we are living on the will of God.

Both people attached importance to perception, "seeing" aid agencies. The lack of precision about which agency was supposed to give the money is emblematic of the particularities of Plas Lapè, as Josselyn's story that began the chapter details. However, the general lack of clarity is a symptom of this larger problem of the population—also known as beneficiaries—not being adequately informed. This is in direct contrast to the precision with which agencies collect information about them.

"They're Just Taking People's Names": Performances

One of the most poignant images Josselyn's testimony evokes is being made to sing for their aid, literally. Adults being schooled on appropriate trash management is another example of infantilization (Louis 2012). Several activist colleagues used the analogy of theater to refer to post-earthquake aid. This language gained currency when Martelly, a popular music performer, became president of Haiti. Camps attracted so much attention from journalists, aid workers, donors, and even foreign researchers that is easy to see how IDPs felt continually "on stage." Being an IDP became a role to play, complete with a script, with humanitarian agencies at once audience and director. The consequence for a bad performance or simply not playing according to script could mean, like in Karade, an NGO pulling out. And IDPs always had to perform.

The basic performance was to give out personal information. Over time, even before I sent college students to the field, people became *bouke*—fed up—with reciting these same lines over and over again, with few changes to their situations they could see, eloquently expressed by Nadine, from Hancho: "Well, myself, to me, they're just taking people's names, and they make a big deal out that. That's what I see, I don't see anything possible. I see nothing." The tense group interview with the Meri Dikini committee included charged accounts of having to perform, including responding to questions:

So for what I see, I am not saying negative, but it's supposed to be so. NGOs don't really care about us, they almost forgot about us on the site. Well. I'll say forget! They always drop by and collect information from us such as: what kind problem we are facing here, and we only expose our complaints: we say that's my problem, they say ok, we are going to think over your problem, but they don't do anything in terms of follow up.

They even ask sometimes "tell us three things that are the most pressing for you."

I can't read this passage, and certainly the addition by the second individual, without wondering whether he was referring to this research, because we too had asked about priorities. The problem wasn't only the indignity of being subjected to the gaze of any onlooker but the lack of any material change that occurred—at least those they could see—as a result of the performance. It was as if the agencies were themselves only play-acting at trying to help, collecting stories and leaving. Josselyn's being made to sing, perform for the cameras, is but one example. Josselyn's performance—the video of people singing—contributed to the agency's authenticity, "street cred," and ultimately a form of capital.

People experience queuing up in line as part of this performance, powerfully captured by Raoul Peck's *Fatal Assistance*. Liza said, "They want to make you suffer before they give you." Marie Hélène, who also stayed at Plas Lapè, detailed this frustration: "They tell you tomorrow, we have to go line up in the little corner. When we go the next day, we spend all day in line. Then they tell you there is nothing, everybody go home. That is how they do it. Since 3 or 4 A.M. we line up, sometimes it's 11 P.M. the night before. We're standing in the hot afternoon sun, and then they tell us 'Everybody go home. There is nothing.' That's how things are." Given this humiliating repeat performance of standing in the hot sun all day, sometimes people eventually did tear up the script and refused to perform. One day in July 2011, when they received only three bars of soap and Aquatabs, some individuals felt this was the last straw, throwing rocks as a form of protest. Although the UN troops, MINUSTAH, were only doing their job, protecting aid workers, it dramatized clearly whose lives mattered more. And it wasn't the residents of Plas Lapè. After this event everyone from Plas Lapè commented on it; some added details that a woman was shot in the neck, and several adding that MINUSTAH shot tear gas. All discussed the revelations about them being thought of as subhuman. Although this incident was admittedly dramatic, this frustration and refusal to comply with humanitarian disciplinary procedures was common, as a Hancho committee member recalled:

They just ask questions anytime they come here. Every day.

They make us talk so much that when one day that we had to take a census of the population, they said that they wouldn't give their names because all that they're doing won't amount to anything, they're not . . .

> I remember one day I grabbed a notebook and I said to a lady, "Ma'am, could you give me your name?" She said, "I'm not giving you my name! All the time you want me to write my name and child's name! All the time!"

Although people living in the camps didn't see benefits accruing to them as a result of these performances, they identified other purposes for their detailed personal information.

"Making Money Off of Us"

One of the most common expressions coming from IDPs is that "NGOs are making money off of us!" This discourse makes sense: in addition to information not trickling down to them, people do not see benefits coming to them, yet they still have to provide information upon request, with their names written down on lists or having their photos taken. The *Nouvelliste*, Haiti's largest daily-circulation newspaper, printed stories almost every day about a promise of aid or new foreign cooperation. At the UN donors' conference on March 31, 2010, the community of nations and multinational agencies pledged more than $10 billion dollars for the Haiti relief and reconstruction effort, $5.6 billion for the following year and a half alone. This on top of more than $3 billion in donations from private citizens. Noted in the introduction, if just donated to everyone in Haiti directly, a household, a *fwaye*, of five would have received $8,000. Lolo, at Karade, exclaimed, "A bunch of NGOs came here after January 12 to make money off our backs. It's a case of *one man's misery being another man's fortune*. Therefore, they're getting rich. You understand?" This discourse about getting rich was quite common. During some of the interviews, people identified what they saw as specific forms of graft, like one of Lolo's neighbors, Mackenson:

> In my opinion, with regard to the large amount of money available to finance the construction, if the NGOs wanted to give us a place to live—I am not saying that the plywood isn't good. You understand?—but they would build us a more comfortable shelter. Considering the amount of money these people have in their hands, what are they doing? They are just laundering the money. As soon as they build the shelters, after two days, you see those shelters collapse.

Note that before he critiqued what he saw as corruption, Mackenson at least paused to give a gesture of appreciation. Their neighbor Maud, generally less prone to rhetorical excess, was even more specific:

> As for the NGO's, they are just making money off our backs. When they collect money for donations, they keep most of it for themselves, and we only get chicken

feed. They organize some activities, they tell people they gave out this or that, but actually, it is no big deal! After getting shelters from CRS for example, we heard that they had cost 20,000 U.S. dollars. They said after they distributed the shelters, because they did not cost 20,000 U.S. dollars, they would give us what is left of the money. But I hear they are leaving and they haven't told us a single thing.

Maud shares a figure without noting where this information came from. This estimate is admittedly very high; figures of seven and eight thousand dollars for temporary shelters floated around cyberspace during 2011, and the website for the Shelter Cluster enumerated a cost of $1,200 to $2,400, depending on factors like local geography. Even this was very high compared to the alternative of people constructing permanent housing with available materials. UN employee Georges was building an extension to his *lakou*, stopped by a yard to look at cinderblocks. They were 26 gourdes, about 60 cents at the time, per block. He calculated for a typical one-room dwelling of the same size as the T-shelter, but a permanent house, the cost of the materials would be $680. This would include iron rebar and corrugated tin roof mounted to allow air in, two design elements deemed especially important after the earthquake. Georges asked rhetorically, "Where are they spending the rest of the money? They certainly aren't paying technicians that much."

Even through the summer of 2014, more than four years after the earthquake, fresh graffiti was written detailing the cost of an NGO project for a particular area, often punctuated by *aba ONG volè* in big letters. Liza didn't mince words: "NGOs have the means to help. They exist because of these problems. If all the problems were solved, organizations wouldn't exist!" In Liza's understanding, NGOs exist off of people's misery. IDPs' performance of misery—the photos, long lines, personal information dutifully given—are capital NGOs sell to donors to get their money. Unfortunately this discourse was quite common after the earthquake, with many expressions relating to food: *faire beurre* (make butter), *pran grès* (skim the fat), *koupe gato* (cut the cake), or simply *manje* (to eat).

Although many people working in NGOs have a sincere desire to help, the contrast between standing in line since 11:00 P.M. the night before or having random strangers take photos of adults clapping their hands singing a song about trash on the one hand while the populations' needs are not met and the trappings of NGO activity on the other is striking. Most commented on were the big white SUVs, windows up and air conditioning running. Frisline shared this analysis in *Poto Mitan*, long before the earthquake: "When foreign countries release aid, it goes to the bigwigs. They're the ones driving the fancy cars. When they pass us on the street, they only give us a coating of dust. As long as aid goes to the bigwigs, we poor won't see a cent." This situation was *abse sou klou* (an abscess on an open wound) after the earthquake, as Liza concluded: "[NGOs] just drive big cars with beautiful air conditioning. At least one person has to hear the little people, to understand the poor majority." We are suffering all the while they are making money off of our misery. This needs to stop!"

Not all people share Liza's radicalism. Some, like Fanfan at Nan Bannann, are able to acknowledge some are still trying: "We are the ones managing ourselves. All the NGOs left! They came to make some money for themselves and they left. Only the Red Cross provides us with a variety of things every month. It has been better than the others." During the group interview with the population at Meri Dikini, one of the most radical critiques was challenged:

> Especially myself, I consider the impact negative. Had it been for NGOs, we would've all been dead.
>
> Well, I wouldn't say if it were for the NGOs, we would've been all dead! Because whatever it was, they're helping anyway. They gave a plastic bag of water when you needed it, you have to consider it! Because if I needed a plastic bag of water this morning, I was thirsty, and somebody gives one to me, I'd value it! Perhaps it gave me what it had, it may give more if it had more!

The first individual's overarching criticism was widespread. One meaning behind it is to highlight all the work that the population had done on their own for their own survival, that they're not dependent on NGOs. Chapter 2 was full of stories of survivors themselves as first responders. Like Yannick, this second individual reigned in this more radical critique by pointing out that all the same, humanitarian agencies did something, recalling the proverb *rayi chen, di dan iblan* (Hate the dog, but acknowledge that its teeth are white).

"Perhaps We Don't Have a President": Government Responsibility

Several individuals who articulated what James Ferguson (1990) called a "foundational" (as opposed to "functional") critique of NGOs nonetheless held the Haitian government responsible for the situation. Franck from Kolonbi, who declared in the previous chapter that he was not dependent on aid, argued that the Haitian government should play a more hands-on coordinating role:

> If you are truly the president of a country, if foreigners come in, you need to be aware of their activities. You should say something like, "I accept that I have problems and you come to help me. But I'm the one to tell you where your help is needed." If everybody comes voluntarily, all the NGOs do whatever they please. They come here and people got money, they buy ten cars, things are good for them. And to make things worse, they take the name and the ID of the population to justify the money toward their donors proving how many people

they help. Therefore if the government involved asked those organizations, "Well. You come. If you want to help me, I want to know what your plan is: what are you doing? Ok so here's my plan, this is how you can help," I think that it would have been better, but they didn't proceed like that.

Franck shares the critique that taking the names of the population justifies their receipt of aid, but he begins and ends with a critique of the government. The conclusion he reached gained wide currency; in 2010 both Bill Clinton and Secretary of State Hillary Clinton identified strengthening the Haitian government as a priority, outlined in the 2005 Paris Declaration. At the UN Donor Conference on March 31, 2010, Secretary of State Clinton said:

> And we in the global community, we must also do things differently. It will be tempting to fall back on old habits—to work around the government rather than to work with them as partners, or to fund a scattered array of well-meaning projects rather than making the deeper, long-term investments that Haiti needs now. We cannot retreat to failed strategies. I know we've heard these imperatives before—the need to coordinate our aid, hold ourselves accountable, share our knowledge, track results. But now, we cannot just declare our intentions. We have to follow through and put them into practice.

As noted in chapter 4, where the government played a coordination role, progress was made. Overall, an additional 4 percent of camps had water and sanitation services (WASH) following the cholera outbreak and a $170 million UN campaign. The progress was concentrated in Cité Soleil, because DINEPA (the National Directorate for Water and Sanitation), a new branch of the Haitian government, made a goal of 100 percent coverage in the camps in that city. Without this prod, NGOs added WASH services only to an additional 1 percent of camps (Schuller and Levey 2014). This 1 percent increase is partially explained by the closing of twelve camps, some by forced eviction, some out of fear of cholera.

Residents' concerns about the government's role vis-à-vis NGOs didn't end at coordination. Robenson, living in St. Louis and with a similar socioeconomic status as Franck, had the following analysis: "Most of the aid, billions were disbursed through NGOs, three-fourths went through NGOs, and one-fourth through the government. As they say, if you don't value yourself, if you don't respect yourself, foreigners won't do it for you. Since they see that our government doesn't give us any importance, any value, the NGOs did the same." The statistic he offered was incorrect: according to the UN Office of the Special Envoy (2011), 0.9 percent of humanitarian aid and 9.1 of development funding went through the Haitian government (see also, for example, Farmer 2011; Katz 2010). However, Robenson's analysis is interesting: foreigners learned to mistreat the poor majority from the Haitian government. Widner, who has been working for NGOs since 1997, and whom we read more about in the next chapter, shares this perspective.

Some of this anti-Haitian discourse has an ideological bent, with people generalizing about how Haitians are bad, contrasted with the good intentions of the foreigners. This discourse also had wide enough currency to reach several foreigners whom I interviewed. Alix from Plas Lapè offers one such example: "Perhaps we don't have a president. But Viva Rio is good, because Haitians wouldn't have given us these two little pieces of wood. Never, Haitians would sell it to us; they wouldn't just give to us." It might be inferred that "Haitians" in Alix's statement are the government, because this was the same person who in chapter 2 said he had come to depend on the generosity of his new neighbors in the camp. However, it is vague, and as a human being Alix might indeed have complex and contradictory thoughts. Jean-Jacques, the Kolonbi committee president, in a long interview rife with such contradictions, focused his critique on not only the government but its current leader: "The population living under tents elected Martelly as president because they no longer believe in popular speeches. But two months after the president had taken his oath of office, the population realized they are still in despair. That's why the only government the population has is God in heaven. After that they don't see anyone else with them and nobody else besides the NGOs." Recall Jean-Jacques was also critical of "bad" NGOs. Of all the groups (committees, NGOs, the government, the United Nations, and donor agencies), NGOs—*enstans*, to include the United Nations and intergovernmental agencies like the Red Cross or IOM—inspired the most ambivalent reactions from the population. At the same time people critiqued NGOs for not bringing aid or not responding to the needs of the population, they also recognized that NGOs have the ability and mission to do so in the first place (and also possibly the source of a job).

This last quote from Jean-Jacques is an example of what Stephen Jackson (2005) called "nongovernmentality," wherein citizens privatize their aspirations and hold non-state actors responsible for fulfilling roles once played by governments. It is a powerful ideological gain of neoliberalism, expressed as TINA: There Is No Alternative. Fanfan from Nan Bannann offers a poignant example of how successful this ideology is: "God knows how much I hate this nation!" In the 2011 household survey, more people (213) said "I don't know" who is responsible for aid than any other responses, just ahead of NGOs at 212. The state received 153 responses, and camp committees 125. This could suggest that people living in the camps, like Robenson, are "following the money." It could also be a manifestation of the contest to win over people "hearts and minds"—one reason why USAID-donated tarps have the Haitian translation of the motto, *èd pèp ameriken an* (Aid from the American people) in big letters. This is a powerful example of what two NGO directors called "planting the flag" in a contest over visibility. However, one of the final questions in the survey asked people to identify who was responsible for moving them out of the camp. NGOs and the state reverse position here, with the difference more decisive: 277 people hold the state and 156 people hold NGOs more responsible (184 people said they did not know). Twenty individuals single out the president as being responsible, with one saying "After God, the president." Most of these people live in Plas Lapè, reflecting his visit during Fritz's interview. Interesting, more people said that they themselves are responsible for moving out than for receiving aid (seventy compared to fifty-two), and, thinking into the future, fewer IDPs (forty-four) imagined a role for the camp committee.

MAKING SENSE OF THESE PERSPECTIVES

There are of course many other things to be said about beneficiaries' perception of NGOs. This sampling represents to the best of my ability the diversity of responses and begins to identify emerging patters or an underlying logic. Most were critical, and a large segment of the population said they didn't know enough to form an opinion. Many who did express appreciation of NGOs also noted that the aid couldn't satisfy the needs of the population. NGOs inadequately communicated with the population, with IDPs knowing little about the aid agencies while having to give out detailed information about their own lives. This imbalance, combined with an extreme disparity of material realities—with life in the camps not changing much and NGOs displaying expenses like SUVs and teams of paid staff—leads many to the critique that NGOs are "making money off our backs." Some even express their critique in capitalist terms, that NGOs are "selling" their personal data or photos in order to receive aid. Though this seems harsh, seen from their perspective it is not that far from the truth. Why is there such a powerful disconnect between humanitarians' good intentions and beneficiaries' perceptions of them? The next chapter presents structural explanations from the point of view of Haitian people who work for humanitarian agencies.

7 · COLONIZATION WITHIN NGOS

Haitian Staff Understandings

After January 12, I had the impression that people thought that there are no more Haitians, that Haitians are not smart anymore. Since it was reported that houses had collapsed, that houses had been destroyed, and rubble had fallen on the population, it seems they thought that rubble fell on our intelligence too. Maybe they think rubble also fell on Haitians' knowledge.

NGOs became overflowing with expatriates. I can personally tell you that at [name withheld] everything was taken over by foreigners. I said foreigners [*etranje*], I didn't say white people [*blan*].[1]

Hmm ... security guard, driver ... those were the only positions available. In fact any simple project manager from any field, a highly qualified Haitian who's been doing a very substantial job for next to nothing was replaced by a foreigner. I said clearly a foreigner, I didn't say white person. They'll be replaced by a foreigner who maybe is fresh from school, without experience, their salary will be five or six times as much as that of a Haitian. The thing is, you need to pay more for them. You need to put her in a guest house or a hotel, or rent a house for him, security agents, cars, the whole works!

The thing is, after January 12, you feel that a colonization occurred within NGOs.

Some people are not aware of the reality, who don't understand the language. They're[2] not used to the country. The way they designed interview questions, for example when we were conducting the *satisfaction survey or needs assessment*,[3] they think they can say anything, while they're actually insulting the Haitian.

The NGOs, together with donors, are the ones that define the projects. People making decisions don't see the reality of the people who are going through it. We don't have the right to speak directly with Mr. Foreigner, who has the power to make decisions.

We wish there would be less participation from foreigners. Of course we need their presence for certain issues, but we don't need them in everything.

Fundamentally, we don't have a strong government so everyone does what they want, the way they want, unfortunately.

I think that the NGOs will always take advantage of this situation. NGOs in general, I think they make more money dealing with emergency than development.

So today is July 17, 2012. Seeing the state of the country, one would think that the catastrophe occurred only yesterday. Because a lot of money was wasted on expatriates. A lot of money was wasted on phony projects. A lot of money was wasted on things that had nothing to do with anything.

When people start having doubts about these activities, there will be social revolts.

Everybody in general, whether Haitians or foreigners, black, white, etc., we have another dimension, a human dimension.

The needs in Haiti *demand attention.*[4] Anyone who enters this country can identify what the population needs. You just need to sit down with them so you figure out how you will help them. The ones you took to be illiterate are ones who are most experienced and more knowledgeable. They have a great deal of knowledge, a lot of things that you with all your education from big universities don't know. Therefore it's important to sit down with them, and you'll see that this new paradigm may bring about more results than the current paradigm.

—Sonson

Although some might find it painful to read, Sonson's testimony offers several lines of critique that were all too common after the earthquake. Sonson had been working in a large international NGO since 2004, during another period of intense mobilization following a crisis, in this case President Aristide's forced departure. So when the earthquake struck, Sonson—"who was a rare Haitian working in follow up and evaluation"—had almost six years of experience with this NGO. Though "Sonson" is a pseudonym, his unique position would give him away if I name the NGO. Also, given how apparently widespread several of the sentiments he expressed are based on my interviews, to single out one NGO for this kind of critique is at once unfair to it and gives the impression of leaving others off the hook. So NGOs and other *enstans* aren't identified in this chapter.

This chapter discusses the perspective of thirty Haitian NGO employees, from front-line worker in the camps to director. Hearing the analyses of people who worked to implement NGO aid after the earthquake gives some clues to what might be behind some of the shortcomings identified in the previous chapter. This chapter is organized into two major sections, clustering analyses from front-line workers and middle management because these two institutional locations tended to play the largest role in shaping responses. Front-line workers tended to focus their analysis downward, on the beneficiary population, whereas middle management tended to focus upward, on their relationship with their foreign coworkers and supervisors. Interviews with the latter population tended to be longer and more involved; a couple of front-line workers literally looked over their shoulder during their interviews. Program supervisors, who like Sonson all had experience working in NGOs before the earthquake, shared their analyses of how the post-quake aid response differed. Several commented on an "internal colonialism" within their agency as they saw decision making and other positions of authority taken over by expatriates, often younger and all less experienced than they, at least concerning Haiti. Workers share their frustrations at being "led into error," as one employee put it, often arising from cultural imperialism. Some of these organic intellectuals (Gramsci 1971) began theorizing about a common experience or knowledge systems, in effect a culture within aid agencies.

FRONT-LINE WORKERS

For the people living in the camps, including camp committees, the faces of NGOs are the individual women and men who visit the camp on a regular basis. They were all Haitian, with one exception. These were the people who had relationships with the population. Françoise explained, "Poor women represent [this NGO] because they're the ones who work in the field, and they're the ones the population gets angry with because when they see [this NGO], it's always these people."

In addition to having a month-to-month contract, all front-line workers I interviewed were hired after January 12. Most individuals got their jobs through some connection with the agency, often through a training: one was a volunteer for the Red Cross, trained in first aid. Another also received first aid training but was involved with the Department of Civil Protection (DPC, in the original French), operating out of the government, through the Ministry of Interior and organized by municipal government. Their instinct to help, or to get a job, or both, led former volunteers to seek out these agencies that trained them. James was the recipient of a scholarship from an organization run by a close friend of the director of the humanitarian agency, who sent out a call for applications to his network.

Several individuals shared their work in the field during their interviews. James presented a simple tautology: "We work in the camps. So we have to find camps in order to work." NGO staff work primarily with camp committees, in the words of one camp manager, "Because we can't have a relationship with everyone." This statement suggests that NGOs preferred the type of hierarchical, federated structure with camp committees as their proxy. This hierarchy was naturalized by some NGO workers, as camp manager Pierre describes: "It's like if you are a president, you have a responsibility to provide electricity for the people. It's the same: you have the responsibility to look out for your people." Pierre's statement reproduces a system of patronage, or at least some form of paternalism. Some religiously oriented individuals used the language of a shepherd and a flock. Testifying to NGOs' attachment to committees, James explained, "The main thing is to have a committee to work with. It's not our job to conduct an analysis to find out if the committee is serious or not." Despite this discourse about how the system is supposed to function, some managers like Gabrielle reported intervening directly in the camp committee. "The first camp where I was working, I didn't find a well-organized committee. I created a committee that was a little better organized." The Plas Lapè manager said that the camp committee has a "problem with harmony: if this one says yes for something, the other says no. And they have personal problems. But they are well structured. If you need help they'll help you." This positive assessment is puzzling, because the committee was dubbed "pockets of tarps," but given Pierre's statement, this makes sense: it's not humanitarian agencies' responsibility to ensure that committees communicate with the population. The committees exist to serve the *enstans*, the aid agencies, not the population.

Some people like Gabrielle, who was paid to be physically present on a daily basis, didn't rely on the committee only. Gabrielle took it as her job to be visible in the camp: "Because if you don't walk around the terrain, how will the people know you?" The camp manager in Plas Lapè acknowledged that "some people aren't aware of my position. We only talk in meetings. Sometimes there's a problem and the committee doesn't know about it. I might be aware of it before them." But the information isn't a two-way street. The camp manager for Plas Lapè reported to me that they were going to relocate the entire camp beginning in March 2012, two months after my interview with her. This information was not shared with even the camp committee. James, who pointed out that "the result is positive, but these days people are hostile to NGOs," also admitted that "we are aware that we need to make more effort to be closer to the population."

Except for Françoise, all were (or had been) students in college. In a country where 1 percent of the population have college degrees, a status of *etudiant(e)* (college student) means something. Most front-line workers displayed very distinct class prejudices, like Gabrielle, a camp manager for one of the eight camps in the study: "The people in the camps, a lot of them are lazy. They think that an NGO will help them during their entire life, whereas it's not true at all. Before the earthquake, everyone used to eat. Everyone used to drink." This discourse of IDPs "bluffing it" went viral, often the first line of defense (or attack) from expatriate staff, some of whom pointed out to me that they were only repeating what "their" staff had said, like James: "However, there are others who choose to remain in it. They are lazies. They take advantage of this disaster. They just sit around the camp, waiting for aid. They don't make any effort." When I inquired about it during the interview, James, who was not a camp manager but a technical staff, said he had proof. I asked about the proof, and he simply repeated what he had said. In the end, he acknowledged that the vast majority of people living in the camps were in need, a point that Gabrielle conceded: "Because after two years, you have to be very brave to stay in the camp if you have your own house." Follow-up research noted that as of January 2012, seven months after the original household survey, 95 percent instead of 80 percent had been renters before the earthquake. Gabrielle estimated 10 percent of people were faking it.

This thinly veiled class prejudice, more important to front-line youth, came through in the interviews. Said someone who worked in Plas Lapè: "The person doesn't understand the strategy. When she gets paid, she spends it all. But the NGO employs him and pays him for a specific purpose. Only, the message isn't completely understood. You may have just told her; they act as if they don't hear." Although communication was identified as a major problem in the previous two chapters, in this retelling, beneficiaries are to blame. Particularly telling, and more than a bit troubling, is the critique that people like Josselyn, Alix, Suze, and Fritz are at fault for spending all the money they received from a cash-for-work program. Most programs, managed by NGOs, were for a short duration like two weeks, paying Haiti's minimum wage of 200 gourdes, less than $5, a day. As Jean-Jacques noted in chapter 1, this two-week salary of 2,000 gourdes, less than $50, would pay for little more than a sack of rice that cost 1,200 gourdes. With people having lost their savings and livelihoods in the earthquake, where were people like Josselyn or Suze going to save money? It was pointed out by many that while people were in the tents, they did not have to pay rent. But the *kriz lavi chè a*, skyrocketing inflation, was already serious before the earthquake.

Some, like the camp manager for Plas Lapè who had by the interview been working there for three months, share a critique of *assistancialisme*: "You can talk to people, telling them don't throw your trash on the street for this, that, and the other. You tell everybody, but people are a little careless because they say to themselves, they pay this person to do that. So, that's why I don't encourage the way the aid is been given, because the people are lazy. The people don't do anything to improve their conditions, those who live here." This testimony demonstrates a powerful class bias and critique, stereotyping thousands of people she had barely met. At the same time it offers a hypothesis, zeroing in on aid policies. Combined with the denigration of the beneficiaries, itself a reflection of class prejudice, this discourse does powerful ideological work, promoting the belief that poor are supposed to "pull themselves up by their bootstraps" as well as blaming the majority who aren't able to do so.

Another component of this neoliberal ideology is an individualist analysis, reversing the sociological imagination (Mills 1959): turning social problems into individual moral failures. One primary job of a camp manager is to train people on doing individual tasks for themselves, to train them on proper hygiene practices, like Pierre, whose job included talking to the population to make them "understand the importance of when the toilets are full, they have to clean them. Why we educate them, we motivate them first so they voluntarily take responsibility. It's not like we're going to pay them because they clean up. Because, they're the ones using it, so we educate them on the importance for a toilet to be clean, to empty it." In the abstract, Pierre's statement follows a certain logic; it is what Gramsci (1971) would call "common sense." People should be expected to clean up after themselves. Most Haitian people would agree; recall Yolette's statement in chapter 2 describing the importance she attached to a clean house. However, in addition to being a vivid example of infantilization (Louis 2012), when a toilet is shared, on average, with 273 people, this is another reality. Certainly it is a problem when an NGO installs the latrine and then abandons it, as in Kolonbi. When I asked Gabrielle about solutions to the social problems she had just detailed, she concluded simply that "each family has to try to find out which life she wants to lead. It's a personal decision." Gabrielle's statement is telling: rather than even attempt to solve camps' structural issues, one should focus on individual families' moral choices (for example, Curtis 2010; Fassin 2012; Redfield 2013; Sharma 2008; Timmer 2010). In the context of her discussion it was clear that the right decision was to leave the camps. The 16/6 relocation program described in chapter 3 followed this individualist logic.

As Françoise notes, sometimes this experience of being the visible representative of a humanitarian agency is frustrating. Sharing Josselyn's and the Hancho committee's frustration, Françoise offered another perspective: "When the people see you, when they see you holding a notebook, they see that you're writing names . . . they have hope. And you're taking names, and there's no hope." Françoise, the only one I interviewed who was not in college, was chosen by this NGO because she was a community leader before the earthquake; this international NGO "bought" her for her access to the population. But the experience with the community soured: in addition to graffiti denouncing it all over the neighborhood, residents held a large community meeting with hundreds of individuals to demand that this NGO leave. François had quit before this. She advises NGOs that "you had better tell it like it is. You don't have anything to give them, just say so. They will warmly welcome you. Because you see Haitians, Haitians understand a lot." Daniel, who worked for an NGO involved in the neighborhood where I live, explained. "Whenever the population hears that a NGO intervenes, it always thinks that the NGO has money in its hands to do the job. And so one way another, it must profit from that money. And that's a recent legacy of the earthquake." Though this NGO may be a small operation and have an "alternative" vision or a grassroots structure, NGOs like the one Daniel worked for fall prey to the realities discussed in the previous chapter: billions of dollars in aid were promised to Haiti. If the $16 billion promised by official agencies or donated by private individuals was simply donated as a cash transfer, each person would get $1,600 and a family of five $8,000. Because the money was ostensibly sent for them, why wouldn't people assume that they "must profit" from it? People in the NGO and intellectual classes used the term *mandyansite*, the condition of begging, to describe this new reality.

Daniel was a student at the State University of Haiti, the School for Human Sciences, and decidedly did not share the neoliberal ideologies of his peers. But he shares their frustration of not being responsible for the policies of the NGO he worked for, and as a month-to-month contractor not being able to respond to residents' questions. When I asked James about the situation in Kolonbi of the toilets being abandoned, this was his response:

> The NGO that was responsible for the latrines no longer works in the camp. Unfortunately, I do not have the name of the institution that took care of the latrines. It even left the country.
>
> The camp committee complained to us about that. There is a unit in [the agency], called WATSAN that works on *water and sanitation*.[5] There was no mention of camp Kolonbi in their annual program. I do not know why.

Jean-Jacques, who was satisfied with the work that James's agency had done in the camp, had given me James's contact. James did not have the power to grant the population's wishes, nor even explain why not. One of the few times that the two researchers saw an NGO representative in Kolonbi during their five weeks of research in 2011, these people asked if the students also worked for the same NGO (Bernard 2013), which speaks volumes about their level of awareness of even their own agency. Daniel explained some of the problems as a result of his structurally marginal position: "You don't have any contact with the person in charge. Your direct supervisor, if he's[6] a flatterer, if he's afraid of losing his job, he just hides the problem." Daniel raises questions about middle management's roles as intermediaries, describing precisely what I call "trickle-down imperialism" (Schuller 2012c): the hierarchical relationship prevents open communication as intermediaries gain power over their subordinates. This series of hierarchical relationships with intermediaries monopolizing contact turns otherwise well-intentioned policies into disastrous results. They often assert a more cautious, conservative interpretation out of fear, and then use their power over their subordinates, who can't independently verify the policies, to define the policy to people lower down the chain. The next section of the chapter outlines the perspectives of people who work with both the front-line staff and foreign supervisors.

MIDDLE MANAGEMENT

Middle management staff played a crucial role in aid delivery; they were the only people who could translate, sometimes literally, the needs of the population. There were some rare exceptions when foreign workers like Emily went to the field (often during a relocation process), but they still needed a translator. Even more exceptional was a Haitian entrusted to represent the NGO as the country director; there were a scant handful. In general, middle management, employed as program or field supervisors, had experience working within NGOs before the earthquake. Everyone I interviewed had, some since the early 1990s. Though some middle management staff had monthly contracts, some had a six-month or a year contract, meaning that they had more stability and greater understanding of their job responsibilities and the politics of the organization.

Middle management's experience and job responsibilities offered them a different perspective than front-line staff, the first point of contact with the beneficiary population. This difference in perspective could partly be explained by front-line workers being afraid to lose their jobs, so they were more cautious in their interviews with me. Most middle management people I interviewed I either knew before the earthquake, or were referred by someone I knew. After Mme. Auguste, whom I knew since 2004 at Sove Lavi, left the room, her new colleagues and I were shooting the breeze. They had joined Mme. Auguste in her critique of their situation. But as soon as I turned on my digital recorder and Mme. Auguste was gone, these two young men waxed about how good the experience was working for an NGO for their future development. It was so different that Mme. Auguste chided them when she came by to have me as the guest of honor taste the sauce. She said, laughing, that she understood this problem. She assured her young colleagues, front-line workers, that they had nothing to fear about being honest with me, that they weren't going to lose their jobs. She recalled the time when Mme. Versailles had first discussed my research with Sove Lavi. The director said, "There's a *ti blan* ['little' foreigner] who wants to do research with us. Go ahead and occupy him, but don't tell him too much." Mme. Auguste got flak from her new boss for a news story posted on the Internet about her latest employer in which I was interviewed. There was absolutely no connection because the journalists were investigating the situation for months, and their foreign collaborator knew I was going to be in town and asked me general questions about the NGO system overall. Mme. Auguste knew she didn't give me any particular details on her current employer, nor did I ask. But her foreign supervisor's paranoia spoke volumes. It was still awkward, as multiple connections were often misread. I had also integrated into this new agency via Lesly, a student who had taken my first seminar on NGOs in 2004, right before his first tour at an NGO.

In addition to not being as worried about losing their jobs as the front-line staff—although the people who talked with me might not be representative of the population, resulting from selection bias—people working in middle management had other experiences to draw from besides life in the camps. Though some shared a critique of the beneficiary population, they also could identify the post-quake situation as either anomalous or at least in some important respects new or different. It is also possible that new, younger staff, on a month-to-month contract and thus more easily falling into poverty, were eager to point out the differences between themselves and the population in much the same way individuals of uncertain class standing in unstable economic times are encouraged to dissociate with the working poor, at least in the United States. It could also be the hubris that often accompanies youthful energy. In addition, people who work both in the field and in the office have more regular contact with decision makers and the internal politics of the organizations. All this explains why people spent much more time processing these realities after the earthquake. Some began with an assessment of how this experience differed from before, particularly other humanitarian crises. Explaining the failures of the earthquake response, some identified worse coordination as a primary cause. However, most analyses centered around the increased presence of foreign workers. Everyone, even those less critical of NGOs overall, shared detailed accounts contributing to Sonson's analysis, testifying to a "colonization" within NGOs. People discussed the impact on their work lives and on the country as foreigners with little to no experience make arbitrary, ill-informed decisions that turn out to be bad for the NGO and the population they are attempting to help.

Previous Experience

Haitian anthropologist Rachel Beauvoir-Dominique wrote a detailed, incisive report (2005) critiquing the response to Tropical Storm Jeanne, which struck the city of Gonaïves in 2004. Not yet a hurricane, Jeanne killed more than three thousand people, most in the capital city of the Artibonite department, Haiti's "bread basket." The loss to the rice crop was devastating. Beauvoir-Dominique's report outlined the lack of coordination, the exclusion of the beneficiary population,

NGOs' working around the government, and a general lack of respect for human rights and international standards and norms such as the Red Cross Code of Conduct or the Sphere standards. The text was eerily prescient of the failures in the post-earthquake humanitarian response.

However, this was not the last major humanitarian crisis before the earthquake: in 2008, following a mass mobilization against the *kriz lavi chè a*—the high cost of living—that brought down Prime Minister Jacques Edouard Alexis, Haiti was slammed with four hurricanes: Fay, Gustav, Hanna, and Ike. There were fewer deaths—793—from a greater cataclysm—four hurricanes compared to one tropical storm, but there were only seven deaths in Cuba, which was also directly hit by Hurricane Ike.

One important difference between the situations of 2004 and 2008 was the government's preparedness and response. In 2004 Haiti was under the administration of a foreign-picked interim government; NGOs played such a heavy role at this time that people called it a "nongovernmental government." Several individuals spoke of their experience in the 2008 humanitarian response; Lesly recalled that "there were many, many, many foreigners. *The departmental delegate at that time was doing his job well.*"[7] Michèle Pierre-Louis, longtime president of the George Soros-supported FOKAL, the Foundation of Knowledge and Freedom, was named prime minister on September 5, days before Ike skirted Haiti. With years of experience in the NGO world, she was able to build bridges to this NGO sector but was viewed with suspicion by the political establishment. Parliament, dominated by the party of President René Préval, spent months interviewing her. She went to Parliament so often that she was called *Pap Padap*, the name for Haiti's newly implanted phone company Digicel's new recharge program. Her biggest opponent, who had engineered Alexis's ouster, was Senator Youri Latortue, who represented Gonaïves and was the cousin of the interim prime minister Gérard Latortue in 2004, who also hailed from the "City of Independence." In part, the string of disasters forced the issue; many people of Gonaïves were again under water for the second time in four years.

All humanitarian staff who worked in Gonaïves in 2008 reported a greater sense of solidarity. NGO staff met as "clusters," according to their sectorial expertise. This was to become a blueprint after Haiti's earthquake, a "lessons learned" in Aceh, Indonesia, in the post-tsunami experience. According to Widner, who had been working in NGOs since 1997, even if there wasn't a cluster, NGOs voluntarily shared information with one another: "I knew the amount of food World Vision would receive for the year for Haiti. I knew the amount of food CRS would receive. I knew the amount of food SAVE would receive. I knew the amount food CARE would receive." Widner even discussed sharing of resources, a program they called "Call Forward" (in English). "If there was a delay in receiving food, I could even borrow from SAVE because I knew the amount of food they had. They could borrow when we needed. Moreover, we shared the same warehouse." Reflecting on this situation, Lesly recalled, "The solidarity I experienced in Gonaïves, I do not see it here in Port-au-Prince after the earthquake. I just see that each institution wants to show that it is the one that does such and such things." What is it about the earthquake that explains this difference in solidarity? Lesly hints that it might be about visibility. Gonaïves is a smaller city, and the areas affected in 2008 were more rural. One difference could be the scale, with many more actors. Lesly, who switched NGO employers after the earthquake, disagreed: "I don't think there is any obstacle. There needs to be the will." Lesly, like all other Haitians working in middle management, held the Haitian government responsible as well as NGOs.

Though the differences between the two humanitarian responses were instructive, people didn't recall only positive experiences from 2008. Widner described a heated debate following a relocation his NGO conducted. On the request of the parish priest, the NGO that Widner and Lesly had worked for moved people off the cathedral grounds in advance of the *fèt chanpèt*, the patron saint festival for Gonaïves. Both Widner and Lesly take credit for the idea of cash assistance, what was to become the 16/6 model. They gave out 6,000 gourdes (about $150) for people to fix up their houses or find apartments. Three days later, with individuals identifying their own "solutions," they gave an additional 4,000 gourdes ($100) and a kit that included food, utensils, and housewares. Lesly recalls cooperation, but Widner bristled as he retold the story:

The next Monday we went to a cluster meeting. Everybody presented what they had done and I presented what I had done. An employee of another NGO was mad at me. The man was upset. He insulted me. He used some pretty foul language.

When I was done presenting the report, I removed my NGO jacket. I told him, I was talking to you as an NGO employee. Now, I am going to speak as a Haitian. I told him they spent four months talking, saying nothing, to relocate people living in the camp. There are 770 families living in the camp, dying under the furnace of the sun. You can't do anything to help them. I asked him if the reason why he talked so much was because he wants us to leave those people in the camp, so you could have a job, or I don't know.

So he tells me that I am being fresh.

I said yes, I am fresh. I'm very sensitive to Haitians. I told him I like and I appreciate the work NGOs are doing. But never dare to talk this way in my presence as Haitian. I never came to any meetings here anymore.

Widner left this NGO months later to work for another. Several things are noteworthy in this passage. First, Widner was the person who was most supportive of NGOs I interviewed, as expressed many times: "As a Haitian, before criticizing an NGO I should help them to perform well." Yet here, his critique of other NGOs resembled that of Liza and other people noted in the previous chapter, that NGOs are making money off of people's misery. Ironically, this cash assistance was to later be hailed by Emily and other foreign NGO workers as the best thing they've done for beneficiaries, yet when the idea was first unveiled (in Haiti—there was some experimentation in Aceh), it triggered a heated reaction. Now, particularly after the Haiti earthquake experience, cash assistance is thought of as a central tool in the humanitarian toolkit. Widner's testimony also brings out competition between NGOs, which Lesly also acknowledged: "This spirit of solidarity has always existed, and this competition has always been around, even though it wasn't revealed."

What about the earthquake encouraged competition instead of solidarity on the part of NGOs? One obvious difference is in the words of Geralda, a Haiti director for an international NGO: "Well, the main change that occurred is known to everyone. There was an invasion of the country, in particular by international NGOs." This language of "invasion" has wide currency since at least 1997, when Sauveur Pierre Etienne published a treatise called *Haiti: Invasion of NGOs* (Étienne 1997). Geralda has worked in NGOs for decades; something about the post-earthquake was qualitatively different. To Geralda, like Sonson, it was the number of foreign workers in these NGOs.

Expatriate "Colonization"

Even someone like Widner who generally defends NGOs has limits, especially when being insulted by a foreigner. All Haitian employees who had experience in the office shared stories of their frustrations at what they took to be mistreatment by their foreign coworkers. The most visible insult was the differential treatment and salaries. At the going-away party for Julie, Mme. Auguste's Canadian supervisor Julie was crying. The driver told Mme. Auguste, "'Yes, she should cry, she makes $7,500 a month.' Not to mention cars, boyfriend for free. Even housing. And I said to myself, 'That's how big her salary was?' I think that 75 percent of our budget goes to those people." People with the information— often the driver, who is sent to deposit checks—reported that the difference in salaries was equivalent to a Haitian staff earning in "Haitian dollars" while the expats make in Mme. Auguste's words, "good, real dollars. Green dollars." Noted in chapter 1, the "Haitian dollar" doesn't exist, referring to one of the first decisions from U.S.-supported Finance Minister Lesly Delatour, who floated Haiti's currency in 1986. It had been fixed to 5 gourdes to the dollar. So a "Haitian dollar" is 5 gourdes. Despite many activists' nationalist railing against the term, many people use it. After the earthquake the exchange rate was about 42 gourdes to the dollar, floating up to 45 by mid-2014 and 53 in August 2015. In other words, Haitian staff were being paid an eighth to a ninth of an expat's salary. This inequality is far from unique to Haiti, as Peter Redfield (2013) discusses: this extreme disparity, though insulting to local staff, results from real inequalities within the global economy.

The inequality and what many Haitian staff took to be discrimination did not end in the salaries. Sonson's quote that opened this chapter identified a range of nontaxable benefits like a car, driver, and a housing allowance. At least eight international NGOs paid a monthly housing allowance of $2,500. By contrast, the monthly rent for the three-bedroom flat I share with a Belgian is around $300 (almost twice our two-bedroom before the earthquake). True, this doesn't include utilities or Internet, but the figure again represents a warped reality, to the benefit of the lucky landlord whose house remained standing after January 12. At the National Forum on NGOs in October 2013, I shared this $2,500 figure to a room of around three hundred professionals, most of whom worked for international NGOs. At the end of the presentation a Haitian woman about my age came to talk with me about this figure. I was braced for the critique, but as she was handing me her card, she explained that the foreign national director of her NGO received a monthly allowance of $8,000. In addition to being insulting, the national director's lavish housing allowance triggered a second displacement, as Geralda and others note: what can be called a "humanitarian gentrification" (Büscher and Vlassenroot 2010; Steineke 2012). In addition, until the U.S. government removed Haiti from the list of "dangerous" countries on January 1, 2014,[8] foreign staffers also earned a "hazard pay" bonus for working in Haiti, also not taxable. Mme. Auguste also slipped in a critique of the way many foreign workers took in Haitian lovers for the duration of their tour in Haiti, also noted in Raoul Peck's (2013) Assistance Mortelle (*Fatal Assistance*). The material benefits are not the only signs of discrimination to Haitian NGO staff, as Mme. Auguste outlined: "When you also consider all their advantages, for example they have access to cars at any time. They do whatever they want. But you who work in the field, they leave with the cars. You don't have access." NGO vehicles were also used after hours, often parked outside of bars, high-end hotels, or the beach. This was a common theme, often repeated during interviews: Daniel noted the use of computer and other equipment, which his foreign colleagues have access to at any time. As explanation, a couple of foreign staff pointed to the policies to root out corruption.

Several Haitian staff theorized that at least a significant part of the explanation for this "colonization" was the global recession and a lack of good jobs for youth in donor countries. Except for Widner, all middle and senior management commented on the fact that their foreign counterparts were young, a fact also noted by Ricardo Seitenfus, a Brazilian professor serving as representative to the

Organization of American States (Robert 2010; Seitenfus 2015). Lesly explained, "And that's frustrating when you are a professional. You have a lot of experience, but it's like someone coming as an intern." But at least in their interviews with me, their foreign colleagues' age by itself wasn't the problem, as Daniel disentangles: "I don't mind that they're young, provided they have the capacity. What I don't like is when the person has no capacity. And that person is the one who leads you to error. That makes me upset! Not only because of the consequences it will have on the country, but also because I could do a better job."

Leaving aside Daniel's lapse in modesty, his statement suggests that expat youths' lack of capacity wouldn't pose a problem to the Haitian staff were it not for the hierarchy within the NGOs. Lesly, who himself left in 2013 to work abroad, said, "*I don't have any problem with the expatriates. On the contrary, I have a very good relationship with expatriates.*[9] But you feel that it's true that there's a problem with resources in Haiti, local resources are under-utilized." At the time of the earthquake, Lesly had had six years of experience working within this NGO, including humanitarian response. This hierarchy also shaped a division of labor wherein field staff were almost entirely Haitian and decision makers were predominantly foreign, as Geralda explained: "So if you conduct a survey today on the NGOs who operated in Haiti, you'll see that 99 percent of the managers were foreign, and all the Haitians were in subordinate positions. Even the highly qualified Haitians." Several people expressed this simply: if you're Haitian you're in the field, if you're *blan* you're at LogBase. LogBase was the Logistics Base for MINUSTAH, the UN troops, inside the international airport. LogBase was where nearly all cluster meetings were held, in English (Klarreich and Polman 2012; Miles 2012).

This role and spatial separation means that some of the biggest communication and coordination problems occurred *within* NGOs. Mme. Auguste's boss Julie did not speak Haitian, and Mme. Auguste did not speak English. This distance was often magnified by humanitarian agencies' specific policies, as Mme. Auguste explained: "Sometimes [Julie] comes, she drops by, but most of the time they're afraid. They say things like the United Nations told them not to go there. The United Nations told you not to do this. They use the United Nations as an excuse." The double standard is not lost on people like Mme. Auguste: Haitian staff can risk their lives to go to these very same places. In addition to this discriminatory treatment, Haitian staff are concerned that policies like these have a bad effect on decision making because the people empowered to make decisions are prevented from contact with the beneficiary population. Therefore if anyone is to be a "voice" of the "voiceless," as IOM un-ironically termed IDPs (Kaussen 2012), it is entirely up to Haitian staff who can translate the population's concerns upward, which as Daniel pointed out is rendered more difficult because middle managers might be afraid of losing their jobs. Sonson, decidedly not afraid for his job, did speak out but was reprimanded for doing so. The "infraction" was minor: "On September 24, 2010, there was a big wind, a kind of tornado. It destroyed three T-shelters [temporary shelters], but imagine, I had to write a report. I reported about the three T-shelters, that's it. *But the president's representative was not,*[10] he was upset because I reported about these three shelters."

Why would foreign NGO staff not want to report on damage? The effect of this is chilling: What else that went up the chain of command is going unreported? What else is simply not going up the chain? Sonson is one of the few Haitian people in his position; one wonders whether foreign evaluation staff would be more or less likely to engage in self-censorship, but the pressure to censor the bad news in Sonson's retelling came clearly from his foreign boss. In large part this explains the disconnect, the cognitive dissonance when reading stories like Josselyn's, Maud's, or Nadine's (or for those of us fortunate enough, visiting the camps) and reading the vast majority of blogs written by public relations staff detailing the good work of this or that agency. More banal, it partially explains a system of poor communications that led to poor decisions.

Cultural Imperialism

This breakdown of communication and the hierarchies wherein less experienced foreign staff are tasked with making decisions without knowing the realities in the field often leads to frustration and ultimately, as Sonson outlined at the beginning of the chapter, to waste of money. This is especially the case during situations when the divisions between deciders and implementers (not to mention the beneficiary population) are cultural as well as social. When I worked in local nonprofits in the mid-1990s, "cultural competence" came into vogue to describe this situation, which some of my colleagues, activists of color, derided as tokenism. Misunderstanding the beneficiary populations, too many expat NGO staff did not attempt to gain cultural competence. Expats often undervalued and underused the experience of their Haitian subordinates, as Lesly lamented, to gain access to the latter's competence. More often, as the following stories attest, inexperienced foreign supervisors took the approach of "schooling" Haitian people. This is a situation beyond a lack of cultural competence wherein expats often fail to notice, or inquire about, Haitian culture. Like all human beings, foreign aid workers have cultures and systems of knowledge of their own, often invisible to them. This cultural baggage is usually carry-on, not checked.

In his eight years of experience, Sonson has come to see NGOs as having a distinct system of knowledge: "The NGOs have their own expertise. There is a type of NGO experience." Daniel referred to this as a "secret society." Even front-line staff like Gabrielle noticed a lack of cultural specificity: "The training they gave is not really adapted to Haiti. It's a training for a country where all necessary structures are in place, a developed country. In Haiti, the realities are different from the training we received." The process of training new employees or potential volunteers is the first point of contact; it is also a cultural exchange, with neophytes often treated as empty vessels for trainers to fill with their own, culturally specific, foreign, knowledge, what Paolo Freire (1985) termed the "banking model." It is an attempt at enculturation, though not usually explicit, because the knowledge conferred is ostensibly universal. Humanitarianism, like its cousin human rights, presuppose a universal subject of "human" (Agier 2010; Barnett 2011; Bornstein and Redfield 2011; Fassin 2012). People like Geralda acknowledge the importance of specific humanitarian knowledge or capacity, but in the end this knowledge needs to be part of a larger vision: "We should not forget that a humanitarian professional is very focused: the professional has a specific capacity on particular humanitarian issues, but has nothing to do with strategic vision." She continues this analysis in the next chapter.

Problems arise when foreign aid workers attempt to impose their own culturally specific ideas, norms, and standards when making decisions without considering the local cultural context. Lesly recalled:

> You find some neophyte foreigners who come and they tell you . . . I remember
> that I had a big discussion with my supervisor, an American woman. She wanted
> our intervention to be done a certain way. I told her that it couldn't be like that.
> It wouldn't be good for the institution or beneficiaries. It would be good for no
> one. She said that there was experience in such and such country. I said no; each
> country has its own realities. Haiti's conditions are different from Afghanistan,
> different from Africa. I explained everything to her. Despite that, since she was
> my boss, she decided to do it. I said, "You can do it as you wish, but I myself
> object to that. I'll carry out what you ask me to but remember what I told you."
> She did it, then . . . protests. Protests. Afterward, she said that I was right.

In Lesly's narrative, her supervisor just wanted to do something. When the agency had only a handful of items to distribute even though there were hundreds of families in need, she felt the urge to just give what she had. This impulse was understandable. But when faced with Lesly's objections, she dug her heels and cited other situations. She thought she could isolate individual families for the purposes of the distribution. As a Haitian, Lesly knew otherwise and advised strongly against it. In the end he respected the institutional hierarchy and did what he was told, being "led to error" in Daniel's words. In the end, this U.S. employee conceded that local knowledge is important.

Because *participation* has been a buzzword of the aid industry for some time (for example, Clark 1992; Cooke and Kothari 2001; Hewamanne 2006; Hickey and Mohan 2004), most people who work for donors and NGOs give at least lip service to its importance. But when faced with sometimes difficult choices about the best way to proceed, some professionals "stick to their guns" and "do what feels right," said a German aid worker. At least Lesly was able to educate his supervisor, but at what cost? Lesly mentioned "protests"—if there were other long-term impacts he either didn't know or didn't tell me. Avoidable errors that result from a hierarchical system in which even technically competent foreign individuals fail to listen to their local subordinates in giving advice are at the root cultural imperialism, with a power imbalance between the cultural frames and knowledge systems of decision maker and implementer (and beneficiary population). This was Mme. Auguste's biggest concern:

> Remember this was all last minute. Julie told me we will need wall lights, this and that. I asked, "Didn't we talk about that?" She told me "Yeah, the Viva Rio people are going to do this and that," but she didn't tell me that they charged too much. And I said, "But Julie, I am a field coordinator. I know what the issues are. You can't do things without letting me know." I told her that the guys who work in Cité Soleil, Delmas 2, dangerous areas, they are the ones working with those populations, so they are in a better position to choose their own people to do the job. It's for their own safety.
>
> So eventually she let me, and we gave them contracts for the job. Then one day Julie sent for me to tell me to tell them where to hang up the banners. I told the messenger that she needed to speak with me in person. She never came.
>
> Then, on day, I was surprised to see the banners up in the streets. We had proposed billboards: big, visible billboards. This forced me to negotiate so they could stay up. Because right after these banners were put up, some people tried to tear them down. You see what I mean? They're in the community, they could have made their own decisions and benefited from a little job. But they saw just like I did one day that the banners were put up, and not even in the most visible places. So I'm not surprised they tried to take the banners down.

Unlike Lesly's supervisor, Julie ignored Mme. Auguste's attempts at an intervention. In Mme. Auguste's retelling, Julie was simply asserting her authority. Mme. Auguste reacted differently than Lesly: she put up resistance, attempting to force Julie to come talk with her directly. Mme. Auguste is at least twenty years older than Lesly, and this was her fifth employer. The institution's education campaign fell flat on its face. No one saw the banners. But this incident took a toll on Mme. Auguste's relationship with the community, as well as Viva Rio's, but Julie was unaffected; she left the country. Implied in Mme. Auguste's discussion about working with local communities in dangerous areas is a threat of violence. Incidents like these, with local leaders cut out of a project, are part of the reason why it was not hard to see protests against a particular NGO, graffiti detailing a critique against a particular NGO, or—Down with all NGOs—or disaffected individuals hurling rocks at aid agencies' big white SUVs as they pass by, or as in Plas Lapè after what the population took to be an insult.

In addition to contributing to project failure and stoking conflict, this cultural imperialism played a role in changing local culture. Referring to the T-shelters built by the NGO where he worked, Sonson said, "They've changed the landscape of the country. Like when you look at them, we call them a cynic view or a panoramic view." Like their name implies, T-shelters, made of plywood, a material that had to be imported, are not intended to last. They are not "sustainable." According to the World Bank's report on housing following disasters, this solution is neither cost-effective nor good for the local environment or economy (Jha et al. 2010). Wendy, a European employed in the UN shelter cluster, threw up her hands when discussing T-shelters. They are costly, fundamentally disempowering, and are forcing another displacement because they take up a larger footprint (while offering only slightly more living space) and cannot be built "stacked," multistory.

Concluding this part of his analysis, Sonson said simply, "Haitians are now starting to develop another culture." In part this is deliberate strategy, especially during training sessions. This is even true of NGOs that consider themselves to be alternative, like Daniel's employer:

> Well, for example I did training on good governance. It was terrible. I am intervening on a concept where a group of institutions come and give you criteria. They tell you this is how to have good governance in your country. They don't take into account the historical perspective of the country, the relationships of dependence between countries. They force you to talk about these criteria. They tell you transparency, because for them it's the easiest thing about good governance.
>
> It's difficult to succeed in doing this for grassroots associations. The model just shows the sponsoring NGO [and country] off as great and they want you to tell the grassroots organizations to function like that. You will decide for them, and they should follow that. That creates problems.

This training is explicitly about changing the culture to fix what some foreign agencies see as deficient in Haitian culture. For the past decade Haiti has been at or near the top of World Bank–founded Transparency International's list of most corrupt countries in the world. The measurement is the "corruption perception index," asking owners of big businesses what they think of the government (Sampson 2010). Taking this statement as unqualified truth, many foreign aid workers brought this up in informal conversations. Even admitting that there is a problem in this arena, as many Haitian people do, a foreign NGO imposing values and definitions about democracy or good governance of a European country, a former colonial power, is hypocritical and problematic. The U.S. government, for example, was shut down in 2013 when Republican members of the House attempted to pressure Obama to un-do "Obamacare." The training fetishizes the outcome of generations of social struggle and concessions made in a law, or legal framework, that can be used as a "check-the-box" legitimation in the end. Selecting transparency above all other elements of good governance—equality, participation, active citizen engagement, or deliberation—is not only easy, foreign NGOs don't, in the words of one NGO worker, "practice what they preach." Though they may be transparent to their foreign donor governments, less so to taxpayers, foreign NGOs are far from transparent to the Haitian people.

Most middle management staff at NGOs also brought up cultural changes resulting from the way in which humanitarian aid was delivered. In Sonson's words, "Because of the presence of the NGOs, the population has developed certain habits." Sonson wasn't talking only about the rise in *assistancialisme* or *mandyansite*, becoming dependent or begging. Many people from different segments of society derided the "yellow T-shirt" phenomenon. Since the beginning of cash-for-work assistance programs, which several people decried for their lack of effectiveness (for example, Ayiti Kale Je 2010), commentators have noted that independent civic activity diminished. Teams were often identifiable by their identical yellow T-shirts, and were paid to do very minor and often degrading tasks. Before the earthquake it was possible to see neighborhood associations engaged in *konbit*, collective labor, working on infrastructural issues like fixing potholes in the street or hauling trash. Now it seems to many that people won't do this kind of work if they didn't have yellow T-shirts, if they weren't paid. Pierre's finger-wagging to the population of the camp was about this. Geralda assessed, "The cash-for-work program supports activities that don't help to construct, whereas it could help create sustainable infrastructure." Going further, she said, "People need jobs to meet their needs, but the question is, what kind of job? A dignified job which helps them feel like people, to help them make decisions in what they're doing, a job that can help you grow."

Several Haitian NGO staff commented on this problem not just for the beneficiary population but for themselves. Despite billions of dollars in aid, the lasting impact in terms of human capacity is limited by the inequality and lack of respect for Haitian staff or accessing local knowledge, as Sonson explained: "Experience can only be acquired through practice. There's no way I can acquire experience, so the next time this happens, you reduced my response capacity because you didn't allow me to learn lessons." This lack of knowledge transfer is, if not by design, then a predictable outcome of the hierarchical relationship within international NGO offices. Mme. Auguste offered an example: "There was a Latino, he really knew the equipment, but he left. He didn't leave any Haitian technician that could handle the equipment. So it's like he left and only another *blan* can come." Though this person may not have intended it, he produced a situation of dependency. Haitian staff are left wondering if this was out of a lack of respect or the protection of another job for a comparatively high-paid foreign staff.

As a deputy director of a Haitian NGO put it, "The problem isn't the presence of NGOs but it how they distributed aid, the management." For example, an NGO had been working with programs relating to children because of their mission and organizational history. "After January 12 they did not work with children anymore, we found them working on agriculture. Instead of reinforcing the capacity of this community, you are destroying it." This NGO, like many others, was "following the money." Haitian people who work for NGOs have a wealth of experience, suggestions, and analyses that unfortunately tend to be marginalized and ignored; this certainly happened with the "colonialism" that followed the earthquake. This silencing is a result of a culture being less valued by foreign aid agencies and foreign staff.

PROGNOSIS

So what happens when the next disaster hits? Unfortunately Haiti, in the middle of the Caribbean "Hurricane Alley," was ranked the third most vulnerable country to climate change (Kreft and Eckstein 2013). It also sits on top of two major fault lines; seismologists warn that kinetic energy that was not released on January 12 will eventually lead to another large-scale event. From the vantage point of Haitian people employed by international NGOs, this chapter offers a sobering assessment of long-term impacts of this "colonization," as Sonson put it. Despite their good intentions, expats who descended on Haiti after the earthquake inherited and reproduced a hierarchy that minimized Haitian knowledge and the staff that possessed it. Though it is certainly not universally true, as we will see in the next chapter, many expats were far less experienced than the Haitian people who worked under them. Even those with specialties and experience in humanitarianism lacked local knowledge. Why did many international NGOs devalue Haitian staff and by extension, culture and local knowledge? What kind of system rewards this inequality? Sonson offers a clue: "There is a type of culture, a rapport they have with the donors."

Though it is true that Sonson and others are bristling at what could be called "expatronizing," foreign workers' condescension, the problem also lies with the model itself. Analyses from Daniel, Lesly, and Mme. Auguste suggest that foreign aid workers attempt to "add culture and stir," maybe adding some local referents and slang terms, but fundamentally the ideas, interventions, and structures, remain foreign (see also Kaussen forthcoming). Why smart, well-intentioned individuals continue to make these same errors suggests a deeper problem: cultural imperialism.

As Sonson voiced, the continued assertion of foreign values, worldviews, and structures suggests that it is makes sense to think in terms of an "NGO culture." In effect, the cultural competency required is fluency in English (or Spanish, or German) and experience interfacing with foreign donor agencies. The fluency in NGO culture, audit culture, trumped understanding the beneficiary population. This suggests "genetic" flaws within the system, problems within the model itself. Drawing from interviews with foreign NGO staff and directors of NGOs, the final chapter in the book attempts to uncover why.

8 · *FOTOKOPI*

Imperialism's Carbon Copy

We should never forget that all these actions are the result of a spirit of generosity and solidarity to help rebuild Haiti. The international community expressed a great solidarity, and the only channel they wanted to use to express this solidarity was NGOs.

Everybody referred to the evaluation of the tsunami in Indonesia. And everybody agreed that in order for reconstruction to work, the local population must stand up and participate. The local government must take leadership of the reconstruction. Despite the publication of these studies very soon after the earthquake, they have never been put into practice.

Humanitarian principles say that the dignity of human beings in vulnerable situations must be respected, but respecting dignity has different aspects. One of them is their capacity to decide, the capacity to stop giving out aid so they can respond with their own means. This humanitarian response here, totally without control, consultation, or participation from the population in the actions and decision-making process, really weakened society even more.

For a long time, the dominant language of the country was English. In a context where English was the dominant language in the decision-making process, in a context where all planning was done in English, and considering cultural aspects were ignored, it was crystal clear that Haitians were outside of everything.

Water distribution began with the international community bringing their own water. Then, they started buying local water trucks, making a few people rich, instead of building water systems that could still be useful to us today. When you distribute water with trucks only, you are spending

millions, but you have to provide water on a daily basis. When the millions are gone, the people don't have drinking water and are exposed once
again to water-related diseases. So you haven't done anything to help them
advance to another stage.

This balance is necessary between long-term work and humanitarian
response that must be quick and must reach the maximum affected people.

There's a total separation: this one is a humanitarian worker, and that one
is a development worker. That's why strategies developed for humanitarian
response are totally opposed to development strategies. Debates are under
way today against this approach, but despite these debates, the separation is
purely mechanical. This mechanical separation damages a country's development, the life of a people, particularly the Haitian people.

International NGOs are leading the reconstruction. They lost all language and approach that we, as international NGOs, are here for back-up
and support. So they are in direct competition in the reconstruction. I know
a lot of cases today wherein either the local NGO can't implement the
project or the project is abandoned because there are conflicts, because the
international NGO won't give up its visibility. It won't give up taking the
lead in decision-making.

Several international NGOs opened an office here! This is direct competition: they cut funding for local NGOs when they come and sit, or the local
NGOs become just a subcontractor for work that has already begun.

An international NGO that captures an amount of money will not succeed in the competition if it doesn't display its flag well hoisted in the center
of Champ-de-Mars [the national palace] or in the center of Léogâne [city
nearest the epicenter]. If funds pass through a national organization, it will
not have this visibility to be able to engage this fierce competition with other
NGOs also looking to capture that same money.

This gaping inequality creates an exodus of qualified professionals from
national NGOs. As soon as they find an opportunity to go, they go, or
people sometimes stop working for a national NGO to sell their labor to an
international NGO.

—Geralda

Geralda is a rarity: one of a scant handful of Haitians who were
national directors for an international NGO. Her perspective is shaped by more
than two decades of experience working in the sector. Geralda's is a structural
analysis. Residents in Karade called UN troops stationed there *fotokopi*—
"photocopies"—because it is as if they hung on the wall, doing nothing (Ulcena
2013). This is an appropriate metaphor for the continuing military occupation

and the proliferation—and competition—of imperialist interests. The plan for Haiti was to repeat the successes in Aceh, Indonesia, while continuing the same failed policies that brought Haiti to the brink of disaster. Many individuals working in the postquake response had in fact come fresh from Aceh with their supposedly universal, generalizable experience, dubbed "Humanitarianism 2.0." By implication of the supposed universal applicability, failures in delivery were not attributed to the model but to "Haitian culture." This chapter analyzes the many differences in context, notably the heavy imprint of the United States and its imposition of what many in Haiti call "the American Plan" (for example, Deshommes 2006; Lwijis 2009), which led to a diminishing of state functions and the creation of the "Republic of NGOs." Provincializing "Western" humanitarianism (Chakrabarty 2007), this chapter analyzes the cultural specificity of the humanitarian toolkit.

This chapter gives voice to the many foreign individuals working for the earthquake response in one way or another. They are a diverse group, like the agencies that employ them. Similarly, their analyses are wide ranging, some more critical and reflexive than others. Although some workers identified technical problems of aid delivery—failures of coordination, Haiti's weak state, and urban challenges—some began to question the model itself. Humanitarian action requires the "photo op"—in Geralda's words, planting the flag—in no small part because of the ever-difficult scramble for funding, which reinforces competition and rewards "just doing something" at the expense of local initiative. The postquake case outlines a need for humanitarian action to be subsumed under a locally defined development and reconstruction plan. Because of Haiti's high profile, these core logics, structures, and "cultures" of aid are more visible, perhaps, than other humanitarian responses.

Even more so than in Haitian NGO staff, there is a pronounced difference between workers fresh from college and those with decades of experience in the field. My own identity as an activist and a blogger definitely shaped not only what people said to me but whether they would talk with me at all. Several twentysomethings had canceled their meetings with me, which I assume was because of a quick Google search on my name. It is possible that some people had heard of me because of a blog or one of a few reports disseminated, or had seen my performance in a documentary video—*Haiti: Where Did the Money Go?*—that was highly critical of the aid response. The interview with me was conducted the week after my intense summer 2010 research. One particularly poignant image from the film—which ends with my "if-then" statement of "Cut the funding"—is of a young, white, bikini-clad aid worker taking her rum punch back to her poolside lounge chair. The conversation got nasty. Representatives of the Red Cross stormed into a January 2012 congressional briefing with two members of Congress present to express their outrage and attack the filmmaker, Michele

Mitchell, and by extension the rest of us. Although this succeeded in derailing the conversation (this was the first I had seen of the film), it also made the Red Cross look bad in front of Congress. Similarly, the Red Cross's vitriolic response on the Internet raised the film's profile. I was similarly collateral damage at a Duke humanitarian conference in a clash between AP correspondent Jonathan Katz and someone who had worked for J/PHRO, Sean Penn's agency, as the latter attacked all who dared to question the humanitarian system, including me. The two tweeted past one another. Accomplished Haitian filmmaker Raoul Peck offered his own critical analysis in *Fatal Assistance*.

I discuss these difficulties in methods classes to interrogate how one's activist identities can affect research, a poignant example of reflexivity: research participants do size us up (Checker, Davis, and Schuller 2014; Ulysse 2002). It certainly also highlights difficulties of what Laura Nader (1969) called "studying up." My advisors admonished me to maintain a low profile during the 2004 coup and its aftermath; in hindsight I am grateful. My increasing visibility came with greater costs to my collaborators in Haiti (Schuller 2010b). It's important, however, not to overstate the case. For example, a graduate student from France also failed to gain access to this closed system—aid veteran Jessica called this a "bubble"—in the summer of 2012. He tried chatting people up in the gyms, meeting people at hotel bars during happy hour, and so on. People's first question was, "Which agency do you work for?" This question suggests whatever differences between *enstans*/agencies—the UN system, other donors, or NGOs—were less important than being an aid worker or not. More important, people in their forties and fifties, with years and sometimes decades of experience in the field, who were definitely not afraid of losing their jobs and who had other humanitarian situations to compare this experience to, saw me as a vehicle to document their lessons learned. Said one, "That's your job." Some wanted to help sharpen my analysis, to correct what they saw as incomplete, and others to push me further. Some explicitly referred to the *Huffington Post* and U.S. Congress, hoping that I could carry their specific critique or suggestion somewhere. Differences between veterans and twentysomethings were stark indeed. Consequently, as a result, I have more critical analyses from veterans, people who are aware of the shortcomings of the humanitarian response and even their own agencies.

"OFF THE RECORD": DISCUSSIONS WITH NEW AGENCY STAFF

Because most conversations with newer staff were "off the record" (by which staff meant unrecorded), I can only paraphrase. Because of this, and because of several people's refusal to participate in the research, this is the segment for which I have the least material. I attempted a bottom-up approach, covering at least the agencies responsible for managing or providing aid to the eight camps in the study. For the most part, I was successful. One particularly defensive agency staff refused. The person, responsible for an admittedly complex relocation for Plas Lapè, had it in her head that I gave a false name—possibly a result of the secretary's confusion. To even think of this would be ridiculous, even if I didn't have a human subjects protocol and a granting agency. I couldn't correct this impression, even after I sent my funded NSF proposal to her, and having a twenty-five-minute conversation with her supervisor about it, until my minutes ran out on my phone (he questioned the study's value, not its methodology). When I showed up to a community meeting at Jean Robert's (a committee leader's) invitation, the staff member adamantly refused my presence. Not wanting to create a stir and thus problems for Jean Robert, the committee, and the population needing relocation assistance, I backed down. This was my last exchange with this individual and agency. I could have persisted: this agency is a member of the Sphere collaborative, one of whose pillars is transparency and principles to be open to research. I could imagine how difficult it was for the staff member, who was handed this job without experience in the middle of a dicey situation. Her predecessor, whom at least a couple of residents praised, had a much longer connection to Haiti than me. But still, this is a hole in understanding one of the most complex camps in the study.

Looking over the interview transcripts it seems all foreign staff, not only the veterans, were keen on getting a message across. Most twentysomethings ended with a plea for understanding that this program is working or doing good. Most offered a good amount of detail about the process of their interventions; a few who conducted research—"satisfaction surveys"—imparted this as well, also in good detail. However, almost no one answered the innocuous question about "what lessons did you learn through your experience?" One said that the program hadn't ended yet, others mentioned they didn't have time to think, and a couple had nothing to say, one because he just imagined himself to be just a worker in the field, and the other just stared blankly. Given that the interviews with these newer staff tended to focus on the agency's program, there are few common points of analysis. The interviews were informative, and a few caused me to rethink some of my admittedly incomplete understandings. None of the foreign staff (a total of twelve) could speak Haitian, and a few barely French. All had college degrees, about half master's degrees. This was the first field-based job for all of the NGO employees, for some the first job after college.

People couldn't project into the future beyond their contract term; an equal number wished they could stay in Haiti past their contract to those who wanted to move on. Some reported "being bit by the Haiti bug" and "falling in love" with the country, and others expressed frustration at the inconveniences associated with poverty and a lack of resources. Some of this latter group shared their greater sensitivity for "things we take for granted" as a result of their experience in Haiti that not only included electricity, running water, Internet access, trash cleanup, and road maintenance, but also what they termed "good governance." If they felt discomfort of having black people (many twice their age) serve them as drivers, guards, maids, or cooks—particularly descendants of the only slaves that successfully drove whites out—they didn't share it with me. Some discussed frustration working with Haitian subordinates, for either being lazy, incompetent, sly, untrustworthy, or just "always trying to get something out of you." The most emotion was displayed when retelling a time in which they "caught" (usually those words) some Haitian attempting to deceive them. Taking me for being ignorant because I did not have this hierarchical relationship, being able to "fly in and out" and "only write" about the country, a couple individuals took it as their duty to educate me on "how things really worked." This sentiment suggests that some people did not understand that some of their difficulties might have been reflections of the specific nature of their relationships, their own attitudes, or both. Some examples stridently denounced as cheating might be better interpreted as a cultural logic, for example, expressing a sense of solidarity: instead of one person receiving a benefit, a person willfully bends the rules and sacrifices half of the goods in question (salary, food, and so on) to share with someone else. Some of the more circumspect of these individuals, like Emily, acknowledged cultural differences and the difficulties of communication.

Most if not all of these individuals have already moved on, out of Haiti, as this chapter is being written. Like them, I also changed jobs, and it was difficult to conduct follow-up with this group. I was wondering if, away from the glare of an admittedly critical media and distance from the daily crises of their work, they could take away some lessons for future humanitarians. The business card I gave them was for my previous employer, and I had only an e-mail exchange with two of them. Luckily, several people in their thirties and upward also shared their analyses.

"I DON'T UNDERSTAND HOW TO DO THIS": LESSONS LEARNED

Either by coincidence or reflecting a general trend, people I interviewed who worked at IOM or other coordinating agency like the United Nations rather than an NGO were at least in their thirties. All had experience working with an NGO, and all had field experience in a disaster "before Haiti happened." This quite common Freudian slip suggests that to many people who either flew into the country afterward or who couldn't but who saw the horrors on televisions or over the Internet, "Haiti" is reducible to the earthquake. More generally, it also speaks to a belief in the universal applicability of humanitarianism, where Haiti can be compared with Afghanistan, Aceh, or Myanmar/Burma. Culture in this accidentally spoken worldview is thus one of many variables, albeit an important one.

As a result of people's greater experience, midcareer humanitarians' responses were more nuanced, and usually more humble. Said William, who worked as a camp manager for an NGO after the earthquake, followed by the IOM: "I've got an undergraduate degree from Oxford, a master's degree from Columbia, and I don't understand how to do this. If someone gives you an answer that is less than a half an hour long, I mistrust it entirely." William's colleague Antonio discussed the challenges within a few "disciplines" (subfields of humanitarian specialties) within the humanitarian toolkit because they were new. IOM published a "Camp Management Toolkit" in several country offices, including Haiti. In effect, Haiti was a testing ground, a very large, complex, and highly visible laboratory for new approaches to humanitarianism. "CMAs, camp management, is a very recent job. I would say it was born in the late '90s. It's ten or fifteen years old. CCM is a class since 2005, so we are talking about six years now. So it's a relatively young discipline and there [are] a few agencies with experience in the job." More specifically, the large scale of the event and response necessitated innovation, as Antonio outlines: "Even camp management, the idea of having a roving camp manager, is something that came up in this country. The doctrine of camp management was one agency to one camp. It was here that we developed a different approach." This experimentation with the humanitarian toolkit led the United Nations to draft what they called a "Transformative Agenda."

Because all had experienced at least one other disaster as basis for comparison, their answers to the "lessons learned" question were to explain the differences between Haiti and the other situation. Likely resulting from the fact that it was the most recent mega-disaster in a "developing country" and had a response of similar scale as that of the 2004 Indian Ocean tsunami, especially Aceh, more people had experience with the 2004 tsunami response than any other. This was a good frame of reference, because Aceh and Haiti were both conflict situations before or during the natural disaster. The humanitarian response in Indonesia also involved Bill Clinton as fundraiser and cheerleader, where he first discussed "building back better." With a roll-out of new approaches to aid provision, particularly in coordination, such as the cluster system, the tsunami response hailed the release of Humanitarianism 2.0. The post-tsunami efforts, particularly in Aceh, were hailed a success, and when compared to the stratospheric promises about "building back better," the effort in Haiti looks particularly lackluster. Humanitarians with experience in both places offered three main explanations, two directly linked. The response in Haiti faltered because of poor coordination, which is linked to Haiti being a "failed state," and that Haiti's was an urban disaster.

Coordination

Coordination was cited as a major concern, which is not surprising given the oft-repeated statement that Haiti was home to ten thousand NGOs. Peter, a U.S.-based humanitarian in his fifties, working for his second NGO post-earthquake at the time of his 2012 interview, said, "In every evaluation of humanitarian response is that the coordination could be improved. So I don't want to say that, because I will sound like everybody else, but it's true." Coordination was noted early on by UN Humanitarian Coordinator Nigel Fisher and Bill Clinton, as well as scholars (for example, Zanotti 2010). Taking a cue from a lesson learned from the Aceh experience, the United Nations organized clusters, bringing together different actors—the UN system, other donors, international NGOs, and, at least in theory, the Haitian government—from the various sectors of the humanitarian response: water and sanitation, health, protection, agriculture, food aid, and so on. Agriculture was a separate cluster from emergency food aid. At least for the first two years, housing was split between three clusters, for emergency shelter (Camp Coordination and Management); temporary, or T-shelters (Shelter); and longer-term housing outside the camps (Housing Reconstruction). Gender-Based Violence was a "subcluster" of Protection. There were twelve clusters overall. All but the water and sanitation and Gender-Based Violence clusters met inside the UN Logistics Base, a military base tucked inside the international airport, called "LogBase" for short. LogBase contained large tents and later shipping containers wherein various UN agencies set up temporary offices, a grocery store, a couple of restaurants serving international fare and the U.S. dollar as the official currency (Klarreich and Polman 2012). The area was patrolled and secured by UN troops, with a solid wall, painted UN colors white and baby blue, that towered more than 6 meters high, topped with barbed wire to keep people out. Armed guards granted access, checking passports. Once cleared, visitors were sent through X-ray, metal detection, and closed-circuit television. Exiting this, they were faced with another guard tower trained down on them. Several Haitian nationals reported that they felt excluded from the space. For example, a high-ranking government official was denied access by the UN guards. Suspecting a racial and national origin bias, I twice attempted to enter without presenting my U.S. passport. Both times I was granted access.

Jessica, who first came to Haiti in March 2010 working for an NGO but was working for a UN cluster as of the 2012 interview, questioned the applicability of the cluster system to this new context: "The cluster system emerged from the disaster coordination after the tsunami, particularly in Aceh, [with] hundreds of agencies descending. Here you had a lot of actors before the earthquake. In Aceh you had hardly any." Clusters thus arose in 2005 as part of UN reform out of a particular context. In Haiti, not only were many NGOs already present, but the Haitian government already had coordination structures, called *tables sectorielles* (sector tables), in place. Some people expressed the concern that the cluster meetings were in addition to their jobs, and some NGO staff with experience before the earthquake chose to opt out. Peter outlined another reason: "A smaller number of people are easier to coordinate. Like we were talking about having different vision, policy, decisions. If you're three [agencies], you can compromise. If you're fifty, it will be more difficult to come to a decision." Despite this understanding of cluster meetings, almost everyone I talked to used the term "clusterfuck" to describe the chaotic, overwhelming, and ineffectual nature of the meetings. Several participants noted that cluster meetings were about "messaging" or sharing information about a particular service contracted by an NGO. They were, in other words, ritual spaces rather than deliberative spaces. In all but the two clusters noted, the language was English, not even French, one of the two national languages accessible to Haiti's NGO class (Miles 2012). As Geralda noted, the linguistic exclusion made it pretty clear who was imagined as the audience and who was welcome: foreign aid workers. Like *kach-fò-wòk* (cash-for-work) and *chèltè* (shelter), the word *klòstè*, a Haitian pronunciation of "cluster," was used among the NGO class, but fewer than 1 percent of IDP camp residents knew what that meant or had even heard of it. Antonio said candidly, "We don't include IDPs in our discussions" (see also Panchang 2012).

Jessica acknowledges another perspective and definition of the word *coordination*: "Looking at coordination through the eyes of the international community and from the government is totally different." Indeed, understandings of the Haitian government differed from that of foreign agencies. The minister of planning and foreign cooperation, who since 2009 has been also the prime minister, has a mandate to coordinate foreign aid response. Students have different interpretations about this position's strategic centrality: given that foreign aid is where the money is, some more cynical students theorized that a head of government would want to have access to skim from the top and/or name contractors. Others argued that this was a reflection of *Realpolitik*, that a prime minister is only as good as the aid she or he can attract to the country, given the weak tax base. The ministry includes the Administration and Coordination of NGOs Unit, UCAONG in the original French, responsible for official definition, reconnaissance, registry, and follow-up with NGOs. After the earthquake killed the UCAONG director, Jesula was thrust to the head of this agency. According to Jesula, the public outcry against what the population saw as NGO corruption and ineffectiveness was so great that the agency felt political pressure from all levels to do something. Before the earthquake, Jesula said that in any given year anywhere between 10 and 20 percent of NGOs gave their annual report to UCAONG, required in order to maintain their tax-exempt status (among other benefits). After the earthquake, UCAONG published a list of NGOs that complied with the law in the *Nouvelliste*, the largest daily circulation newspaper, and mailed a copy to donor agencies. If an NGO received assistance from a donor, and they weren't on the list, the more powerful donors could pressure them into respecting Haitian law. This worked; Jesula estimated that more than half of NGOs complied with this requirement in 2012. Beginning in late 2011, UCAONG also organized departmental councils with local (department, Haiti's equivalent of states) representatives from donors, the Haitian government, and NGOs. At least initially, these councils were well received by all three stakeholder groups as an important space for coordination. In October 2013 UCAONG organized a First National Forum on NGOs, originally scheduled for May of that year, to have the space for dialogue but also to announce a bill revising the NGOs regulatory framework in place since 1989. According to event organizers, more than three hundred people attended, the majority international NGO staff.

"Weak State"

Several people theorized the difference in coordination in Aceh and Haiti as a direct result of the relative strength of the government. For at least a decade, Haiti has been declared a "weak state" (Rotberg 2003a and b). This phrase was repeated so often as to be a throwaway line. For some foreign staff, "weak state" seemed to have talismanic qualities, magically explaining the failures in aid delivery, just like "coordination" in some sectors of the Haitian government, and certainly the NGO Forum. Discussed in chapter 6, DINEPA, the National Directorate for Water and Sanitation (WASH), was singled out as a government agency that engaged in effective coordination: "If we consider the WASH sector, DINEPA, there was coordination between the Health Ministry and all the NGOs that work on WASH. There was a national structure, and the initiatives were coordinated, so you began to see results." For some, DINEPA was the "exception that proves the rule." WASH meetings were held in city halls across the metropolitan area. Some noted that, as a new agency, formed just before the earthquake, DINEPA's office was not downtown and under rubble, like nearly all the ministries. So therefore it could play a lead role in coordination. The destruction of government buildings was often cited as justification for foreign agencies—donors, intergovernmental organizations like the Red Cross and IOM, and NGOs—taking charge of the effort. This didn't sit well with Haitian government employees. A member of the Haitian government retorted, "So we didn't have a space to meet. That doesn't mean you exclude us from the conversation." By and large, government agencies made do with what they had. According to a foreign NGO worker, he was given the choice to meet either "in the small conference room" or "in the large conference room," indicating two different tables under trees on the ministry grounds. Though not universally true, and notwithstanding the populations' belief in government capacity noted in chapter 6, even though government buildings collapsed, the government itself continued to function.

As IOM employee Antonio explained, "Two years after the earthquake, one and a half year after the earthquake, and we still don't have a government. We still don't have the means." At the time of this interview, July 2011, Michel Martelly had just taken office as president but his first choice for prime minister was rejected (noted in chapter 4), and a second wasn't yet named. Several commentators, most visibly in Raoul Peck's *Fatal Assistance*, noted the heavy-handed role the so-called international community, especially the United States, played in bullying the government into reversing first-round election results (Blot 2012; Katz 2013; Seitenfus 2015). *Fatal Assistance* implied that Bill Clinton hand-picked Martelly, and Hillary Clinton threatened President René Préval. Senior OAS Representative Ricardo Seitenfus detailed an attempted coup d'état. In the second round, with the lowest voter turnout since Haiti's transition to democracy began, Martelly received 67 percent of the vote. Following Martelly's installation, aid began to trickle to Haiti, for example, from the U.S. government, which had pledged 1.15 billion. Almost a third was reimbursement for U.S. military and a sizeable portion was debt relief. The international community support to the Martelly administration, from Venezuela to the European Union, remained steady, despite alarming reports even from the State Department about patterns of human rights abuses.

Despite funds being sent to Haiti, the discourse of "failed state" remained. Several times in the interview, Antonio pointed to specific things that were "technically the responsibility of the government." Some expressed off the record that they would have liked very much to follow the lead of the Haitian government, but there was no government to follow. Sophie, who was working in a second national branch of the same international NGO since the earthquake, explained, "In Haiti, there is very low capacity in government in responding to situations. So the exit strategy for NGOs has been to transfer responsibility to national authority. Well, you are transferring many responsibilities to a government that does not have capacity, so there is a risk." Addressing this issue of government capacity, the Spanish government gave direct support to both DINEPA and UCAONG, believing that if coordination is important, then donors must support that role of the Haitian government. For its part, Venezuela, which outpledged even the United States, gave direct cash support—much in the form of loans—to the Haitian government through the PetroCaribe program.

However, Spain and Venezuela were exceptions; nearly all other donors continued to support NGOs headquartered in their countries or gave to a new international body. Solidifying this tendency, following the UN donor conference the end of March 2010, donors asked the Haitian Parliament to vote to dissolve itself and endorse the creation of the Interim Haiti Reconstruction Commission, the IHRC. The IHRC was composed of twenty-six members, half of them foreign, cochaired by Bill Clinton and then-Prime Minister Jean-Max Bellerive. In theory this was a symbol of shared governance. The IHRC's mandate was to review and approve projects for reconstruction. Once approved, the Haiti Reconstruction Fund had the authority to release the funds. In the words of a World Bank official, "It was the way we could convince donors to let go of the money. In effect we were holding onto it." Jessica continued her earlier line of analysis: "And everything the donors were trying to say, it was like this was some big breakthrough giving more trust to the Haitian government. I think that message was lost, one of the huge gaps in perspectives. Many of the donors felt that they were showing more trust, when the Haitian government saw it as not enough." The IHRC was structured in such a way that the major donors—the United States, Canada, France, and the European Union—had individual seats, while the entirety of the Caribbean Community (CARICOM) shared a seat (Willems 2012). Commentators across the political spectrum in Haiti saw the IHRC as a symbol of Haiti's sovereignty being violated (Bélizaire 2010; Willems 2012). One international aid worker reported that a senior government official characterized it as *comment est-ce qu'on va foutre la gueule du peuple haitien*, which can be translated as "How can we fuck the snout of the Haitian people?" Prime Minister Bellerive, who was to be IHRC cochair, responded to senators, "I hope you sense the dependency in this document. If you don't sense it, you should tear it up" (Dupuy 2010, 15). Several Haitian members of the IHRC denounced that they were shut out of the process of meaningful participation, publishing a scathing open letter on December 14, 2010, before a meeting in the Dominican Republic when borders were closed to Haitian people because of the cholera epidemic caused by the United Nations.[2] At least it was more open, to some, reflecting the reality of an occupation: UN troops on the ground since 2004 and an even longer foreign control of finances and aid. Testifying to this exclusion, even fewer IDPs had heard of the IHRC, known in French as CIRH, than even clusters. One foreign aid worker simply said succinctly, "The big problem of this country is Haiti." However many in Haiti view this discourse of "failed state" differently, including this organization director: "The *blan* came here after the earthquake and asked, 'where is the state?' But it's these same people, the same World Bank, IMF, USAID, European Union that forced Haiti to reduce the public sector during the 1995–1996 Structural Adjustment Programs." Possibly Haitian actors' memory is longer than foreign institutions, certainly staffed by young expats; this recalls a Haitian proverb, *bay kou bliye, pote mak sonje*. One who hits another forgets, but one with the scar remembers.

Urban Disaster

A third major "lesson learned" from the Haiti earthquake response was that it was an urban disaster. Antonio outlined the set of issues: "When you are looking at the camp in the middle of nowhere, it is a very closed environment you can control. When you are dealing with an urban environment you don't have as much control: it keeps changing and it keeps moving, and it's very different." I find it significant that he used the word *control*. He might have used the word *secure* if security or safety was the primary issue, or something like *monitor* if that was the primary concern. This statement recalls a Médecins Sans Frontièrs (MSF) worker telling Michel Agier (2010, 29) that "the camp does not need democracy in order to function." Setting aside this word choice, given that Antonio's first language is not English,[3] the fact that the earthquake struck the urban center of Haiti presented logistical challenges to the humanitarian response for which they were not prepared. Noted above, most government buildings were destroyed in the earthquake.

This is possibly one major difference between IDP and refugee camps. Refugees, officially stateless, can be moved to locations convenient to humanitarian providers. Another difference could be the proximate cause of the migration, violence or war on the one hand or a natural phenomenon like an earthquake or a hurricane (Agier 2011; Feldman 2008, 2010) on the other. Antonio did not explicitly discuss this question in his assessment of the humanitarian toolkit. In rural settings, humanitarian agencies might engage in negotiations between two warring factions but not with a multitude of individuals claiming to be landowners. The concept of humanitarian space was developed with the former set of negotiations in mind, at the macro level (Acuto 2014). As many like Antonio acknowledged, the urban nature of the disaster and response presented challenges in gaining access to camps. In the 2010 random survey of camps from the IOM database, 71 percent were on private land. By Antonio's assessment late summer 2011, 10 percent of camps were on public land: "When you're dealing with rural displacement, government usually owns the land where the camps are built. Here, the government doesn't own land and most of the land is private, so people are forced to go or relocate." As Antonio stated, this fundamentally pit two rights in direct competition: "As you know, we are dealing with two conflicting rights. The right to live in dignified conditions and the right of owners to exercise the right of private property." In the end, private property won, as the cases of forced eviction escalated, increasingly accompanied by violence.

Land tenure shaped the humanitarian response. In the 2010 study, we found that camps on public land had better access to services than those without. Camps on public land were more likely to have water (75.0 percent) than those on private land (51.8 percent), although this gap is not statistically significant.

Clinics existed in 39.1 percent of camps on state land, whereas only 12.9 percent of camps on private land did, a significant gap in services (Schuller and Levey 2014, S12). Said one humanitarian staff, "When landowners don't want us there, there's not much we can do." This at least partially explains the gap in services between camps on public and private land noted in chapter 4, which also reports that a medical team waited sheepishly outside of the St. Louis camp for authorization to enter. They were refused, so they left.

Echoing others, including Paul Farmer (2011), Antonio pointed out that "in general terms, I think we have been doing okay when it comes to responding to such a big-scale event. What I think we are not doing well is the reconstruction. By now we should have had options for people to leave the camps, many more options than we have so far." To Antonio and many others, although the humanitarian phase was a good response, the situation in Haiti remained "stuck" in this "emergency phase." Antonio continued, "If by now, we were already in the reconstruction phase and we had houses coming up and reconstruction taking place in the neighborhoods, services being moved to the neighborhoods, by now people would be moving out of the camps and it would be fine. It would be a proper progression." Putting aside the supposed naturalness of these phases for the moment, why was Haiti "stuck" in this phase? Why didn't it properly progress? One reflex within the humanitarian sector was to cast blame on individuals for gaming the system. The rhetoric was so powerful that even William recoiled, saying, "Even though I'm going to make mistakes and some scoundrel is going to get away with it, that's kind of the cost of doing business." William's approach may be fatalistic, but at least it does not contribute to Haitian exceptionalism, implying that this occurs everywhere.

Another response focused not so much on defective individuals as a defective land tenure system, again associated with the urban nature of the disaster. Several media accounts detailed difficulties to assess legal ownership given the state of the national archives and almost nonexistent cadaster, land title registry. Both Antonio and William noted that in their conversation. A couple of news stories pointed to situations in which the same parcel of land was claimed by multiple individuals, each having some written document they considered to be a title. As Antonio noted, "It has taken months to organize tools, to try to identify who was living in the house before the earthquake, and having that information validated by the community." Antonio is alluding to a local process of community enumeration piloted by the elected mayor of Carrefour (where two of the camps in the study were located, CAJIT and City Hall, Meri Dikini) and neighborhood associations. A community gets together and decides as a collective the land usage and rights to what part of the land. If there are competing claims people work it out. Although they may not have a paper with a title, they have long and detailed histories of usage, building, and improvements. Wendy, who worked on the other side of the housing issue in the Shelter Cluster, explained some of the unexpected benefits of this process:

> The value is not only that this process unblocked the reconstruction but it also created an address, with street names. People value the place names and there is a sense of place. You look at the map and all these areas are just gray, without any details or streets. Now we have that.
>
> And also with recognition they become able to pay taxes and they become stakeholders in the local government. So with a tax base and some say in it as taxpayers, they will be able to break the cycle of dependency.

This process, initiated by Haitian local government and grassroots organizations, was given support from the United Nations and replicated all over Port-au-Prince. This final lesson learned offers a positive example of a bottom-up solution, locally led, receiving international support. It directly addressed challenges associated with an urban disaster. One key reason for its success was local ownership, a core principle enshrined in several recent declarations on aid effectiveness, such as the 2005 Paris Declaration and the 2011 Busan Global Partnership for Effective Development Cooperation.

THE MODEL ITSELF

These lessons that humanitarian actors took away from Haiti—the need for coordination, the importance (or the lack) of state leadership, and the urban realities of the affected area—are not particularly earth shattering. The UN Office of the Special Envoy has already distilled these lessons on the "Lessons from Haiti" page (http://www.lessonsfromhaiti.org), and the United Nations has noted experience in Haiti as inspiring its Transformative Agenda.[4] Indeed, future humanitarian efforts would do well to heed these lessons. However, for several reasons, this book isn't done. These are critiques that leave intact the possibility that these factors are outside of the control of humanitarian agencies, that they are somehow external to humanitarian action. To continue the dialogue with Peter, one might ask why does coordination continue to be lacking? To Antonio, one might wonder why the humanitarian toolkit is so ill equipped to deal with messy urban legal frameworks and as a consequence side with elite landlords, even as some agencies win awards for their courage in negotiating with warlords?

In addition to these questions remaining unanswered, these "external" self-critiques of the humanitarian response have limited utility in addressing some of the more gripping realities articulated by Haitian "actors" (who again have their say in the conclusion). This book has presented several problems that demand interrogation of the logic behind the humanitarian impulse itself. Thankfully a handful of individuals with years and often decades of experience working in the field engaged in this self-evaluation. They mostly sought me out, although some were introduced by colleagues. These agency staff call into question the model itself, what Didier Fassin (2010, 2012) called "humanitarian reason." The first factor internal to the humanitarian enterprise that impeded progress is the photo op, the omnipresence of media. Directly related to this need for visibility, behind it, is a competition over funding. Also connected is the need to "just do something," which leads into doing *for* instead of working *with* beneficiary communities. This is a core difference in the ideology of development and humanitarian aid.

The "Photo Op"

As several analysts have noted (for example, Brauman 1993; Benthall 1993), disaster aid feeds off media coverage. Olsen et al. (2003) demonstrated a correlation in the amount of seconds allocated on prime time news to a particular disaster and the generosity of the response (see, for example, Brown and Minty 2008). The article was published before the mega-disasters of the past decade, including the 2004 Indian Ocean tsunami and Hurricane Katrina, in 2005, as well as the Haiti earthquake. Although the article didn't lay out a formula for a precise prediction of private and public donations to a humanitarian effort, the hypothesis seems validated by the differences in donations after the Haiti earthquake, the 2010 floods in Pakistan, and the "triple threat"—the earthquake, tsunami, and nuclear fallout—in 2011 in Fukushima, Japan. The Pakistan flood that displaced 20 million people was almost entirely ignored in U.S. media; only $687 million was donated, with pledges totaling just over a billion dollars. Even though Japan is one of the world's wealthiest countries, the disaster attracted 530 billion yen during the first year, almost $5 billion. Humanitarian staff, particularly those engaged in public relations or fundraising, are acutely aware of this: their organizations live (none have died so far) from media coverage. Therefore, decisions about particular courses of action on the ground are guided at least in part for the opportunity to stage a photo op. Some staff grumbled about their roles as "PR tools" even when they knew better. "Remember how your salaries are being paid," one person sardonically retold when I asked why she did things she knew to be ineffective, inefficient, or inappropriate. She left this agency a month after our interview.

This mantra, directive, or logic of visibility was evident in many sectors of the humanitarian response. Despite that T-shelters were inappropriate and created pressures that swelled the shantytowns on dangerous mountainsides, and despite that the Haitian government and the Shelter Cluster issued a moratorium in 2011, temporary shelters were still the solution of choice for several NGOs. Explaining why, Wendy argued, "It's also the most visible, providing the photo opportunity, to show off what our structures are." This logic of visibility was also behind the choice of which camps were to be closed during the controversial 16/6 relocation program. Andrea, who like William came to Haiti working for an NGO and later joined the IOM, said, "They might not be the most vulnerable sites, but they are sites with the most visibility." Aside from the Champs-de-Mars, the epicenter of the photo op across from the crumbled National Palace, which was not part of the program, these locations, including the area around the airport and the main two plazas in the suburb of Pétion-Ville, were the most highly visible to journalists. Camps were a visible reminder of poverty and the failures in reconstruction, a thorn in the side of President Martelly's slogan that "Haiti is open for business." This slogan just happened to coincide with Bill Clinton's.[5] For his part, William, who worked more directly on relocation, was unmoved by this critique: "There are humanitarian actors and donors who are very upset that the six camps have been chosen quite clearly on political grounds. My view on that is you were never going to get them to start on any other grounds other than political." The need for visibility also encouraged private water trucks instead of reinforcing public taps that existed before the earthquake, as Geralda critiqued, in part because in the camps people like Josselyn in Plas Lapè could be seen— and photographed—standing in long lines (see Figure 4.1). Recall also Josselyn's aversion to having to perform, singing and clapping hands, for the cameras. Beneficiaries' performance becomes "cred" for the humanitarian agency filming it; it becomes capital they can leverage, in effect to sell to donors for more aid, or to justify its receipt. AP journalist Jonathan Katz (2013) came close to suggesting that this tendency to play to the international media led many NGOs to force people into the camps in order to receive aid.

Wendy noted the tendency for humanitarian agencies to look for visible signs of distress and send aid there, so it would be expected that NGOs not even look for the strategic points, local providers, or local leaders. This is one reason why the international response missed a golden opportunity to decrease the vulnerability that neoliberalism engendered when 630,000 people fled the city.[6] Agencies have to be seen giving aid. This tendency was also behind a finding of our 2010 study that camps in peripheral municipalities have fewer services than those near the urban core. This might explain why CAJIT was not "found" until the food aid had already stopped in April 2010. Those of us in the solidarity movement might have contributed to these tendencies by the lack of clarity of our rhetoric. If the only question (that was heard, at least) was "Where did the money go?," then understandably, NGOs needing to justify their receipt of $3.06 billion in private donations and $6.43 billion in official sources went for the "quick wins" in the words of one, the photo op. Said another, "If I can see it, I can sell it." This simple statement says a lot: in the first several months of the recovery it was enough to show pictures of usually young, usually white, workers carrying boxes of aid to demonstrate effort.[7] But when the image of the country did not change as a result of foreigners' good intentions, journalists began questioning (some had all along, a strange mix of Fox News and leftist non-mainstream sites) the overall effort and its effectiveness. In response, some humanitarian actors went on the offensive.

Competition

A corollary of the need for visibility stemming from the same source of funding allocations is competition. Andrea was quite agitated when reporting from her time working for an NGO: "What I did see before in the cluster meetings was big fights. 'This is my camp! You don't go in there even if you provide services that we can't provide. This is my camp!' People were very, very territorial." This statement is particularly disheartening; some agencies would prefer to sacrifice well-being on the part of "their" IDPs in order to maintain this monopoly on service provision. In Washington I have heard NGO representatives jockey for position for "their" Haitian, said without irony or consideration of the postcolonial ramifications, particularly that Haiti is the world's only free nation resulting a from slave revolt. Some Haitian staff outlined some of these same analyses, like Sonson's statement in the previous chapter that the NGOs were "colonized" by foreign staff. And this competition increases along with the opportunity for funding, as Lesly theorized in the previous chapter, comparing the 2008 hurricane season and 2010 earthquake. This competition over the flood of donor money privileged large international NGOs, as Jessica noted: "There was a lot more engagement from the local NGOs, partly because there wasn't this huge flood of money in Myanmar." At the time of his interview, Widner worked for an INGO that had opened up an office in Haiti after the earthquake. In other words, it was now directly competing with the NGOs that it used to fund. This tendency to, in Geralda's words, plant the flag is not only true at the NGO level. The rubble from a hospital in the apparently gentrifying neighborhood of Turgeau, near the Digicel headquarters, also the site for a Marriott hotel opened in 2015, was the site for four national flags: in addition to the Haitian, the U.S., French, and Canadian flags were hoisted (see Figure 8.1). This quite visible reminder of the competition over Haiti remained through much of 2010.

Plas Lapè is a perfect case in point. Josselyn named five *enstans* as having some responsibility for the camp: three NGOs (Viva Rio, Concern Worldwide, and the Salvation Army) and two intergovernmental organizations (IOM and the Red Cross). All three NGOs had legitimate claims on the neighborhood, having worked there before the earthquake. Because of this work, which was

FIGURE 8.1. Remnants of a hospital in the Turgeau neighborhood, August 2010. Photo: author

rare in pre-quake Port-au-Prince,[8] each had its own network of local leaders. Noted in chapter 5, the Salvation Army succeeded in becoming the officially recognized camp management agency and therefore selected the camp committee. But they retreated after a few months, leaving Viva Rio and Concern. Staff at one was highly critical of the other for their management style and for destroying the soccer field in the process of providing camp amenities. Residents like Josselyn and Fritz were confused about who was responsible for exactly what, which led to a great deal of frustration. They did not know where to direct their concerns and felt they were getting less because of the tension, and sometimes conflict, between the agencies, sometimes played out by *moun pa*, their contacts. This situation exploded when "as typically happens" residents stoned the Red Cross trucks delivering a couple of bars of soap and Aquatabs that fateful day in July 2011. In this situation some individuals reacted violently, but this was unfortunately the only mechanism for speaking out that they felt they had (see also Maternowska 2006, 128).

The relocation process was another *tèt chaje*, headache. Martelly's visit a few days after this incident promised relocation to newly constructed homes in a demonstration, model village. One of the NGOs began relocation, but in the end the funds did not materialize. An example of the phenomenon noted in chapter 5, that it is easier to critique those in proximity, committee members like Jean-Robert blamed the NGO more than the Haitian government for this failure. And the IOM gave out the IDP cards. In the end, the other NGO organized the relocation plan that was interrupted by arson. It is not so far afield to imagine in this context that the *moun pa*, the people, of the other NGO were acting out, as one person whispered to me. NGO aid and certainly relocation is big business: the cash assistance alone for the camp would have been $3 million.[9] Although Plas Lapè is admittedly an extreme example, it throws into relief the challenges associated with competition. Zoomed out to the country level, the Haiti earthquake response was so much more money than the response to other disasters, sent so quickly, that it exposed latent tendencies in other, less well funded and certainly less visible disaster responses. Scholars have identified these as problems in other humanitarian settings (for example, de Waal 1997; Malkki 1995, 1997; Uvin 1998).

"Just Do Something"

Directly related to this visibility is the humanitarian impulse to "just do something," as Jessica described: "You put your finger on it earlier, the humanitarian mentality is that you have to do something. And they measure themselves like that." Immediately following the earthquake, the speed of delivering medical assistance was the difference between life and death. But this emergency medicine may not be the most appropriate model or metaphor for all aid. This pressure to just do something can often lead to doing for, not working with, the beneficiary population. Andrea offered an example of this tendency: "Let's do massive importing of NFIs [nonfood items] while everything is available on the local market and maybe some early livelihood projects would be better." Andrea's statement might be a little exaggerated, given that all these NFIs are imported, a reflection of neoliberal macroeconomic policy for decades, and given that the port and airport were seriously damaged. However, there is still an important lesson here; Matt Marek, the country director of the U.S. Red Cross at the time of the earthquake, shared a story at a conference on humanitarianism at Duke University. Right after the earthquake, someone had asked what he would do if he were king. He said he would give everyone cash so they could create their own solutions and not become aid dependent. This is being attempted, and at least one field study demonstrated success (Haushofer and Shapiro 2013). Marek stepped down soon after the quake, and the Red Cross did not follow his suggestion. In fact, it came under fire for planning to build a high-end hotel with donations. Andrea argued that this *assistancialisme*, dependency, started long before the earthquake: "We are responsible for a lot of the ways that they are behaving. We have created this codependency over years."

I too had inadvertently adhered to this logic. Among other critiques of my 2010 report, Wendy took issue with one of my recommendations being to "bring services to the neighborhoods." She argued that I should have said "reinforce, repair, and support services in the neighborhoods" because aid agencies too often consider urban neighborhoods to be *terra nullius*, empty land, a legal term justifying colonialism. Though I was using Haitian social movement colleagues' language of rights to dignity and pointing to shortcomings before the earthquake, my recommendation didn't acknowledge that people somehow managed to get water before the earthquake. The humanitarian impulse to *do for* precluded the solutions that would have been the most durable and far more cost effective. Instead of paying upward of ten times the amount to politically connected private water companies to truck in water, humanitarian agencies could have simply asked residents where they got water before the earthquake, often a municipal tap, and repaired or reinforced those structures. This idea, like having large community meetings wherein residents state their priority concerns and identify solutions as someone at the Carrefour City Hall camp suggested, noted in chapter 6, was unimaginable to many. One person erroneously said that I wasn't in Haiti in January and begin telling me that this kind of public meeting was impossible. Not only were they possible, these kinds of town-hall-style meetings were held in places like l'Etoile Brillant, the Mausolée (tomb of liberator Jean-Jacques Dessalines), and in CAJIT.

This tendency to just do something is too often connected to paternalism and dependency. Many people in Haiti are concerned about the impact of pending closure of the MSF trauma hospitals in Port-au-Prince and Léogâne, because their opening after the earthquake drew resources, patients, and doctors from existing hospitals (Trouillot 2012). Particularly Léogâne risks not having any hospital at all. Whether conscious or not (I suspect not, given the interviews I had), expat humanitarians often asserted that they knew better, expatronizing. In Jessica's words, "It is the whole culture of experts, right. Culture of 'step aside' mentality." The growth of master's degrees in the humanitarian enterprise, not to mention the advance of new technologies and "disciplines" as Antonio called them, hails the emergence of a specialized, professionalized knowledge. But what is the context and content of this knowledge, and how is it to be applied? Indeed, much of the logistics of delivery of humanitarian aid is specialized; I do not know how to dig a pit latrine, for example, that is deep enough to be useful and separates potential disease vectors from humans but not so deep so as to contaminate the water table. Andrea noted the difference between building houses and latrines, structurally. Haitian engineers were trained on the former, not the latter, "and this is normal." After their shared experience, Andrea reported that her team gained this technical competency. Andrea's experience was not universal, as sometimes a paternalistic attitude got in the way. William held that foreign agencies can and should wield power over even the host government: "I don't doubt for a second that since they are politicians that their primary [goal] is to look popular with donors. I also don't have a problem with that. That is what donors are there for: to put pressure on people to behave in ways we find ethically appropriate." In his analysis, William mixes scales of analysis, from politicians to people. Note also the primary role of donors to set priorities: in other words, donors' primary purpose is to set up a reward structure. That is, in fact, what they did: food aid had a tendency to splinter households, rewarding smaller nuclear families at the expense of Haitian sociocultural practice. Similarly, emergency aid reinforced matrifocality, although this form is considered abnormal, even pathological, in some donor countries like the United States. Sometimes foreign agencies do not even possess this technical knowledge. Wendy noted that only one NGO working in housing in Haiti had experience in the field; however, their model was a 100 percent dependency model because foreign volunteers build the structures. She referred to a global survey of two hundred NGOs intervening in housing, whereas only eight had the requisite expertise. One might ask, why are these institutions receiving the funding, and what exactly are they transferring? The dilemmas surrounding housing construction clearly expose the final shortcoming in the humanitarian model itself.

Development

Recalling Antonio's statement separating the humanitarian response from the reconstruction effort, embedded in this language was a "normal progression" from relief to development. Antonio and some of his colleagues posted the lack of formal legal titles and functioning regulatory agencies—a deficiency in Haiti—as barriers. Turning the gaze back on themselves, other people pointed to the fact that tools in the supposedly universal humanitarian "toolkit" were inappropriate for the urban setting. However, even this hypothesis leaves intact the supposedly universal progression from emergency aid to reconstruction (for example, Harmer and Macrae 2004; Macrae et al. 1997; Macrae and Leader 2001; Mosel and Levine 2014). The experience following Haiti's earthquake calls into question the appropriateness of this separation.

Haiti's earthquake is an example of what practitioners and scholars call a "complex emergency" (Dillon and Reid 2000; Duffield 1994; Fairweather 1997; Minn 2007). Using a medical metaphor, Paul Farmer (2011) described the situation as "acute-on-chronic." William acknowledged the difficulties of an arbitrary distinction between humanitarian aid and development: "It is impossible to distinguish between those who were earthquake affected and those that were poor beforehand. As a result, dealing with the visible consequences of the earthquake, you are having to take on the structural problems of Haiti, which are long standing and certainly won't get dealt with in the sort of short-term emergency cycle that emergency donors deal with." Working for IOM, a decidedly humanitarian agency, William articulates the necessity to have a developmentalist approach as well, taking on the structural roots of the extreme vulnerability. William recalls that Bill Clinton, ever an optimist, was looking for a silver lining to the tragedy, focusing efforts on "building back better." Clinton's optimism has historical precedent: The story often told about my hometown of Chicago is that the 1871 fire provided the impetus and opportunity for the city to become a gleaming modern metropolis, complete with rational city planning and towering skyscrapers. Not coincidentally, "build back better" was also the slogan Clinton used in the 2004 tsunami relief effort. William expressed his frustration: "You listen to the rhetoric the first couple of months, you'll have your hair pulled back a hell of a lot. You hear it out of Bill Clinton's mouth, you hear it out of [Haitian Prime Minister] Bellerive's mouth, you hear it out of a hell of a lot of people's mouths. Go back, look at public statements, you have not heard 'Build back better' anymore." Relieved at this retreat, William calculated that, for the 16/6 program he was managing, to redevelop neighborhoods would cost $10 billion. He continued, "No way. There is no way $10 billion is going to come this way. . . . It took a long time for the rhetoric to come back down to earth. I have a problem with that. It is papering over the cracks. But you can't give me a buck and ask me to do ten bucks worth of work."

William's calculation is based on the assumption that foreign "actors" were to do all the work that others, like Jessica and Wendy, criticized for erasing local initiative. Again critiquing my work, a 2012 report about relocation, this time a line about housing that was built, Wendy noted: "Whether it's 5,000 or 20,000, this number only includes housing built by international agencies. Why is that? Why don't they have an interest in reporting the construction that Haitian people are doing for themselves?" Wendy said that in Kanaran, where not a single NGO intervened, residents invested $64 million of their own private capital in the first two years after the earthquake. Wendy pointed to a document of the World Bank (Jha et al. 2010), officially published three days after the earthquake, distilling twenty years of experience in housing. "You'd be amazed that no one reads it." Agreeing with the report's findings, Wendy's experience in Afghanistan and Pakistan similarly showed her that the way to rebuild homes and communities is to empower people to rebuild their own homes: "Sure, they'd need to learn antiseismic techniques, but you could condition the receipt of the second tranche of funds on passing a workshop and having the building inspected." In general, aid, and particularly post-disaster aid, works best, according to Wendy, when it reinforces and supports local initiatives. "Our eye is off the ball. We need to play an accompanying role, not a directing role." Farmer (2011) has also underscored accompaniment as the appropriate role for foreign agencies.

Jessica shared a critique similar to William's: "After the kind of disaster you had in Haiti, yes you need humanitarian assistance, but you need to have a reconstruction approach. You cannot just say, 'Let's come in here and have a humanitarian response.' It should be a part of something larger it should be subservient to." Given that people such as Antonio argued that there wasn't the progression toward reconstruction, it is obvious that what Jessica and William outlined didn't occur. However, diverging from William's point of view, Jessica argued that the primary reason the postquake response remained stuck in the emergency phase was that humanitarian agencies assumed control: "If you have responses being led by humanitarian actors, very few humanitarian actors really see what transition means and where they need to fit in the larger reconstruction plan. I think that was one of the problems here. You could have had clarified and articulated what precisely the humanitarian response should be responsible for. And that line was never drawn."

One might ask to whom humanitarian agencies should have been accountable: Who was to draw this line? Was this the role of the UN clusters? Haitian government agencies like UCAONG or DINEPA? International donors? The agencies themselves? Jessica theorized that the reason why the agencies couldn't—or wouldn't—submit to something larger was because of what she called the project mentality: "Donors and international agencies need to be thinking about development and need to be thinking about the next twenty or thirty years and not just about their particular achievements and projects. Get out of the project mentality." The late Haitian sociologist Janil Lwijis (1993, 2009) shared this critique of the project mentality and logic, as have others (for example, Freeman 2014; Meinert and Whyte 2014). Embedded in Jessica's analysis, behind the project mentality is the need for visibility and taking credit for achievements. The project mentality is an expression of a capitalist logic of production, as Wendy details: "It's the logic of production: building becomes about logistics, not about consultation, not about development, not about choice, not about working with the neighborhood. It's about efficiency. It's a very supply-driven industry. So the imperative is to spend." Wendy (and several other interlocutors, some who preferred not to be recorded) told me that some donors, particularly USAID, rate NGOs by their "burn rate," or how quickly they can spend money, as well as their "surge capacity."

A couple of discussion points arise from these interviews, relating to the relief to development continuum. Media accounts of the earthquake, which was widely credited for the generosity of the response, were greatly aided by the "photogenic" nature of the disaster, that is to say, the sheer scale of human misery and large slabs of concrete seemingly everywhere (at least on camera). As William, Jessica, and others note, the "complex emergency"—the poverty and inequality, the UN troops on the ground following a foreign-engineered regime change—required a development response. Further, most of the organizations that received private and official assistance had been in the country before the earthquake, with Chemonics a notable exception. Most of these organizations were multi-mandate—the Red Cross was a notable exception—engaging in development interventions for years before the earthquake.

There is still debate about the "continuum" (Mosel and Levine 2014). It is also important to keep in mind the clear failures in development by the "Republic of NGOs" in a neoliberal policy regime. Chapter 1 details how these failures structured Haiti's vulnerability to disasters. However, given that the generosity was in part because of development failures, despite the work of many in-country NGOs, and the fact that most were engaged in development, what accounts for the humanitarian mandate assumed by these same NGOs? For answers a structural analysis is required.

"The Machine"

Jessica, who had experience with a dozen disasters by the time of her 2012 interview, identified "the problem" as "the machine of the humanitarian system, globally. A lot of it as well is the problems in Haiti but also this bubble system. . . . It's not really perfect anywhere. Rather than encouraging more cohesion, I think it encourages more fragmentation." To Jessica, and others, Aceh was the outlier for being successful. A key problem involves hierarchy, as Wendy noted: "What is the point of being here on the ground if we can't transmit this information upward?" Wendy notes the frustration of hierarchy preventing field experience from guiding humanitarian action.

Peter noted a critical element of this failure to learn on the ground: "So you could write a book about this: two months after the earthquake, all of the largest NGOs changed their directors, including this one. So people who had been here for three years or four years, either transferred out, or were PTSD, or somebody brought in the superstar of the humanitarian response. So it is only now that people come here who plan to stay for a while." The interview was conducted in July 2012. Each of the "Big Ten" NGOs may have had a different story, but this change in leadership disrupted much of the work. Andrea noted that in the beginning NGOs had different staff every two weeks, making coordination and decision making near impossible and institutional memory nonexistent. Geralda noted that after she left—coincidentally she was scheduled to step down on January 12—there were five different in-country directors during the first several months. An acquaintance from long before the earthquake outlined this significance in her NGO, pointing out that the former country director—when it was a "rinky-dink" operation of $9 million a year—had lived in Haiti for nine years, had a Haitian wife, and children in the Haitian school system. When the "big star" came in to run the agency, the former director left, taking his Rolodex of contacts with him. As Geralda noted, "And precisely because there were many new managers, sometimes they didn't know their local partners and how they should work with them."

Jessica also detailed a problem with these humanitarian superstars, their lack of understanding of the local context:

> Sadly, I think that if there is one thing that is institutionalized, it is an incredible disregard for context. And it is very sad, I mean you can look through any report from [her institution] and you know we are always making the same point. Understand fucking context. Is it that difficult?
>
> Maybe it is because I have been trained as an anthropologist and that stuff is not negotiable. Shocking. It was not just a linguistic issue. People could speak perfect French and could have access to a lot more information that was coming out in the French-Haitian media. Did they read the French-Haitian media? NO. Because the reference point is yourself. You are not looking at your role in a country and what you are doing in that country to support. You are kind of looking in a little bubble.

Several commentators from the previous chapter share similar critiques about Haiti having its own on-the-ground realities and context, and having to work for expats who lacked this understanding. Lesly, Mme. Auguste, and Daniel all point to the consequences of their foreign supervisors' bad experience: protests, program failure, and threats of violence.

In addition to this micro-structural analysis of the hierarchies within *enstans*, the earthquake response was hampered by macro-structural forces. The 2008 financial crisis marked a steady decline in "development" funding (Development Initiatives 2013). Although the world and certainly the United States was still reeling from the crisis, the 2010 Haiti earthquake dramatically demonstrated that funding for disasters was still available.

A couple of interlocutors identified imperialism as lurking beneath many of these problems. Again comparing the Aceh experience, explaining its success, Jessica outlined the role played by the Indonesian government: "I mean obviously Jakarta was much stronger than the Haitian government, but nonetheless, the most important ingredient was that it was genuinely led by the Indonesian government. The thing that was critical was that the international community recognized the legitimacy of the Indonesian government and they got behind them." Haiti, by contrast, was deemed a "weak state," in effect becoming a self-fulfilling prophecy, despite the fact that there were and are many skilled professionals working in government and NGOs, as Jessica pointed out. She adamantly rejected the argument of Haitian exceptionalism: "You will always be

in a difficult context. Aceh was a difficult context. You will always have a complicated transition. I don't think that is something that we should be blaming the
government for having a difficulty."

A key difference to Jessica and others, explaining why foreign donors and
NGOs willingly submitted to the authority of the Indonesian government but
not that of Haiti, is U.S. hegemony: "In a place like Indonesia for example, the
U.S. does have a lot of power but they are not the only actor. You know, the com-
mitment to a place like Indonesia . . . they were already committed to strengthening institutions." Another career aid worker pointed out that the Australian
government provided immediate budget support to the Indonesian government. As a strong centralized government, Jakarta could "second" its workers
from elsewhere to Aceh. In Haiti, Spain was alone in supporting two central government agencies to fulfill their coordination role. In contrast, the earthquake
provided an opportunity for the United States to regain some of its "influence"
in the region, as a January 13, 2010, memo from the right-wing Heritage Foundation argued (Vorbe 2011). This influence had gradually waned as a result of
the UN military force led by Brazil and largely staffed by Latin Americans and
PetroCaribe from Venezuela. Several commentators point to the role played by
the U.S. military in edging out French NGO MSF even as they granted travel to
two twenty-something orphanage staff at the request of the Pennsylvania governor Ed Rendell.[10]

Why would Spain support the Haitian government when neoliberal United
States and other donors did not? In part, Spain was one of the only socialist
governments in Europe at the time. In addition, Spain had long given up imperial ambitions on the colony, ceding it to France in 1697, so there was less need
to "plant the flag." The earthquake also offered an opportunity for a display of
French largesse and also the *mission civilatrice* (civilizing mission) that only the
colonial power, and only France, could bring, an assertion of French neocolonial
legitimacy. Explaining why the World Bank team that had published the housing
report never came to Haiti, Wendy argued:

> The World Bank people here say that they already know Haiti, that they know what will
> work and will not work in Haiti, so this housing team has never been invited to Haiti
> to offer their expertise, or even have one workshop or training with the housing actors.
> This is particularly true of the World Bank: all of the leaders are French. They have the
> attitude that only they can work in Haiti because they have the right to do so. They
> have the language, the technical knowhow and they set up the education system, etc.

Although she didn't use the language of Haitian exceptionalism, that is what she
was describing. Wendy is not from the colonial power but from another European Union country. This last discussion suggests a limit to a strictly structural

analysis. Despite my misgivings of the ways that culture has been deployed within the Haitian context, and certainly the earthquake (especially coming from commentators like Pat Robertson or the more mainstream David Brooks), culture offers necessary context to complete the understanding of the humanitarian ruptures.

Culture of and inside the "Bubble"

Jessica's term "bubble" offers a good explanation for the closed, self-referential system epitomized by LogBase, a foreign military base protected from Haitian people, the supposed beneficiaries. She relates, "There is only so much that the agencies can do to get out of that bubble. As much as some of them might be aware that it is a bubble, the cluster system doesn't become the place where they interact with local groups." The term *bubble* is not only useful in LogBase and the clusters that met there. Postquake aid solidified and accelerated trends already begun in Port-au-Prince, as commentators like Department of Development Sciences chair Ilionor Louis, argued: since 2004, a foreign-supported and engineered crisis, there has been a continuous presence of NGOs and expats. Commentators have dubbed Haiti the "Republic of NGOs." Some of the impacts are increasing housing costs and the proliferation of high-end hotels, restaurants, and large, air-conditioned grocery stores selling almost entirely imported goods, mostly geared to foreign palates, protected by armed guards. Andrea Steinke (2012) calls this process "humanitarian gentrification" (see also Büscher and Vlassenroot 2010). Well into 2011, foreign agency staff and volunteer mission trips used so many rental cars that for the first time since 2001, since I have been going to Haiti, the streets were jammed with cars with Dominican license plates. As the French PhD student noted, foreign aid workers live and work in a closed system, attempting to bring their middle-class lifestyles and consumption patterns with them. This is what Heather Hindman (2013) calls "expatria." As the armed guards painfully attest, this lifestyle, protecting the bubble by keeping out all but the wealthiest Haitian people and those selected to join the NGO class (Schuller 2009), is not sustainable. In a very real sense these are mobile borders, in space and time, given curfews. Steinke inadvertently got an NGO driver in trouble by noting the route home they took to avoid a *blokis*, a traffic jam, that was caused by the influx of NGO vehicles. This was NGO policy, largely dictated from LogBase. When she protested, saying that Haitians do this all the time, the foreign NGO supervisor said point blank that foreign lives are worth more to the NGO. This was so because of the ransom they would have to pay in the case of kidnapping. Steinke also noted that this agency was looking for reasons to downsize their staff.

Generally speaking, inside the bubble, expats reproduce their structures, consumption patterns, language, communication systems, habits, values, and worldview. In other words, a culture. This final section of the chapter discusses expat culture that shapes, closes off, structures, and illuminates the choices and actions of the foreign humanitarians and the agencies for whom they work. Critiquing some of his colleagues and certainly the acerbic public discussions, William pronounced, "If we come in here with our Occidental view of what corruption means, then we are idiots." His statement suggests what one discerns from reading the press releases, blogs, news stories, "Situation Reports" (called SitRep for short), and other communiqués from humanitarian NGOs: they took their own cultural frames of reference, and the humanitarian toolkit, as universal. Differences between foreign humanitarians' models and on-the-ground realities are evidence of a "deficiency" in Haitian culture. For example, Wendy discussed the noise about the lack of formal land titles as an excuse to not build (as Antonio expressed—see also de Soto 2000) as reflections of culturally specific, foreign worldviews: "The fact that there is no court and no legal document does not inhibit people from building or repairing. That's a Western legal fiction that donors, particularly the U.S. and French government, are trying to establish." Exceptions to this are numerical standards expressed in the Sphere Project's *Humanitarian Charter and Minimum Standards* (2004). For example, UN Humanitarian Coordinator Nigel Fisher backpedaled from the standard that a single toilet be shared by no more than twenty people. The goal he set was one hundred people (Panchang 2012). As the 2010 study found, not even this was met: on average, there was one toilet per every 273 people. Wendy argued that the authors of the Sphere standards never meant for the standards to be considered a bible but a living document. She brought this up in the interview to discuss the minimum standards of 18 square meters for a decent house, a point discussed in the conclusion.

Language is a key marker for this exclusion, at once justifying and reproducing the bubble, not just within LogBase and in the cluster meetings but within the agencies themselves, as Andrea explained: "In emergencies in countries that are not native English speakers, you have a limit to the amount of qualified personnel that you can employ. So what happens is that you employ your standard roster, people don't speak the standard language of the country. French in this case, not even Creole." Why might this be the case? Because the predominant language of donors, international agencies, and finance, is English. And not just any English but "legalese," in the words of one international agency staff. She might have also said "NGOese." This presents a problem when front-line workers like Gabrielle, Françoise, Daniel, and James cannot speak English. Given their class status within Haitian society and their educational privilege, all but Françoise, who was chosen from the beneficiary population, could be assumed to speak French. This presents a barrier in intra-NGO communication: How can people meeting in LogBase accurately report what front-line staff observe?

NGO workers, and not just NGOs themselves, are expected to translate. As Daniel noted in the previous chapter, not only the words but the ideas, beliefs, and ideologies behind them are foreign.

Andrea gestured toward another set of realities that are often lost in translation, which explains why Haitian staff like Mme. Auguste worked for people half her age: "The system is not really set up for low-cost staff that is not already in the system, and knows how to work in the system. And you need to have some experience in it to be able to deal with it. Once you have worked for an NGO, it's basically similar in all of it. But you need to get used to it." Once you're in "the system," you can move around within it: Andrea began working in Haiti with an NGO and moved, like William, to the IOM. Both Peter and Sophie were in their second office post-earthquake. Working in the system requires fluency in rules, hierarchies, reporting, accounting, and so on, as Andrea defines: "That is what I would call the NGO system. Massive amounts of rules, massive amounts of coordination, reports that you have to write. Which all, in theory, makes sense, but in real-life work, it's more hindering energy than it is advancing work."

This critique was shared by many with Andrea's experience, in part because it is a common frustration, or to use a value-neutral term, a common experience, of people working for NGOs. As an "organic intellectual" (Gramsci 1971; Susser 2011), Andrea's analysis suggests thinking of NGOs as a culture in and of itself. So while Mme. Auguste may have had much more experience with the system in Haiti, Julie, her supervisor, was "fluent" (or "culturally competent") in international NGO culture. It is this expertise, this set of knowledge, this fluency in NGO-speak, this familiarity with a "culture of NGOs," that is required to be an in-country director, to move resources around, to be a broker for these billions in aid. This is why, from this logic, that "big stars" were moved into Haiti after the earthquake. Andrea also noted that this bureaucratic culture of NGOs tends to reproduce itself, discussing the creation and universal use of committees in camps. Her guess was that these hierarchical bureaucratic structures, these "mini-NGOs," existed before the earthquake: "And it is probably just a result of this long-term presence of the NGOs. So they learned that NGOs like to work with committees, and so they started organizing in committees." This is a prime example of the *fotokopi*, the photocopy phenomenon.

A "Culture of NGOs"?

This chapter has provided an essential set of perspectives coming from humanitarian expats. Although they are, like the agencies they work for, a diverse bunch, they share a *habitus* of working within a culture of NGOs. Whether or not they are aware of this fact—some are more than others—they also live in a bubble, an artificially constructed, closed system that makes possible the attempt to reproduce the middle-class, "Western" lifestyles they left back home. UN troops were often derided because they came from less powerful, lower-status countries. Like MINUSTAH, the UN mission, the postquake response also brought Latin American people to Haiti in large numbers. Because of the expats living and working in this bubble, one can identify some core challenges that explain the difficulties, missteps, gaps, and shortcomings identified by the Haitian people in this book. Moving beyond the technical critiques of coordination, weak state, and rural-model-meets-urban realities, this chapter has raised questions about the DNA of humanitarian action itself. These contradictions, this tension and disjunctions across the various cultures, are exposed by the magnitude and visibility of the response to the Haiti earthquake. This chapter also suggests that humanitarian aid is not universal but culturally specific. It suggests that this cultural difference, and the insularity of the bubble—and possibly a culture of NGOs—explains the shortcomings.

Still to be done is making an explicit analysis of the problems discussed in this book. What lessons writ large does this ethnographic study of the postquake humanitarian aftershocks reveal? What does the Haiti case contribute to general theory? Answering these questions, the conclusion brings Haitian perspectives back to the fore.

CONCLUSION

I have an ongoing critical position toward humanitarian logic. And my position remains systematically critical. And at the same time it proposes to build the alternative model. And I think neither of these options excludes the other. They are not exclusive.

NGO1 supported a project in Gressier, in ITECA and communities in the area. What's important, the NGOs don't have time to think over this logic. They just came and planted a flag, and considered that their first step.

The first thing is, we call the shots around here, not the humanitarian organization. The logic of the humanitarian organization didn't determine the choices, we determined the choices.

Many develop an ideology: there's a reality that humanitarian NGOs engage in mystification. They act like they are the ones who donate the funds, when in fact it is a solidarity from one country to another.

Well, they said the quality beneficiaries have now is the same as they had before. And what they receive is better than what they had. I didn't agree with that. This almost terminated the collaboration. We finally doubled the size of the houses to thirty-six square meters. This is the first element.

The second element relates to experiences with management. Humanitarian NGOs are currently spending money any which way because they say Haitians can't manage. Constructing autonomy begins here as well.

We reject in advance all attempts to say that Haitians can't manage.

They considered isolated families. They came and built houses and sold these pictures to receive charity overseas. We say no. In order words, they've tooted their own horn; they had huge media coverage. That's not the point. It's out of the question to let their actions reinforce individualism among us.

The biggest lesson I learned is that you make as little concessions as possible when you discuss your work with humanitarian organizations.

And the second lesson is a humanitarian market. Beyond what they say, beyond solidarity, in fact, it's a market: a market following the currently prevailing market logic. It's a market logic because from a crisis situation, from disasters or misfortune, they can mobilize capital. And predatory organizations suck most of the funds dry, you see? And just a relatively small amount of money reached the people.

There's a third lesson that we learned. They don't care a great deal about the community. They show little interest. Most of them don't make the effort to learn the language. The community is like an object instead of a potential subject.

National organizations must affirm their leadership. First and foremost, your funds don't give you leadership. First and foremost, it's your presence on the ground. You have to value yourself. It's a market, so you have to increase your value.

Not all our relationships are like that. We have a strong relationship. We have a partnership with NGO2. It's an organization affiliated with the Catholic Church, close to liberation theology movements but with a certain margin of autonomy enabling them to mobilize funds in its country of origin. And it allows them to have some negotiating power that is impossible with USAID.

I think the best instrument to evaluate a project is to ask the question whether or not there's a new community dynamic springing up in the process.

—Chenet Jean-Baptiste, ITECA

I am using Chenet's real name because he is, like Malya Villard of KOFAVIV who began chapter 4, highly visible. He is also not only an "organic" intellectual, he is a scholar and a professor, publishing and presenting in conferences in his name. I have cited him in this book. The experience of ITECA, the Institute of Technology and Community Organizing, is so singular that I couldn't hide his identity while drawing necessary lessons from it. Although Chenet's tone is militant, he is also pragmatic, at once criticizing the system as a whole and constructing alternatives. This is a good summary of what I've been attempting to do throughout this book: engaging in fundamental critique while attempting to grapple toward solutions. This conclusion attempts both.

Chenet's ambivalence is also visible in his recommendations to other local organizations to increase their value within the prevailing humanitarian market logic. ITECA was founded in 1978 by development professionals and liberation theology-inspired religious leaders of the *ti legliz* (the "small" or the people's church). Up until the earthquake, ITECA had been working in long-term, bottom-up, development: hosting trainings and incubators to empower local residents to stand up and be involved in their community, transforming local relationships.

ITECA is headquartered outside of Port-au-Prince, in the town of Gressier, the epicenter of the earthquake. Not surprisingly, the earthquake had a great impact on Gressier, affecting many ITECA members: sixteen hundred families had lost their homes as a result of the tremors. In this situation, thrust into humanitarianism, they felt an obligation to respond without the means to do so. But as Chenet noted, they also had an obligation to stay true to their mission and their members, promoting the dignity and worth of everyone as human beings.

Chenet's militancy comes from experience: he shares with Geralda the concern of foreign *enstans* "planting the flag." Headquartered in the epicenter, ITECA's value in the humanitarian market, their ability to negotiate, was thus increased. A dozen international NGOs descended on Gressier after the earthquake. The municipal government estimated that three hundred international NGOs came to the bigger city of Léogâne, just to the south. I begin with Chenet's analysis to remind readers that Haitian people are analyzing this humanitarian experience, drawing lessons that are useful to those of us who are concerned with humanity, who are compelled to act as agency staff, journalists, solidarity activists, and/or scholars. Like Chenet, many of us play more than one role. Chenet also offers guidance for building the road ahead.

This conclusion summarizes the lessons Haitian individuals, from Chenet to IDPs like Manolia, have drawn from the humanitarian aftershocks. Why did so much money, media attention, and tens of thousands of well-meaning people not only fall so short of our goals but also inflict damage that may be long lasting on Haitian people's resilience and vulnerability to disasters? People's stories of collectivism, solidarity, and survival—like Nadege's, Robenson's, or Claudine's—should have, in a different media context, been an inspiration the world over (Solnit 2009). Answering these questions requires that we interrogate humanitarianism itself: the logic of the photo op, the disaster narrative, the structures, "culture," and the power dynamics inherent to the gift. Thus, far more than add-culture-and-stir or check-the-box solutions, the "Haiti case" demands a rethinking of the fundamental logics and structures of humanitarian aid. Drawing inspiration from Chenet, Geralda, and others, this conclusion sketches an outline of new humanitarian models, what might be called "Humanitarianism 3.0."

"DICTATORSHIP OF AID": HAITIAN UNDERSTANDINGS

Analyses of humanitarian aid by practitioners and scholars, including anthropologists, have proliferated and professionalized in recent years. Building on insights in excellent recent reviews of this emerging field, including from

Michael Barnett (2013) and Myriam Ticktin (2014), this conclusion adds Haitian people's analyses, from lived experience from a diverse range of perspectives, to this conversation.

Haitian filmmaker Raoul Peck began the concluding section of *Fatal Assistance* by narrating, "The dictatorship of aid is violent, arbitrary, blind, self-impregnated, a paternalistic monster that speaks sweetly of its passage." As evidenced by this quote, research from within Haiti itself tends to be critical, with many studies focusing on long-term cultural changes. The first scholarship on NGOs shared an optimism that they could inspire change, including democratization (for example, Ethéart 1991; Mangonès 1991; Mathurin 1991; Mathurin, Mathurin, and Zaugg 1989). However, after it became clear that NGOs, empowered by donors' promotion of neoliberalism, presided over declining development indicators, Haitian intellectuals began decrying what they saw as an "invasion" (Étienne 1997). Sharing a radical analysis with critical globalization scholars (Hardt and Negri 2001; Houtart 1998; Petras 1997) and following a Haitian culturalist analysis of Price-Mars (1983) and Barthélémy (1990), interpretivist Haitian scholars critiqued NGOs for being harbingers of imperialism, implanting foreign cultural values, notably neoliberalism and the market economy (Lwijis 1993, 2009; Theus 2008). Other social science studies of humanitarian aid, with a more explicit methodology, engage humanitarian agencies on their own terms, noting their failures (for example, Beauvoir-Dominique 2005; Louis 2013; Vorbe 2011).

There is a growing preoccupation among Haitian scholars, activists, and government with NGOs. The national regulatory framework discussed in the previous chapter explicitly defined NGOs as working in development. Further, the bulk of international NGOs have worked on development, and despite this NGO aid, development indicators have seen a steady decline. So the focus on humanitarianism is new. For obvious reasons, the word *imanitè*, quite similar to *imanite* (humanity), entered mainstream lexicon—at least among Haiti's NGO class and universities—only after the earthquake. Several conferences and teach-ins at various institutions, from well-heeled foreign-funded think tanks holding conversations in posh hotels to grassroots groups engaging people living in the camps, were held after the earthquake to try and make sense of this "paternalistic monster." Some more radical activists, pointing out the all-too-obvious (to Haitian people, at least) contradictions in the United Nations' role conducting a military occupation while simultaneously coordinating the humanitarian response, have begun to use the term "humanitarian occupation." This language reflects the sentiments of being shut out of conversations about the future of the country, either at LogBase or at the IHRC. This critique is only likely to grow with the contradictions: the United Nations asked for money through "flash appeals" to combat cholera while blocking all efforts to recognize its responsibility for bringing the disease to the troops. The year 2015 also marks the centennial of the nineteen-year U.S. occupation of Haiti; events are already being planned to critically reflect on the parallels in these two foreign occupations as of the time of this writing.

In this conclusion I am attempting to give Haitian people the last word, especially important considering Haiti is already being described as a "must" on one's CV if one is to have a humanitarian career. But in most ways that matter—my language, worldview, foreign passport, habitus, frequent flyer status . . . all this is to say, my privilege—I more closely resemble the foreign humanitarian. James Ferguson (2005) described development as being anthropology's "evil twin." Sometimes I felt like the evil twin: although as a professor I can say that my livelihood doesn't directly depend on people's misery, this rings hollow when I tell people that this research is financed by the National Science Foundation, a branch of the U.S. government. So if it is painful to read these critiques coming from Haitian beneficiaries in one of the world's biggest, best-funded, and mediatized humanitarian efforts ever launched, it's equally hard to write. And I know that I am not spared these critiques. What gives me the right to speak on Haitian people's behalf, even as I critique others like myself for the same? The short answer is nothing, of course. Like Antonio, Peter, and Wendy, it is far easier to count my "outputs"—number of articles on *HuffPo*, how many times I've been invited to Washington—than the outcomes. Although I might not have the right, talking with hundreds of individuals, peering into their subhuman conditions, and taking their time, gives me a certain responsibility, an obligation. Like the *enstans* working in the camps, I too have been asked numerous times about the concrete results of this work. Although she never saw people move into a new home, at least Emily could point to a roster of people who moved out of Nan Bannann. As I answered in the best, most direct Haitian possible: I hope this research will shed some light on the reasons why you find yourself in this situation. Together, we'll be able to identify solutions. In other words, not much at all.

But here goes.

HUMANITARIAN AFTERSHOCKS

Haiti's earthquake broke the charts in terms of media coverage. For weeks, multinational media outlets like CNN were broadcasting Haiti nearly all the time. It is, with few parallels, one of the most visible catastrophes of our age, and given the proliferation of media forms as well as outlets, the most well documented. This visibility was a double-edged sword: on the one hand, the response had few equals in terms of generosity. Chenet didn't mince words: humanitarianism is a market, and the suffering of individuals became a form of capital for humanitarian agencies, as Widner, taking off his NGO jacket, noted in disgust. On the other, this hypervisibility put enormous pressure on agencies to show results. Hence, photogenic, highly costly, and unsustainable "solutions" were chosen as opposed to those that might have long-term impact. As Geralda noted, "The principle, to be honest, is that a humanitarian intervention is more expensive than a development intervention." In part this is because logistics are more expensive when speed of response is paramount, when saving lives. But Chenet forces us to question why, as Jessica and others noted, humanitarian agencies assumed control of the response and wouldn't subsume their activities under a development framework. Is it because of the "burn rate," so that donors and NGOs can show that they've spent the money? Haitian people throughout this book, from Liza, to Josselyn, to Sonson, to Geralda, suspect so. Chenet offers a Marxist language and framework to understand why top-down, high-cost solutions were repeated despite opposition from local communities: humanitarianism is a market. The late Janil Lwijis, who died from a politically motivated assassination minutes before the earthquake, shared this analysis (2009). Thinking of humanitarian aid as a form of capital also helps to understand Josselyn's and others' performances. If the photo op is the operating principle based on a market logic, performances such as standing in line, repeating one's name to anyone conducting a census, singing a song about trash are indeed capital for the *enstans* providing the aid.

Given the singularity of the media attention and therefore generosity, it is tempting to once again exceptionalize Haiti. However, Chenet's and Lwijis's analyses also offer insights into other humanitarian situations. Haiti's case is more visible and therefore the contradictions within the humanitarian system are easier to notice. But the need for visibility, photo op, project mentality, market logic, and turning people's suffering into capital are unfortunately realities of a humanitarian system that relies on generosity of individual donors and states, particularly in a lingering financial crisis (for example, Agier 2006; Barnett 2011; Duffield, Macrae, and Curtis 2001; Fassin 2012; Feldman 2010; Scherz 2013). People employed in public relations and especially fundraising intimately understand this reality. The Haiti case, perhaps because of its visibility, makes these contradictions—and their consequences—more difficult to ignore. As Maud, Lise, and many others exclaimed, "They are making money off us!"

Related to this point, the postquake aid response highlights what can be called the "disaster narrative." Although the nonstop barrage of media coverage engendered generosity, most stories also normalized foreign control. They did so first by portraying the most abject misery, framed in a narrative of a nation brought to its knees. Second, by systematically ignoring the everyday heroism and solidarity of tens of thousands of ordinary people like Manoucheka and Manolia, framing them outside the story, media accounts painted a picture of *terra nullius*, if not *Lord of the Flies*. This served to justify a fear-based, militarized response. Recall Sonson's quote: "It seems that they thought that the rubble fell on our intelligence too." If we foreigners were responsible for everything, from security to nation building, because everything was destroyed and there was nothing left of the state, or local capacity, then why not continue to forge ahead with the war surgeries and "cigar cuts" (a military term roughly meaning "cutting people's limbs off as one would a cigar"), continuing to build T-shelters when the government said no? Structuring this expatronizing, Chenet discussed the tendency to turn recipients into objects, and Ilionor Louis (2012), into children.

The paranoia discussed in chapter 2 that Hugo Chávez helped to spread notwithstanding, few people questioned what Paul Farmer (2011) called the "proximate" cause of the suffering: the earthquake itself. The coverage focused almost entirely on this immediate level, the hazardous conditions (Wisner et al. 2004). Lost in the majority of discussions in the media are the distal, more structural, causes: hyper-urbanization triggered by one of the most successful implantations of free-market capitalism the world has ever seen on the heels of a U.S. military occupation, and the ways in which structural adjustment weakened the government. Consequently, the opportunity to reinforce what Haitian people were actually doing was lost (Jean-Baptiste 2012). Rather than seize this opportunity to undo this urbanization and rebuild Haiti's rural peasant economy agencies contributed to the centralization, overcrowding, and individualism. As Wendy noted, it wouldn't have even occurred to humanitarian agencies. Geralda and Chenet argued that this is because of their need to plant the flag, to be seen where the journalists were. It was, in effect, a vicious cycle. Aid attracted journalists to the epicenter and the national plaza, to the camps. Meanwhile, quietly, 630,000 Haitian people like Maud, Mackenson, and Frisline sought refuge with their rural family members, and even more individuals in Port-au-Prince were piecing together their homes, families, and neighborhoods outside the camps.

Like the inseparability of media from modern humanitarian action, the central role of the photo op in humanitarian logic, insights from understanding these disaster narratives are certainly not limited to Haiti. Discussing multiple cases of industrial accidents, from *Exxon Valdez* to the BP *Deepwater Horizon* spill, Gregory Button (2010) demonstrated how hotly contested the disaster narrative can be. Accounts that portray spills as accidents and without precedent actively discourage public recognition of these as systemic, portraying these excesses of corporate greed and lack of accountability as normal. And thus the response is usually woefully inadequate, and certainly we are no better prepared against future catastrophes. Mahmood Mamdani (2009) analyzes the disaster narrative coming from Darfur that mapped onto global anti-Islamic discourses, turning the "Responsibility to Protect" into a "right to punish." Chenet challenged one of these narratives, rejecting the notion that Haitians cannot manage, that justified exclusion.

As scholars, particularly anthropologists (for example, Agier 2010; Bornstein and Redfield 2011; Fassin 2012), have noted, humanitarianism presupposes a universal human subject: humanity (see also Barnett 2011). Taken out of their specific historical contexts, which highlight particular origins addressing actual events, humanitarian models—the toolkit—are presented as having universal applicability. The experience in Haiti shows otherwise, in effect "provincializing" (Chakrabarty 2007) humanitarianism, uncovering its cultural specificity. Chenet rejected the individualism that he observed often accompanies humanitarian aid projects. Individualism is a powerful ideology of U.S. exceptionalism, the "rags to riches" and "bootstraps" mentalities; it is also a central cultural logic of neoliberalism and belief in the free market, as Margaret Thatcher once opined, "There is no such thing as society, only individual men and women, and there are families." Humanitarian aid also envisions a culturally specific model of family as well. As chapters 3 and 4 document, policies of aid envisioned and thus encouraged the formation of a nuclear household that is the norm—if increasingly not the practice—in advanced post-industrial capitalist societies such as the United States. Although it might be tempting to hypothesize that this is an outcome of disasters overall, this book has documented greater disruption of traditional multigenerational *lakou*-style households where NGOs played a greater role. Franck noted in chapter 3 that aid caused children to grow up quickly. And although it was one of the more successful outcomes of the international effort, the advocacy around women, particularly against gender-based violence, reinforced a single-issue feminist praxis rooted in middle-class, white, U.S. experience. The disconnect between this foreign model imposed on and structured in the aid response had consequences of reinforcing gender-based stereotypes, at once demonizing men and letting them off the hook for child rearing. The ways in which aid was gendered also had the paradoxical impact of targeting women for acts of sexual violence and transactional sex, as Evrance and Fabiola detailed in chapter 4.

Like other conclusions about the photo op and disaster narrative, I argue that it's best to look at Haiti not as an outlier but as a bellwether, an invitation to look more closely into other humanitarian spaces. As a product of a particular cultural context, humanitarian aid can trigger cultural change (Hours 2003). Michel Agier (2003) called humanitarian agencies the "left hand of empire." Scholars have noted that humanitarianism shares a cultural value system with individualism (Fassin 2012; Thomas 2013). Aspects of aid, and its impact, are also gendered (Ticktin 2011). For one example, Misha Quill has documented conditions and impacts in Bangladesh that eerily resemble those discussed here. Quill examines how the structures of humanitarian aid in refugee camps and aid policies similarly reproduce and escalate gender-based violence.

Despite the pretentions of universality in the multibillion-dollar response, in practice, not all humans are equally valued. There are too many examples coming from people in Haiti, people from the IDP camps like Claudine or Nadege, to directors of agencies like Chenet and Geralda, to repeat them all here. First, many people in the camps referred to living "like animals"; Yves noted that they were treated "worse than dogs." The differential value attached to human lives was made crystal clear during Hurricane Emily in August 2011. Jean-Robert from Plas Lapè called their camp manager and asked where he was. This individual said that MINUSTAH had informed the agency to not go outside, because it was too dangerous, to which Jean-Robert responded, "But we in the camp are outside. If it's too dangerous for you, what about us?" As Chenet said, "Humanitarian NGOs came with this model, the Sphere minimum standards, to school us on the proper way of doing things. Since we didn't have experience directly in humanitarian aid, we were happy to read it. Then we found out that they are not following their own rules, their own standards. When we call them on that, they say that we're stirring up trouble. They say Haiti is a case of its own. So we deserve less? We aren't human beings like everyone else?" People who work in NGOs like Daniel or Mme. Auguste also noted other differential treatment between Haitian and expat staff, Haitian staffers not being able to use the company vehicle or computer for fear of "corruption" when their foreign coworkers routinely did so, a lower regard for the Haitians' safety, and their lower pay. Geralda noted that "the more international staff your structure has, a greater percentage of your administrative costs goes to salaries and benefits." In the first months following the earthquake, foreign specialists were often paid $1,000 per day, which could pay for two families' rental subsidies for one year. More than just feeling valued differently, this inequality makes life more difficult for Haitian staff. The previous chapter discussed a secondary displacement, a "humanitarian gentrification" (Büscher and Vlassenroot 2010; Steinke 2012), as expat staff are given monthly housing allowance many times greater than the previous market value. Geralda noted that "the house where I lived before the earthquake, I now can't afford that kind of house at all because the rent is five times more. Landlords haven't dropped the prices of houses yet. Although people increase their rent four–five times higher, they don't pay the state four–five times more, and the NGOs know that."

Unfortunately this is not unique to Haiti. Peter Redfield (2013) discusses a dilemma within MSF regarding the pay differentials between foreign volunteers and in-country workers. In justification, agencies could point to the inequalities in the world economy, the prevailing wage in places like Japan or the Netherlands compared to those in Burkina Faso or Bangladesh. To attract the most qualified professionals, NGOs have to provide a competitive salary for people from a host of countries. Several people in Haiti, like Sonson and Lesly, have theorized that the recession and rising unemployment explains why many young foreign professionals found themselves in Haiti after the earthquake. It not only provides a good job and a rite of passage for individuals (Bornstein 2012), it eases the burden on the labor market in the North. In addition to the inequalities within the world economy, Steinke uncovered a different value attached to the lives themselves. Generally speaking, humanitarian agencies face a dilemma when crossing enemy lines to offer life-saving assistance: their workers can be more valuable as hostages, or even martyrs. One cost to their rushing "where angels fear to tread" (Barnett and Weiss 2011) is that foreigners have a higher premium on their lives compared to the recipient communities.

People living in camps can distinguish among agencies that are providing aid. However, the Haitian term *enstans* is deliberately vague, blurring institutions such as NGOs, intergovernmental organizations, foreign governments, and the United Nations. It provides a linguistic clue to the growing ambivalence toward NGOs. Chapter 6 shared many recipients' gratitude toward NGOs and other humanitarian agencies. This is mixed with a growing fatigue of not seeing better results.

Sonson and Andrea both suggest thinking about a "culture of NGOs." If culture is defined as creative, adaptive responses to particular situations, languages, and explanatory frameworks ("worldview"), as systems of knowledge that shape action, NGOs may have a shared culture. Based on experience shared across NGOs, this culture supersedes national (foreign) origin of the agency and of the worker. This worldview shapes humanitarian action as surely as other factors, including being protected by what Jessica called "the bubble," by militarized checkpoints, with armed guards at home, at the office, grocery stores, and leisure spaces and the drivers to shuttle from them: not so much *without* borders as *mobile* borders. Inside this bubble or mobile sovereignty (Pandolfi 2003) is a system constrained by rules, hierarchy, procurement procedures, curfews, forms, reports, and RFPs (requests for proposals) sustained by a shared belief in doing something, an affirmation of a challenging if rewarding job. Fluency in NGO culture helps a given worker translate available aid into "deliverables." The challenge of moving aid is in no small part logistical, as much the mountain of paperwork from "above," but also understanding the culture, the contacts, and the context from "below." Those with decades of experience have also developed abilities to move these worlds together, systems for dealing with the cognitive dissonance when these worlds collide, and motivation to continue when they don't.

Management scholars and organizational sociologists often discuss an organizational culture within single institutions, often a recourse to explain an inability to adapt to change. Taking Haitian people's experience with the earthquake response as a cue, it might be worth exploring possible commonalities across organizations. These similarities, or NGO culture, are structured in part by what has been called the "audit culture" (Power 1997; Shore and Wright 2000; Strathern 2000; Vannier 2010), the ever-present reality that requires NGOs and government offices to be able to produce documentation. All actions are therefore potentially auditable, and all decisions justified by the paper trail. As Sonson, Geralda, and Andrea have noted, this is a key feature to a larger NGO culture, what Daniel called a "secret society."

Haitian perspectives, realities, and analyses might also be useful to address a core dilemma about conceptualizing NGOs. Scholars of NGOs have noted that "NGO" is frustratingly difficult to define, easier to define what it is not (Bernal and Grewal 2014; Fisher 1997). Scholarship has long deconstructed the term, arguing that it has little utility to describe the multitude of experiences, organizational types, and realities lumped under the term "NGO." This said, there has yet to be a term proposed in its place that has been widely adopted. The humanitarian aftershocks in Haiti suggest that it might be more productive to think of NGOs as a verb, and not a noun, marked by the actions they do and the internal activities that distinguish the organizational type (see also Sharma 2014). A common critique I heard after the earthquake among people involved in social movements is *"ah! W ap fè ONG"* (You are NGO-ing), by which the speaker usually meant adopting a bureaucratic structure or adopting a project logic, justifying the use of foreign funding, often arising from my efforts. "NGO-ing" might make more sense as a signifier than "NGOs" as a noun, even outside Haiti (see also Hilhorst 2003, 5). But still, it would be misguided to look for rigid criteria that must always be met. Here, Wittgenstein's "family resemblances" (2010) might be a useful way to think through the similarities of experience while acknowledging that a given NGO may be more or less hierarchical, have greater or lesser bureaucratic structures, diversity of funding, national origin, or domain of interventions.[1] This way similarities can be sought without ignoring specificities. But NGOs all act, and these actions serve as justifications for their existence and use of funds. One manifestation of this is the language of humanitarian aid, which includes actors and solutions. During the cholera crisis, the main goal of the Haitian government in the WASH (Water, Sanitation, and Hygiene) cluster was to identify both. Actors are agencies that assume responsibility to bring a particular WASH service or "solution" to a camp: usually an NGO or an intergovernmental organization like the Red Cross or IOM. As the cochair of the WASH cluster, UNICEF was the provider of last resort.

One of the biggest problems with the aid response was that the word *actor* usually did not include Haitian people, and certainly not recipient communities. At LogBase, Haitian people were shut out of discussions about humanitarian aid. IDPs were not even imagined as having a seat at the table. Chenet is clear about how aid turns recipient communities into objects. This relegation of Haitians to passive recipients or spectators, *assistancialisme*, might be a manifestation of the power imbalance inherent to the gift. French anthropologist Marcel Mauss (1990) argued that the act of offering a gift creates a permanent state of indebtedness, an obligation, of the recipient toward the giver. This obligation accrues over time until the receiver is able to offer a gift to her or his benefactor. As Erica Bornstein (2012, 14) noted, Jacques Derrida called Mauss to task for mistaking reciprocal exchange for the gift. The only true gift is done anonymously, so there are no possibilities for this relationship of obligation to take root. Individual people overseas who contributed to the earthquake response might have taken advantage of the tax incentives to donate, but most did not imagine any ongoing relationship with Haiti. Most people did not contribute to Haiti at all; they contributed to an array of aid agencies, mostly NGOs or the Red Cross. Meanwhile, the *enstans* delivering this humanitarian aid did manage relationships with a range of Haitian individuals, communities, organizations, and government agencies. Recipients like Chenet felt this paternalism, this sense of entitlement, resulting from the mystification wherein the agencies pretend to be the actual givers of the aid.

This mystification is by no means limited to Haiti. Several scholars of humanitarianism have also discussed Mauss and the tyranny of the gift (for example, Barnett 2011; Bornstein 2012; Fassin 2012; Minn 2007; Redfield 2013). People in this book like Robenson, Nadege, and Lesly challenge us to reflect in new ways, to imagine and dare to put into practice new forms of humanitarianism that fully respect our shared humanity, what might be called an "anthropological imagination." Saddled with the ambitious name of the study of *anthropos*, "man" (now humankind), anthropologists have unique responsibility to define, deconstruct, and ultimately defend a common humanity. Joel Robbins (2013) argued that what unites us is our capacity to suffer, and he argued that we move beyond the "savage slot" (Trouillot 2003). However, this book has demonstrated that this capacity is by no means equal; they are products of a world system set up to benefit the few at the expense of the many. Thus we need to look at the local community level, real peoples' lived experience while at the same time paying attention to the global level and humanity as a construct and a species. Tracking back and forth, this anthropological imagination acknowledges the ties that bind us and our specific places within the world system, our differential privilege, but also respects our differences. Given that this requires fundamentally challenging the assumptions, the worldview, logic, and structures of the current system, the humanitarian aftershocks in Haiti suggests a reboot, a new operating system: Humanitarianism 3.0.

HUMANITARIANISM 3.0

A first recommendation for Humanitarianism 3.0 builds directly on Mauss, as well as Chenet's discussion of the humanitarian market system. When I've facilitated discussions on the earthquake following a screening of *Poto Mitan* or discussing this research, I am often asked to offer my recommendations or, worse, on-the-spot evaluation of this or that NGO. Rather than endorse this approach, I always turn the conversation to our roles as citizens and taxpayers. The word *citizen* connotes active involvement and responsibility, even as it excludes, dramatized by recent debates on immigration policy in the United States, France, and Germany, among others. Collectively, individuals donated $3.02 billion to the earthquake response, which, however generous, was less than a quarter of what our governments pledged—$13.34 billion—nearly half of which had been disbursed as of the end of 2012. More important, citizen (taxpayer) action is required to keep an eye on our governments, undoing the policies that rendered Haiti vulnerable to disaster in the first place. The tax code rewards individuals for making voluntary contributions to registered, recognized, and regulated charities in the United States through the 501(c)(3) designation. Some grassroots or radical groups reject the designation and status of "charity" as complicit with the nonprofit industrial complex (INCITE! Women of Color Against Violence 2007), but it allows taxpayers—at least those of us who earn enough income to itemize deductions—to select where common pool resources are to be directed. The reflex to give may feel good, but, as this book and countless others demonstrate, individual acts of charity do not even attempt to address larger, structural, often global, root causes.

If people still felt compelled to make a voluntary contribution, I ask individuals to, in effect, call in their obligations to the recipient NGOs. Whether as gift givers or consumers, most people did not ask any questions of recipients or about the relationships that the donation facilitated. Three days after the earthquake I published a blog on *Common Dreams*, outlining an example of these questions, which boil down to relationships and decision making: Who are the ultimate recipients of this aid? How were these recipients chosen? How long has this relationship existed? Who makes decisions about this aid? Simply put, NGOs that raised funds for earthquake relief did not feel it necessary to provide these details, as the Red Cross scandal hammers home, in no small part because the media's hyperbolic disaster narrative already tugged on people's heartstrings. As donors or potential donors to humanitarian causes, we have the ability to make these changes. But we're not sitting in the chair that's set at the table for us; many intermediaries speak for us, invoking our name. If we're concerned about making even short-term impact—not least medium- or long-term change—without the problems discussed in this book being attached, we can simply ask. One thing we could do, mirroring the solidarity that Chenet and other organic intellectuals in this book describe, is send a check for $25 to an *enstans*, an agency, with a handwritten note asking these questions and a promise to help solicit more aid from members of a campus group, women's organization, labor union, faith community, or neighborhood fundraiser with those answers. It's also easier to make an impassioned pitch for donations if you can also provide these details.

As citizens and taxpayers we can also make structural changes. As the Disaster Accountability Project (2011) demonstrated, almost no NGOs offered basic information beyond that required from the U.S. government. NGO "watchdog" sites like Charity Navigator and GuideStar use the 990 form required by the IRS. But groups are not required to be more detailed than, for example, "disaster relief-Caribbean" as a single expense item. In part kicked off at the fateful *Haiti: Where Did the Money Go?* congressional hearing discussed in the previous chapter, an advocacy effort finally resulted in the passage of the Assessing Progress in Haiti Act, signed into law by President Barack Obama on August 8, 2014. This is a good start at asking and getting answers to the difficult questions. But it is only a start: as this book has shown, accountability means so much more than "Where did the money go?" Although it has been appropriated in the service of neoliberalism, a weapon in downsizing government and social services, accountability also means attention to process, that information about strategies, about funders, and about relationships need to be shared with beneficiaries. In the case of Haiti, that means that they make effective use of radio not only as PR tools but to inform about the structure of the humanitarian aid system, decision making, priorities, and with individual NGOs doing what and where. And reporting results, budgets, funds and employees need to be shared with beneficiaries, at the very least in summary form in Haitian. The preoccupation with numerical results has primarily resulted in more rigid management and better NGO regimes of producing numbers. By and large, this "Audit Culture" has not solved problems; it has only proliferated justifications for receipt of funds and, as Andrea noted, increased bureaucracy, making NGO interventions more costly and lethargic. The people in this book challenge us to come up with new metrics, calibrated to justice and long-term effectiveness.

Moving away from outputs and into outcomes, we must also ask Chenet's question about assessing long-term impact, about looking at the local-level social changes. Admittedly, this is difficult. Although this book doesn't provide answers, it urgently sharpens the focus on what we should ask, charting directions for future studies. We need to move well beyond the project cycle and ask about long-term changes engendered by the aid: What capacities are built or reinforced even after the *enstans* leaves? How do people—individually and in communities—understand themselves, define success, and envision their future? Some of these new dynamics, like the blowback of violence against women, of disrupting solidarity networks and the household structure, are not welcome, as Chenet and Geralda forcefully articulate.

Solidarity, as opposed to charity, also can disrupt the "tyranny of the gift." Solidarity, focused on rights and justice, implies an exchange, of shared struggle because our liberation is tied up with the liberation of others. We are all in this together. Nothing less than our humanity itself is at stake. People like

Manoucheka, Yves, and Allande denounced their being thought of, and treated, as animals. This same struggle of the value of human life is being waged in the United States, given renewed urgency since August 9, 2014, when a police officer in Ferguson, Missouri, shot and killed an unarmed Black teen, Michael Brown. Although the issue of state violence against Black communities certainly did not begin here, Ferguson became a symbol and place for a movement affirming that #BlackLivesMatter. This movement draws on shared and specific histories—from the middle passage, to slavery, to lynchings, Jim Crow, and the prison industrial complex—confronting the ways in which the U.S. state, tacitly if not actively supported by its constituents, targets black individuals for violence (Bonilla and Rosa 2015; Falcón 2015; Lindsey 2015). These ongoing, specific forms of state violence call into question the ideology of a universal humanity. The Church debated for centuries whether people in Africa were, in fact, human (Trouillot 1995). Located differentially within the world system, Haiti and Black America may have different economies, life chances, and what the United Nations call "human development indicators," but they share a history of struggle and what Kamari Maxine Clarke (2010) called "humanitarian diasporas," specific circuits of engagement. Those engaged in solidarity, shutting down commerce through using their bodies in "die-ins" are asserting and affirming the rights and value of human beings. Some activists point out the irony that the status of "persons" and citizenship rights won for former slaves following the Civil War by the Fourteenth Amendment were conferred onto corporations in the 2010 *Citizens United* decision, granting unlimited access to buying elections.

It is this system, this state, which extended globally through the United Nations, is being resisted by movements in Haiti. New social movements sprang up to promote the right to decent housing, to combat violence against women, to seek reparations from the United Nations for the cholera epidemic, to defend food sovereignty alongside peasants facing eviction from top-down development models of export processing factories in Caracol or high-end tourism in Île-à-Vache, to demand government regulation and protection, public participation, environmental impact mitigation, and profit sharing regarding mining. Each of these movements invited foreign citizens and taxpayers to fulfill our responsibilities, demanding that the governments acting in our names and with our resources stop their role in the abuses. Bottom-up, citizen-to-citizen solidarity requires that we each keep an eye on what our governments are doing. Being in solidarity also means dismantling both the "left hand" and "right hand" of empire (Agier 2003) and rebuilding a global system that privileges human relationships based on equality and mutual respect. According to Myriam Chancy (2013, 212), the current situation "maintains an ideological stronghold that perpetuates hegemonic relationships between the global North and South, and most pertinently for the United States, the subjugation of the only symbolic 'African' nation in the hemisphere." Being in solidarity means disrupting systemic racism at home while at the same time addressing the white supremacy it supports abroad, because these two are intimately linked institutionally as well as ideologically (Willoughby-Herard 2015). Solidarity is also expressed in thousands of individuals within the Haitian Diaspora donating time, talents, and millions of dollars, donating even greater resources to their families and communities back home.

The lessons we as humanity might have learned from the Haiti earthquake would have been priceless (Solnit 2009): dignity, solidarity, the value of collective action, humility, and resilience. Had we accepted this gift from people like Manolia or Claudine, ours of funding would not have been "poisoned," as Mauss holds. More work needs to be done on identifying and supporting the first responders to any disaster: the affected communities themselves. Had we followed the 630,000 people like Marie-Jeanne, Yves, or Nadege back home, reimbursed peasant families for their generosity, and engaged people on rebuilding those communities hollowed out by the neoliberal economic policies our governments imposed, this would have created much less pressure on the areas like Port-au-Prince that were directly affected by the earthquake. In addition to ITECA, some individual efforts were waged by Haitian organizations like the Papaye Peasant Movement (MPP) and Group of Support for Repatriated People and Refugees (GARR). Both bristle at the term "NGO" and blend activism and direct service. The world might have also gained new ideas about community organization, about prioritization, and local logistics in the process, to say the least about directing resources to solve locally defined priorities.

Participation is so much more than checking off the box. Rather than creating "Mini-Me" camp committees, the reward structure of a transformative humanitarian aid could have encouraged large, open, town-hall-type meetings for people in the neighborhood, whether or not they were in a camp. Asking questions like "Where did you get your water before the earthquake?" might have resulted in long-lasting reinforcements at a fraction of the cost. Thinking of IDPs as people with capacities in addition to needs might have led to identifying teachers, nurses, masons, or carpenters, as the Karade leaders suggested. Connecting these skills to resources to meet these locally identified needs, while offering jobs with dignity and breaking a cycle of dependency, would have likely been far more cost effective and expedient. Houses certainly would have been rebuilt more quickly, as locally identified solutions like the community enumeration unblocking land tenure could have been accompanied with funds and specific training on anti-seismic techniques.

Importantly, this would have also reinforced human capacity, even after the aid was gone. There are obviously skills and expertise required, like architects in Andrea's team needing to learn about latrines. And certainly resources like medical assistance, food, and building materials. But, to borrow Bill Clinton's question in early 2010: "Are we serious about putting ourselves out of a job?" Clinton's comment, leading up to the UN Donors Conference, did not specify which job—disaster response or development—but he continued, "Are we helping them become more self-sufficient?" Sonson was adamant about the need to learn from this experience. Geralda agreed: "Because people learn too, when they do." She outlined a lesson learned for future humanitarian efforts: "We didn't feel the need to invest in training a critical mass of local NGOs, which would have influenced and changed the global trend. So, maybe this should have been our main role at that time."

The scale of the disaster in Port-au-Prince requires an appropriate scale of response. Addressing housing density and (re)building necessary infrastructure requires a role for centralized planning and resource allocation. This is one of the main functions of the government. The WASH cluster achieved results in cholera prevention in no small part because the Haitian government coordinated and set mandates for NGOs. Local governments also gained relevance in Haiti because of the Department of Civil Protection tasked with emergency response. There was also a simulation of a large-scale disaster in 2009 and a report to be published. Like the report coming from the Aceh experience, this wasn't applied. Geralda argues, "The structure already exists in theory, so the aid must follow this circuit." To not do so is to create a self-fulfilling prophecy. One way to get there, if, as Geralda noted, our solidarity was only expressed through NGOs, is for foreign donors to voluntarily "tax" our aid to offer minimal resources to the ministry and local governments to coordinate NGO projects financed by our governments. That could help build this capacity over time. However, barely 50 miles across the sea, Cuba is a textbook model for emergency disaster preparedness and response. In 2004, Oxfam published a report (Thompson and Gaviria 2004) distilling Cuba's formula. Between 1996 and 2002, six major hurricanes struck the island. In that period, only 16 people died in Cuba, compared to 649 for its island neighbors. This disparity with Haiti was made even starker during Tropical Storm Jeanne in 2004. The report presented twelve major themes, among which are communication, government priorities, social cohesion, and community-based institutional reinforcement in the Civil Defense and Community Based Disaster Management approach as keys to Cuba's success at reducing vulnerability. Although it certainly isn't perfect, Cuba's medical system was built with resources limited by centuries of plantation slavery exploitation and an embargo from the United States. And as they demonstrated in Haiti, Cuban and Cuban-trained doctors are effective at preventing and treating illnesses common to the tropical region with a limited budget and available technologies.

Humanitarianism 3.0 should deliberately be part of a larger framework addressing development and human rights. As Chenet pointed out, "The previous living condition of the population, if we really analyze it, was already a humanitarian crisis situation." If we are serious, not only to assuage our feelings of guilt or powerlessness, then we should look at this previous humanitarian crisis situation and interrogate the reasons for it, and also our complicity. Again, though it is not perfect, and Afro-Cubans still face inequality and racism, Cuban society has made remarkable achievements in human development: it has a literacy rate higher than the United States, for example, and universal health care. As chapter 1 demonstrated, the Haiti earthquake is the clearest example of the failures of free-market-only approaches. As such, disaster response must address these structural roots to vulnerability head on. Geralda concluded quite simply that "there mustn't be any humanitarian intervention outside a development framework." But what kind of development? Chenet's warning about Haiti being in a humanitarian crisis before the earthquake is a powerful reminder that in Haiti, with foreign-directed development initiatives, largely implemented by NGOs within a neoliberal policy framework that undermined government capacity, the development experiment has mostly failed. Therefore, a Humanitarianism 3.0 requires radically different approaches.

ITECA offers another example. By the time of the earthquake, ITECA had worked and had its headquarters in the town of Gressier, the epicenter, for twenty-seven years. They conducted a community evaluation and found that sixteen hundred families lost their homes. ITECA lacked the financial means to rebuild them, but they had decades of local experience and relationships, requiring them to have foreign partners. As Chenet alluded to, they engaged in long and often heated negotiations with several agencies, many of whom went to Gressier to plant the flag on the quake's epicenter. Knowing their value in a humanitarian market, ITECA insisted that the local community have a say in the final product and that the process be dignified. Because of ITECA's mission of community empowerment, social justice, and dignity, they stood their ground. As part of developing local human and institutional capacity, a large component of the project involved training and locally resourced materials. The first beneficiaries of the training were individual homeowners: an important element of the project was active participation and volunteer labor from recipient households, in part to disrupt the obligations arising from a gift. ITECA decided, after long discussions during several meetings, to become an NGO in order to be able to import building materials. Although this opened ITECA up to greater scrutiny and criticism, they also had a seat at the table, elected to be the NGO representative to the Departmental Council and the national council. As Chenet said, "Guarding against the problems about bureaucratization requires constant vigilance, self-critique, and a solid relationship to the local community, to whom we feel accountable." According to Chenet, a main benefit of the new NGO status, "while keeping our spirit of activism and solidarity as a social movement," was to build capacity. To feed local demand, for logistical reasons and cost effectiveness, and to create jobs, ITECA opened up a factory to fabricate cement blocks and other building materials. This factory not only offered jobs, it allowed them to locally source materials that also supplied other community groups' and individuals' rebuilding efforts. ITECA was hailed as a model for autonomy and local self-determination by other groups in Haiti, even as it sometimes frustrated their foreign partners who were used to being in the driver's seat. In the first year ITECA built three hundred houses, and then with the new partner, they built an additional five hundred. As of 2014, they have built more than nine hundred homes. Chenet reported that they continue to run into difficulties; their first foreign partner, a European NGO, has attempted to smear ITECA's reputation there.

ITECA's success offers glimmers of humanitarianism rethought. Geralda noted that logistics are often the most expensive for humanitarian agencies, in large part because they involve foreign staff, equipment, and materials. Because a medical team needs water, electricity, and a functional system of roads to save lives, a demand-driven humanitarian development could build local capacity. Rather than do it all themselves or offering contracts to for-profit private companies in the countries of their origins, humanitarian *enstans*, even in the emergency phase, could contract local government to provide their immediate logistical needs, building local capacity and sustainably providing their public water, public electricity, and roads. Doing away with the "step aside mentality" requires trust, respect, and belief in a common, shared humanity.

A final element to Humanitarianism 3.0 is that it should be about our shared connections to our common humanity, dignity, and self-worth. There are Fergusons in every corner of the world. Just as the Haitian Revolution was a logical conclusion to the egalitarian ideology expressed in the French Revolution, that local groups like ITECA and the organized social movements are demanding full participation and a new model is affirmation of the highest ideals of humanitarianism. If we only follow their lead, we as humanity can imagine and bring into being better humanitarian practice, animated by solidarity and respecting rights, in effect ripping it from empire. Geralda inspires us to live up to these ideals:

> If we want to do better next time, we have to learn lessons from our experience, and our humanitarian strategy must tell us what to avoid and how to do it. Actually practice the lessons learned. The level of solidarity was extraordinary. It's important to continue to look at the level of solidarity from one people following a disaster from another people. For us to continue to have this level of solidarity, we need to deliver this aid another way.

APPENDIX

CAMPS IN THE STUDY

CAJIT   Support Committee for the Youth of Impasse Thomas, in the hills above the Paloma neighborhood, Carrefour

Hancho I   Camp straddling factory parcels on the edge of the Industrial Park and the Cité Jacques Roumain neighborhood

Karade   Carradeux, officially a neighborhood but came to denote a cluster of seven contiguous camps

Kolonbi   "Colombia," in Delmas 19, near the Industrial Park

Meri Dikini   "The municipal office of Diquini," the city hall of the suburb of Carrefour

Nan Bannann   "In the banana trees," straddling three private properties in a residential neighborhood, Delmas 32

Plas Lapè   "Peace Plaza," in a lower-income neighborhood, Delmas 2

St. Louis   A wealthy Catholic school for boys, in Delmas 31 and 33

NAMES OF CAMP RESIDENTS INTERVIEWED

Alix	Plas Lapè
Allande	Kolonbi
Carolle	Karade
Cassandra	Hancho
Charlène	CAJIT
Claudine	St. Louis
Edwidge	CAJIT
Emile	Plas Lapè
Esaie	St. Louis
Eveline	Nan Bannann
Evrance	Kolonbi
Fanfan	Nan Bannann
France	CAJIT
Franck	Kolonbi
François	Hancho
Fritz	Plas Lapè

Ghislaine	St. Louis
Gladis	Nan Bannann
Gracia	Hancho
Jean-Claude	Kolonbi
Jean-Jacques	Kolonbi
Jhon	CAJIT
Jorel	Kolonbi
Josselyn	Plas Lapè
Jozi	St. Louis
Katiana	Hancho
Liline	Meri Dikini
Linda	CAJIT
Lolo	Karade
MacDonald	Meri Dikini
Mackenson	Karade
Magalie	Kolonbi
Manno	Nan Bannann
Manolia	Hancho
Manouchka	Hancho
Margo	Hancho
Marie-Hélène	Plas Lapè
Marie-Marthe	Meri Dikini
Marjorie	St. Louis
Maud	Karade
Michaëlle	Nan Bannann
Michèle	Hancho
Murielle	Meri Dikini
Nadege	St. Louis
Nadeve	Karade
Nadine	Hancho
Nelson	CAJIT
Paul	Kolonbi
Rachelle	St. Louis
Robenson	St. Louis
Roody	Karade
Rose-Anne	Hancho
Sabine	CAJIT
Sandy	Nan Bannann
Sophonie	Meri Dikini
Suze	Plas Lapè

Tatiana	Meri Dikini
Ti Wobè	Nan Bannann
Tracey	CAJIT
Wedly	Kolonbi
Yannick	St. Louis
Yolette	St. Louis
Youyou	Karade
Yves	CAJIT

NOTES

INTRODUCTION

1. Names of most individuals are changed to protect people's anonymity. However, where the individuals are public figures, and already in the media, their real, full names are used. An activist colleague has sensitized me to the postcolonial patronization inherent in the common anthropological practice of giving interlocutors only a first name. Given the sheer number of individuals profiled in this book, however, having an invented first and last name in this project risked even greater confusion.

2. The low figure was established by a report commissioned but not published by USAID: (Schwartz and with Yves-François Pierre and Eric Calpas 2011). This report was aimed at critiquing the official statistic put out January 12, 2011, by the government of Haiti. See, for example "Haiti Revises Quake Death Toll Up to over 316,000" (2011).

CHAPTER 1. HAITI'S UNNATURAL DISASTER

1. I follow eminent Haitian scholar Patrick Bellegarde-Smith, who uses the word *Haitian* to denote the language that has been around for five hundred years. We do not call French a "creole" of Latin, for example. Haiti beyond Coasts conference keynote, Northwestern University, April 17, 2015.

2. In addition to being a mismatch with "South," to use the term "West" is a holdover from imperialism, and geographically inaccurate. New York is due north of Haiti, for example.

3. See, for example, Curtin 1990; Higman 1984; Hoetink 1973; James 1989 (1938); Knight 1997; Mintz 1985.

4. This includes scholars such as Michel Foucault (1979), whose narrative about the more "civilized" form of discipline in bourgeois society skips over what France (and other European nations) was doing in the Caribbean. Sibylle Fischer (2007) similarly calls Agamben (1998)—whose notion of "bare life" built on Foucault's (1978) notion of "biopower"—to task.

5. This was the argument put forth by Tannenbaum (1947). This was challenged by other scholars for its lack of historical specificity, notably that the Spanish Caribbean intensified slavery after British (1838) and French (1848) emancipation, and with it the intermediate social categories. See, for example, Wade 1995; Whitten 2007.

6. Toussaint Louverture has been the subject of many scholarly analyses, beginning with Trinidadian revolutionary C.L.R. James (James 1989 [1938]). This text has inspired a plethora of literary criticism and reinterpretations, especially from within the Caribbean (Fick 1990; Fischer 2004; Scott 2004).

7. Recently republished, his Creole language *Ti dife boulè* (Little Burning Fires) (Trouillot 1977) interrogates this thesis.

8. Dessalines also formally did away with racism in his 1805 constitution, claiming all inhabitants as "black" and offering Haitian citizenship to anyone who sought it.

9. Trouillot (1995) and others criticize the brutality and inequality that went into Christophe's imperial ambitions, including the building of the Citadel and his palace.

10. This act is often cited as justification for persistent anti-Haitian racism, finding expression in a 2013 Supreme Court ruling stripping Dominican citizenship for anyone with foreign ancestry born after 1929. See Chancy 2012; Sagás 2000; Simmons 2009; Suárez 2006; Wucker 1999.

11. It is debatable whether this was ever a credible threat because Napoleon sold the entire middle third of the United States to Jefferson at rock-bottom prices in 1803, when it was about to lose its "pearl of the Caribbean."

12. An additional four held slaves at one point in their lives.

13. The formal policy was to be adopted in 1834, but it took four years for the word to reach the crown colonies and to be enforced.

14. The precise figure printed on banners and sung on radio spots was $21,685,135,571.48.

15. The percentage represents 561 of 785 who responded.

16. Measured in purchasing power parity. In April 2013, a large factory collapsed in Dhaka, Bangladesh's free trade zone, killing 1,129 workers and injuring more than 2,500.

17. President Préval, faced with pressure from Bill Clinton, recently named UN Special Envoy, unconstitutionally reduced the wage.

18. In 2003, Haiti's scheduled debt service was $57.4 million, whereas the entire scheduled grants for education, health care, environment, and transportation combined was $39.21 million (IMF 2005, 88; World Bank 2002, vii).

19. According to the Organisation for Economic Co-operation and Development (OECD), the average in member countries is 22 percent; U.S. investment is among the lowest, at around 15 percent.

20. State socialism led to massive urbanization, whereas in the deindustrializing North there were rust belt cities.

21. Despite this parity, legislation establishing the Creole Academy had not been passed until 2014.

22. These are often invisible to many foreign onlookers, including aid workers.

23. Although nearly all NGOs had their headquarters in Port-au-Prince before the earthquake, only a handful actually worked there.

24. "Extended" family is in quotes because this is an ideologically laden term, and as such has many different definitions. It is often deployed to critique entire social groupings. See Arneil (2006) for a detailed analysis and critique.

CHAPTER 2. RACING FROM THE RUBBLE

1. Her journalist/agronomist husband, Jean-Leopold Dominique, was murdered in 2000, in a high-profile and as-yet uninvestigated case.

2. I am leaving this word in its original quotes, such as "the thing," to respect people's word choice. When it is simply "earthquake" the word *tranblemanntè* was used. Note the lack of definitive article. As Schwartz (2011) pointed out, some people treat Goudougoudou as a proper noun, referring to it as if it had agency. There are some parallels within the disaster literature about referring to disaster "agents" (Oliver-Smith 1999).

3. I could have chosen to gender *nèg* as masculine, as many have. It is often used to also signify "guy."

4. This is measured by the Gini coefficient.

5. The expression was in French: *"lorsque l'on ne trouve pa ce qu'on aime, on aime ce qu' on a."*

6. See Glick Schiller and Fouron (2001) for a discussion of the naming of these places like "Boston" or "Brooklyn."

7. Castelot Val, the research assistant who conducted research at the camp, had difficulty obtaining the etymology of *Hancho*. Sheepishly, at the end of the fieldwork, after I specifically prodded, he said that it was Haitian slang, referring to gangs, "Let's be hot," with "hot" referring to levels of violence, or a rap song of the name, "Head Honcho."

8. There is no such thing as a "Haitian" dollar; the concept refers to the many years of the gourde being fixed as five to one U.S. dollar, before Leslie Delatour floated the currency.

CHAPTER 3. HITTING HOME

1. *Lakou* is a culturally specific form of household and tradition; *fwaye* is the general term for household (or house).

2. Slavery had a different character in the Caribbean, and certainly in Haiti, with more "Bossale," born in Africa. This means that fewer people were born into slavery and processes of disidentification with one's homeland were more severe.

3. Haitian anthropologist Rachel Beauvoir-Dominique (personal communication) pointed to regional differences in practices of food and language between the "Grand South" and "Grand North," and these are identifiable in the northern and southern zones in the Port-au-Prince metropolitan area.

4. The word is *li*, which isn't gendered. Sometimes it is clear with context.

5. *Lakou* can be single or plural. A plural form of *lakou* is denoted by placing *yo* after it. Some people (for example, Smith 2001) have tried to denote this by adding -*s* at the end. Its usage is imperfect and often difficult to read.

6. According to several Haitian historians, agronomists, and anthropologists the use of rice as a daily staple in Port-au-Prince was only generalized after the flood of cheaper, subsidized, imported rice.

7. These were quantitative interviews with self-reported choices, so it is not clear from the context what kind of "service" people engaged in, but research assistants who were curious asked the young women. It appears that at least a few (out of sixteen overall) were engaged in some form of sex work.

8. Interestingly this intensive, hands-on surveying was far from the norm before the earthquake. One of the main problems in planning was this lack of verifiable census data.

9. Although depending on the question, there could be multiple "true" responses, because it indeed varied based on context.

10. As of May 1, 2014, the State Department per diem rate was $266 for Port-au-Prince and Petion-Ville, $241 for Cap-Haïtien, $239 for seaside resort town Montrouis, $173 for Jacmel, and $180 for "Other." The latest effective date was May 1, 2013.

11. As of January 1, 2014, Haiti was taken off the list of countries that the U.S. government pays this bonus to salaries. It is still, however, on a list of countries that are deemed too dangerous to send undergraduate students.

12. Next chapter discusses research about rape and sexual violence.

13. This is not in quotes because this interview was not audio-recorded. I took detailed jottings during the interview and wrote field notes within an hour of the end of the interview in most cases. This was in part because some international aid representatives preferred to be off the record.

14. A listing can be found on http://www.amnesty.ie/our-work/forced-evictions-haiti.

15. For the purposes of data analysis *family* was defined as anyone with a blood or marriage relation. Sometimes individuals did not select "family" but said husband, and so on.

16. Ilionor Louis (2012b) reported that actually people had more space in the Petion-Ville club camp than Corail. The Morne à Cabrit project was not even intended for camp residents, for but middle-class government professionals.

CHAPTER 4. *PA MANYEN FANM NAN KONSA*

1. Martelly dropped Rouzier not long after this.

2. In 2006, the Minister of Women's Condition presented a law recognizing paternity to Parliament, who passed it in 2007, officially ending this discriminatory practice.

3. Women's International Network of the World Association of Community Radio Broadcasters (AMARC), Equality Now, Gender and Disaster Network, Groots International, Huairou Commission, Lambi Fund of Haiti, MADRE, ORÉGAND (Observatoire sur le développement régional et l'analyse différenciée selon les sexes), PotoFanm+Fi: Rebuilding Haiti Initiative, g+dsr.

4. The word used was *bouda*, which is a sexually explicit form of the word, not *dèyè*, "behind."

5. United Nations Office of the Special Envoy for Haiti 2012.

6. As of September 2013, the database arbitrarily excluded informal settlement of Kanaran/Canaan, home to some 130,000 people. Therefore the most recent statistic before this political decision is used in the chapter.

7. Haiti's violent crime rate ranks below median within the region. Haiti's homicide rate of 8.2 per 100,000 is consistently more than three times lower than that of Brazil (26.4), the country at the head of MINUSTAH's military unit, and almost seven times lower than Jamaica (54.9), across the Windward Channel. Source: U.S. Department of State, Bureau of Diplomatic Security, *Haiti 2011 Crime and Safety Report*, https://www.osac.gov.

CHAPTER 5. *PÒCH PRELA*

1. The original Haitian is *entelijan*, "intelligent," used in the sense of being manipulative.

2. With much reflection, I have decided to use the real NGO names in this chapter because the real camp names are used. CRS's institutional identity played a significant role in the rapprochement, given the relationship with the Catholic priest. Readers should not interpret these as representatives of all their work in all the camps, and certainly not the work of all NGOs.

3. The original Haitian is *tonbe*, to "fall (into)."

4. For the sake of clarity I'm using the word *camp* even though the language she used was *site*.

5. It would be understood to be in French or even English because aid agencies wouldn't be expected to understand Haitian.

6. Even though I began the interview in Haitian, he chose to switch to English. This is the original transcript.

7. This was both his house and traditional religious space as well, as he was an *oungan*, a religious leader.

8. The italicized phrase was in French, not Haitian. I follow this convention.

9. It was also the institution that offered T-shelters in the neighborhood where I lived. They were invited into the neighborhood by Hospice St. Joseph, a Catholic parish organization that had been active in the neighborhood for twenty years.

10. The language of "guiding principles" and "standards" in the case of the Sphere Project and humanitarian charter is less binding than those of "rights."

11. *Èske gen yon komite nan kan isit? Kijan komite sa rele? Kiyès ki lidè nan komite kan an? Ki estrateji/aktivite komite sa a ap mennen? Kilè rankont komite a fèt? Kijan yo chwazi moun pou rantre nan komite a? Èske ou gen dwa patisipe nan rankont komite?*

12. The word *participation* was one of the three pillars of the platform of Aristide during the first democratic election in 1990. It was a very powerful political term meaning the inclusion of Haiti's poor majority in matters of the government. Since the rise of NGO influence in the mid-1990s, participation has come to mean the receipt of aid from an NGO, as it is in this case, as well as for an individual to contribute his or her dues or portion.

13. Literally, *gen je pou ou wè*, "have eyes that see."

CHAPTER 6. *ABA ONG VOLÈ*

1. Said a twenty-five-year veteran of a Red Cross, "The ICRC is created by an international conference of states, although it is actually run by an international committee which is basically Swiss. Not quite sure what the status of the IFRC is, but probably has a similar status. The reality of how national societies of the RC or Red Crescent are perceived on the ground is a totally different matter. The Syrian Arab Red Crescent, for example, is seen by most as an emanation of the Syrian state. Most Red Cross societies have some affiliation or get support from the state but the degree to which they are or are seen as 'independent' obviously varies."

2. I searched the site several times throughout 2014; the last search was conducted on October 15.

3. The methodology was never made explicit, but it might be a compilation of any association or organization registered with one or another government ministry. Research in 2009 verified that a very small percentage of these groups still existed in two neighborhoods, fewer than 5 percent (Schuller 2012a).

4. The word is *yo* in the original Haitian. The interviewer used the word *yo* in the question.

5. Original text is *afè pawòl, afè pawòl, afè twalèt la*, the "affairs of speaking of, speaking of, affairs of toilets."

6. The original was *li*. I am keeping this term broad because it is possible that the speaker was referring to a person or an NGO.

7. The word was not *yès*—from the English "yes," meaning excellent, great.

8. *Èske yo di nou poukisa se èd sa a yo pote.*

9. This is correct spelling for neither French nor Haitian, but this was what the communication included.

10. Later, during relocation, "Federation" of Red Cross agencies.

11. Both phrases were *ti pèp la*.

CHAPTER 7. COLONIZATION WITHIN NGOS

1. *Blan* also means foreigner, but *etranje* is the more polite form.

2. Original in this passage was *li*, "(s)he." For the sake of clarity the original was changed to the plural form.

3. Original in English.

4. Original in French. Literally "crave eyes."

5. Original in English.

6. In this instance the supervisor was a male.

7. Original in French.

8. The State Department still issues a travel warning advising people away from traveling to Haiti, a ban in place since at least 2001, when I first visited.

9. Original in French.

10. Original in French.

CHAPTER 8. *FOTOKOPI*

1. Hurricane Katrina in 2005 and the 2008 Sichuan earthquake notably occurred in two of the world's most powerful economies.

2. The full text of the letter is posted online, unnamed, published originally in *Le Matin*, unofficial translation from Isabeau Doucet. *Letter from the Haitian Members of the Interim Haiti Reconstruction Commission to Co-Chairmen of the Commission*, http://www.normangirvan .info/protest-letter-haitian-ihrc-members/.

3. The word *control* has less ominous connotations in French, for example.

4. Inter-Agency Standing Committee, *IASC Principals Transformative Agenda*, http://www .humanitarianinfo.org/iasc/pageloader.aspx?page=content-template-default&bd=87.

5. In *Fatal Assistance*, there was a strong implication that Bill Clinton backed Martelly in the elections. The documentary also showed Secretary of State Hillary Clinton strong-arming President Préval about the election results.

6. There were some individual efforts, notably a settlement built in the Belladères–Las Cahobas border region and in Papaye.

7. For an example, see the cover photo of Frédéric Thomas's *Haiti: l'Echec humanitaire*.

8. Schuller (2007b): 89 percent of NGOs in the official database were headquartered in the Port-au-Prince metropolitan area, whereas 85 percent said their work was outside of Port-au-Prince.

9. Because I was unable to interview them, and this information was not made public, I do not have the precise figure.

10. These staff flew fifty-three orphans without Haitian government permission or awareness, with no proposals for adoption.

CONCLUSION

1. William Fisher (2014) also invoked Wittgenstein, but to suggest that the term "NGO" was useful to help us climb the ladder, and now it may be time to throw it away.

GLOSSARY

assistancialisme: French term referring to a condition of dependency, an individual turning into a spectator

blan: Foreigner, also white person

deplase: Haitian term meaning "displaced" and "internally displaced person" (IDP)

enstans: Literally "instance," a deliberately vague term to refer to the multitude of organizational types, including nongovernmental organizations

fanmi: Family

fwaye: Literally "foyer," referring to household space, also households

goudougoudou: Term for the earthquake

istwa: Both "story" and "history"

kan: Camp

konbit: Collective work group

kotizasyon: Practice of voluntary contribution, used by grassroots organizations and social movements

kriz estriktirèl: The "Structural" crisis, neoliberal policies and structures that are manifest in outcroppings of particular identified crises. It can be correlated to either what scholars term "vulnerability" or "structural violence"

kriz lavi chè a: The crisis of inflation, exploding in 2008 with mass mobilization

lakou: Traditional extended family compound, referring to the space, practice, and belief system

moun pa: Your people, often referring to a situation of nepotism

pòch prela: Literally, "pockets of tarps," referring to camp committees, beyond "deep pockets"

sòl: Solidarity lending practice, organically organized in groups

tí sourit: Literally, "little mouse," meaning the majority of people, as opposed to "rats," or big men

youn ede lòt: One helping the other, a traditional value in Haitian social life

REFERENCES

Abu-Lughod, Lila. 1991. "Writing against Culture." In *Recapturing Anthropology: Working in the Present*, edited by Richard G. Fox, 137–162. Santa Fe, NM: School of American Research Press.

Acted, and International Organization for Migration (IOM). 2011. *Enquête IOM—ACTED: Intentions des deplaces Haïti*. Port-au-Prince: Acted and IOM.

Acuto, Michele. 2014. *Negotiating Relief: The Dialectic of Humanitarian Space*. London: C. Hurst.

Adams, Vincanne. 2013. *Markets of Sorrow, Labors of Faith: New Orleans in the Wake of Katrina*. Durham, NC: Duke University Press.

Agamben, Giorgio. 1998. *Homo Sacer: Sovereign Power and Bare Life*. Stanford, CA: Stanford University Press.

Agence France-Presse. 2011. "Haiti Cholera Death Toll Tops 4,000." *Agence France-Presse*, January 28. http://www.nanodaily.com/reports/Haiti_death_toll_from_cholera_tops_4000_999.html.

Agier, Michel. 2003. "La Main Gauche de l'Empire: Ordre et désordres de l'humanitaire." *Multitudes*. 11 (1): 67–77.

———. 2006. "Le gouvernement humanitaire et la politique des réfugiés." In *La Philosophie déplacée: Autour de Jacques Rancière, Colloque de Cerisy*, edited by Laurence Cornu and Patrice Vermeren. Paris: Horlieu Editions.

———. 2010. "Humanity as an Identity and Its Political Effects (A Note on Camps and Humanitarian Government)." *Humanity: An International Journal of Human Rights, Humanitarianism, and Development* 1 (1): 29–45.

———. 2011. *Managing the Undesirables: Refugee Camps and Humanitarian Government*. Malden, MA: Polity.

Alexander, David E. 1997. "The Study of Natural Disasters, 1977–97: Some Reflections on a Changing Field of Knowledge." *Disasters* 21 (4): 284–304.

———. 2013. "Resilience and Disaster Risk Reduction: An Etymological Journey." *Natural Hazards and Earth System Sciences* 13 (11): 2707–2716.

Alvarez, Sonia E. 1999. "Advocating Feminism: The Latin American Feminist NGO 'Boom.'" *International Feminist Journal of Politics* 1 (2): 181–209.

Anastario, Michael P., Ryan Larrance, and Lynn Lawry. 2008. "Using Mental Health Indicators to Identify Postdisaster Gender-Based Violence among Women Displaced by Hurricane Katrina." *Journal of Women's Health* (15409996) 17 (9): 1437–1444. doi: 10.1089/jwh.2007.0694.

Arneil, Barbara. 2006. *Diverse Communities—The Problem with Social Capital*. Cambridge: Cambridge University Press.

Atmar, Mohammed Haneef. 2001. "Politicisation of Humanitarian Aid and Its Consequences for Afghans." *Disasters* 25 (4): 321–330.

Ayiti Kale Je. 2010. *Cash for . . . What? Argent contre . . . Quoi? Dinero para . . . Que?*, November 9. http://haitigrassrootswatch.squarespace.com/journal/2010/11/8/cash-for-what-argent-contre-quoi-dinero-para-que.html.

Bankoff, Greg. 2004. "The Historical Geography of Disaster: 'Vulnerability' and 'Local Knowledge' in Western Discourse." In *Mapping Vulnerability: Disasters, Development, and People*, edited by Greg Bankoff, Georg Frerks, and Dorothea Hilhorst, 25–36. London: Earthscan.

Bankoff, Greg, Georg Frerks, and Dorothea Hilhorst, eds. 2004. *Mapping Vulnerability: Disasters, Development, and People*. London: Earthscan.

Barnett, Michael. 2011. *The Empire of Humanity: A History of Humanitarianism*. Ithaca, NY: Cornell University Press.

———. 2013. "Humanitarian Governance." *Annual Review of Political Science* 16: 379–398.

Barnett, Michael, and Thomas G. Weiss. 2011. *Humanitarianism Contested: Where Angels Fear to Tread*. New York: Routledge.

Barrios, Roberto. 2014. "'Here, I'm Not at Ease': Anthropological Perspectives on Community Resilience." *Disasters* 38 (2): 329–350.

Barthélémy, Gérard. 1990. *L'univers rural haïtien: Le pays en dehors*. Paris: L'Harmattan.

Bastien, Rémy. 1961. "Haitian Rural Family Organization." *Social and Economic Studies* 10 (4): 478–510.

Bazin, Marc. 2008. *Des idées pour l'action*. Port-au-Prince: Imprimateur II.

Beauvoir-Dominique, Rachel. 2012. "Humanitarian Assistance in Gonaïves after Hurricane Jeanne." In *Tectonic Shifts: Haiti since the Earthquake*, edited by Mark Schuller and Pablo Morales, 13–17. Sterling, VA: Kumarian.

Beauvoir-Dominique, Rachel, Centre de Recherches Urbaines—Travaux (CRU-T), and Plateforme des Organisations Haïtiennes de Défense des Droits Humains (POHDH). 2005. *Impact de l'assistance humanitaire aux Gonaïves suite au cyclone Jeanne au regard des droits humains fondamentaux*. Port-au-Prince: Plateforme des Organisations Haïtiennes de Défense des Droits Humains (POHDH).

Beckles, Hilary McD. 2013. *Britain's Black Debt: Reparations for Caribbean Slavery and Native Genocide*. Kingston, Jamaica: University of the West Indies Press.

Behar, Ruth, and Deborah Gordon. 1995. *Women Writing Culture*. Berkeley: University of California Press.

Bélizaire, Roland. 2010. *Politiques publiques en Haïti: A quand la rupture avec la dépendence?* Port-au-Prince: Plateforme Haïtienne de Plaidoyer pour un Développement Alternatif (PAPDA).

Bell, Beverly. 2001. *Walking on Fire: Haitian Women's Stories of Survival and Resistance*. Ithaca, NY: Cornell University Press.

———. 2013. *Fault Lines: Views from across Haiti's Divide*. Ithaca, NY: Cornell University Press.

Bengtsson, Linus, Xin Lu, Anna Thorson, Richard Garfield, and Johan von Schreeb. 2011. "Improved Response to Disasters and Outbreaks by Tracking Population Movements with Mobile Phone Network Data: A Post-Earthquake Geospatial Study in Haiti." *PLOS Medicine*. August 30. http://journals.plos.org/plosmedicine/article?id=10.1371/journal.pmed.1001083

Benoit, Olga. 1995. "Women's Popular Organizations." *Roots* 1 (3): 26–29.

Benthall, Jonathan. 1993. *Disasters, Relief, and the Media*. London: I. B. Tauris.

Bergan, Renée, and Mark Schuller. 2009. *Poto Mitan: Haitian Women, Pillars of the Global Economy*. Watertown, MA: Documentary Educational Resources.

Bernal, Victoria, and Inderpal Grewal. 2014. *Theorizing NGOs: States, Feminism, and Neoliberalism*. Durham, NC: Duke University Press.

Bernard, Jean Maxius, and Julio Desormeaux. 1996. *Culture, santé, sexualité à Cité Soleil.* Port-au-Prince: Centres pour le Développement et la Santé.

Bernard, Sabine. 2013. "Finding My Cultural Identity: Experience from a 'Dyaspora' in Haiti's Internally Displaced Persons Camps." *Practicing Anthropologist* 35 (3): 8–11.

Bessis, Sophie. 2001. "The World Bank and Women: 'Institutional Feminism.'" In *Eye to Eye: Women Practising Development across Cultures,* edited by Susan Perry and Celeste Schenck, 10–24. London: Zed Books.

Bhavnani, Kum-Kum, John Foran, and Priya A. Kurian. 2003. *Feminist Futures: Re-imagining Women, Culture, and Development.* London: Zed.

Blot, Jean-Yves. 2012. "The November 28, 2010 Elections: Another Catastrophe for Haiti." In *Tectonic Shifts: Haiti since the Earthquake,* edited by Mark Schuller and Pablo Morales, 195–199. Sterling, VA: Kumarian.

Bonilla, Yarimar. 2012. "The Past Is Made by Walking: Labor Activism and Historical Production in Postcolonial Guadeloupe." *Cultural Anthropology* 26 (3): 313–339.

Bonilla, Yarimar, and Jonathan Rosa. 2015. "#Ferguson: Digital Protest, Hashtag Ethnography, and the Racial Politics of Social Media in the United States." *American Ethnologist* 42: 4–17.

Bornstein, Erica. 2012. *Disquieting Gifts: Humanitarianism in New Delhi.* Stanford, CA: Stanford University Press.

Bornstein, Erica, and Peter Redfield. 2011. *Forces of Compassion: Humanitarianism between Ethics and Politics.* Santa Fe, NM: School for Advanced Research Press.

Bourdieu, Pierre. 1998. *Practical Reason: On the Theory of Action.* Stanford, CA: Stanford University Press.

Brauman, Rony. 1993. "When Suffering Makes a Good Story." In *Life, Death, and Aid: The Médecins sans Frontières Report on World Crisis Intervention,* edited by François Jean, 149–158. London: Routledge.

Brenner, Johanna. 2000. *Women and the Politics of Class.* New York: Monthly Review Press.

Brown, Philip H., and Jessica H. Minty. 2008. "Media Coverage and Charitable Giving after the 2004 Tsunami." *Southern Economic Journal* 75 (1): 9–25.

Brun, Cathrine. 2003. "Local Citizens or Internally Displaced Persons? Dilemmas of Long Term Displacement in Sri Lanka." *Journal of Refugee Studies* 16 (4): 376–397.

Büscher, Karen, and Koen Vlassenroot. 2010. "Humanitarian Presence and Urban Development: New Opportunities and Contrasts in Goma, DRC." *Disasters* 34 (S2): S256–S273.

Button, Gregory V. 2010. *Disaster Culture: Knowledge and Uncertainty in the Wake of Human and Environmental Catastrophe.* Walnut Creek, CA: Left Coast Press.

Cadet, Jean-Robert. 1998. *Restavec: From Haitian Slave Child to Middle-Class American.* Austin: University of Texas Press.

Carsten, Janet. 2000. *Cultures of Relatedness: New Approaches to the Study of Kinship.* Cambridge: Cambridge University Press.

Cayemittes, Michel, Marie Florence Placide, Bernard Barrière, Soumaïla Mariko, and Blaise Sévère. 2001. *Enquête mortalité, morbidité et utilisation des services (EMMUS III) Haiti 2000.* Port-au-Prince: Institut Haïtien de l'Enfance, Pan American Health Organization.

Center for Economic and Policy Research (CEPR). 2015. *Haiti by the Numbers, Five Years Later.* January 8. Washington, DC: Center for Economic and Policy Research.

Chakrabarty, Dinesh. 2007. *Provincializing Europe: Postcolonial Thought and Historical Difference.* 2nd ed. Princeton, NJ: Princeton University Press.

Chancy, Myriam. 2010. "Hearing Our Mothers: Safeguarding Haitian Women's Self-Representation and Practices of Survival." March 12, 2010, edited by Bard College

Presentation for Human Rights Project. http://www.myriamchancy.com/post
-earthquake-%E2%80%9Chearing-our-mothers-safeguarding-haitian-women%E2%80
%99s-self-representation-practices-of-survival-%E2%80%9D/.

———. 2012. *From Sugar to Revolution: Women's Visions of Haiti, Cuba, and the Dominican Republic*. Waterloo, ON: Wilifred Laurier University Press.

———. 2013. "A Marshall Plan for a Haiti at Peace: To Continue or End the Legacy of the Revolution." In *Haiti and the Americas*, edited by Carla Calargé, Raphael Dalleo, Luis Duno-Gottberg, and Clevis Headley, 199–218. Jackson: University Press of Mississippi.

Charles, Carolle. 1995. "Gender and Politics in Contemporary Haiti: The Duvalierist State, Transnationalism, and the Emergence of a New Feminism (1980–1990)." *Feminist Studies* 21 (1): 135–164.

Charles, Jacqueline. 2011. "Evictions Ramp Up for Haitian Quake Victims." *Miami Herald*, May 28. http://www.haitian-truth.org/evictions-ramp-up-for-haitian-quake-victims/.

Charnovitz, Steve. 1997. "Two Centuries of Participation: NGOs and International Governance." *Michigan Journal of International Law* 18 (2): 183–286.

Checker, Melissa. 2005. *Polluted Promises: Environmental Racism in a Southern Town*. New York: New York University Press.

———. 2008. "Eco-Apartheid and Global Greenwaves: African Diasporic Environmental Justice Movements." *Souls: A Critical Journal of Black Politics, Culture, and Society* 10 (4): 390–408.

Checker, Melissa, Dàna-Ain Davis, and Mark Schuller. 2014. "The Conflicts of Crisis: Critical Reflections on Feminist Ethnography and Anthropological Activism." *American Anthropologist* 116 (2): 408–420.

CIA World Factbook. 2015. https://www.cia.gov/library/publications/the-world-factbook/rankorder/2172rank.html.

Clark, John. 1992. "Democratising Development: NGOs and the State." *Development in Practice* 2 (3): 151–161.

Clarke, Edith. 1957. *My Mother Who Fathered Me: A Study of the Family in Three Selected Communities in Jamaica*. New York: G. Allen and Unwin.

Clarke, Kamari Maxime. 2010. "New Spheres of Transnational Formations: Mobilizations of Humanitarian Diasporas." *Transforming Anthropology* 18 (1): 48–65.

Clifford, James, and George Marcus. 1986. *Writing Culture: The Poetics and Politics of Ethnography*. Berkeley: University of Calfornia Press.

Clitandre, Nadege. 2011. "Haitian Exceptionalism in the Caribbean and the Project of Re-building Haiti." *Journal of Haitian Studies* 17 (2): 146–153.

Collier, Jane, and Sylvia Yanagisako. 1987. "Theory in Anthropology since Feminist Practice." *Critique of Anthropology* 9 (2): 27–37.

Collier, Paul. 2007. *The Bottom Billion: Why the Poorest Countries Are Failing and What Can Be Done about It*. Oxford: Oxford University Press.

———. 2009. *Haiti: From Natural Catastrophe to Economic Security—a Report for the Secretary General*. New York: United Nations Secretary General.

Collins, Patricia Hill. 1990. *Black Feminist Thought: Knowledge, Consciousness, and the Politics of Empowerment*. 2nd rev. 10th. Anniv. ed. New York: Routledge.

Colten, Craig E. 2006. "Vulnerability and Place: Flat Land and Uneven Risk in New Orleans." *American Anthropologist* 108 (4): 731–734.

Cooke, Bill, and Uma Kothari. 2001. *Participation: The New Tyranny?* New York: Zed.

Corvington, Georges Jr. 2009. *Port-au-Prince au cours des ans*, vol. 8, *La Ville contemporaine, 1950–1956*. Port-au-Prince: Éditions Henri Deschamps.

Cox, Oliver Cromwell. 1948. *Caste, Class, and Race: A Study in Social Dynamics.* New York: Doubleday.

Crenshaw, Kimberle Williams. 1991. "Mapping the Margins: Intersectionality, Identity Politics, and Violence against Women of Color." *Stanford Law Review* 43 (6): 1241–1299.

Crowley (née Donovan), K., and J. R. Elliott. 2012. "Earthquake Disasters and Resilience in the Global North: Lessons from New Zealand and Japan." *Geographical Journal* 178 (3): 208–215.

Curtin, Philip. 1990. *The Rise and Fall of the Plantation Complex: Essays in Atlantic History.* 2nd ed. Cambridge: Cambridge University Press.

Curtis, Jennifer. 2010. "'Profoundly Ungrateful': The Paradoxes of Thatcherism in Northern Ireland." *Political and Legal Anthropology Review* 33 (2): 201–224.

d'Adesky, Anne-Christine, and Poto Fanm+Fi. 2012. *Beyond Shock—Charting the Landscape of Sexual Violence in Post-quake Haiti: Progress, Challenges, and Emerging Trends, 2010–2012.* Foreword by Edwidge Danticat and photo essay by Nadia Todres. San Francisco and Port-au-Prince: Poto Fanm+Fi Initiative.

Daniel, Trenton. 2011. "US: Flaws in Death Toll Report on Haiti Quake." Associated Press. June 4. http://www.jamaicaobserver.com/US—Flaws-in-death-toll-report-on-Haiti-quake.

Danticat, Edwidge. 2007. *Brother, I'm Dying.* New York: Knopf.

David, Emmanuel, and Elaine Enarson. 2012. *The Women of Katrina: How Gender, Race, and Class Matter in an American Disaster.* Nashville, TN: Vanderbilt University Press.

Davies, Thomas. 2014. *NGOs: A New History of Transnational Civil Society.* New York: Oxford University Press.

Davis, Angela Yvonne. 1983a. "The Legacy of Slavery: Standards of a New Womanhood." In *Women, Race and Class*, 3–29. New York: Vintage.

———. 1983b. "Rape, Racism and the Myth of the Black Rapist." In *Women, Race and Class*, 172–201. New York: Vintage.

Davis, Coralynn. 2003. "Feminist Tigers and Patriarchal Lions: Rhetorical Strategies and Instrumental Effects in the Struggle for Definition and Control over Development in Nepal." *Meridians: Feminism, Race, Transnationalism* 3 (2): 204–249.

Davis, Mike. 2006. *Planet of Slums.* London: Verso.

Deleuze, Gilles, and Félix Guattari. 1987. *A Thousand Plateaus: Capitalism and Schizophrenia.* Translated by Brian Massaumi. Minneapolis: University of Minnesota Press.

Denis, Lorimer, and François Duvalier. 1965. *Problème des classes à travers l'histoire d'Haïti.* Port-au-Prince: Imprimerie de l'État.

Deshommes, Fritz. 1995. *Néo-libéralisme: Crise économique et alternative de développement.* 2nd ed. Port-au-Prince: Imprimateur II.

———. 2006. *Haïti: Un nation écartelée, entre "plan américain" et projet national.* Port-au-Prince: Éditions Cahiers Universitaires.

———. 2011. *Et si la Constitution de 1987 était porteuse de Refondation?* Port-au-Prince: Éditions Cahiers Universitaires.

De Soto, Hernando. 2000. *The Mystery of Capital: Why Capitalism Triumphs in the West and Fails Everywhere Else.* New York: Basic Books.

Development Initiatives. 2013. *Global Humanitarian Assistance Report 2013.* Bristol, UK: Development Initiatives.

———. 2014. *Global Humanitarian Assistance Report 2014.* Bristol, UK: Development Initiatives.

De Waal, Alexander. 1997. *Famine Crimes: Politics and the Disaster Relief Industry in Africa.* African Issues. London: African Rights.

DeWind, Josh, and David H. Kinley III. 1988. *Aiding Migration: The Impact of International Development Assistance on Haiti*. Boulder, CO: Westview.

Diamond, Jared. 2005. *Collapse: How Societies Choose to Fail or Succeed*. New York: Viking.

Diederich, Bernard. 1985. "Swine Fever Ironies: The Slaughter of the Haitian Black Pig." *Caribbean Review* 14 (1): 16–17, 41.

Dillon, Michael, and Julian Reid. 2000. "Global Governance, Liberal Peace, and Complex Emergency." *Alternatives: Global, Local, Political* 25 (1): 117–143.

Disaster Accountability Project. 2011. *One Year Followup Report—Transparency of Relief Organizations Responding to 2010 Haiti Earthquake*. Washington, DC: Disaster Accountability Project.

Donini, Antonio. 2012. *The Golden Fleece: Manipulation and Independence in Humanitarian Action*. Sterling, VA: Kumarian.

DuBois, Laurent. 2012. *Haiti: Aftershocks of History*. New York: Metropolitan Books.

Duffield, Mark. 1994. "Complex Emergencies and the Crisis of Developmentalism." *IDS Bulletin* 25 (4): 15. Birmingham, UK: Institute of Development Studies.

———. 2014. *Global Governance and the New Wars: The Merging of Development and Security*. 2nd ed. London: Zed.

Duffield, Mark, Joanna Macrae, and Devon Curtis. 2001. "Editorial: Politics and Humanitarian Aid." *Disasters* 25 (4): 269–274.

Duhaime, Eric. 2002. *Haïti: Pourquoi payer la dette de Papa Doc?* Port-au-Prince: Jubilé 2000 Haïti.

Duncan, Christopher. 2005. "Unwelcome Guests: Relations between Internally Displaced Persons and their Hosts in North Sulawesi, Indonesia." *Journal of Refugee Studies* 18 (1): 25–46.

Dupuy, Alex. 1989. *Haiti in the World Economy: Class, Race, and Underdevelopment since 1700*. Boulder, CO: Westview.

———. 2010. "Disaster Capitalism to the Rescue: The International Community and Haiti after the Earthquake." *NACLA Report on the Americas* 43 (5): 14–19.

———. 2014. *Haiti, from Revolutionary Slaves to Powerless Citizens: Essays on the Politics and Economics of Underdevelopment, 1804–2013*. New York: Routledge.

Dyson, Michael Eric. 2005. *Come Hell or High Water: Hurricane Katrina and the Color of Disaster*. New York: Basic Civitas.

Edelman, Marc. 2005. "When Networks Don't Work: The Rise and Fall and Rise of Civil Society Initiatives in Central America." In *Social Movements: An Anthropological Reader*, edited by June C. Nash, 29–45. Malden, MA: Blackwell.

Edwards, Michael, and David Hulme. 1996. "Beyond the Magic Bullet? Lessons and Conclusions." In *Beyond the Magic Bullet: NGO Performance and Accountability in the Post-Cold War World*, edited by Michael Edwards and David Hulme, 254–266. West Hartford, CT: Kumarian.

Elliot, Justin, and Laura Sullivan. 2015. "How the Red Cross Raised Half a Billion Dollars for Haiti and Built Six Homes." ProPublica and NPR, June 3. https://www.propublica.org/how-the-red-cross-raised-half-a-billion-dollars-for-haiti-and-built-6-homes.

Enarson, Elaine. 1998. "Through Women's Eyes: A Gendered Research Agenda for Disaster Social Science." *Disasters* 22 (2): 157–173.

———. 2012. *Women Confronting Natural Disasters: From Vulnerability to Resilience*. Boulder, CO: Lynne Reinner.

Esteus, Sony. 2013. *L'experiences des Radios Communautaires en Haïti. A partir des resultats de plusiers evaluations effectuées de 2002 à 2007*. Port-au-Prince: Sosyete Animasyon ak Kominikasyon Sosyal.

Ethéart, Bernard. 1991. "Les organisations non-gouvernementales: Definition, caracteristiques, mode de fonctionnement." In *Definition, rôle et fonction des ONG: Cahier 2,* edited by HAVA, 10–12. Port-au-Prince: HAVA.

Étienne, Sauveur Pierre. 1997. *Haiti: L'Invasion des ONG.* Port-au-Prince: Centre de Recherche Sociale et de Formation Économique pour le Développement.

Etienne, Yolette. 2012. "Haiti and Catastrophes: Lessons Not Learned." In *Tectonic Shifts: Haiti since the Earthquake,* edited by Mark Schuller and Pablo Morales, 27–32. Sterling, VA: Kumarian.

Exantus, Carine. 2010. "Diary of a Survivor in Haiti." In *Conversations for a Better World.* http://www.conversationsforabetterworld.com/2010/03/diary-of-a-survivor-in-haiti-part-i/.

Fairweather, Ian. 1997. "Crisis Anthropology and the New Dialogue." *Anthropology Today* 13 (4): 19.

Falcón, Sylvanna. 2015. The Globalization of Ferguson: Pedagogical Matters about Racial Violence. *Feminist Studies* 41:218–221.

Fan, Lilianne. 2012. "Shelter Strategies, Humanitarian Praxis, and Critical Urban Theory in Post-Crisis Reconstruction." *Disasters* 36 (S1): S64–S86.

Fanon, Franz. 1965. *Studies in a Dying Colonialism.* Translated by Haakon Chevalier. New York: Monthly Review Press.

Farmer, Paul. 1992. *AIDS and Accusation: Haiti and the Geography of Blame.* Berkeley: University of California Press.

———. 2004. "An Anthropology of Structural Violence." *Current Anthropology* 45 (3): 305–325.

———. 2011. *Haiti after the Earthquake.* New York: Polity.

Fassin, Didier. 2010. *La raison humanitaire: Une histoire morale du temps présent.* Paris: Gallimard/Seuil.

———. 2011. "Noli Me Tangere: The Moral Untouchability of Humanitarianism." In *Forces of Compassion: Humanitarianism between Ethics and Politics,* edited by Erica Bornstein and Peter Redfield, 35–52. Santa Fe, NM: SAR Press.

———. 2012. *Humanitarian Reason: A Moral History of the Present.* Translated by Rachel Gomme. Berkeley: University of California Press.

Fassin, Didier, and Mariella Pandolfi. 2010. *Contemporary States of Emergency: The Politics of Military and Humanitarian Interventions.* New York: Zone.

Fatton, Robert. 2002. *Haiti's Predatory Republic: The Unending Transition to Democracy.* Boulder, CO: Lynne Reinner.

———. 2004. "The Haitian Authoritarian *Habitus* and the Contradictory Legacy of 1804." *Journal of Haitian Studies* 10 (1): 22–43.

———. 2007. *The Roots of Haitian Despotism.* Boulder, CO: Lynne Rienner.

Feldman, Ilana. 2008. *Governing Gaza: Bureaucracy, Authority, and the Work of Rule, 1917–1967.* Durham, NC: Duke University Press.

———. 2010. "Ad Hoc Humanity: UN Peacekeeping and the Limits of International Community in Gaza." *American Anthropologist* 112 (3): 416–429.

Ferguson, James. 1987. *Papa Doc, Baby Doc: Haiti and the Duvaliers.* Oxford, UK: Basil Blackwell.

———. 1990. *The Anti-Politics Machine: "Development," Depoliticization, and Bureaucratic Power in Lesotho.* New York: Cambridge University Press.

———. 2005. "Anthropology and Its Evil Twin: 'Development' in the Constitution of a Discipline." In *The Anthropology of Development and Globalization: From Classical Political Economy to Contemporary Neoliberalism,* edited by Marc Edelman and Angelique Haugerud, 140–153. Malden, MA: Blackwell.

Fick, Carolyn. 1990. *The Making of Haiti: The Saint Domingue Revolution from Below*. Knoxville: University of Tennessee Press.

Fischer, Sibylle. 2004. *Modernity Disavowed: Haiti and the Cultures of Slavery in the Age of Revolution*. Durham, NC: Duke University Press.

———. 2007. "Haiti: Fantasies of Bare Life." *Small Axe: A Caribbean Journal of Criticism* 23: 1–15.

Fisher, William. 1997. "Doing Good? The Politics and Antipolitics of NGO Practices." *Annual Reviews in Anthropology* 26: 439–464.

———. 2014. Discussant comments. For *What's in a Name? Tracing Anthropology's Uneasy Ethnographic Engagement with NGOs*, Mark Schuller and David Lewis, organizers. Washington, DC: American Anthropological Association.

Florvilus, Patrice. 2012. "Workshop on the Right to Housing." In *Tectonic Shifts: Haiti since the Earthquake*, edited by Mark Schuller and Pablo Morales, 133–138. Sterling, VA: Kumarian.

Fothergill, Alice. 1999. "Women's Roles in a Disaster." *Applied Behavioral Science Review* 7 (2): 125–143.

———. 2004. *Heads above Water: Gender, Class, and Family in the Grand Forks Flood*. New York: State University of New York Press.

Foucault, Michel. 1978. *The History of Sexuality, an Introduction*. Translated by Robert Hurley. 3 vols. New York: Vintage Books.

———. 1979. *Discipline and Punish*. Translated by Alan Sheridan. New York: Vintage Books.

Freeman, Scott. 2014. "'Cutting Earth': Haiti, Soil Conservation, and the Tyranny of Projects." PhD diss., Teachers College.

Freire, Paulo. 1970. *Pedagogy of the Oppressed*. Translated by Myra Bergman Ramos. New York: Continuum

Frerks, Georg, and Stephen Bender. 2004. "Conclusion: Vulnerability Analysis as a Means of Strengthening Policy Formulation and Policy Practice." In *Mapping Vulnerability: Disasters, Development, and People*, edited by Greg Bankoff, Georg Frerks, and Dorothea Hilhorst, 194–205. London: Earthscan.

Gabaud, Pierre Simpson. 2000. *Associannisme Paysan en Haïti: Effets de Permanence et de Rupture*. Port-au-Prince : Éditions des Antilles.

Gaillard, Jean-Christophe. 2007. "Resilience of Traditional Societies in Facing Natural Hazards." *Disaster Prevention and Management: An International Journal* 16 (4): 522–544.

Galtung, Johan. 1980. "'A Structural Theory of Imperialism'—Ten Years Later." *Millennium: Journal of International Studies* 9 (3): 181–196.

Gilbert, Myrtha. 2001. *Luttes des femmes et luttes sociales en Haïti*. Port-au-Prince: Imprimateur II.

———. 2010. *La catastrophe n'était pas naturelle*. Port-au-Prince: Imprimateur II.

———. 2012. *Shada, chronique d'une extravagante escroquerie*. Port-au-Prince: Éditions Université d'État d'Haïti.

Glick Schiller, Nina, and Georges Fouron. 2001. *Georges Woke Up Laughing: Long-Distance Nationalism and the Search for Home*. Durham, NC: Duke University Press.

Gold, Herbert. 1991. *Best Nightmare on Earth: A Life in Haiti*. New York: Touchstone Books.

Government Accountability Office. 2013. *Haiti Reconstruction: USAID Infrastructure Projects Have Had Mixed Results and Face Sustainability Challenges*. Washington, DC: Government Accountability Office.

Gramsci, Antonio. 1971. *Selections from the Prison Notebooks of Antonio Gramsci*. Edited and translated by Quintin Hoare and Geoffrey Nowell Smith. New York: International Publishers.

Greenhalgh, Susan. 1990. "Toward a Political Economy of Fertility: Anthropological Contributions." *Population and Development Review* 19 (2): 303–321.

Guest Editorial. 2011. "Disaster Resilience: A Bounce Back or Bounce Forward Ability?" *Local Environment: The International Journal of Justice and Sustainability* 16 (5): 417–424.

Hachette, Dominique. 1981. *Haiti: Economic Memorandum, Recent Economic, Industrial, and Sector Developments.* Washington, DC: World Bank.

"Haiti Revises Quake Death Toll Up to over 316,000." 2011. Reuters. http://www.reuters .com/article/2011/01/12/haiti-quake-toll-idUSN1223196420110112.

Hardt, Michael, and Antonio Negri. 2001. *Empire.* Cambridge, MA: Harvard University Press.

Harmer, Adele, and Joanna Macrae. 2004. *Beyond the Continuum: The Changing Role of Aid Policy in Protracted Crises.* London: Humanitarian Policy Group, Overseas Development Institute.

Harrison, Faye Venetia. 1997. "The Gendered Politics and Violence of Structural Adjustment: A View from Jamaica." In *Situated Lives: Gender and Culture in Everyday Life,* edited by Louise Lamphere, Helen Ragone, and Patricia Zavella, 451–468. New York: Routledge.

———. 2008. *Outsider Within: Reworking Anthropology in the Global Age.* Urbana: University of Illinois Press.

Harvey, David. 2005. *A Brief History of Neoliberalism.* New York: Oxford University Press.

———. 2006. *Spaces of Global Capitalism: Toward a Theory of Uneven Geographical Development.* New York: Verso.

Haushofer, Johannes, and Jeremy Shapiro. 2013. *Household Response to Income Changes: Evidence from an Unconditional Cash Transfer Program in Kenya.* Cambridge, MA: Massachusetts Institute of Technology, Abdul Latif Jameel Poverty Action Lab.

Hefferan, Tara. 2007. *Twinning Faith and Development: Catholic Parish Partnering in the US and Haiti.* Bloomfield, CT: Kumarian.

Hendriksen, Rene, Lance B. Price, and James M Shupp. 2011. "Population Genetics of *Vibrio cholerae* from Nepal in 2010: Evidence on the Origin of the Haitian Outbreak." *mBIO* 2 (4): 1–6.

Henrici, Jane. Forthcoming. "Disasters, Gender, and the Americas in Resilience, Recovery, and Research." In *A Progressive Feminist Reader,* edited by Ida Susser and Christine Gailey. Boulder, CO: Paradigm.

Henrici, Jane M., Allison Suppan Helmuth, and Jackie Braun. 2010. *Women, Disasters, and Hurricane Katrina.* Washington, DC: Institute for Women's Policy Research.

Henrici, Jane M., Allison Suppan Helmuth, and Angela Carlberg. 2012. "Doubly Displaced: Women, Public Housing, and Spatial Access after Katrina." In *The Women of Katrina: How Gender, Race, and Class Matter in an American Disaster,* edited by Emmanuel David and Elaine Enarson, 142–154. Nashville, TN: Vanderbilt University Press.

Hewamanne, Sandya. 2006. "'Participation? My Blood and Flesh Is Being Sucked Dry': Market-Based Development and Sri Lanka's Free Trade Zone Women Workers." *Journal of Third World Studies* 23 (1): 51–74.

Hickey, Samuel, and Giles Mohan. 2004. *Participation: From Tyranny to Transformation? Exploring New Approaches to Participation in Development.* London: Zed.

Higman, B. W. 1984. *Slave Populations of the British Caribbean, 1807–1834.* Baltimore, MD: Johns Hopkins University Press.

Hilhorst, Dorothea. 2003. *The Real World of NGOs: Discourses, Diversity and Development.* London: Zed.

Hindman, Heather. 2013. *Mediating the Global: Expatria's Forms and Consequences in Kathmandu.* Stanford, CA: Stanford University Press.

Hochschild, Arlie Russell. 1989. *The Second Shift: Working Parents and the Revolution at Home.* New York: Viking.

Hoetink, H. 1973. *Slavery and Race Relations in the Americas.* New York: Harper and Row.

Hours, Bernard. 2003. "Les ONG: Outils et contestation de la globalisation." *Journal des Anthropologues* 94–95: 13–22.

Houtart, François. 1998. "Éditorial—les ONG: Instruments du projet néoliéral ou bases solidaires des alternative populaires." In *Les ONG: Instruments du néo-libéralisme ou alternatives populaires?,* edited by François Houtart, 5–33. Paris: l'Harmattan.

Humanitarian Accountability Partnership (HAP), and International Organization for Migration (IOM). 2010. *Camp Committee Assessment: A Tool for Deciding How to Work with Camp Committees.* Port-au-Prince: Humanitarian Accountability Project.

INCITE! Women of Color against Violence. 2007. *The Revolution Will Not Be Funded: Beyond the Non-Profit Industrial Complex.* Cambridge, MA: South End Press.

———. 2012. "INCITE! Statement on Hurricane Katrina." In *The Women of Katrina: How Gender, Race, and Class Matter in an American Disaster,* edited by Emmanuel David and Elaine Enarson, 3–6. Nashville, TN: Vanderbilt University Press.

International Monetary Fund. 2005. *Haiti: Selected Issues.* Washington, DC: International Monetary Fund.

International Organization for Migration (IOM). 2011. *IOM Haiti Transitional Shelter Program Monthly Report—December 2011.* Port-au-Prince: International Organization for Migration.

INURED. 2010. *Voices from the Shanties: A Post-Earthquake Rapid Assessment of Cité Soleil, Port-au-Prince.* Miami and Port-au-Prince: Institut Inter-Universitaire de Recherche et Développement.

Jackson, Stephen. 2005. "'The State Didn't Even Exist': Non-Governmentality in Kivu, Eastern DR Congo." In *Between a Rock and a Hard Place: African NGOs, Donors, and the State,* edited by Jim Igoe and Tim Kelsall, 165–196. Durham, NC: Carolina Academic Press.

James, C.L.R. 1989 (1938). *The Black Jacobins: Toussaint Louverture and the San Domingo Revolution.* New York: Vintage.

James, Erica Caple. 2010. *Democratic Insecurities: Violence, Trauma, and Intervention in Haiti.* Edited by Robert Borofsky. Berkeley: University of California Press.

Jean, J. A. Gracien. 2002. *Sociétés civiles en mutation.* Edited by Philippe Fils-Aimé. Port-au-Prince: Centre International de Politologie Appliquée-Haïti.

Jean-Baptiste, Chenet. 2012. "Haiti's Earthquake: A Further Insult to Peasants' Lives." In *Tectonic Shifts: Haiti since the Earthquake,* edited by Mark Schuller and Pablo Morales, 97–100. Sterling, VA: Kumarian.

Jean-Charles, Régine. 2014. *Conflict Bodies: The Politics of Rape Representation in the Francophone Imaginary.* Columbus: Ohio State University Press.

Jha, Abhas K., Jennifer Duyne Barenstein, Priscilla M. Phelps, Daniel Pittet, and Stephen Sena. 2010. *Safer Homes, Stronger Communities: A Handbook for Reconstructing after Natural Disasters.* Washington, DC: World Bank.

Johnson, Cedric. 2011. *The Neoliberal Deluge: Hurricane Katrina, Late Capitalism, and the Remaking of New Orleans.* Minneapolis: University of Minnesota Press.

Kamat, Sangeeta. 2002. *Development Hegemony: NGOs and the State in India.* Delhi: Oxford University Press.

Karim, Lamia. 2011. *Microfinance and Its Discontents: Women in Debt in Bangladesh.* Minneapolis: University of Minnesota Press.

Katz, Jonathan. 2010. "Billions for Haiti, a Criticism for Every Dollar." Associated Press. March 6. http://www.boston.com/news/world/latinamerica/articles/2010/03/05/billions_for_haiti_a_criticism_for_every_dollar/.

——. 2013. *The Big Truck That Went By: How the World Came to Save Haiti and Left Behind a Disaster.* New York: Palgrave Macmillan.

Kaussen, Valerie. 2012. "Do It Yourself: International Aid and the Neoliberal Ethos in the Tent Camps of Port-au-Prince." In *Tectonic Shifts: Haiti since the Earthquake,* edited by Mark Schuller and Pablo Morales, 125–130. Sterling, VA: Kumarian.

——. Forthcoming. "Haitian Culture in the Informal Economy of International Aid." In Alessandra Benedicty, Jhon Picard Byron, Kaiama Glover, and Mark Schuller, eds. *The Haiti Exception: Haiti and the Predicament of Narrative.* Liverpool: Liverpool University Press.

Kempadoo, Kamala. 2004. *Sexing the Caribbean: Gender, Race, and Sexual Labor.* New York: Routledge.

Klarreich, Kathie, and Linda Polman. 2012. "The NGO Republic of Haiti." *The Nation,* November 19. http://www.thenation.com/article/170929/ngo-republic-haiti.

Klein, Naomi. 2007. *The Shock Doctrine: The Rise of Disaster Capitalism.* New York: Metropolitan Books.

Knight, Franklin W. 1970. *Slave Society in Cuba during the Nineteenth Century.* Madison: University of Wisconsin Press.

——. 1997. *The Slave Societies of the Caribbean.* London: UNESCO.

Kreft, Sönke, and David Eckstein. 2013. "Global Climate Risk Index 2014." Bonn and Berlin: Germanwatch.

Laguerre, Michel. 1973. "The Place of Voodoo in the Social Structure of Haiti." *Caribbean Quarterly* 19 (3): 36–50.

——. 1982. *Urban Life in the Caribbean: A Study of a Haitian Urban Community.* Cambridge, MA: Schenkman.

Lahens, Yanick. 2010. *Failles.* Paris: Sabine Wespieser.

Lang, Sabine. 2000. "The NGO-ization of Feminism." In *Global Feminisms since 1945,* edited by Bonnie G. Smith, 290–304. London: Routledge.

Lawless, Robert. 1992. *Haiti's Bad Press.* Rochester, VT: Schenkman.

Leth, Asger, and Milos Loncarevic. 2006. *Ghosts of Cité Soleil.* Nordisk Films.

Let Haiti Live. 2011. "Violent and Destructive Eviction at the Kafou Ayopo, Haiti." http://www.lethaitilive.org/nouvel/2011/5/23/violent-and-destructive-eviction-at-the-kafou-ayopo-haiti.html.

Lewis, David, and David Mosse. 2006. *Development Brokers and Translators: The Ethnography of Aid and Agencies.* Bloomfield, CT: Kumarian.

Lewis, Oscar. 1966. *La Vida: A Puerto Rican Family in the Culture of Poverty—San Juan and New York.* New York: Random House.

Lindsey, Treva B. 2015. "Post-Ferguson: A 'Herstorical' Approach to Black Violability." *Feminist Studies* 41: 232–237.

Litt, Jacquelyn, Althea Skinner, and Kelley Robinson. 2012. "The Katrina Difference: African American Women's Networks and Poverty in New Orleans after Katrina." In *The Women of Katrina: How Gender, Race, and Class Matter in an American Disaster,* edited by Emmanuel David and Elaine Enarson, 130–141. Nashville, TN: Vanderbilt University Press.

Louis, Ilionor. 2012a. "La fracture (2)." *Haïti en Marche* 26 (8): 12–14.

———. 2012b. "La relocalisation des familles victimes de catastrophes naturelles à Port-au-Prince." *Sapiens Research* 2 (2): 71–16.

———. 2013. *Des Bidonvilles aux camps: Conditions de vie à Canaan, à Corail Cesse-Lesse, et à la Piste de l'Ancienne Aviation de Port-au-Prince.* Port-au-Prince: Faculté d'Ethnologie.

Low, Setha M., and Denise Lawrence-Zúñiga. 2003. "Locating Culture." In *The Anthropology of Space and Place: Locating Culture,* edited by Setha M. Low and Denise Lawrence-Zúñiga, 1–47. London: Blackwell.

Lubiano, Wahneema. 2008. "Race, Class, and the Politics of Death: Critical Responses to Hurricane Katrina." In *Capitalizing on Catastrophe: Neoliberal Strategies in Disaster Reconstruction,* edited by Nandini Gunewardena and Mark Schuller, 117–122. Lanham, MD: AltaMira.

Lucien, Georges Eddy. 2013. *Une modernisation manquée: Port-au-Prince (1915–1956). Vol. 1: Modernisation et centralisation.* Port-au-Prince: Éditions Université d'État d'Haïti.

Luft, Rachel. 2009. "Beyond Disaster Exceptionalism: Social Movement Developments in New Orleans after Hurricane Katrina." *American Quarterly* 61 (3): 499–527.

Lundahl, Mats. 1984. "Papa Doc: Innovator in the Predatory State." *Scandia* 50 (1): 39–78.

———. 1989. "History as an Obstacle to Change: The Case of Haiti." *Journal of Interamerican Studies and World Affairs* 31 (1–2): 1–21.

Lwijis, Janil. 1993. *Entè OPD: Kalfou Pwojè.* Port-au-Prince: Imprimateur II.

———. 2009. *ONG: Ki gouvènman ou ye?* Port-au-Prince: Asosyasyon Invèsite ak Invèsitèz Desalinyèn—ASID.

Maclin, Beth, Jocelyn Kelly, Justin Kabanga, and Michael VanRooyen. 2014. "'They Have Embraced a Different Behaviour': Transactional Sex and Family Dynamics in Eastern Congo's Conflict." *Culture, Health & Sexuality: An International Journal for Research, Intervention and Care* 17 (1): 119–131.

Macrae, Joanna, Mark Bradbury, Susanne Jaspars, Douglas Johnson, and Mark Duffield. 1997. "Conflict, the Continuum, and Chronic Emergencies: A Critical Analysis of the Scope for Linking Relief, Rehabilitation, and Development Planning in Sudan." *Disasters* 21 (3): 223–243.

Macrae, Joanna, and Nicholas Leader. 2001. "Apples, Pears, and Porridge: The Origins and Impact of the Search for 'Coherence' between Humanitarian and Political Responses to Chronic Political Emergencies." *Disasters* 25 (4): 290–307.

MADRE, CUNY School of Law, and IJDH. 2011. *Our Bodies Are Still Trembling: Haitian Women Continue to Fight against Rape: One Year Update.* New York: MADRE, City University of New York School of Law, and IJDH.

Malkki, Liisa. 1995. "Refugees and Exile: From 'Refugee Studies' to the National Order of Things." *Annual Review of Anthropology* 24: 495–523.

———. 1997. "National Geographic: The Rooting of Peoples and the Territorialization of National Identity among Scholars and Refugees." In *Culture, Power, Place: Explorations in Critical Anthropology,* edited by Akhil Gupta and James Ferguson, 52–75. Durham, NC: Duke University Press.

Mamdani, Mahmood. 2009. *Saviors and Survivors: Darfur, Politics, and the War on Terror.* London: Verso.

Mangonès, Kathy. 1991. "Reflexion sur l'élaboration d'une politique de développement." In *Définition, rôle et fonction des ONG: Cahier 2,* edited by HAVA, 5–9. Port-au-Prince: HAVA.

Manjoo, Rashida, and United Nations. 2011. *Report of the Special Rapporteur on Violence against Women, Its Causes and Consequences.* New York: United Nations General Assembly.

Mars, Kettly. 2013. *Aux frontières de soif.* Paris: Mercure de France.

Maternowska, M. Catherine. 2006. *Reproducing Inequities: Poverty and the Politics of Population in Haiti*. New Brunswick, NJ: Rutgers University Press.

Mathurin, Alliette, Ernst Mathurin, and Bernard Zaugg. 1989. *Implantation et impact des organisations non gouvernementales: Contexte général et étude de cas*. Port-au-Prince: Groupe de Recherche et d'Appui au Milieu Rural.

Mathurin, Maguy. 1991. "La participation dans le développement en Haiti: Bilan et perspective." In *Définition, rôle et fonction des ONG: Cahier 2*, edited by HAVA, 13–16. Port-au-Prince: HAVA.

Mauss, Marcel. 1990. *The Gift: The Form and Reason for Exchange in Archaic Societies*. London: Routledge.

Mazzeo, John. 2009. "Lavichè: Haiti's Vulnerability to the Global Food Crisis." *NAPA Bulletin* 32 (1): 115–129.

McAlister, Elizabeth. 2013. "Humanitarian Adhocracy, Transnational New Apostolic Missions, and Evangelical Anti-Dependency in a Haitian Refugee Camp." *Nova Religio* 16 (4): 11–34.

McLanahan, Sara S., Annemette Sorensen, and Dorothy Watson. 1989. "Sex Differences in Poverty, 1950–1980." *Signs* 15 (1): 102–122.

Mead, Margaret. 2001. *Coming of Age in Samoa: A Psychological Study of Primitive Youth for Western Civilisation*. New York: Perennial Classics.

Meinert, Lotte, and Susan Reynolds Whyte. 2014. "Epidemic Projectification: AIDS Responses in Uganda as Event and Process." *Cambridge Anthropology* 32 (1): 77–94.

Merry, Sally Engle. 2006. *Human Rights and Gender Violence: Translating International Law into Local Justice*. Chicago: University of Chicago Press.

Miles, Melinda. 2012. "Assumptions and Exclusion: Coordination Failures during the Emergency Phase." In *Tectonic Shifts: Haiti since the Earthquake*, edited by Mark Schuller and Pablo Morales, 45–49. Sterling, VA: Kumarian.

Mills, C. Wright. 1959. *The Sociological Imagination*. New York: Oxford University Press.

Ministère de la Santé Publique et de la Population. 2012. "Rapport de cas." Port-au-Prince: Gouvernement d'Haïti, Ministère de la Santé Publique et de la Population.

Minn, Pierre. 2007. "Toward an Anthropology of Humanitarianism." *Journal of Humanitarian Assistance* 51. http://sites.tufts.edu/jha/archives/51.

Mintz, Sidney. 1985. *Sweetness and Power: The Place of Sugar in Modern History*. New York: Viking.

———. 2010. *Three Ancient Colonies: Caribbean Themes and Variations*. Cambridge, MA: Harvard University Press.

Mitchell, Michele. 2012. *Haiti: Where Did the Money Go?* Public Broadcasting Corporation.

Montas-Dominique, Michèle. 2011. "Sim Pa Rele (If I Don't Shout)." In *Haiti after the Earthquake*, edited by Paul Farmer, 259–272. Philadelphia: Public Affairs.

Moon, Ban Ki. 2010. *Report of the Secretary-General on the United Nations Stabilization Mission in Haiti*. New York: United Nations Security Council.

Mosel, Irina, and Simon Levine. 2014. *Remaking the Case for Linking Relief, Rehabilitation, and Development: How LRRD Can Become a Practically Useful Concept for Assistance in Difficult Places*. London: Humanitarian Policy Group, Overseas Development Institute.

Moynihan, Daniel Patrick. 1965. *The Negro Family: The Case for National Action*. Washington, DC: Office of Planning and Research, United States Department of Labor.

Muggah, Robert. 2011. *Security from the Bottom Up in Haiti: Before and after the Quake*. Geneva: Small Arms Survey.

Nader, Laura. 1969. "Up the Anthropologist—Perspectives Gained from Studying Up." In *Reinventing Anthropology*, edited by Dell Hymes, 285–311. New York: Pantheon.

Nagar, Richa, and S. Raju. 2003. "Women, NGOs, and the Contradictions of Empowerment and Disempowerment: A Conversation." *Antipode* 35 (1): 1–13.

Nagar, Richa, and Sangtin Writers. 2006. *Playing with Fire: Feminist Thought and Activism through Seven Lives in India.* Minneapolis: University of Minnesota Press.

Nelzy, Sandy. 2013. "The Impact of NGOs in Saint-Louis de Gonzague Camp, Haiti." *Practicing Anthropology* 35 (3): 20–22.

New York Times Editorial Board. 2014. "Haiti, Unfinished and Forsaken." *New York Times,* January 10. http://www.nytimes.com/2014/01/11/opinion/haiti-unfinished-and -forsaken.html?_r=0.

Nicholls, David. 1996. *From Dessalines to Duvalier: Race, Colour, and National Independence in Haiti.* 2nd ed. New York: Cambridge University Press.

Nixon, Rob. 2011. *Slow Violence and the Environmentalism of the Poor.* Cambridge, MA: Harvard University Press.

Noël, Adlin. 2013. "Lack of Transparency, Accountability, and Victims' Participation in Decision Making: Haiti's Major Threat." *Practicing Anthropologist* 35 (3): 14–16.

Nolan, Clancy. 2011. "Haiti, Violated." *World Policy Journal* 128: 93–102.

NYU School of Law Center for Human Rights and Global Justice. 2011. *Sexual Violence in Haiti's IDP Camps: Results of a Household Survey.* New York: New York University School of Law Center for Human Rights and Global Justice.

O'Brien, Geoff, Phil O'Keefe, Joanne Rose, and Ben Wisner. 2006. "Climate Change and Disaster Management." *Disasters* 30 (1): 64–80.

O'Grady, Mary. 2014. "Bill, Hillary and the Haiti Debacle" *Wall Street Journal,* May 18. http://www.wsj.com/articles.SB10001424052702304547704579564651201202122.

Oliver-Smith, Anthony. 1999. "What Is a Disaster?" In *The Angry Earth: Disaster in Anthropological Perspective,* edited by Anthony Oliver-Smith and Susanna M. Hoffman, 18–34. New York: Routledge.

———. 2004. "Theorizing Vulnerability in a Globalized World: A Political Ecological Perspective." In *Mapping Vulnerability: Disasters, Development, and People,* edited by Greg Bankoff, Georg Frerks, and Dorothea Hilhorst, 10–24. London: Earthscan.

———. 2010. *Defying Displacement: Grassroots Resistance and the Critique of Development.* Austin: University of Texas Press.

———. 2012. "Haiti's 500-Year Earthquake." In *Tectonic Shifts: Haiti since the Earthquake,* edited by Mark Schuller and Pablo Morales, 18–23. Sterling, VA: Kumarian.

Olsen, Gorm Rye, Nils Carstensen, and Kristian Hoyen. 2003. "Humanitarian Crises: What Determines the Level of Emergency Assistance? Media Coverage, Donor Interests, and the Aid Business." *Disasters* 27 (2): 109–126.

Ong, Aihwa, and Stephen J. Collier. 2005. *Global Assemblages: Technology, Politics, and Ethics as Anthropological Problems.* Malden, MA: Blackwell.

Oxfam. 2013. *No Accident: Resilience and the Inequality of Risk.* Oxfam.

Paley, Julia. 2001. "The Paradox of Participation: Civil Society and Democracy in Chile." *Political and Legal Anthropology Review* 24 (1): 1–12.

Panchang, Deepa. 2012. "'Waiting for Helicopters'? Perceptions, Misperceptions, and the Right to Water in Haiti." In *Tectonic Shifts: Haiti since the Earthquake,* edited by Mark Schuller and Pablo Morales, 183–187. Sterling, VA: Kumarian.

Pandolfi, Mariella. 2003. "Contract of Mutual (In)difference: Governance and the Humanitarian Apparatus in Contemporary Albania and Kosovo." *Indiana Journal of Global Legal Studies* 10: 369–381.

Parpart, Jane. 1999. "Rethinking Participation, Empowerment, and Development from a Gender Perspective." In *Transforming Development: Foreign Aid for a Changing World*, edited by Jim Freedman, 250–267. Toronto: University of Toronto Press.

Patterson, Orlando. 1982. *Slavery and Social Death: A Comparative Study.* Cambridge, MA: Harvard University Press.

Pearce, Jenny. 1997. "Between Co-Option and Irrelevance? Latin American NGOs in the 1990s." In *NGOs, States, and Donors: Too Close for Comfort?*, edited by David Hulme and Michael Edwards, 257–274. New York: St. Martin's Press in association with Save the Children.

Peck, Raoul. 2013. *Assistance Mortelle.* Paris: Arte France. Running time 99 minutes.

Petras, James. 1997. "Imperialism and NGOs in Latin America." *Monthly Review* 49 (7): 10–17.

Piarroux, Renaud, Robert Barrais, Benoît Faucher, Rachel Haus, Martine Piarroux, Jean Gaudart, Roc Magloire, and Didier Raoult. 2011. "Understanding the Cholera Epidemic, Haiti." *Emerging Infectious Diseases* 17 (7): 1161–1167.

Pierre-Louis. Forthcoming. "Urban Poetics." In *The Haiti Exception: Haiti and the Predicament of Narrative*, ed. Alessandra Benedicty, Jhon Picard Byron, Kaiama Glover, and Mark Schuller. Liverpool: Liverpool University Press.

Plummer, Brenda Gayle. 1988. *Haiti and the Great Powers, 1912–1915.* Baton Rouge: Louisiana State University Press.

Polanyi, Karl. 2001. *The Great Transformation: The Political and Economic Origins of Our Time.* Boston: Beacon.

Polyné, Millery. 2010. *From Douglass to Duvalier: U.S. African Americans, Haiti, and Pan Africanism, 1870–1964.* Gainesville: University Press of Florida.

Porter, Marilyn, and Ellen R. Judd. 1999. *Feminists Doing Development: A Practical Critique.* London: Zed.

Power, Michael. 1997. *The Audit Society: Rituals of Verification.* Oxford: Oxford University Press.

Preston, Caroline, and Nicole Wallace. 2011. "American Donors Gave $1.4-Billion to Haiti Aid." https://philanthropy.com/article/Haiti-Aid-Falls-Short-of-Other/159311.

Price, Sally. 1982. *Co-wives and Calabashes.* Ann Arbor: University of Michigan Press.

Price-Mars, Jean. 1919. *La vocation de l'élite.* Port-au-Prince: Imprimerie E. Chenet.

———. 1956. *Formation ethique, folk-lore, et culture du peuple haitien.* 2nd ed. Port-au-Prince: Imprimerie N A Theodore.

———. 1983. *So Spoke the Uncle.* Translated by Magdaline W Shannon. 3rd ed. Washington, DC: Three Continents Press.

Putnam, Robert D. 1995. "Bowling Alone: America's Declining Social Capital." *Journal of Democracy* 6: 65–78.

———. 2001. *Bowling Alone: The Collapse and Revival of American Community.* New York: Touchstone.

Racine, Marie M. B. 1995. "The Long Journey toward Freedom." *Roots* 1 (3): 7–12.

Redfield, Peter. 2013. *Life in Crisis: The Ethical Journey of Doctors without Borders.* Berkeley: University of California Press.

Regan, Jane. 2003. *ONG "altènatif"—zanmi oswa ennmi lit radikal?* Port-au-Prince: Institut Culturel Karl Leveque.

Renda, Mary. 2001. *Taking Haiti: Military Occupation and the Culture of U.S. Imperialism, 1915–1940.* Chapel Hill: University of North Carolina Press.

Richard, Analiese. 2009. "Mediating Dilemmas: Local NGOs and Rural Development in Neoliberal Mexico." *Political and Legal Anthropology Review* 32 (2): 166–194.

Richardson, Laurie, and Grassroots International. 1997. *Kenbe Peyi a Sou Kontwòl, Demokrasi Nan Grangou—Men Politik USAID an Ayiti.* Boston: Grassroots International.

Richman, Karen. 2014. "Possession and Attachment: Notes on Moral Ritual Communication among Haitian Descent Groups." In *Spirited Things: The Work of "Possession" in Afro-Atlantic Religions,* edited by Paul C. Johnson, 207–224. Chicago: University of Chicago Press.

Robbins, Joel. 2013. "Beyond the Suffering Subject: Toward an Anthropology of the Good." *Journal of the Royal Anthropological Institute* 19: 447–62.

Robert, Arnaud. 2010. "Haïti est la preuve de l'échec de l'aide internationale." *Le Temps,* December 20. http://www.letemps.ch/Page/Uuid/2a1b8ado-0bb8-11eo-91f4-4e4896afb50210.

Robinson, Randall. 2001. *The Debt: What America Owes to Blacks.* New York: Plume.

Rodney, Walter. 1972. *How Europe Underdeveloped Africa.* Washington, DC: Howard University Press.

Rona, Gabor. 2014. *The ICRC's Status: In a Class of Its Own.* International Committee of the Red Cross 2004. http://www.icrc.org/eng/resources/documents/misc/5w9fjy.htm.

Rosaldo, Renato. 1984. "Grief and a Headhunter's Rage: On the Cultural Force of Emotions." In *Text, Play, and Story: The Construction and Reconstruction of Self and Society,* edited by Stuart Plattner, 178–195. Washington, DC: American Ethnological Society.

Ross, Loretta J. 2012. "A Feminist Perspective on Katrina." In *The Women of Katrina: How Gender, Race, and Class Matter in an American Disaster,* edited by Emmanuel David and Elaine Enarson, 15–23. Nashville, TN: Vanderbilt University Press.

Rotberg, Robert. 1997. "Preface: Haiti's Last Best Chance." In *Haiti Renewed: Political and Economic Prospects,* edited by Robert I. Rotberg, vii–xiii. Cambridge, MA/Washington, DC: World Peace Foundation/ Brookings Institution Press.

———. 2003a. *Haiti's Turmoil: Politics and Policy under Aristide and Clinton.* Cambridge, MA: World Peace Foundation.

———. 2003b. *State Failure and State Weakness in a Time of Terror.* Cambridge: Cambridge University Press.

Ryan, William. 1971. *Blaming the Victim.* New York: Pantheon.

Sagás, Ernesto. 2000. *Race and Politics in the Dominican Republic.* Gainesville: University Press of Florida.

Sahlins, Marshall. 1972. *Stone Age Economics.* New York: Aldine de Gruyter.

Said, Edward. 1979. *Orientalism.* New York: Vintage.

Sampson, Steven. 1996. "The Social Life of Projects: Importing Civil Society to Albania." In *Civil Society: Challenging Western Models,* edited by Chris Hann and Elizabeth Dunn, 121–142. London: Routledge.

———. 2010. "The Anti-Corruption Industry: From Movement to Institution." *Global Crime* 11 (2): 261–278.

Sassen, Saskia. 2001. *The Global City: New York, London, Tokyo.* 2nd ed. Princeton, NJ: Princeton University Press.

Scherz, China. 2013. "Let Us Make God Our Banker: Ethics, Temporality, and Agency in a Ugandan Charity Home." *American Ethnologist* 40 (4): 624–636.

Schneider, David M. 1984. *A Critique of the Study of Kinship.* Ann Arbor: University of Michigan Press.

Schuller, Mark. 2006. "Jamming the Meatgrinder World: Lessons Learned from Tenants Organizing in St. Paul." In *Homing Devices: The Poor as Targets of Public Housing Policy and Practice*, edited by Marilyn Thomas-Houston and Mark Schuller, 159–180. Lanham, MD: Lexington Press.

———. 2007a. "Haiti's 200-Year Ménage-à-Trois: Globalization, the State, and Civil Society." *Caribbean Studies* 35 (2): 141–179.

———. 2007b. "Invasion or Infusion? Understanding the Role of NGOs in Contemporary Haiti." *Journal of Haitian Studies* 13 (2): 96–119.

———. 2009. "Gluing Globalization: NGOs as Intermediaries in Haiti." *Political and Legal Anthropology Review* 32 (1): 84–104.

———. 2010a. "From Activist to Applied Anthropologist to Anthropologist? On the Politics of Collaboration." *Practicing Anthropologist* 32 (1): 43–47.

———. 2010b. "Mister Blan: The Incredible Whiteness of Being (an Anthropologist)." In *Fieldwork Identities*, edited by Erin Taylor, 125–150. Coconut Creek, FL: Caribbean Studies Press.

———. 2010c. *Unstable Foundations: The Impact of NGOs on Human Rights for Port-au-Prince's 1.5 Million Homeless*. New York and Port-au-Prince: City University of New York and the Université d'État d'Haïti.

———. 2011. *Mèt Ko Veye Ko: Foreign Responsibility in the Failure to Protect against Cholera and Other Man-Made Disasters*. New York and Port-au-Prince: City University of New York and l'Université d'État d'Haïti.

———. 2012a. "Genetically Modified Organizations? Understanding and Supporting Local Civil Society in Urban Haiti." *Journal of Haitian Studies* 18 (1): 50–73.

———. 2012b. *Homeward Bound? Assessing Progress of Relocation from Haiti's IDP Camps*. DeKalb and Port-au-Prince: Northern Illinois University and Faculté d'Ethnologie.

———. 2012c. *Killing with Kindness: Haiti, International Aid, and NGOs*. New Brunswick, NJ: Rutgers University Press.

———. 2014. "Being an Insider Without: Activist Anthropological Engagement in Haiti after the Earthquake." *American Anthropologist* 116 (2).

Schuller, Mark, and Tania Levey. 2014. "Kabrit Ki Gen Twop Met: Understanding Gaps in WASH Services in Haiti's IDP Camps." *Disasters* 38 (S1): S1–S24.

Schwartz, Timothy. 2009. *Fewer Men, More Babies: Sex, Family, and Fertility in Haiti*. Lanham, MD: Lexington Books.

Schwartz, Timothy, with Yves-François Pierre and Eric Calpas. 2011. *BARR Survey Report: Building Assessments and Rubble Removal in Quake-Affected Neighborhoods in Haiti*. Washington, DC: United States Agency for International Development.

Scott, David. 2004. *Conscripts of Modernity: The Tragedy of Colonial Enlightenment*. Durham, NC: Duke University Press.

Seitenfus, Ricardo. 2015. *L'echec de l'aide internationale à Haïti: Dilemmes et égarements*. Port-au-Prince: Éditions Université d'État d'Haïti.

Sharma, Aradhana. 2006. "Crossbreeding Institutions, Breeding Struggle: Women's Empowerment, Neoliberal Governmentality, and State (Re)Formation in India." *Cultural Anthropology* 21 (1): 60–95.

———. 2008. *Logics of Empowerment: Development, Gender, and Governance in Neoliberal India*. Minneapolis: University of Minnesota Press.

———. 2014. "Notes on the Difficulty of Studying NGOs, with a Nod to Philip Abrams." For *What's in a Name? Tracing Anthropology's Uneasy Ethnographic Engagement with NGOs*. Mark Schuller and David Lewis, organizers. Washington, DC: American Anthropological Association.

Sharpe, Christina. 2010. *Monstrous Intimacies: Making Post-Slavery Subjects (Perverse Modernities)*. Durham, NC: Duke University Press.

Sheller, Mimi. 2004. "'You Signed My Name, but Not My Feet': Paradoxes of Peasant Resistance and State Control in Post-Revolutionary Haiti." *Journal of Haitian Studies* 10 (1): 72–86.

———. 2012. *Citizenship from Below: Erotic Agency and Caribbeam Freedom.* Durham, NC: Duke University Press.

Shore, Cris, and Susan Wright. 2000. "Coercive Accountability: The Rise of Audit Culture in Higher Education." In *Audit Cultures: Anthropological Studies in Accountability: Ethics and the Academy,* edited by Marilyn Strathern, 57–89. London: Routledge.

Simmons, David. 2010. "Structural Violence as Social Practice: Haitian Agricultural Workers, Anti-Haitianism, and Health in the Dominican Republic." *Human Organization* 69 (1): 10–18.

Simmons, Kimberly Eison. 2009. *Reconstructing Racial Identity and the African Past in the Dominican Republic.* Gainesville: University Press of Florida.

Slocum, Karla, and Deborah Thomas. 2003. "Rethinking Global and Area Studies: Insights from Caribbeanist Anthropology." *American Anthropologist* 105 (3): 553–565.

Smith, Jennie Marcelle. 2001. *When the Hands Are Many: Community Organization and Social Change in Rural Haiti.* Ithaca, NY: Cornell University Press.

Smith, Matthew. 2009. *Red and Black in Haiti: Radicalism, Conflict, and Political Change, 1934–1957.* Chapel Hill: University of North Carolina Press.

Smith, Neil. 1984. *Uneven Development: Nature, Capital, and the Production of Space.* Oxford: Blackwell.

Smith, Raymond Thomas. 1956. *The Negro Family in British Guiana.* London: Routledge and Paul.

Solnit, Rebecca. 2009. *The Paradise Built in Hell: The Extraordinary Communities That Arise in Disaster.* New York: Penguin Books.

Sphere Project. 2004. *Humanitarian Charter and Minimum Standards in Humanitarian Response.* Geneva: Sphere Project.

Spillers, Hortence J. 1987. "Mama's Baby, Papa's Maybe: An American Grammar Book." *Diacritics* 17 (2): 64–81.

Spivak, Giyatri. 1988. "Can the Subaltern Speak?" In *Marxism and the Interpretation of Culture,* edited by Cary Nelson and Lawrence Grossberg, 271–313. Urbana: University of Illinois Press.

Steineke, Andrea. 2012. "Republik der NGOs." *Analyse und Kritik* 568. http://www.akweb.de/ak_s/ak568/16.htm.

Strathern, Marilyn. 1985. "Kinship and Economy: Constitutive Orders of a Provisional Kind." *American Ethnologist* 12 (2): 191–209.

———. 2000. *Audit Cultures: Anthropological Studies in Accountability, Ethics, and the Academy.* London: Routledge.

Suárez, Lucía. 2006. *The Tears of Hispaniola: Haitian and Dominican Diaspora Memory.* Gainesville: University of Florida Press.

Susser, Ida. 2011. "Organic Intellectuals, Crossing Scales, and the Emergence of Social Movements with Respect to AIDS in South Africa." *American Ethnologist* 38 (4): 733–742.

Tannenbaum, Frank. 1947. *Slave and Citizen: The Negro in the Americas.* New York: Knopf.

Tarrow, Sidney. 2011. *Power in Movement: Social Movements and Contentious Politics.* 3rd ed. Cambridge: Cambridge University Press.

Terry, Fiona. 2014. "Humanitarian Diplomacy: The ICRC Experience." In *Negotiating Relief: The Politics of Humanitarian Space,* edited by Michele Acuto, 247–257. London: Hurst.

Theus, Béguens. 2008. *Haïti, ONG et la misère.* Port-au-Prince: Éditions Automne.

Thomas, Frédéric. 2013. *L'échec humanitaire: Le cas haïtien*. Bruxelles: Couleur Livres.

Thompson, Martha, with Izaskun Gaviria. 2004. *Weathering the Storm: Lessons in Risk Reduction from Cuba*. Boston: Oxfam America.

Ticktin, Miriam. 2011. "The Gendered Human of Humanitarianism: Medicalizing and Politicizing Sexual Violence." *Gender and History* 23 (2): 250–265.

———. 2014. "Transnational Humanitarianism." *Annual Review of Anthropology* 43: 273–289.

Tierney, Kathleen. 2012. "Critical Disjunctures: Disaster Research, Social Inequality, Gender, and Hurricane Katrina." In *The Women of Katrina: How Gender, Race, and Class Matter in an American Disaster*, edited by Emmanuel David and Elaine Enarson, 245–258. Nashville, TN: Vanderbilt University Press.

Tierney, Kathleen, Christine Bevc, and Erica Kuligowski. 2006. "Metaphors Matter: Disaster Myths, Media Frames, and Their Consequences in Hurricane Katrina." *Annals of the American Academy of Political and Social Science* 604: 57–81.

Timmer, Andrea. 2010. "Constructing the 'Needy Subject': NGO Discourses of Roma Need." *Political and Legal Anthropology Review* 33 (2): 264–281.

Tobin, Graham A., and Linda M. Whiteford. 2002. "Community Resilience and Volcano Hazard: The Eruption of Tungurahua and Evacuation of the Faldas in Ecuador." *Disasters* 26 (1): 28–48.

Toussaint, Herold. 2012. *Salt in the Wound: The Urgent Need to Prevent Forced Evictions from Camps in Haiti*. Port-au-Prince: Oxfam GB.

Trouillot, Evelyne. 2012. "*Abse sou Klou*: Reconstructing Exclusion." In *Tectonic Shifts: Haiti since the Earthquake*, edited by Mark Schuller and Pablo Morales, 103–107. Sterling, VA: Kumarian.

Trouillot, Michel-Rolph. 1977. *Ti dife boule sou istoua Ayiti*. Brooklyn: Koleksyon Lakansyèl.

———. 1990a. *Haiti, State against Nation: The Origins and Legacy of Duvalierism*. New York: Monthly Review Press.

———. 1990b. "The Odd and the Ordinary: Haiti, the Caribbean, and the World." *Cimarrón: New Perspectives on the Caribbean* 2 (3): 3–12.

———. 1992. "The Caribbean Region: An Open Frontier in Anthropological Theory." *Annual Review of Anthropology* 21: 19–42.

———. 1994. "Culture, Color, and Politics in Haiti." In *Race*, edited by Steven Gregory and Roger Sanjek, 146–174. New Brunswick, NJ: Rutgers University Press.

———. 1995. *Silencing the Past: Power and the Production of History*. Boston: Beacon.

———. 2003. *Global Transformations: Anthropology and the Modern World*. New York: Palgrave Macmillan.

Troutman, Emily. 2011. "US Report Queries Haiti Quake Death Toll, Homeless." *Agence France-Presse*, May 27.

Ulcena, Tracey. 2013. "Survivors, Not Victims." *Practicing Anthropology* 35 (3): 17–19.

Ulysse, Gina Athena. 2002. "Conquering Duppies in Kingston: Miss Tiny and Me, Fieldwork Conflicts, and Being Loved and Rescued." *Anthropology and Humanism* 27 (1): 10–26.

———. 2008. *Downtown Ladies: Informal Commercial Importers, a Haitian Anthropologist, and Self-Making in Jamaica*. Chicago: University of Chicago Press.

———. 2010. "Why Representations of Haiti Matter Now More Than Ever." *NACLA Report on the Americas* 43 (5): 37–41.

———. 2011a. *Fascinating! Her Resilience*. Middletown, CT: Wesleyan University Center for the Arts.

———. 2011b. "Pawòl Fanm sou Douze Janvye (Women's Words on January 12th)." *Meridians: Feminism, Race, Transnationalism* 11 (1): 91–162.

United Nations News Centre. 2011. "Haiti: UN concerned at forcible evictions of quake survivors from camps." http://www.un.org/apps/news/story.asp?NewsID=39526# .VXMKnoYzF5M, 13 Septmber.

United Nations Office for Coordination of Humanitarian Aid (OCHA). 2001. *Guiding Principles on Internal Displacement.* New York: United Nations.

United Nations Special Envoy to Haiti. 2011. *Has Aid Changed? Channelling Assistance to Haiti Before and After the Earthquake.* New York: United Nations Office of the Special Envoy to Haiti.

———. 2012. *Haiti: Lessons Learned.* New York: United Nations Office of the Special Envoy to Haiti.

Uvin, Peter. 1998. *Aiding Violence: The Development Enterprise in Rwanda.* West Hartford, CT: Kumarian.

Vanderkooy, Patricia Noelle. 2004. "'Who Speaks for Us?': Representation and Accountability within Grassroots Organizations in Port-au-Prince, Haiti." MA thesis, University of Guelph.

Vannier, Christian. 2010. "Audit Culture and Grassroots Participation in Rural Haitian Development." *Political and Legal Anthropology Review* 33 (2): 282–305.

Victor, Gary. 2010. *Le sang et la mer.* La Roque d'Anthéron, France: Vents d'Ailleurs.

Vorbe, Charles. 2011. "Séisme, humanitarisme et interventionnisme en Haïti." *Cahiers du Centre de la Population et du Développement (CEPODE)* 2 (2): 71–86.

Wade, Peter. 1995. *Blackness and Race Mixture: The Dynamics of Racial Identity in Colombia.* Baltimore, MD: Johns Hopkins University Press.

Watts, Michael, and Richard Peet. 1996. *Liberation Ecologies: Environment, Development, Social Movements.* London: Routledge.

Weber, Max. 1946. "The Sociology of Charismatic Authority." In *Max Weber: Essays in Sociology,* edited by H. Gerth and C. Wright Mills, 245–264. New York: Oxford University Press.

———. 1985 (1904–1905). *The Protestant Ethic and the Spirit of Capitalism.* Translated by Talcott Parsons. London: Unwin Paperbacks.

Weston, Kath. 1997. *Families We Choose: Lesbians, Gays, Kinship.* Rev. ed. New York: Columbia University Press.

Whitten, Norman. 2007. "The *Longue Durée* of Racial Fixity and the Transformative Conjunctures of Racial Blending." *Journal of Latin American and Caribbean Anthropology* 12 (2): 356–383.

Willems, Joris. 2012. "Deconstructing the Reconstruction: The IHRC." In *Tectonic Shifts: Haiti since the Earthquake,* edited by Mark Schuller and Pablo Morales, 41–45. Sterling, VA: Kumarian.

Williams, Eric Eustace. 1961. *Capitalism and Slavery.* New York: Russell and Russell.

Williams, Patricia J. 1991. *The Alchemy of Race and Rights.* Cambridge, MA: Harvard University Press.

Willinger, Beth, and Janna Knight. 2012. "Setting the Stage for Disaster: Women in New Orleans before and after Katrina." In *The Women of Katrina: How Gender, Race, and Class Matter in an American Disaster,* edited by Emmanuel David and Elaine Enarson, 55–75. Nashville, TN: Vanderbilt University Press.

Willoughby-Herard, Tiffany. 2015. *Waste of a White Skin: The Carnegie Corporation and the Racial Logic of White Vulnerability.* Berkeley: University of California Press.

Wisner, Ben, Piers Blaikie, Terry Cannon, and Ian Davis. 2004. *At Risk: Natural Hazards, People's Vulnerability, and Disasters.* 2nd ed. New York: Routledge.

Wisner, Ben, and Peter Walker. 2005. *Beyond Kobe: A Proactive Look at the World Conference on Disaster Reduction, 18–22 January 2005, Kobe, Japan.* Medford, MA: Tufts University—Feinstein International Famine Center.

Wittgenstein, Ludwig van. 2010 (1953). *Philosophical Investigations,* 4th ed. Hoboken, NJ: Wiley.

Woods, Clyde. 2010. *In the Wake of Hurricane Katrina: New Paradigms and Social Visions.* Baltimore, MD: Johns Hopkins University Press.

Woodward, Susan. 2001. "Humanitarian War: A New Consensus?" *Disasters* 25 (4): 331–344.

Worker Rights Consortium. 2013. *Stealing from the Poor: Wage Theft in the Haitian Apparel Industry.* Washington, DC: Worker Rights Consortium.

World Bank. 2002. "Haiti: External Financing Report: October 1, 2000—September 30, 2001." Washington, DC: World Bank.

Wucker, Michele. 1999. *Why the Cocks Fight: Dominicans, Haitians, and the Struggle for Hispaniola.* New York: Hill and Wang.

Young, Iris Marion. 1994. "Gender as Seriality: Thinking about Women as a Social Collective." *Signs* 19 (3): 713–738.

Zanotti, Laura. 2010. "Cacophonies of Aid, Failed State Building, and NGOs in Haiti: Setting the Stage for Disaster, Envisioning the Future." *Third World Quarterly* 31 (5): 755–771. doi: 10.2307/27896575.

Zaoudé, Aster, and Joanne Sandler. 2001. "International Organizations: Women's Rights and Gender Equality." In *Eye to Eye: Women Practising Development across Cultures,* edited by Susan Perry and Celeste Schenck, 25–40. London: Zed.

INDEX

Page references with f indicate figures; those with t, tables.

ABOUT THE AUTHOR

MARK SCHULLER is an associate professor of anthropology and NGO Leadership and Development at Northern Illinois University and affiliate at the Faculté d'Ethnologie, l'Université d'État d'Haïti. Having begun work in Haiti in 2001, supported by the National Science Foundation Senior and CAREER Grant, Bellagio Center, and others, Schuller has done research on globalization, NGOs, gender, and disasters in Haiti published in two dozen book chapters and peer-reviewed articles as well as public media, including a column in *Huffington Post*. He is the author or coeditor of seven books, including *Killing with Kindness: Haiti, International Aid, and NGOs* (Rutgers, 2010), which won the Margaret Mead Award. He is codirector/coproducer of the documentary *Poto Mitan: Haitian Women, Pillars of the Global Economy* (2009). He guest curated an award-winning museum exhibit: "Fragments: Haiti Four Years since the Earthquake." Schuller is coeditor of Berghahn Books' "Catastrophes in Context: A Series in Engaged Social Science on Disasters," board chair of the Lambi Fund of Haiti, and is active in several solidarity efforts.

CPSIA information can be obtained
at www.ICGtesting.com
Printed in the USA
LVOW13s1728211216
518300LV00016B/298/P